# GREEN AND SAFFRON

**HEDGEHOG AND FOX**

HISTORY AND POLITICS SERIES

*"The fox knows many things,*
*but the hedgehog knows one big thing"*

**General Editor**

**RUDRANGSHU MUKHERJEE**

MUKUL SHARMA

# Green and Saffron

## The RSS, Modi, and Indian Environmental Politics

*Foreword by Jonathan Olsen*

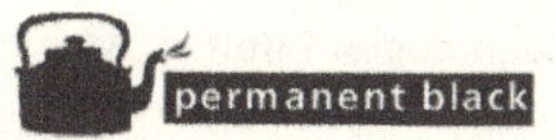

*and*

*Published by*
PERMANENT BLACK
'Himalayana', Mall Road, Ranikhet Cantt,
Ranikhet 263645
perblack@gmail.com
*and*

*Distributed by*
ORIENT BLACKSWAN PRIVATE LTD
Bangalore Bhopal Bhubaneshwar Chandigarh Chennai
Ernakulam Guwahati Hyderabad Jaipur Kolkata
Lucknow Mumbai New Delhi Patna
www.orientblackswan.com



ISBN 978-81-7824-685-7

This book is a revised, new edition of Mukul Sharma,
*Green and Saffron: Hindu Nationalism and Indian Environmental Politics* (2012)

Typeset in Adobe Garamond Pro
by Guru Typograph Technology, Crossings Republic, Ghaziabad
Printed and bound by Manipal Technologies Limited, Manipal

*for*

two *anands* in my life
Anand Swamy and Anand Pradhan

# Foreword

THE FIRST SCHOLARSHIP on the nexus between modern right-wing nationalist/far-right thought and environmentalism emerged in the 1990s. Although some might place this scholarship slightly earlier – in the mid 1980s with the publication of Anna Bramwell's *Blood and Soil: Richard Walther Darré and Hitler's "Green Party"* (or more properly, the reactions to that 1985 book) – it was really a variety of academic researchers in the 1990s who were the first to comprehensively interrogate the environmental politics and ecological thought of the contemporary far right. This first generation of scholars – above all, Thomas Jahn and Peter Wehling's *Ökologie von rechts* (1991), Janet Biehl and Peter Staudenmaier's *Ecofascism: Lessons from the German Experience* (1995), Oliver Geden's *Rechte Ökologie* (1996), and my own book *Nature and Nationalism: Right-Wing Ecology and the Politics of Identity in Contemporary Germany* (1999, and now celebrating the 25th anniversary of its publication) – set up the basic parameters of future research by taking this topic seriously and on its own terms. As most accounts of modern environmentalism and environmental ideology still place these firmly on the left (as a post-materialist expression of the 1960s generation of New Left actors in Europe and the United States), the novelty of these accounts and the scepticism surrounding them was a chief obstacle to overcome. Yet, these scholars did not by and large dismiss "right-wing ecology" as simply an avenue for far-right actors to smuggle in extremist ideas in green packaging. Instead, they carefully analysed the actors, concepts, and ideological framing of a new and distinctive right-wing ecological worldview.

In my own book, I argued that (contra Bramwell) modern environmentalism was not "beyond left and right" but rather traversed by already existing, but nevertheless contrasting, ideological visions of what environmental politics is and should be, this being based on a political reading of humans' relationship to the natural world. In my empirical investigation of various far-right parties and grouplets as well as the history of the modern environmental movement in Germany, I concluded that left and right ecology were deeply intertwined with the identity building of a community – one more universalist and globalist in its objectives, the other a narrower, nationalist particularism. Finding most of the existing literature still insufficiently theoretical, I set out to identify the central concepts of the latter – what I called "right-wing ecology". In addition, I argued that what undergirded the central concepts I identified – eco-naturalism, eco-organicism, and eco-authoritarianism – was the intertwining of notions of pollution and the purity of nature with the pollution and purity of the national community: what and who belong, and what and who do not, or rather shouldn't, in this worldview.

Although works from this first generation articulated the central ideas within far-right ecological ideology, set out broad conceptual categories for understanding this worldview, and identified some key actors, the approaches – and I once again include my own book here – were not as methodologically rigorous as they could have been, their conceptual terminology was not systematically explored (e.g. eco-fascism, right-wing ecology, or far-right ecology?), their geographic scope was limited (mostly to Europe, and mostly still to Germany), and the central environmental concern of our time – climate change – was not on their radar.

Starting in the 2010s, the next generation of scholars (such as Bernhard Forchtner, Kristian Voss, Balsa Lubarda, Kristy Campion, and many others) have largely improved on these deficits. In particular, they have employed more systematic empirical approaches, have provided more rigour in conceptualisation and categorisation, have addressed the important issue of climate change (and the far right's stance towards this issue), and have deepened some research foci (e.g. gender and environmentalism/anti-environmentalism). Above all, and though still in its infancy, a new generation of scholars has started to significantly widen the geographical scope of their investigations.

It is to this second generation of scholars that Mukul Sharma's book *Green and Saffron: Hindu Nationalism and Indian Environmental Politics*, originally published in 2012, belongs. I became acquainted with Professor Sharma's book only a few years ago (something that speaks to the fact that scholars in our still rather new sub-field are regrettably often unaware of new developments in the scholarly literature). What I appreciated above all in his work was the way in which he employed much of my theoretical and conceptual framework in *Nature and Nationalism* to explore a vastly different cultural setting, adding new theoretical insights and conceptual refinements within a rich and textured empirical exploration of the relationship between modern environmental movements in India and contemporary ultra-nationalist Hindu politics – the "green and saffron" of the title. Sharma's book was an extremely important contribution to the academic literature. Thus, when I heard that he was planning a new, updated edition of *Green and Saffron* and had asked me to write a foreword for this new edition, I was honoured. I was also excited and curious to see how this geopolitical phenomenon had further developed in the years since the book's original publication and how Professor Sharma, after additional research and reflection, would refine and further build upon his understanding in this already fascinating work.

This new edition of *Green and Saffron* does not disappoint. As in the original edition of the book, Sharma argues that Indian politics over the last decade and a half has been marked by both a "greening of saffron" and a "saffronizing of green". Saffron, as Sharma presents this colour imagery, represents Hindutva or "Hinduness", a cultural and political practice of Hindu nationalism that lies at the heart of the Modi regime, and which attempts to mobilise supporters through an identity-building project celebrating India's pre-colonial past, Hindu cultural achievements and religious practices, and the myths of ancient Hindu culture. However, as identity building necessarily involves a demarcation of "us" from "them", defining the in-group substantially through the description of out-groups, Hindutva also identifies its "other" – Muslims, the West, and the colonial history of India more broadly.

The "greening of saffron", according to Sharma, signifies the increasing use of environmental discourse, rhetoric, and policy as a way to undergird this Hindu nationalist project and the demarcation between "us" and "them". Meanwhile, the "saffronising of green" signifies the way in which, as Sharma states, "independent environmental movements and organisations make Hindutva's cultural politics a fundamental aspect of their environmental discourse." In other words, parts of India's environmental movement have adjusted their language, practice, and concerns to accommodate this modern Hindu right-wing nationalism. Although the rise of Hindu nationalism under Modi is a well-chronicled tale, Sharma's book is unique in identifying ecology as a key factor in the shaping of the Hindu nationalist ideological agenda. This interweaving of "nature and nationalism" – a tradition which I located in my own book as central to understanding the German far right and its engagement with environmentalism – thus appears in a different form, with different cultural and (especially) religious expressions, in modern Hindu nationalism. Moreover, similar to other movements, groups, and parties in Europe, the integration of ecology into nationalist/far-right thought ultimately serves here too as a nationalist project of both identity conservation and creation as well as social exclusion.

This new edition of *Green and Saffron* preserves the strengths of the original edition while tightening up the argument and ploughing new empirical fields. After its opening introductory chapter, Chapter 2 details the ideological thrust of the Rashtriya Swayamsevak Sangh (RSS) and the Bharatiya Janata Party (BJP) – the latter the Hindu nationalist party led by Prime Minister Narendra Modi, the former a Hindu nationalist organisation founded in 1925, which serves as an umbrella for a large and diverse group of ethno-nationalist organisations collectively known as the Sangh Parivar (Sangh family) – and demonstrates how the RSS and BJP have gradually moved environmental concerns to the centre of their nationalist discourse.

The empirical heart of *Green and Saffron*, however, remains three well-researched case studies: Anna Hazare's impact on the watershed management programme in Ralegan Siddhi, Maharashtra; the Chipko leader Sunderlal Bahuguna's opposition to the Tehri dam in the Garhwal Himalaya; and Vrindavan's forest revival and conservation project in Mathura, Uttar Pradesh. In his extremely detailed and masterful narrative of these cases, Sharma argues that in all of these environmental movements, environmental conservation and nationalist Hindu politics have developed close ties, revealing the infiltration of environmental conservation projects by the rhetoric and categories of Hindutva.

In the first case study, that of Ralegan Siddhi (a self-proclaimed "ideal village" for rural development and water conservation) and its leader Anna Hazare, Sharma shows how Hindu nationalist concepts and ideas of authority have gradually come to inform his work. Authoritarian moralism infiltrates Hazare's implicit linking of environmental conservation with the social stratification of caste and gender (as well as draconian punishments for violations of religious codes of personal conduct) in an attempt to create a harmonious relationship between the governed and the governing. Meanwhile, nationalism is embodied in Anna Hazare's nationalist discourse and a championing of an India in conflict with its enemies. As Sharma writes, "narratives of the war, the army, and the enemy remain core points of reference within the discourse on nation and rural development in Ralegan Siddhi."

The next case study, that of Sunderlal Bahuguna and his opposition to the Tehri dam in Garhwal, illustrates how opposition to the dam has occurred simultaneously on two fronts. On the one hand, the dam has been criticised for its giganticism and potential for large-scale environmental damage and social dislocation. At the same time, opposition to the dam has also increasingly centred around its supposed violation of sacred spaces, cultural/religious pollution, and the havoc it can wreak on the nation and Hindutva. Indeed, in reading Sharma's account, it is difficult today to disentangle purely environmental objections from those engaging on religious, cultural, and (ultimately) political grounds. The infusion of religious and cultural concerns – all, of course, in service to the agenda of modern Hindu nationalism – into the language and practices of this modern environmental movement makes for extremely compelling reading.

The final case study, that of the Vrindavan Forest Revival and Conservation Project, demonstrates the influence of religious imagery and myth on the articulation of environmental policy, imagery, and myths which promote the central pillars of Hindutva and an accompanying exclusivistic nationalism. Throughout the case studies, Sharma shows how religious and cultural discourse at the centre of an ultra-nationalist project of identity building has been married to diverse environmental social movements.

The key concepts found in all three case studies are, as in my own work, purity, and pollution. These concepts can be understood in both their socio-cultural/religious meanings as well as in their environmental meanings. Purity signifies the undiluted and unadulterated, that which is untouched by the foreign and alien. Pollution, conversely, signifies that which spoils or defiles those things in the natural order. The incorporation of Hindu nationalism within diverse environmental movements reveals itself in the ways in which these concepts are used to posit a pure ethno-nationalist community of Hindutva juxtaposed to foreign influences and domestic opponents. As Sharma writes, "this is a discourse within which understandings of the violation of nature are based on particular assumptions about what the natural and social orders should look like, who they should belong to, and how."

One of the key features of this revised edition of *Green and Saffron* is a new chapter concerning India's response to global climate change, or rather how this response has also served to promote both the Hindu nationalist agenda and the Modi personality cult. An embrace of the fight against climate change by a right-wing nationalist leader and party is a rather curious phenomenon if we keep in mind the fact that far-right parties in Western Europe today are overwhelmingly hostile to serious efforts to combat climate change. Their responses range from outright climate change denialism to various forms of scepticism – attribution scepticism (admitting the climate is changing while simultaneously denying humans' role in this change) to response scepticism (admitting the climate is changing but arguing that mitigation efforts are either pointless, counterproductive, or too expensive). Indeed, populist far-right parties in Europe see Green parties as their main enemies and mobilise their own supporters through a backlash to environmental regulations and unnecessary alarm over climate change. Nevertheless, it should be pointed out that among a subsection of the far right in Europe, climate change acceptance is gradually growing, along with a new frame – a "green nationalism" combining climate change acceptance with far-right ecological positions. Although this subset is still small and that line of discourse still rather marginal, in the future – if this ideological position gains in strength – it might mean that the far-right posits the fight against climate change as a protection of the homeland (a national rather than international struggle); that it cultivates national traditions as essential tools in this fight; and it casts climate migrants as cultural pollutants in this struggle. Could these still marginal voices and evolving ecological ideas within the far-right scene in Europe become a more dominant force, updating the basic tenets of this worldview to accommodate climate change acceptance and mitigation?

Perhaps India might show the way. As Sharma chronicles, Modi, the RSS, and the BJP have embraced the fight against climate change. Indeed, starting around 2002, Modi gradually positioned himself as a modern icon of sustainable development, emphasising the significance of climate change (even publishing a book in 2011, entitled *Gujarat's Response to Challenges of Climate Change*) while championing the role of renewable energy as an important, technocratic solution to this global problem. Lauded by some independent Indian climate experts as a "climate leader", Modi has also attempted to burnish his international reputation as a leader in the fight to combat climate change (despite India's rising contribution to greenhouse gases). Thus, he was recognised by the UN in 2018 with its "Champions of the Earth" award, visited the White House in 2014 while articulating a vision of how to combat climate change, and stands committed to the goals of the Paris accords.

A right-wing nationalist/far-right politician and party who not only do not deny the reality of climate change, but seek to actively combat it, would, on the surface, appear to be an alloyed good. Yet Sharma shows how Modi, the BJP, and RSS have also used climate change and renewable energy as political tools to advance their Hindu nationalist agenda. At the same time, they have sidelined or co-opted independent environmental organisations and instituted a top-down, centralised approach to environmental policy-making. Sharma clearly laments the disappearance of heterogeneity and political pluralism in Indian civil society represented by the saffronising of green. Above all, Sharma perceives the danger of the ethno-nationalist discourse central to the BJP's and Modi's environmental vision. Indeed, from the very beginning, Modi and the BJP have linked the fight against climate change to Hindutva, exalting the historical grandeur of ancient India and "asserting the powerful civilisation of the Indian nation." For example, he has praised "India's ancient wisdom", extolled its purportedly unique reverence for nature, linked Hindu cultural and religious practices regarding the Sun in the Vedas to modern forms of solar energy and the promotion of solar power, and claimed that modern environmentalism and the fight against climate change demand a reassertion of ancient Hindu values. The RSS, meanwhile, draws upon references to ancient mythology and pre-modern Hindu science to support the Modi government's initiatives to combat climate change, even invoking Yoga as one of the key ways to overcome the climate crisis! Not surprisingly, the RSS also presents Modi as the "Solar Superman" and solar power as a "Saffron supergrid".

While Modi, the BJP, and the RSS have infused climate change mitigation and renewable energy with the myths and cultural and religious practices of Hindu nationalism, they have also juxtaposed directly or indirectly those responsible for the problem in the first place – foreign invaders, colonial powers, and domestic enemies of Hindutva, i.e. Muslims. As Sharma writes, the environmental rhetoric of Modi, the BJP, and RSS is an "exclusive narrative that emphasises the Hindu religion and traditions as the sole foundation for addressing climate change and embracing renewable energy." Those who are not with us on Hindu-centric solutions to climate change, it seems, are against us. The outgroups demarcating identity have been clearly identified.

Meanwhile, Sharma argues, Modi's and the BJP's renewable energy policy is deeply enmeshed with big corporate interests. Indeed, certain elements of the private sector have been among the biggest winners of the Modi/BJP energy policy. Sharma discusses, for example, how the Adani Group – Indian's largest coal miner and thermal power producer blamed for environmental destruction and violations of indigenous land rights – has seen its profits and share prices rise dramatically over the last several years as it has invested in the areas of solar and wind power. Overall, Modi has found a way to be seen as a leader on climate change while marrying a technocratic vision of sustainable environmental development with an ethnonationalist project.

To conclude: the new edition of *Green and Saffron* thus represents a laudable addition to the academic literature on right-wing ecology/far-right ecologism. Sharma's unique strengths – his attention to detail, masterful narrative, sensitivity to nuance, analytical insights, and theoretical and conceptual innovations – make this a first-class book which engages both the reader who knows very little on this topic as well as academics already working in this field. It explores significant new terrain as well as raises important questions which will keep scholars busy in the coming years. With the rise of a global far right, the emergence of new authoritarian strongmen within established democracies, and the increasingly urgent need to find solutions to our imperilling climate crisis, this new edition of *Green and Saffron* could not be more timely. I recommend it highly.

Jonathan Olsen is Professor and Chair, Texas Woman's University (USA). He is the author or co-author of four books, including *Nature and Nationalism: Right-Wing Ecology and the Politics of Identity in Contemporary Germany* (New York and London: Palgrave, 1999), and dozens of articles in academic journals. He has held visiting appointments at the University of Münster (Germany), Europa University-Viadrinna (Frankfurt-Oder, Germany), and the University of Potsdam (Germany).

# Contents

# Preface to the New Edition

THIS NEW EDITION represents my effort to comprehend changes and continuities over the years 2014 to 2022 within the intricate interplay recorded in an earlier incarnation of *Green and Saffron* (2012). The subtitle of this updated edition has been changed to "The RSS, Modi, and Indian Environmental Politics", whereas in the first edition it was "Hindu Nationalism and Indian Environmental Politics". The subtitle change is on account of the RSS and Modi emerging as the driving forces of Hindu nationalism and environmental politics after 2014. The fundamental premise of the book, emphasising the interconnectedness of *Green and Saffron* within Indian environmental politics, remains as pertinent as ever. In fact, this new edition highlights the notable trend of "saffronising" the environmental discourse to the extent that it can be described as the emergence of a saffron civil society.

The present edition contains approximately 50,000 words more than its predecessor, including a newly incorporated chapter centred on Narendra Modi, climate change, and renewable energy. Over the past decade we have witnessed profound transformations in Hindu nationalism and environmental politics. On the surface, these changes are stark: the rise of Hindu nationalism and the RSS, the establishment of a BJP-led national government, and the emergence of Narendra Modi on one side; and on the other the weakening of environmental organisations and movements, coupled with the ascent of a formidable saffron civil society within the environmental domain. Yet, beneath the surface there exist more profound shifts in environmental politics, particularly those distinctive to the landscape of right-wing ecology in India, setting it somewhat apart from its counterparts in other areas of the world.

This edition is also distinct from the 2012 version in two other ways: its concentrated focus on "the greening of saffron", and a foreword by Jonathan Olsen. The new focus delves comprehensively into the environmental politics and practices of the Rashtriya Swayamsevak Sangh (RSS), the BJP (Bharatiya Janata Party), and Modi, taking into account the latest published as well as unpublished literature and activities of Hindutva forces since 2014. Consequently, Chapter 2, "Hindu Nationalism and the Environment: Elements and Themes", has undergone significant expansion. Additionally, an entirely new chapter, Chapter 6, has been added: in it I dissect Hindu nationalist politics vis-à-vis climate change and renewable energy. A Postscript has also been added to provide insights into RSS shakha/grassroots events focused on the environment.

It is important to clarify, however, that these additions do not aim to analyse the performance of Modi and his government in the environmental arena since 2014. Instead, this edition focuses on exploring Hindu nationalist politics in relation to the environment, and how this ideology is applied to articulate environmental issues in pursuit of the Hindutva political agenda. A comprehensive assessment of Modi's government in the environmental sphere would, in my opinion, necessitate a separate work. I also want to emphasise that this book does not explore the relationship between Hindu religion and ecology within the context of religious ecology. Instead, its primary focus is on the politics of ecology within the framework of the Hindu nationalist ideology apparent in contemporary India.

The Introduction, and the final chapter "Features of Hindu Environmentalism: The Convergence of Green and Saffron", have been thoroughly revised to encompass a comprehensive examination of the elements that have emerged since 2014.

Regarding the subject of the saffronising of green, on which my focus in the earlier edition was written up as three case studies based on fieldwork in two locations – Ralegan Siddhi and Vrindavan – I undertook further fieldwork in both locations over 2023. Consequently, I have incorporated postscripts into the two chapters that look at these areas, thereby shedding light on the new dimensions that have emerged in them.

Since this edition primarily emphasises India post-2014, I have removed the chapter on conservative environmentalism in Europe which featured in the 2012 version.

Overall, the present edition aims to broaden our understanding of right-wing ecology during the ascendancy of Hindu nationalism, particularly under the leadership of the authoritative-authoritarian figure of Narendra Modi. No single book can comprehensively cover all developments in this domain: entirely new chapters could be written on topics such as Hindu nationalist environmental politics regarding technology, science, food, animals, and specific geographical locations. This edition aims to capture overarching trends in the hope that future works and emerging scholars will delve deeper into these subjects.

# Acknowledgements

In June 2020 I received a communication from Dr Bernhard Forchtner, University of Leicester, UK, asking for an essay in his forthcoming edited book, *Visualising Far-right Environments: Communication and the Politics of Nature*. I accepted his invitation. Unfortunately, my plans were disrupted by the outbreak of the Covid-19 pandemic, which made it impossible for me to meet the initially agreed deadline. Throughout this challenging period, Dr Forchtner showed remarkable patience and courtesy, generously extending the time line to allow me to finalise my contribution. Ultimately, my essay titled "Homeland, Cows, and Climate Change: The Visualisation of Environmental Issues by the Far Right in India" found its place within the pages of his book. More than its value as academic collaboration, this whole experience served as a catalyst for my reconnection with the themes of *Green and Saffron*, prompting me to contemplate a new edition. Therefore I express my utmost gratitude to Dr Bernhard Forchtner for his contribution. Although I have never met him in person, I have gained invaluable insights from his extensive work in this field, as well as from his outstanding communication, editing, and overall professional abilities.

In the late 1990s, as I embarked on my journey as a journalist and researcher focused on *Green and Saffron*, a serendipitous discovery shaped the trajectory of my work. It was a book authored by Jonathan Olsen explaining the phenomenon of right-wing ecology in Germany. This tome swiftly became an invaluable compass guiding my research in India. Fast forward to 2020, and a communication from Jonathan made me turn attention to my own book. This unexpected connection, too, led me to contemplate the possibility of this revised edition. Jonathan's pioneering insights on the subject were pivotal in my decision-making. Over a series of email exchanges and zoom conversations I reached out to him, requesting the foreword that he has very generously provided: my heartfelt gratitude to him. I eagerly anticipate continuing to garner wisdom from his future contributions.

In 2020, following my appointment to the Department of Environmental Studies at Ashoka University, I taught a course on Indian environmental politics woven around aspects of *Green and Saffron*. The academic environment at Ashoka University, coupled with the enthusiastic interest of my students, proved a significant motivating factor. My course students consistently enquired about recent developments, particularly those after 2014. I am gratified that some of them have chosen to pursue research assignments independently within this very domain.

Since the 1990s, work on this book has gone through many phases on account of changes in my life: from professional journalism to doctoral research and academia, from the world of universities to national and international non-governmental organisations (NGOs and INGOs) to social-political activism. The subject lived on within me anyhow, and even when it seemed I was losing the threads they found their way back via some coincidence, event, or discussion.

If I had to name one person who had to go through all this with me, who shared the beginning, end, pain, joy, happiness, and burden, and yet offered support all the time with her academic rigour, comments, and suggestions, it would be Charu Gupta. This book would not have begun or been concluded without her – which also holds true for this revised edition.

The second-most important person, who has been with me throughout in one way or another, is Mahesh Rangarajan, a friend possessed of a unique combination of energy, talent, intellect, and much more. His detailed handwritten comments on my several drafts, his many emails providing references, his queries, discussions, and concern over my progress all meant a lot to me. Mahesh has diligently reviewed the new chapter featured in this edition and provided me with comprehensive feedback. His insights and comments have proven incredibly valuable during the revision process.

As regards some circumstances in which this book originated more than a decade back: it started when I was a journalist working for the *Navbharat Times* in Delhi, closely monitoring environmental issues and movements. I was lucky at the time to gain first-hand knowledge of environmentalist politics and practices on the ground. I read everything I could lay my hands on around the subject, I made intensive notes. In London for a few months I mulled matters and finally mustered up the courage to call Professor Gyanendra Pandey to explore the possibility of a PhD under his supervision. Gyan played a decisive role in helping me shape, develop, and make my research proposal concrete. As my PhD adviser it was he who first read the initial drafts of two chapters and engaged with me in long discussions at the India International Centre. My teacher, he also became a friend; he was always a great communicator, charmer, and supporter. When he left Delhi I virtually lost my bearings. Now I remember Gyan every time I look at sections of this book and think that in some ways it was completed because I wanted to convey my respect for him and repay his confidence in me.

It was around the time Gyan left Delhi that I began sharing the bedrock of ideas on which this book is built with my friends Aditya Nigam and Nivedita Menon. Always intellectually sharp and politically alert, they offered support, comments, and encouragement. Later, when I was applying for a Sephis scholarship and gaining affiliation to the Centre for the Study of Developing Societies (CSDS) to complete this book, Aditya did all he could to help my work. Nivi's support was especially critical at one point of time and I acknowledge it with deep personal regards.

I also connected quite often with two acknowledged scholars, Ramachandra Guha and Jean Dreze, to get their comments and suggestions. Ram Guha provided written suggestions and references for many chapters, and during my times of confusion and conflict stood by the value of my work. His support has been invaluable and I thank him for all he has done for me. Jean Dreze commented on several chapters, reminding me of certain gaps, nuances, and new dimensions in dealing with my case studies, and suggesting certain positive changes. I was surprised and touched when, after a gap of several years, he asked after the status of my research. Jean is a man difficult to thank – a wisp of a man, he becomes a will-o'-the-wisp before you can catch him to thank him.

I had heard of "blessings in disguise" but saw one take shape as Dilip Menon when he became my new research supervisor. It was a matter of pride and privilege for me that a distinguished historian like Dilip accepted me as his student. He was pleasant, thorough, innovative, and provocative, providing me with new references, books, and methodologies. His immense knowledge was never intimidating, on the contrary it was comforting. I owe him my sincere thanks and an apology for being a student drop-out.

Support and encouragement also came from several other distinguished scholars: Nandini Gooptu of Oxford University, when I was a visiting fellow at Queen Elizabeth House, discussed my topic threadbare. As a fellow at the Asia Centre of the London School of Economics and Political Science I had the benefit of comments on a draft chapter from Meghnad Desai, who showed keen interest in my work. Ghanshyam Shah, David Hardiman, Jonathan Parry, the late M.S.S. Pandian, and the late Krishna Raj contributed with suggestions. I also offer my sincere thanks to Ulbe Bosma and Ingrid Goehard from Sephis for supporting my research.

Following the publication of my book in 2012, I delivered talks at numerous universities in India and abroad. I would like to express my heartfelt gratitude to Professor Ujjwal Singh, Professor Maninder Thakur, Professor Barbara Harris-White, Professor Gunnel Cederlöf, and Professor Bengt G. Karlsson for the invitations that took me to these institutions.

Satyadeep helped with the editing and proof-reading, for which I thank him.

Finally, Rukun Advani, my editor and publisher, took great interest in this work and, with encouraging words and instant responses, got me in the end to part with the manuscript. The book is what it is considerably due to him. When contemplating the necessity of a revised edition, I reached out to Rukun in 2021 to explore the idea, and he responded encouragingly. During our subsequent communications in 2023, he expressed unequivocal commitment to proceed with the new edition. His clear support as my publisher – seconded by Rudrangshu Mukherjee's generous financial and intellectual support via the Ashoka University series he runs – worked as a powerful motivator for me to complete this new edition.

In the world of NGOs and INGOs within which I have worked the past several years, I remember and thank two of my former colleagues in the Heinrich Boell Foundation, an organisation close to the Green Party in Germany. These colleagues saw the broad relevance of this topic and, driven by supportive feeling for a friend and colleague, selflessly helped me collect documents, translated them into English, and went over the text. For various reasons, they do not wish to be named, but I will always remember them for their solidarity and comradeship.

Other colleagues, friends, and acquaintances in this sector have shown their appreciation at different points and in various ways. To name a few, I acknowledge the support of Sumedha Basu, Anand Pradhan, Aniket Aga, John Samuel, Yamini Mishra, Salil Shetty, Richa Singh, Sana Das, Sheeba Mathew, and Sibha Mohanty.

Vijay Pratap, a political and social activist and visible figure in civil society initiatives, gave critical comments and showed a lot of interest in the course my work was taking. I have learned and gained a lot from him. Ashish Kothari, a fine writer and long-standing professional on environmental issues; and Aseem Srivastava, an economist, commentator, author, and friend, have been sources of support.

In the field of media and journalism, within which I still have a deep sense of belonging, the *Economic and Political Weekly*, *Frontline*, and *Seminar* have given space to my writings. N. Ram, editor, *Frontline*, was the first to publish my piece "Nature and Nationalism" in that magazine and, as always, I wish to convey warm thanks to him for his constant support. Ram Manohar Reddy, formerly editor of the *Economic and Political Weekly*, published three special articles of mine that prompted many people from India and abroad to send me enriching comments: my special thanks to Ram Reddy. Harsh Sethi of *Seminar* published an article based on this work: I have always found him generous and positive and thank him. I sincerely thank Suhas Palshikar, editor, *Studies in Indian Politics*, who published a research article titled "Hindu Nationalism and Right-wing Ecology: RSS, Modi and Motherland Post-2014". The insightful comments provided by anonymous referees, coupled with the editors' timely and constructive feedback, significantly enhanced the quality of this book's chapters.

Some people become integral to one's life, whatever one does and wherever one lives. For me they are my friends Anand Swamy and Jeremy Seabrook, and my son Ishaan Sharma. Without them I am incomplete. They make me and my work whole. I would like to acknowledge here their life-saving importance for me and this book.

I began with Charu but would like to end with another dedication: to Chandi Prasad Bhatt. An environmentalist, activist, amazing human being, father-figure, concerned neighbour, writer, communicator, villager, and traveller who inspires countless people like me in their everyday journeys of environmentalism and social activism.

In Charu and Chandi Prasad-ji I see all that is most precious to me.

# Prologue

## An Annual Puja, an Animal Sacrifice, a Fair

### In the State of Bihar, District Khagaria, Block Auololi, Village Sonmanki

FOUR KILOMETRES south from Khagaria town, at the Sonmanki ghat on the Bagmati river, a religious ceremony is beginning. The purpose of the ceremony, called Maa Kosi ka Mela (a fair in honour of Mother Kosi), held on the auspicious day of Paus Purnima, is to control land erosion caused by the Kosi and Bagmati rivers, which seasonally change course, bringing devastating floods in their wake. There is a chill in the morning air, but that does not deter the few hundred villagers – men, women, and children – of Sonmanki, Koyla, and Ladaura villages from attending the fair.

On the river bank's sandy surface a temple of bricks and cement is constructed, but it is left incomplete. Here a big idol of Mother Kosi is installed. The idol-maker, Dinesh Kumar Paswan, explains to me that the idol broadly resembles that of the goddess Durga. Shown riding a crocodile, the idol has four arms; one of these holds a conch shell, another a discus. Along with the main idol is a small idol of Koshlaveer, bearing in his hand a spade. Four other idols are installed alongside – of Saraswati, Ganesh, Laxmi, and Kartik.

A head Brahmin arrives with his two disciples after a dip in the river. They don new clothes and sacred threads (*janeu*), then come into the temple and arrange prayer material in front of the idols – *chandan, dhoop, agarbatti,* fruits, flowers, coconut, sweets, and several other things. A fasting Brahmin, who has to be from the village, must now join in prayer. The head Brahmin begins the puja by chanting mantras in Sanskrit. He lights the fire and periodically consigns various offerings to the flames. His disciples and the villagers follow him with offerings and chants. After an hour of prayer, an *arti* takes place in which everyone assembled participates. Dalits of the villages gather outside the temple and wait for the *arti* to come out; they are not allowed inside. The *arti* concludes and the chief Brahmin proceeds towards the river water. Everybody follows. Here a small goat is ready with red ribbons. The goat is bathed in the river, worshipped, and then drowned as a sacrifice to placate the river. Erosion, changes in river courses, and floods are wished away. A Dalit *ghatwar* is allowed to take possession of the drowned goat.

The beginning of the ceremony – the prayer – is over. Now the Sonmanki mela has formally begun and will continue for four days. A few women serve specially cooked food to the Brahmin and his disciples. He is given money and *dakshina.* He leaves the venue and will return on the fourth day to conclude the ceremony – to perform puja and *omjaap*, organise the idol immersion, and accept offerings and his service fees.

Indian culture has a long tradition of worshipping rivers. We worship the Ganga, Yamuna, and Saraswati. We live with rivers, and thus on some occasions like Kartik Purnima, Agahan Purnima and Magh Purnima, we first bathe in the sacred rivers and then worship them. The emergence of Kosi worship and fair is a reflection of our faith in rivers, in their flow in whatever form, and our deep commitment to environmental values inherent in our traditional culture. In flood-affected areas, this has a special significance.

So says a report entitled *Nadiyon ka Swarup Murtiyon ke Roop Mein* (The Nature of Rivers in the Form of Idols), prepared by a local NGO which actively supports this kind of environmentalism. The fair looks like a shop window for various activities. There are swings, recreational performances, edibles, village plays, small circuses, wrestling and *kushti,* song and dance. Pappu Kumar, a major organiser of this fair, narrates that in the year 2000 four *natuas* (jesters) came to perform the dances and a city group enacted a play, *Sasta Khoon, Mahanga Pani* (Blood is Cheap, Water is Dear) and charged Rs 6000 to perform it. Altogether, about ten or twelve villages, including Sonak, Sonmanki, Koyla, and Ladaura, have joined in the festivities.

Kosi worship began in 1990 and the fair came into being in 1995. It began first in Sonmanki, Koyla, and Ladaura villages. A few years later, in 2001–2, it was also happening in slightly far-off villages such as Mohanpur. Some local NGOs began working to spread its appeal. Twenty-six-year-old Umesh Gupta claims to be the initiator of Mother Kosi worship, and the villagers acknowledge this. A petty trader and transport operator of Sonmanki village, Umesh is also a local leader. He says, "Erosion due to the river changing course was fast approaching our village and, therefore, I thought of offering our prayers to the beloved river. When I shared my ideas with some other villagers and organizations active in the village, they gave a positive nod. In any case, we have long been worshipping the river in one way or the other." Umesh and other villagers in Sonmanki now believe that from the time the worship of Mother Kosi began, the erosion affecting their village has decreased. They also believe this is so because the fair is held at a sacred place where ten years earlier the river flowed. The river is seen as an integral part of their collective life, being the source of all joy and sorrow. It is to be both loved and feared. "We have always been with the Kosi river, and seen its different changing courses. The river gives us life. It can do anything to anybody": this is the refrain of Rajvir, a villager. Indeed, the Kosi is the source of everything – agriculture, fish, and fodder – and makes life possible for the majority of the people here.

Sonmanki is located between Kosi and Bagmati, two well-known rivers of the region. Land erosion, often caused by regular floods, affects the village seriously. The village is a large one, a big settlement with a long history. The people here, mostly Brahmins, Rajputs, Yadavs, Kurmis, and Musahars, cultivate the land and grow rice, maize, and sometimes vegetables – all at the mercy of rains and floods. A few families here own all the land, even as the majority of the population is landless. Most households have some cattle, but that is hardly sufficient for their food, nor even to provide supplementary income. A large number of people leave the village to seek casual employment, venturing to cities nearby and far off. The few who have land and money or access to private or government jobs live in nearby towns and "do some side business" in the construction and transport sectors. Here, there is no primary school, health centre; no roads and no electricity. Sonmanki and the villages nearby are situated precariously at the edge of every erosion. The regular floods, displacement, and destitution, make life difficult and uncertain for most villagers. Crisis-ridden agriculture and seasonal labour remain the basis of the economy; living and working are often seen as endless, painful chores. Employment and food are scarce; getting a bare minimum entails tiring and unremunerative work. There are many additional dangers to cope with: rains and floods ruin the harvest; diseases break out and, with no immediate ways of getting medical attention, are a constant worry. Snakes are a real and persistent threat to life.

The villagers do not regard themselves as capable of controlling these events. They live in a world where things happen to them. Although a few developments are attributed to personal agency – habits like drinking liquor and gambling – most misfortunes are blamed on spirits or the anger of Mother Kosi. "Mother Kosi is punishing me. She is unhappy; we all neglected and forgot her these many years," says Akhouri. Another says: "We had always been blessed by our Mother Kosi and had lived happily here. However, in present times, this has stopped. The government and development projects are ruining us." These too are beyond the control of the villagers, so they are responsible for their present misfortune. It follows that a range of methods are suggested to guard against environmental destruction.

It is possible that the villagers also have other methods, values, and traditions for environmental protection, for a variety of experiences and influences are at work. However, the villagers know beyond all argument that they are at the mercy of forces largely beyond their control. This sense of powerlessness pervades everything. It is the very context in which all cultural and environmental practices must be negotiated. A sense of low self-efficacy prevails in a range of situations, and the villagers are on the constant lookout for various personal agents. Traditional medicines, charms, and ritual offerings offer some protection in specific situations, but there are always others waiting in the wings. Ma Kosi ka Mela is one of them.

The physical environment that dictates the fortunes of Sonmanki and other villages is no different from the social environment. Five upper-caste landowners own a hundred acres of agricultural land. A dozen more own a sizeable proportion of the agricultural land in the region. There are also some new landowners from the city who are buying land for farms, brick kilns, plantations, and non-farm activities. "We work on the land owned by *babu log* [masters]. The employment here is only for a few months in a year, but that is the only stable earning within our normal reach. The daily wages are Rs 30 to Rs 40, depending on the decision of the landowners," says Hariom, a scheduled caste landless worker in Ladaura village. In the recent past, landless labourers have been migrating more and more to various cities in search of work, and for this they depend on their masters. They need loans for their journey and the expenses back home; their families are given repeated loans or other help by the landowners' families. These relationships of power and protection operate in many ways: "Every few months, the money orders come to the post office. Since the post office is at the *babu*'s place, he receives it and gives us the money only after deducting some amount as interest. The draft can only be encashed through *babu saheb*'s account,"' says a villager.

The balance of power lies here, with the landowner, the rich, upper-caste man. Physical and social environments feed into each other; both share a common feature: they are more powerful than the populace. Pappu, Umesh Gupta, and Rajeev Singh have land, money, and power. They spend thousands initiating the worship, the fair, the temple, the animal sacrifice. Umesh Gupta and Pappu claim to spend Rs 25,000 to Rs 30,000 every year on the puja and mela. They are the ones who invent, prevail upon, and manage traditions and cultures to suit their environment, to get what they need. Through this reinvention of traditional environmental and cultural values, a new fatalism is induced and celebrated. The power and will of the people to exert an influence on environmental processes is taken over by the dominant social powers. The powerful stand to gain the most from a conservative assertion of the status quo. They live at the cost of most of the rest, condemned to a sapping and fatalistic powerlessness.

# 1

# Introduction

In its present updated and expanded form this book explores the intersection of environmental politics and the ideology of Hindu nationalism, in both present-day and historical settings. Starting from 2014 the ascent of Hindu nationalism, led by entities like the RSS, the BJP, and the BJP's leader Narendra Modi, has been closely intertwined with specific environmental narratives, initiatives, and messaging. These efforts serve a dual purpose: firstly, to broaden the political and ideological influence of these entities and the leader, and secondly, to contribute to the emergence of a new and assertive Hindu nationalist environmental perspective. My work has emerged from my interest in contemporary environmental issues and movements in independent India, as well as in the development of Hindu nationalist ideology and politics over the same period. Both these developments have been significant in the late-twentieth and early-twenty-first centuries. Most of the existing academic and journalistic literature tends to treat the two – environmentalism and Hindu nationalism – as discrete and autonomous, seldom perceiving that environmental issues have often been constructed and defined in new ways by Hindu nationalism. Complementing this, certain environmental movements and discourses, consciously or unconsciously, overtly or covertly, have expressed themselves in ways that aid articulations of revivalist and nationalist Hindu thought; in fact certain core components of Hindutva ideology have become crucial rallying points for these movements.

My book explores the interrelationships between the two. It does so by examining the articulation and activities of Hindu nationalist forces on environmental issues, specifically focusing on some prominent environmental initiatives in the various regions of India. It studies the process by which a particular political ideology becomes infused with and takes shape through conceptions of nature, culture, and the nation. Moreover, it investigates how a prevailing political entity in contemporary India substantially amplifies its engagement with environmental politics.

The term "saffron" has specific connotations. It is often a religiously significant colour, particularly in Hinduism, within which it is associated with renunciation. In this book, however, "saffron" is not intended to denote any specifically religious activity, such as asceticism or the life of itinerant monks. Nor, by using the term, am I setting out to unravel Hindu religious thought, which is a separate subject for philosophical and historical exploration.[1] Rather, I use the word saffron to denote the political dimensions of drawing on colour imagery. Specifically, I look at the political practice of Hindutva ("Hinduness") which deploys the religious associations of the colour saffron for mobilisations – environmental and otherwise – that are unconnected with the practice of religion as ordinarily understood. In this sense, therefore, my book delves into the ideological and mobilisational core of Hindutva or Hinduness as politics, distinct from religiosity.

Looking more microscopically, my work is therefore also closely concerned with those who may not always see themselves as carriers of an ideology, but who in practice implicitly advance the logic, objectives, and ways of seeing of that ideology. I argue that there is a "greening of saffron" when Hindutva organisations make nature conservation part of their political ideologies and agendas. The other side of the same coin shows a "saffronising of green", which happens when environmental movements and organisations make Hindutva's cultural politics a fundamental aspect of their environmental discourse.

[1] As, for instance, studied in Chapple and Tucker, eds, *Hinduism and Ecology*.

Hindu nationalism encompasses authoritarian cultural nationalists as well as Hindutva adherents and supporters, all of whom are out to remake Indian society, polity, ecology, and culture in myriad ways. This brand of nationalism has also played a critical role in shaping communal identities in India. Naturally, there is a rich and varied analytic literature on the subject which looks at Hindu nationalism's projects historically and as contemporary practice.[2] The India under Modi's leadership and the rise of Hindu nationalism since 2014 have garnered substantial attention in the recent past.[3] But this is not a literature that, for all its insight, has recognised the importance of ecology as a factor in shaping the contours of Hindu nationalism. By the same token, environmental movements in contemporary India have been extensively covered in the media, being complemented by a rich corpus of academic writings on the subject.[4] Significant in their own right, this again is a literature, largely celebratory in tone, that has ignored the frequent intertwining of green politics with saffron imagery.

There are probably many reasons for writers on the environment missing seeing these links: political colour-blindness; anti-Nehruvianism or an anti-science worldview; hostility to modernist visions of development; a contempt for centralised planning, technology, and progress; upper-caste predilections; the valorisation of and nostalgia for a supposedly more environmentally friendly past; a view of

[2] Some of these are: Pandey, *The Construction of Communalism*; Freitag, *Collective Action and Community*; Das, ed., *Mirrors of Violence*; Van der Veer, *Religious Nationalism*; Brass, *Ethnicity and Nationalism*; Jaffrelot, *The Hindu Nationalist*; Hansen, *The Saffron Wave*.

[3] See, for example, Jaffrelot, *Modi's India*; Gudavarthy, *India after Modi*; Rehman, ed., *Rise of Saffron;* Sardesai, *How Modi Won*; Prabhu, *Middle Class, Media*; Mehta, *The New BJP*.

[4] To mention just a few, Agarwal and Narain, eds, *The State of India's Environment*; Agarwal, D'Monte, and Samarth, eds, *The Fight for Survival*; Baviskar, *In the Belly*; Chhatre and Saberwal, *Democratising Nature*; Fernandes, Menon, and Viegas, *Forests, Environment and Tribal*; Shiva, *Staying Alive*; Guha, *The Unquiet Woods*; Guha, ed., *Social Ecology*; Gadgil and Guha, *Ecology and Equity*; Pathak, ed., *Pahar* (Mountain), vols 1, 2, 3–4, Delhi, 1983, 1986 and 1989, respectively.

ecological activism as broadly benign; and a desire to celebrate the small, the rural, and the traditional.[5] Feminist scholars have been more perceptive: unlike analysts of environmentalism they have frequently seen the links between gender issues and Hindu nationalism.[6]

This book attempts to bridge the lacuna. Unlike work on statist authoritarian interventions,[7] or on the mobilisation strategies of a democratising under-class,[8] it focuses on the unexplored cultural, ethnic, and sectarian dimensions of green issues in India, with an emphasis on the past fifteen years, including the Modi era. It reflects on the general political trajectory of Indian politics over this period and locates environmental movements and debates within the contexts of that trajectory. It also seeks to reveal the transition from secular environmentalism to an environmentalism imbued with religiously emotive and sectarian issues, leading therefrom to the intermeshing of identity, power, and nature.[9]

In a wider historical and geographical context this subject – the coalescence of environmentalism with specific varieties of political activism and mobilisation – has been sporadically documented in the West.[10] Scholars have pointed out that far-right parties and organisations in Europe and the United States have sometimes taken a Green perspective onto their platform, the ideological product of which has been called "right-wing ecology" or far-right ecologism.[11] The environmental communication of the "far-right" party and non-party

[5] These are taken up in greater detail in various parts of the book.

[6] See, for example, Sarkar and Butalia, eds, *Women and the Hindu*; Sarkar, "The Woman as Communal Subject", 2057–62; Jayawardena and De Alwis, eds, *Embodied Violence*; Bacchetta, *Gender in the Hindu*; Jeffery and Basu, eds, *Resisting the Sacred.*

[7] For instance, Jalais, *The Forest of Tigers.*

[8] For instance, Subramanian, *Shorelines.*

[9] In this sense this book develops and amplifies issues raised in my essay "Saffronising Green".

[10] For example, Bramwell, *Ecology in the 20th Century*; Schama, *Landscape and Memory.*

[11] Olsen, *Nature and Nationalism*; Lubarda, *Far-Right Ecologism.*

actors offers distinctive ecological visions of community life and also points to a close connection between the politics of identity and the imagination of nature.[12] These formations have also shown that biological explanations and ecological justifications have frequently been used to support fascism: many neo-Nazis, for instance, replicate Hitler's vegetarianism, as well as "back to the land" movements and biodynamic farming.[13] Others have reflected on similar dangers in present-day Green politics within the West, where traditional ecological conservation can easily shade into right-wing irrationalism or extreme romanticism. The key elements in such instances include the use of biological metaphors, a stress on the "organic community" and the individual's need to merge with it, a Laurentian glorification of ritual, intuition, and the mystical, and a distrust of the rational.[14] There is a significant level of denial of climate change among right-wing parties. However, researchers have pointed out that some far-right populist parties are adopting climate-protection policy positions, showing much more flexibility and adaptability than previously anticipated, and using these issues strategically for the benefit of their organisation.[15] Indeed, some have acknowledged climate change, incorporating such a stance to blame immigrants and to advocate stronger borders, which has been referred to as "eco-bordering".[16] These elements can all be found in certain kinds of ecological writing, especially those that promote "deep ecology" activism – which shows an affinity with what might legitimately be called eco-fascism.[17] While

[12] Forchtner, ed., *The Far Right.*

[13] Bookchin, "A Green Course", 10–13. Bookchin shows how nature philosophy can be gravely abused. Hitler, for example, used biological analogies, notably those of race, soil, homeland, folk, and blood to underpin his viciously fascist-imperialist theories, and spoke of the homeland almost in an ecological sense.

[14] The oeuvre of D.H. Lawrence and writers of his ilk is widely recognised as crucial to the formation of this ideology in the twentieth century, though detailed consideration of such writers is obviously not part of the scope of this book.

[15] Oswald, Fromm, and Broda, "Strategic Clustering", 185–205.

[16] Turner and Bailey, "Ecobordering", 110–31.

[17] Hay, "Ecological Values", 22–9; Peet and Watts, eds, *Liberation Ecologies,* 268–9.

providing important references and examples, there are crucial differences between these on the one hand, and roughly analogous Indian instances on the other – as I will try to show.

At stake in this intermeshing of Green and Saffron is nothing less than the way people understand their humanity. It is paradoxical that the environmental concerns of Hindu nationalists are occasionally expressed in virtually the language used by radical environmental and social movements. This simple and disingenuous appropriation of language points to a serious problem: the emergence of communal and authoritarian discourses within the new social movements in India. Simultaneously, it indicates the ambivalences and multivalences in the vocabulary that is deployed: we are often faced with a situation where a single set of words can mean quite different things, depending on the discourse within which such words are placed. It would be naive to assume that the entire content of the emerging environmental issues and movements is progressive, which is their claim. A large part of the panoply of environmental politics in India today in fact reveals some political allegiances or affinities with Hindu nationalist and authoritarian forces. Therefore, rather than uncritically endorse all environmental movements, or all visions of the environment, I analyse their limitations, as also the intractability and contradictions in their relationship to Hindu nationalism and communalism. It is now often said that "those who want to reform society according to nature are neither Left nor Right, but ecologically minded."[18] Individuals, groups, and campaigns that take up environmental causes either see environmental work as political work, or claim that their politics lies beyond or above both Left and Right. At times, such activity is categorised as non-party, independent, or alternative political work. How tenable are these claims?

Environmental ideologies and worldviews define politics, nations, and development in diverse ways, with sharply contesting and contrasting visions of how to structure society, resources, classes, castes, people, landscapes, and culture. Today's environmentalism defines and proposes the contours of culture, community, tradition, and place

[18] Bramwell, *Ecology in the 20th Century*, 48. She also says that politics according to nature is unambiguous.

in significant ways; it also helps perform important roles in identity creation and conservation. If this is true, then it is impossible to maintain that environmental politics is beyond Left and Right, nationalism and communalism, Brahmin and Dalit, authority and democracy, nationalism and ultra-nationalism. Far from transcending these categories it is, in fact, being transformed by them.

## The Greening of Saffron

The idea of dharma and activities based on it, and its exploitation for political purposes, have been central to the theory and practice of Hindu communal organisations. The RSS regularly plugs into issues of ecology and world peace, and the interrelated critiques of Western materialistic and monolithic notions of truth that lead to the imperialist suppression of non-Western identities.[19] There exist a series of teachings and activities pertaining to conservation, purification, and cleanliness – carried out through local organisations working among tribals, youths, students, women, workers, and farmers – which use a local idiom and vocabulary replete with alternative local epithets, but which are essentially the branch propaganda or local projects of the RSS and the Vishwa Hindu Parishad (VHP). For instance, the RSS argues that "The genesis of the Chipko movement is not only in the ecological or economic background, but in religious belief . . . The religious basis of the movement is evident in the fact that it is inspired and guided by women."[20] Further, "The minds of Hindu people are slowly being awakened through Chipko, Appiko, Bishnois, Chetna Manch and other environmental movements."[21]

The scope of "environmental" activities by Hindu communal forces has widened since the 1980s. The VHP joined the anti-Tehri dam movement in a big way in the late 1980s; the former Shiv Sena supremo Bal Thackeray repeatedly claimed to be a pure naturalist and

[19] Sarkar, "The Woman as Communal Subject", 2059.

[20] Anonymous, *Desh ki Chinta* (Concern for the Nation), RSS pamphlet, Delhi, 1988, 4. All translations from the Hindi are mine, unless otherwise specified.

[21] Ibid.

environmentalist; the BJP–Shiv Sena combine actively participated in the first phase of the anti-Enron agitation, which brought it global attention; the Hindu Right's overwhelming support to and initiatives in the coastal fishworkers' movement of the 1990s coincided with reclaiming the "authentic" name for Bombay, namely Mumbai (after Mumbadevi, the goddess traditionally worshipped by Bombay's fisherfolk); the BJP and its affiliates actively campaigned "to save Ram Setu" in the name of environment, religion, and society. These examples reveal not only a proactive concern for the environment but also political support for some well-known environmental movements.

Starting from 2014, there have been discernible shifts in both the quantity and quality of environmental initiatives carried out by the RSS–BJP combine. This amalgam of organisations, including the ruling BJP at the national level and within several states, has adopted a more systematic, organised, and widespread approach to addressing environmental concerns. Their agenda encompasses a diverse array of topics, such as rural development, agriculture, organic farming, nutrition, cattle, wildlife, rivers, sanitation, hygiene, pollution, urbanisation, industry, scientific advances, energy, climate shifts, urban planning, and responses to natural calamities. Among these themes, certain concepts stand out prominently. They include the notion of an expansive and sacred natural "Motherland" rooted in Hindu traditions, encompassing its historical, contemporary, and future dimensions. This vision often centres around icons symbolising the maternal figure, embodied in elements like rivers and animals, while also identifying perceived adversaries. Additionally, a significant emphasis is placed on praising Narendra Modi as a champion of environmental causes. Notably, climate change and renewable energy have risen to the forefront as critical arenas for environmental discourse within the Hindu nationalist framework. These topics are intricately linked, with the RSS advocating for active participation of industries, scientists, and technocrats in combating climate change. Simultaneously, they position the large-scale renewable energy sector as a solution to address this issue. In parallel, there is a selective targeting of practices, individuals, locales, and political entities. These are either criticised and condemned for ecological reasons or lauded to elevate a strong leader who is portrayed as guiding and acting to cleanse the nation of perceived cultural pollutants.

The environmental concerns of Hindu authoritarianism can be broadly classified into certain themes that are valorised or demonised, depending on political context and requirement. These include eco-nationalism, eco-primitivism, eco-naturalism, the eco-enemy, the eco-saviour, Brahmanical models, and cow protection. Focusing on these themes, Hindu environmental politics fabricates glorifications of "Hindu" mother/fatherland, rivers, forests, community, tradition, self-reliant villages, and the science, technology, and knowledge of ancient "Bharat" and its nature philosophy; simultaneously it condemns modernisation, Westernisation, and globalisation. Many of these elements can also be observed in various other prominent environmental movements and organisations in the country, though their perspective may vary somewhat. Overall, this is a scenario which shows the grounds being created for building a relationship between these two apparently opposed forces.

Hindutva's political agenda is often articulated via weaving environmental issues into its popular discourses. The vocabulary of environmentalism is deployed to censure "foreign cultural domination", "imported culture", "the continued domination of Muslim culture", "British-induced Christianity", and "Western secular institutions and values". Traditional environmental terms tie in nicely with the religious repertoire of sanitation, pollution, sacredness, purity, and purification, and these then link with aggressive right-wing idiom and political metaphor. The "other" – not only excluded from the Hindu Right's environmental activities but also described as "poison" in the blood of India – is thereby eliminated, at least discursively. The effect is to forge the Hindu Right's environmental discourse as a consciously planned extension of old boundaries into new frontiers. If the old boundaries involved a rational environmentalist pedagogy and the everyday practice of environmentalism, the new frontiers involve a militant posture on environmental issues within a larger metanarrative of Hindu nationalism, Hindu superiority, national purity, and the need for mass movements supporting these. Since the year 2014, the RSS and the BJP have adeptly merged governance strategies with political agendas, seamlessly blending Hindu nationalism and environmental ideologies, as well as aligning eco-activities with corporate interests. This strategic fusion has enabled them to engage in extensive organisational and political outreach, on a wide range of environmental issues.

There are obvious paradoxes and contradictions within this Greening of Saffron. For one, the animosity and call for brutal elimination of the other also find expression in the Hindu Right's relationship with environmental movements which challenge its views and domination within its traditional strongholds. For another, this situation is pregnant with possibilities as well as problems for Hindutva: to first nullify and then renegotiate the Enron power project; to oppose the Tehri dam but support the Sardar Sarovar dam; to oppose globalisation and westernisation but to mobilise global corporations and mega "clean" industrial projects, to try and extend its appeal to the marginalised within Hindu society while marginalising all "others"; to make alliances with some prominent environmental movements but secede from a large number of others.

## The Saffronising of Green

This book, however, focuses significantly on the obverse, namely the Saffronising of Green. It does so by looking at some of the political shades within various environmental discourses, organisations, and movements over the past few decades, centrally Anna Hazare's Watershed Programme in Ralegan Siddhi, Maharashtra; Sunderlal Bahuguna and opposition to the Tehri dam in Garhwal; and the World Wildlife Fund for Nature's Vrindavan–Mathura Revival Project in Uttar Pradesh (UP). These three are used as umbrella case studies to explicate a constructive work effort (Ralegan Siddhi), a popular movement (Tehri), and a major NGO-backed reafforestation campaign in the North Indian area of Vrindavan which is considered sacred by many. In a variety of ways and contrasting styles, the politics of Hindu cultural nationalism infuses, interacts with, overwhelms, and retreats from the public and intellectual spaces represented by these sites. Different players enter the stage, and not all lines or roles are prescripted. What unfolds may come as a surprise both to those who study ecological movements in India as well as to those familiar with Hindu nationalist politics.

The "Vrindavan Forest Revival Project" in UP was jointly initiated by certain prominent environmental and religious organisations in 1991. Vrindavan has for long been constructed by folklore as the birthplace of Krishna, and, after what Hindutva terms the "Ram Janmabhoomi liberation campaign" and the destruction of the Babri mosque, the "liberation of Krishna Janmabhoomi" has become an ongoing part of its agenda. The vocabulary used to mobilise in favour of this environmental project underlines the causes of Vrindavan's environmental problems: these are the "abandonment of traditional Hindu values and technology", "centuries of Muslim and British rule detrimental to traditional Hindu culture and practices", and "forgetting injunctions such as those found in the *Manu Smriti*". The solutions suggested are based on an entirely new socio-political grounding which goes far beyond tree planting and improvements to the sewage system.[22] Part of this discourse provides a defence of the caste system, which is increasingly being challenged by the rising lower and intermediate castes, especially in North India, the heartland of communalism. For instance, Kailash Malhotra, an anthropologist, claims that

> The caste system . . . was actually based on an ancient concept of sustainable development which disciplined the society by partitioning the use of natural resources according to specific occupations (or castes); and "created" the right social milieu in which sustainable patterns of resource use were encouraged to "emerge".[23]

Or, as someone else puts it, "The Hindu caste system can be seen as a progenitor of the concept of sustainable development."[24] This variety of environmentalism involves a politics of both inclusion and

[22] Flyer, *Vrindavan Forest Revival Project*; Das (project director), "Reviving the Forests", 27.

[23] Quoted in Malhotra, *The State of India's Environment*, 162.

[24] Dwivedi, "Satyagraha for Conservation", 159.

exclusion. Far from being a binding factor in Vrindavan conservation, Krishna becomes an entity claimed by a few to the exclusion of many. In fact, the deity becomes one of the symbols of discord and resistance because its adoption has led to specific groups in society being excluded from the conservation project.

Similarly, in Ralegan Siddhi, a supposedly ideal village which showcases rural development and water conservation, the integration of Dalits is based on a double-barrelled prescription: they have to perform duties and services in accord with the best traditions of the past; their salvation lies in accepting the Brahmanical fold by adopting certain dietary, sartorial, and cultural habits laid down for them by caste Hindus. Nation, nation-building, nationalism, and ultra-nationalism, which have become the hallmarks of some prominent environmental initiatives, all find an echo in Ralegan Siddhi. The meaning of the Indian nation also takes specific shape here in the context of wars or the threat of war from neighbouring countries. Narratives of the war, the army, and the enemy remain core points of reference within the discourse on nation and rural development here. This particular developmental discourse of Anna Hazare, in which the army, war, and environmental engineering become one, as well as aspects of villager consciousness, are articulated in the form of a strict code and discipline. They are also linked to the ways in which the nation and its culture get conceptualised – nation as ideal, sufferer, and victim which must thus assert itself against the enemy. The efforts of rural development and its agents are intended to aid this process.

The enemy and threat perceptions occupy a similarly special place in the environmental identity of Sunderlal Bahuguna and the anti-Tehri dam activists. This identity is never fixed, it is always in a flux, in part because the threats change as the occasion demands. Mainly, the threats are seen as emanating from China and Chinese missiles, as also from "internal" enemies of India's national integrity and cultural unity. Environmentalism becomes part of a toolkit to protect this putative unity and integrity against internal and external aggression.

All three environmental movements studied herein reveal that purity and pollution, the sacred and the non-sacred, the holy and the unholy, the indigenous and the foreign, and in some cases the local and the migrant, all have an important bearing on notions of identity and the nation. Whereas pollution, in the modern environmental sense, normally relates to the material conditions of our natural surroundings, in the discourse of right-wing environmentalism pollution is additionally understood as the defilement of our natural, social, and cultural worlds by all that is declared unwanted, unwelcome, and alien. In this discourse certain things are decreed as heritage or as belonging to self and the nation, the purpose being to decree by implication that certain other things are alien. By this method some human groups are rendered clean precisely in order to render others dirty. This is a discourse within which understandings of the violation of nature are based on particular assumptions about what the natural and social orders should look like, who they should belong to, and how. The argument is that "we", the pure, need a sacrosanct moral regime not only to be rid of liquor, smoking, non-vegetarian food, and promiscuity, but also in order to exercise a hypothesised Hindu control over the private and the public, the personal and the political. In this way environmental discourses, however well intentioned, fall into the trap of valorising and romanticising dangerous forms of indigenism and obscurantism.

In order to look in detail at what has been outlined in this Introduction, Chapter 2 explores the views of the Hindu communalists – including parties, groups, and thinkers – on the environment. It focuses on some of the central principles that comprise the core of their environmental ideology. This core often shows a startling similarity with the ecological principles of some Indian environmental organisations and initiatives. An overriding concern with social pollution, the invocation of a mythical "golden age" of Vedic India, the valorisation of countryside and community, the idea of the nation as a product of nature, the defence of nature, nation, and nationalism, and a stress on the naturalness of the social order – all these are important environmental concerns in the ideology of Hindutva. Subsequent to 2014, a handful of pervasive environmental motifs have been utilised to portray India as a venerable historic Hindu nation deeply rooted in ecological principles. Simultaneously, this narrative has been manipulated to propagate hostility and aggression towards perceived "contaminated" Muslim communities, shaping perceptions around topics like food, animals, spaces, places, cultures, and traditions. The deployment of this world-view entails making common cause with environmental groups and movements. Environmentalism is therefore used as a Trojan horse to carry an authoritarian ideology into the citadels of ordinary discourse and political debate. Hyperbolic crisis narratives of environmental collapse also provide an opportunity to rework and re-energise the categories of Indian national identity as Hindu and its enemies as all that true Hinduism must shun.

The three chapters that then ensue carry the central argument of the book via detailed analysis of three environmental initiatives. Chapter 3 examines Anna Hazare's programme of watershed development in Ralegan Siddhi and provides insights into ways in which an individual and his organisation can play a central role in reshaping rural life. It explores the elusive but crucial element of a "moral authority" which presupposes the existence of a traditional culture conducive to the exercise of such authority. The hegemonic functions of consent and conservatism come into the picture here. It seems peculiar that accounts of this important movement remain largely commemorative in nature and do not examine the ideology and politics of the experiment. It seems to me crucial not only for us to understand the present and future of these "green villages", but also to interrogate the brand of environmentalism which underpins their greening. In spite of the apparent diversities that characterise Anna Hazare and Ralegan Siddhi, there is an underlying thread of unity within the ideological system of this form of green village, and this singularity of vision is what I try to show. Authority and legitimacy are a kind of double key to Anna Hazare's experiment. His is an authority deeply rooted in the dominant socio-political tradition of the region which often blinds the movement to many basic and universal issues connected with rights, democracy, and justice. An individual's overly personal moral authority, even as it substantially improves economic conditions within a village, also makes one ask if it is also improving (or worsening) the possibilities for democratically organised and thinking communities that are being made free of the burdens of force, punishment, coercion, obligation, patronage, charity, and piety from, if not authoritarianism, then its close kin paternalism and patriarchy.

Chapter 4 focuses on Sunderlal Bahuguna and his opposition to the Tehri dam in Garhwal. The movement has been significant for Indian environmentalism in general and struggles against big dams in particular. Big dams have been criticised both for the large-scale environmental transformation that they cause and for the social dislocations that inevitably follow their construction. Opposition to the Tehri dam began in the 1970s and much has been written about the dam's hazards and safety, about Sunderlal Bahuguna and his movement. Yet the language and politics of the movement, its visions of nation, history, and culture, and its alliance with specific varieties of politics have received scant attention. Least analysed seem to have been the shifts in the movement after the 1990s. I look specifically at these alterations, at the shifting contours of the movement and their implications. My attempt in doing this is to illuminate the changing declarations about and evocations of nature, religion, and nation by Sunderlal Bahuguna and the Tehri Bandh Virodhi Sangharsh Samiti on the one hand, and on the other of the VHP, which too is deeply implicated in anti-dam politics.

Such analysis shows that opposition to the Tehri dam has never been some simple disagreement about viability or non-viability, costs and benefits, and the displacement and resettlement issues thrown up by large dam construction. The debate has been far deeper, striking at the heart of philosophical, cultural, religious, political, and moral issues within the idea of "development". Prominent environmental activists and groups have pitched in with arguments in support of the age-old purity and holiness of the Ganga. Hindu myth and belief, ideas of cultural pollution, and a variety of fears and conspiracy theories have been brought in too, transforming a supposedly environmental platform into a breeding ground for Hindu nationalism. The possibilities of enhancing their credibility by moving beyond the traditional and familiar politics of hate has made it seem imperative to Hindutva to make common cause with Green issues. So the movement against the Tehri dam has become a means for combining everyday sacredness with protective impulse, the gravity of high politics with the solemnity of daily worship, and nature with nationalism. It has re-envisioned a river as a source of water into a political, moral, and emotional idea.

Naturally, such collaboration between Green and Saffron raises larger questions about Hindu nationalism and Indian environmentalism. It would be simplistic to see the VHP's involvement with opposition to the dam as only a political attempt to harness votes for the BJP. In fact, it is their comfortable intermeshing with a stream of environmental discourse that needs to be taken into account. The Tehri movement always had within it the seeds of Hindu conservatism. But, with its political course, the Hindu Right has also shown that it has the power to absorb, co-opt, and re-orient the political trajectory of an environmental movement.

I then move on to the Vrindavan Forest Revival and Conservation Project in UP, initiated by certain prominent environmental and religious organisations in 1991. We see here how the imagery and myth of a specific location reappear within an environmental context and encompass a whole environmental programme. It is apparent in this instance that the concern to protect and improve the environment of a religious location is not just a consequence of spirituality, imagination, and deep personal feeling among the proponents. Rather, valued places, powerful symbols, and representations work at different levels to create an intersection where place-specific religiosity, environmentalism, and Hindu authoritarian politics converge. Here, environmentalists transform a diversity of understandings, knowledges, myths, epics, and religious histories into a fixed and singular story that promotes a homogeneous and exclusive Hindu community. They use and manipulate, for their convenience, the various faces of Krishna offered in religious texts, transforming him into a deity that fits with the broader agenda of Hindutva.

Chapter 6 focuses on the recent history of Hindu nationalist engagement with climate change and renewable energy in the post-2014 era, particularly through the actions of Narendra Modi. It raises questions about the character of climate politics within the Hindu nationalist leadership, the role of key cultural and political concepts like a pure and powerful nation, the influence of Bharat's civilisational identity on the global stage, and the strategic utilisation of climate change to enhance the popularity and legitimacy of an authoritarian leader and his government. The analysis expands to explore the transformation in India's climate discourse post-2014, where social movements and grassroots organisations in the climate and renewable-energy sector have diminished. The shift in policies towards big industry-driven development under Modi's leadership has radically altered the sector. This has paradoxically aligned significant civil society groups with Modi's agenda while the RSS-BJP co-opt the traditional space of social movements.

So there is a history to this convergence between Green and Saffron, as well as contemporary concerns animating it. Although recent as a phenomenon on this scale in India, many elements within these movements have roots in earlier notions of environmental protection or preservation. Chapter 7 examines some of the major lines of argument about development and environmentalism in India before and after Independence. Special attention is paid to a continuing "nature and nationalism" tradition which is crucial for an understanding of the contemporary juncture.[25] Although this tradition was not the only form of environmental reasoning that existed earlier, it has been one of the most visible, and its arguments have had a powerful resonance. So I explore the ideological continuities and discontinuities that exist between this earlier tradition and its recent editions, placing particular emphasis on Gandhian environmental thought and beliefs.

In recent versions of the tradition, environmental degradation is the result of the imposition of modernisation and development by a Western colonial civilisation upon a rooted and indigenous Indian culture. This view is accompanied by a specific reading of Indian, largely Hindu, tradition. In the years following 2014, India under Modi's leadership has come to be recognised as a pivotal hub for "Bharatiya" contributions to environmental knowledge, science, and technology.

[25] Olsen, *Nature and Nationalism*.

A strain of nostalgia colours several of the arguments that are provided by what some scholars have referred to as a "new traditionalist" discourse. The pre-colonial Indian rural past is imagined to have been marked by harmonious social relationships and ecologically sensitive resource-use practices. If there is here a Proustian remembrance of time past, it is one which shows idealised local self-contained communities managing their own resources sustainably and equitably. Consequently, the logical consequence involves the depiction of a contemporary decline and deterioration, a narrative that can be revitalised through the adoption of Hindu nationalist environmental ideology. This renewal is sought through the amalgamation of green practices intertwined with corporate motivations, extensive organisational and political efforts on environmental issues, and a strong alignment with states governed by the BJP.

The last chapter sums up the major themes and features of the authoritarian environmentalism and its politics which the preceding chapters have analysed. It argues that such environmentalism, far from being a specifically Indian phenomenon, is to be found in various countries in different forms. This coalescence of authoritarian politics and environmental values therefore confronts us with further questions pertaining to dissemination, reach, impact, and likely durability – nationally and internationally. In the specific context of the convergence between Green and Saffron in India, I try to tease out some conclusions about the nature of contemporary environmentalism and its complex relationship with Hindu nationalism.

Within the academic literature Hindu nationalism has been examined mainly in relation to communalism, culture, and religion. This is insufficient. In our time this political programme encompasses a wide range of new themes as well as non-market and non-materialist issues, including those pertaining to the environment. True, Hindu nationalist forces are scattered and often inconsistent when taking up environmental issues; true also that their electoral dividends are not heavily dependent on their cultivation of an environmental constituency. Likewise, it is true that environmental groups and movements with a tendency towards authoritarianism and communalism are only a few among very many. All these truths notwithstanding, the important point is that this kind of environmentalism has made huge inroads into popular consciousness and, in our time, gained a far wider acceptance in India and elsewhere, in theory and in practice. The impact of this convergence cannot therefore be gauged only by analysing electoral gains and extreme manifestations during apocalyptic moments of upheaval. They must also be seen at the macro level of changes in political-environmental discourse.

Explorations such as those provided in this book offer certain critical tools as well as a textured analysis for, I hope, an improved understanding of the complexities, nuances, and ambiguities of environmental and social politics. I believe it is not only unnecessary to falsely valorise the past in order to critique modern development paradigms, but that such valorisation needs to be exposed for the political damage that it does. Environmental discourses which function in this manner are unacceptable because of their implications for social relations, as also their consequence for the distribution of benefits from resource-use and, indeed, ecological sustainability. A socially just and ecologically sustainable society cannot be created via the atavistic recrudescence implied in postulating the value of traditional socio-ecological relations, nor by religious, economic, and cultural nationalism. Fortunately, several environmental movements and activists are consistently and spiritedly resisting Hindu communalism. My intention in this book is to both record a history and outline a politics which alerts secular environmental and social movements in independent India to the problems that arise by the coming together of Saffron and Green.

# 2

# Hindu Nationalism and the Environment

## Elements and Themes

"Hindutva is an environmental movement and the Sangh promotes sustainable development" – Sunil Ambekar, RSS Akhil Bharatiya Prachar Pramukh[1]

ENVIRONMENTALISM IN THE saffronised colour of Hindu nationalism has arrived in India and assumed a full-fledged shape. For the past decade the RSS–BJP combine has been making concerted efforts to build its environmental politics, simultaneously speaking in many tongues and languages – of environment conservation and protection of the great Hindu "natural" motherland; of community and co-operation, force and authority; of pure, sacred, ancient traditions and "impure", imported, "polluted" people and cultures. Since the BJP's meteoric rise and advance post-2014, Hindu nationalist organisations have evolved a long-term political and organisational approach towards the environment, delving deep into issues of ecology and nature as well as launching campaigns around sacred rivers and animals. Many of the initiatives they have launched are new and well synchronised. In this chapter I first draw on contemporary and historical empirical evidence to document how RSS-led Hindu

[1] Ambekar, *The RSS Roadmaps*, 89.

nationalist organisations have evolved their environmental initiatives. Next, in the second section, I deal with the main themes and features of Hindutva environmentalism. I take pointers from studies on the far right and ecology: this provides me a framework for understanding Hindu nationalist environmental politics in India. The third section discusses the main ideas and subjects of Hindu nationalist organisations that continue throughout the Sangh Parivar, and their programmes and political discourses that yearn for the restoration of an ancient, Brahminical, Hindu, natural and sacred world. In the fourth section, through a close reading of issues between 2014 and 2019 of the *Organiser* – the RSS' official journal – I highlight the continuities and changes in Hindu nationalist politics on the environment post-2014, after the BJP came to power. Throughout these four sections I foreground the need to recognise the political reality of Hindu nationalism, and to unravel its environmental manifestations.

## The Emergence of an RSS Ecology: Present and Past

On 30 September 2017, RSS Sarsanghchalak (chief) Mohan Bhagwat, in his Vijayadashami speech – an important annual statement that traditionally lays out the goals and priorities of the organisation for the following year – emphasised the importance of environmental issues in India.[2] Thereafter, the Akhil Bharatiya Karyakari Mandal of the RSS,[3] at its Mumbai meeting in October 2018, decided to focus on five things in the "near future": "environment protection and water conservation initiatives taken up by swayamsevaks, along with society at large", "training swayamsevaks in handling natural calamities", "protection of Indian cows and cow-oriented farming and health care",

[2] Rashtriya Swayamsevak Sangh, "Summary of the Vijayadashami 2017 Address of Sarsanghchalak Dr Mohan ji Bhagwat", https: // www.rss.org/ Encyc/2017/9/30/mohan-bhagwat-vijayadashami-speech-2017. html.

[3] This is the highest country-level body of the RSS, in which *sanghchalak, karyawah, pracharak* and their deputies from all zones and state bodies in the country meet twice a year to decide on important contemporary issues to be taken up by the organisation.

"rural development activities", and "the construction of Ram temple as an issue of national self-respect and honour." The meeting was attended by Sarsanghchalak Mohan Bhagwat, Sarkaryawah Suresh Bhaiyaji Joshi, Sah Sarkaryawah Manmohan Vaidya, and 350 delegates from across the country.[4] Further, the AKBM (Akhil Bharatiya Pratinidhi Sabha Baithak), the top decision-making body of the RSS,[5] met in March 2019 and concretised the "new initiatives", i.e. to "take up various activities along with the society in the field of environment protection and conservation through initiatives in three key areas – water conservation and water management, planting trees, and eliminating use of plastic and other non-biodegradable materials like thermocol." They adopted resolutions on the "need to protect the traditions and beliefs of Hindu society" and "the construction of Ram temple", and congratulated the BJP government for carrying out air strikes on terror camps in Pakistan, and for their stand on Article 370. Regarding Hindu environmental traditions, culture, and relig ion in the contexts of Jallaikattu, Deepawali crackers, and Sabarimala, Sarkaryawah Suresh Bhaiyaji Joshi said that "along with the Constitution, one cannot ignore the importance of traditions and culture. Giving a decision according to the law is one thing and its acceptability in the society is another thing. So, such issues should be dealt in the light of our values and culture."[6]

Following the decisions of the ABKM and AKBM, the RSS created a separate Paryavaran Vibhag (environment wing) within the organisation and a senior *pracharak*, Gopal Arya, was made its national convener. The RSS has also floated autonomous organisations

[4] Rashtriya Swayamsevak Sangh, "Focus on Environment and Water Conservation", 31 October 2018, https://www.rss.org/Encyc/2018/10/31/ABKM2018Begins.html.

[5] AKBM is the general body of the RSS, comprising representatives of provinces. The number of representatives is proportionate to the number of *swayamsevaks* in each province. They meet every year to decide on important issues for the organisation.

[6] Rashtriya Swayamsevak Sangh, "RSS' New Initiative to Focus on Environment Conservation – Bhaiyyaji Joshi", 10 March 2019, https://www.rss.org//Encyc/2019/3/10/ABPS-press-briefing-by-rss-sarkaryavah.html.

and publications to promote their environmental activities. Paryavaran Sanrakshan (environment conservation) is one such all-India organisation which narrates the "story" of its origin through RSS decision-making processes:

> Rashtriya Swayamsevak Sangh Sarkaryavah Shri Bhaiyya ji Joshi officially announced the Sangh's new environment program: "The RSS' work has reached a certain level and now we feel that it is time to take a big leap in terms of expansion of the work" . . . The Karyakari Mandal had also decided to assign a dedicated team to inculcate an integrated approach to address environment-related concerns, which was later implemented in the Pratinidhi Sabha. Though these concerns are global, many a times their solutions are rooted in the local geo-cultural approach and conventional wisdom. Societal participation will ensure the integration of different approaches, while addressing the problems.[7]

This particular organisation claims to be present in 45 zones and 1105 districts of the country, with 394 zone teams and 60 zone conveners, 294 district teams, 1010 district conveners, and 307 district co-ordinators. It organised several public awareness activities in 2020–1: all-India poster/art/home decoration/eco-brick competitions on World Earth Day, Nature Worship, Media Conclave, University Vice-Chancellor Conclave, NGO Jal Samvad, All-India School Environment Competition, Online Conclave, Haridwar Kumbh-Polythene-free MahaKumbh, Eco-Brick, and Polythene-free Bharat. It publishes an e-magazine called *Paryavaran Perspective*. The "Prakriti Vandana Pledge" of the organisation narrates its nature philosophy:

> Our *Sanatan* culture considers not only the human being, but the entire world as the manifestation of Supreme God. According to *Sri Bhagwad Gita, Sanatan* means the one who cannot be destroyed by fire, water and weapons, who is present in every living-non-living. Our culture is the only one in the world which sees an individual connected to family, family connected to society, and society connected to the world, as one entity. Hindutva is not only a religion, it is a scientific life system. The

[7] Paryavaran Sanrakshan, "Our Story", https://paryavaransanrakshan.org/our-story/.

> roots of our culture are so refined and widespread that the scientific nature of all our works is self-evident . . . Let us come back to our traditions to worship nature.

It pledges the protection of land, water, and homes. Ultimately, there is a pledge to be a Paryavaran Prahari – a soldier of nature – who "pledges to protect, conserve and sustain our environment."[8] The organisation is focused more on the peoples' outreach of the RSS, where environmental issues are couched in Hindu religious discourse.

The Hindu Adhyatmik Evam Sewa Foundation is another new organisation established by the RSS to organise campaigns on environmental and nationalist agendas. Working closely with Paryavaran Sanrakshan, the foundation articulates the environmental agendas of Hindu nationalism. The foundation's activities are patronised and propagated by senior functionaries of the RSS–BJP, including Mohan Bhagwat and Narendra Modi. An all-India nature worship programme organised by the foundation in August 2020 pledged to protect nature and "war heroes", to embrace trees and the "Hindutva organisation", to recite nature songs and "Vande Mataram". Inaugurated by Mohan Bhagwat, this programme was observed by all the major organisations of the RSS in many parts of the country.

The RSS has initiated or supported several organisations and their activities at the local level, which is normally not known or visible at the national level, and they regularly pursue Hindu nationalist agendas through environmental work. For example, on the River Ganga, other than the RSS and the VHP there are at least six organisations – Ganga Mahasabha; Patanjali Vidyapeeth, Haridwar; Ganga Sewa Abhiyan, Varanasi; Ganga Samagra Abhiyan; Matrisadan, Haridwar; and Hindu Janjagriti Abhiyan, which champion RSS ideologies. The Hindu Janjagriti Abhiyan states in its literature that the Ganga, a critical symbol of Hindu culture, civilisation and tradition, is in danger and this must be addressed by every Indian. However, it argues:

[8] There are many pledges on environmental conservation by the organisation. For details: Paryavaran Sanrakshan, "Prakruti Vandana Pledge", https://sankalp.paryavaransanrakshan.org/.

> In the present democracy, Ganga protection has limitations. The establishment of *Ram Rajya*-based ideal nation, and religion-based Hindu nation is the only effective way to defend the holy Ganga . . . On reading this material, every Indian should work together with *Gangabhats*, and should contribute actively for the establishment of a "Hindu Nation".[9]

The sacred rivers and their insertion into the construction of a Hindu nationalist identity are pivotal in other RSS-linked organisations as well. In Uttar Pradesh, Lok Bharti launched a Gomti-Ganga yatra in 2011 which crossed thirteen districts of the state and formed a "Gomti family" and a "Gomti Friends Circle". In 2018 it organised a meeting in the state capital and decided to launch a government-led consciousness campaign for the cultural rejuvenation of the Gomti River, which they argue has a deep religious value originating in the Rigveda, the Shiv Mahapuran, and the Hindu gods Ram and Lakshman.[10]

The RSS has recently floated an ideological forum for its environmental activities. "*Sumangalam* – Developing Sustainable Life on the Basis of Five Elements" – is a new physical and digital platform aimed at presenting profound and pragmatic solutions based on "Bharatiya" thought. Its objective is to present a unique concept of, firstly, securing purity of the five basic elements of nature, i.e. the Panch Mahabhoot – earth, water, fire, air, and space; and secondly, attaining order and balance, or rather harmony between them for the survival and sustainability of life on earth.[11] Five regional conferences have been planned in collaboration with five union ministries on the "unique Indian concept of the purity of five basic elements of nature – earth, water, fire, air and space – to address the challenges of environmental issues and climate change." The RSS' organisations – Deendayal Research Institute and Vijnan Bharti – will work with the ministries of Environment, Forest and Climate Change, Science,

[9] Athawale and Pingale, *Devnadi Ganga ki Raksha Kare!*, 3.

[10] Negi, "Gomti Sanrakhshan Abhiyan", 18–21.

[11] Sumangalam: Framing Indian Narrative of Environment, https://jal.panchmahabhoot.in/about-us/.

Renewable Energy, Earth Sciences, and Water Resources. These conferences will culminate in a final conference in the national capital, where an "India Declaration on Environment" will be adopted as a "charter of solutions", based on Bharatiya thought, and solutions will be offered for "contemporary problems caused by rapidly changing climate."[12] The initiative on the water element has been titled SuJalam, which is dedicated to creating a "discourse on the sacrality of water, and juxtaposing it with scientific thoughts."

Along with the RSS, the militant Hindutva outfit Vishwa Hindu Parishad (VHP), which has been focusing on the Ram temple, cow protection, and religious conversion, has continued with its campaigns on "protecting Ganga" (Shri Ganga Raksha). The 2019 Kashi Dharma Sansad, led by Shankaracharya Swami Swaroopanand and attended by hundreds of sadhus and *dharmacharyas* (scholars of dharma), passed a resolution to "demolish all the dams built on river Ganga, enact a law to stop future dam construction on the river and immediate closure of industries on the river banks."[13] Other older organisations of the RSS family – the Swadeshi Jagaran Manch, Akhil Bharatiya Vanvasi Kalyan Ashram, Seva Bharti, Bharatiya Shikshan Mandal, and Saraswati Shishu Mandir – have also started raising environmental issues in their sector-specific nationalistic modes. A senior *pracharak* asserts that "green activities are plentiful in Sangh and Parivar organisations." For example, the ABVP's Students for Development (SFD) and Vigyan Bharati have taken on several environment-related works. One of their members says: "Parivar organisations have conversational skill, an immense emotional connectedness with society and a social competence to coordinate multifarious views."[14]

The RSS annual report 2021–2, presented at the Akhil Bharatiya Pratinidhi Sabha by Sarkaryawah Dattatreya Hosabale, gave for the first time a detailed account of their "environment conservation"

[12] Smriti Kak Ramachandran, "RSS-inspired Groups Plan Indian Declaration", *Hindustan Times*, 27 June 2022, 8.

[13] Vishwa Hindu Parishad, https://vhp.org/dharma_sansad.

[14] Ambekar, *The RSS Roadmaps*, 134–5.

works, organisationally and programmatically: in 44 zones, the responsibility of "co-ordinator" has been assigned. Groundwork has started in 667 districts and 177 city centres. In 36 zone-level activities, 1380 activists from 564 districts have participated. In school-level special programmes, 8,46,443 students from 55,062 schools have participated, and 50,000 university students joined the Rashtriya Paryavaran Yuva Samsad. According to the report, over 53 lakh people from 4 lakh families took part in the Prakruti Vandan programme organised by the Hindu Spiritual & Seva Foundation, and 7,61,742 people have downloaded the Eco Mitram App of Paryavaran Samrakshan Gatividhi. Programmatically, the activities were carried out in the areas of water, forest, waste, sanitation, and public space.[15] The report has separate sections on rural development and cow service, each with a distinct environmental content.

The RSS and the BJP, widely seen as representing facets of Hindu communalism and nationalism, have become powerful forces in Indian politics over the past three decades. Electorally and politically, the BJP has been growing nationally and regionally: in the 1989 parliamentary elections its vote share had risen to 11.4 per cent from 7.4 per cent in 1984 (when it had won only two seats), and it won 89 seats in the Lok Sabha, emerging as the third largest party in the country. By early 1991, with 119 seats in the Lok Sabha, and a 19.9 per cent share of the total votes, it had become the second largest party.[16] In the 1996 national elections it emerged as the largest single party in the country. In the February 1998 general election it polled more than a quarter of the popular vote in India and emerged as the largest party in the Lok Sabha. In late March 1998 the party's leader Atal Bihari Vajpayee became the prime minister in a coalition government formed by the BJP and twelve regional parties. The BJP contested the 1999 parliamentary elections as the leader of the National Democratic Alliance (NDA), a coalition of more than twenty national and regional parties. The alliance secured a governing majority, with the BJP winning 182 of the coalition's 294 seats. Vajpayee, as

[15] Rashtriya Swayamsevak Sangh, "Annual Report 2021–22", https://www.rss.org/Encyc/2022/3/11/ABPS-Annual-Report-2021-22.html.

[16] Hansen, *The Saffron Wave,* 3–5.

the leader of the largest party in the alliance, was again elected prime minister. The 2014 parliamentary elections, and several other state elections – for example of Maharashtra and Haryana in October 2014, Jammu and Kashmir in November–December 2014, Assam in 2016, Uttarakhand, Uttar Pradesh, Gujarat, and Himachal Pradesh in 2017, Tripura and Nagaland in 2018 – highlight the meteoric electoral growth of the BJP. Under Narendra Modi the party secured a majority of seats (282) in the Lok Sabha elections of 2014, with 31 per cent vote share, and its partners won 54 more seats. In the 2019 parliamentary elections the Modi-led BJP's vote share increased to 37.36 per cent (winning 303 seats), and they once again formed the central government. Students of Hindu communalism have offered various interpretations regarding its ideology, and the reasons for its growth. Some explain this party's current power as a result of decades of systematic, painstaking organisational work and imaginative political strategies.[17] Others understand this growth in more cultural and historical terms, arguing that Hindu nationalists may have been successful because they drew on older reserves of "religious nationalism" that had long been central to most forms of Indian nationalism.[18] Others not only emphasise the institutional groundwork that supports the politics of the Hindu Right and the long history of its meticulously organised efforts towards a Hindu Rashtra, but also underline that, particularly in its existing incarnation, it is engaged in fundamental forms of religious engineering – which is how its political agenda differs most significantly from that of other right-wing formations.[19] It has also been argued that saffron politics has emerged and taken shape neither in the political system as such nor in the religious field, but in the broader realm of what we may call public culture – the public space in which a society and its constituent individuals and communities imagine, represent, and recognise themselves through political discourse, commercial and cultural expression, and the representation of state and civic organisations.[20]

[17] Jaffrelot, *The Hindu Nationalist.*

[18] Van der Veer, *Religious Nationalism.*

[19] Basu, *et al.*, *Khaki Shorts, Saffron.*

[20] Hansen, *The Saffron Wave.*

Political scientists and commentators have also offered varied explanations for the dominance of the BJP since 2014. India under Modi has been seen as an Indian variant of an "ethnic democracy", which is informed by the promotion of a Hindu definition of the nation, in opposition to the principle of secularism enshrined in the 1950 Constitution, and by its opposition to Christian and Muslim minorities. A Hindutva interlaced with populism and alchemy, achieved by Modi, is considered significant here.[21] Others have explained the electoral ascendance of the BJP and Modi as a gradual shaping of new hegemonies, i.e. a set of dominant ideas and sensibilities based on "new Hindu nationalism", "new developmentalism", and an extensive organisational network. The logic of Hindu majoritarianism is skilfully aligned with ideas of a "new India".[22] Some have drawn attention to the nexus between Hindu nationalism and political economy, where there is kinship between a political economy of nationhood and a nativist cultural project. This is implicit in the dominant nationalist discourse, which has allowed violent religious majoritarianism to develop in the country.[23] Bio-nationalism is seen as central to the politics of Hindu nationalism, i.e. the centrality of "biology" and "scientific temperament" within the imagination, teaching, and practice of political Hindu nationalism. Claims of common blood, indigenous DNA, unique theories, native ecologies, and regimes of bodily discipline are grounded in a vision of Hinduism as a modern scientific religion.[24]

The saffron brigade, in this period of its phenomenal growth, has taken up environmentalism as one of its important planks in order to articulate its broader socio-political goals. Environmental issues have become vehicles to carry forward sectarian politics. Some researchers have viewed this as an invention of "new areas of social politics" by political and social groups inspired by the Hindutva of the RSS, where issues related to ecology, environment, and water acquire

[21] Jaffrelot, *Modi's India.*

[22] Palshikar, "Towards Hegemony", 36–42.

[23] Balasubramanian, "A More Indian Path", 333–78; Goswami, *Producing India.*

[24] Subramaniam, *Holy Science.*

special significance. As one scholar puts it: "Keeping the river in the backdrop as a source of water linked with both sacred and profane meanings, these groups are working to evolve with a new social politics around various local, regional and great rivers of India such as Ganga, Narmada, Brahmaputra and Godavari."[25] The Ganga Yatra in January 2020, initiated by Yogi Adityanath, a key Hindutva leader and chief minister of Uttar Pradesh, provided an opportunity to transform the social into the political. The river became a combined symbol of culture, religion, politics, and socio-economic life. Further, humanitarian work by the RSS in disaster situations, in the form of socio-environmental "seva" – which has been quite frequent in the past two decades – also represents political exercises for organisational expansion and an ideological entrenchment of Hindutva. The disaster management and relief-rehabilitation work of the Sangh in Gujarat and Odisha was strategically used to advance the idea of a strong Hindu Rashtra.[26]

Since the BJP started gaining ground in Indian politics, the environment has appeared prominently in its political documents. For example, in its election manifesto of 1998, it says

> The BJP believes in the traditional Indian position that Nature is sacred. The *Atharva Veda* sets out the principle that nature is the mother of humans and that human beings owe a responsibility to maintain the ecological balance. The BJP will ensure institutional measures to bring about ecological security so that all developmental programmes are in conformity with the principles of sustainable development.[27]

Earlier, during the mid-term elections of 1991, the BJP had pledged to halt the "degradation of the environment and disturbance of the eco-system" because "our land, air and waters, our hills, forests, flora and fauna, are all sacred to us. We will keep them neat, clean and intact."[28] The party's ally at the time, the Shiv Sena,

[25] Narayan, *Republic of Hindutva*, 87.

[26] Bhattacharjee, *Disaster Relief.*

[27] Bharatiya Janata Party (BJP), *Election Manifesto 1998*, 44.

[28] BJP, *Towards Ram Rajya: Mid-Term Poll to Lok Sabha, May 1991 – Our Commitments*, 28–9.

followed suit. Suresh Prabhakar Prabhu of the Shiv Sena became the union minister for environment and forests in the BJP-led government in 1998 and undertook "a series of measures for imparting a new impetus to the task of protecting the environment and conserving forests and wildlife."[29]

The landmark 2014 parliamentary elections, which made the BJP and Modi the dominant force in Indian politics, had strong Hindu nationalist environmental elements. The much-publicised election manifesto of the BJP – "Ek Bharat Shreshtha Bharat: Sabka Saath Sabka Vikas" – prefaced the environmental subject in several ways:

> India is the most ancient civilisation of the world and has always been looked upon by the world as a land of wealth and wisdom. India has been credited to have developed, apart from philosophy and mathematics, science and technology of a very high order, which had attracted scholars from all over the world . . . Historical records establish the level of progress and prosperity attained by India before the advent of the Europeans. Indian advancement in mathematics, astronomy, physics and chemistry along with the biological sciences has been well recognised. India was a land of abundance, prosperity, affluence, a land of sharing and caring, living in perfect harmony and peace with the nature.[30]

The Union Environment Minister in the 2014 era explained "his priority as a Minister" by invoking Hindutva and the RSS ideology: "As we love our mother, we must love your nature – the mother earth. Our guide and philosopher Deen Dayal Upadhyaya has very finely explained the relationship between the self, society, nature and the universe as one continuous chain."[31]

The VHP plugs into issues of ecology along the same lines. A series of teachings and activities pertaining to conservation, purification, and cleanliness have been organised through local organisations, using alternative local vocabularies. Essentially these have

[29] Ministry of Environment and Forests, *125 Days of New Government: New Programmes and Initiatives*, Delhi, n.d., 1.

[30] Bharatiya Janata Party (BJP), *Election Manifesto 1998*, 1.

[31] "Priority as an Environment Minister: An Interview with Union Environment Minister Prakash Javadekar", http://pibmumbai.gov.in/scripts/detail.asp?releaseId=E2014FR22.

worked as branches or local projects of the VHP among tribals, students, women, workers, and farmers.[32] The VHP took up the issue of the Tehri dam's location on the Ganga. Swami Chinmayanand, a BJP MP who has been closely associated with the VHP's anti-Tehri-dam campaign and who also works actively in other programmes of the organisation, claims:

> Environmental issues and concerns are nothing new for the VHP. The purity of Ganga is not the only issue that we are taking up. The sanctity and sacredness of our environment is closely related with the sanctity of our culture. Since the early 1990s, we have been raising the issues of environmental and cultural pollution, and organising *yatras*, campaigns and meetings on these.[33]

The RSS-affiliated Akhil Bharatiya Vanvasi Kalyan Ashram, which works on tribal issues – in their understanding tribals are Hindus and should be kept in the Hindu fold through various activities like education, hostels, healthcare, sports, rural development, preservation of culture, *satsangs*, and *bhajani mandalis* – has added a new activity named *vanvasi hit raksha* (protection of tribal's interests) on *jal* (water), jungle, and *jameen* (land).[34]

In these various ways and through its different organisations, the saffron brigade has launched specific campaigns on environmental issues and evolved environmentalism as a running theme which continues beyond election times. Their eco-vision showcases India as a

[32] Sapre, *Param Vaibhav ke Path Par*, Delhi. This book gives a detailed account of organisations affiliated with the RSS. For example, the Akhil Bharatiya Vanvasi Kalyan Ashram works among tribals to conserve forests and forest regions. The Bharatiya Kisan Sangh is active among farmers for cow and cattle protection, and for the conservation and development of flora and fauna. In the hill region, Uttaranchal Utthan Parishad works for rural and environmental development. The Bharat Vikas Parishad works on environmental issues. The Akhil Bharatiya Adhivakta Parishad takes up issues related to environmental laws. The Laghu Udhyog Bharti is active in relation to environment-friendly technology, polluting industries, and the small-scale sector.

[33] Interview with Swami Chinmayanand in Haridwar, 26 July 2000.

[34] Vanvasi Kalyan Ashram, "Our Aaayams", https://vanvasi.org/projects/#our-aayams.

holy land whose earth, air, water, hills, forests, flora, and fauna are sacred. What is sacrosanct needs to be kept "pure":

> The attachment to forests, trees, flora and fauna is part of India's ethical consciousness. There is a need to revive this and to involve the people in this concern. We need to comprehend that ecological and environmental concerns are not mere elitist posturing. Unfortunately, this is precisely what they have been reduced to by the present generational order. In our context it does not make sense to mouth borrowed Western clichés on the theme.[35]

Such constant engagement, apart from being an attempt to capture public space for immediate electoral ends, bears an uncanny resemblance to some of the prominent environmental movements in the country. At a conceptual and programmatic level, paradoxically, Hindu nationalist environmentalism and progressive environmental movements and organisations have a great deal in common. Probed deeper, the Hindu Right's environmental concerns reveal how these two apparently opposed forces can be interrelated.

Though the saffron brigade comprises different sets of organisations, emphases, and programmes, their environmental concerns can be broadly classified into three themes: eco-nationalism, eco-primitivism, and eco-naturalism. The prism of pollution shines through all three. At one level pollution is a physical, material fact – "the external environment", which has to do with contamination in general – of land, water, and air by industries and urban centres, and via non-biodegradable materials and hazardous chemical wastes.[36] At another, it is specific to developing countries, which are often the dumping grounds and waste disposal heaps of some advanced countries.[37] At a third level pollution is a socially constructed cultural phenomenon. Pollution dilutes and vitiates a hypothetically pristine socio-cultural fabric. As an identifiable alien element in a given natural order, its removal becomes the necessary condition for the restoration of that order. That which is natural and native is a priori superior to the foreign. From this it follows that cultural pollution is an inva-

[35] BJP Pamphlet no. 30, quoted in Ahuja, *BJP and the Indian Politics*, 5–7.
[36] BJP, *Election Manifesto 1998*, 44.
[37] Thengadi, *Global Economic System*, 10–11.

sion against the values and lifestyles of time-tested Hindu codes and honour, a conspiracy which shows the evil designs of Christianity, Islam, and others.[38]

Another dimension of this is "internal pollution", which signifies a "distortion", a "distorted state" of mind and thought. This pollution is internalised in "word, touch, feature, feel and smell" of the people. Internal and external pollution are closely interrelated: "The problem of pollution cannot be resolved only by focusing on external, and internal issues must also be addressed simultaneously."[39] In this vision, there are "enemies" who are responsible for spreading pollution, and they should be eliminated, just as the Hindu deity Vishnu changed his appearance to kill devils.[40] An extended identification of spheres of pollution within the human and natural worlds, nature and culture, is characteristic of Hindu communalism. The native and the foreign, those who belong and those who do not, are carefully separated.[41]

## Eco-Nationalism, Eco-Primitivism and Eco-Naturalism

"The unified national consciousness of the people can be roused only by appealing to the inherent spirit of nationalism dormant in every heart. The first and foremost aspect of this spirit is to look upon Bharat not merely as a territorial entity but as our adored Motherland." – H.V. Seshadri, RSS[42]

[38] *Organiser*, "RSS Calls for Atmosphere Free of Cultural Pollution", 26 March 2000, 9–10. Also see SJM, *Rebuilding the Nation,* 28. In this pamphlet, "resisting cultural pollution" and "protecting national interests" are emphasised together. Kumaris, "World Spiritual University", 14–23. The explanation here is that the most significant variety of pollution – the seed of all other types – is mental pollution. This makes it essential to safeguard ourselves from both environmental as well as mental pollution.

[39] Gupta, *Paryavaran Premi Hindu,* 4–7.

[40] Ibid., 27–8.

[41] The work of Jonathan Olsen has been especially valuable in conceptualising right-wing ecology and the politics of nationalism. I would like to formally record my debt to his analysis. Olsen, *Nature and Nationalism.*

[42] Seshadri, "Thinking Workers", 13.

Exploring right-wing ecology in Germany, its ideological underpinnings, historical evolution, and relationship to mainstream political-environmental discourse, Jonathan Olsen, the leading scholar on the subject, identifies certain major themes of the far Right's conception of ecology and politics. According to him, right-wing ecology is based on an ultra-nationalism which has at least three characteristics, i.e. naturalism, organicism, and the call for a national renewal. Naturalism conceptualises the existence of a nation by natural factors like ethnicity, blood, and language, where consent and the sovereignty of individuals are given away for a natural creation. Related to naturalism, the characteristic of organicism is to view nation "as a living organism, complete, unique, and self-contained";[43] in it individuals are incomplete and subordinate to the supreme value of allegiance to the nation. Ultra-nationalism calls for a national renewal, which is expressed in an exclusionary, quasi-religious, and mystic language that marginalises certain targeted people on the grounds of culture, religion, blood, or ethnicity.

Elaborating on the features and themes of right-wing ecology through three main categories – eco-naturalism, eco-organicism, and eco-authoritarianism – Olsen explains eco-naturalism as one of the pillars of right-wing ecology. It prescribes the laws of nature as models for social order, understands society itself in the language of nature, maintains social relations as per the natural order, and considers the nation as a product of nature.

This naturalisation of social and political phenomena asks humans to submit to nature and natural orders. Alongside eco-naturalism, eco-organicism, by viewing society as a natural eco-system based on complete unity between society and nature at a collective level, makes certain national cultures, and ethnic and blood groups dominant and "native", much like native flora and fauna. The survival and development of the nation, considered as a unified and closed eco-system, depends on maintaining the ecological balance and the unique characteristics of the system. Following the corollary of eco-naturalism and eco-organicism, where nature and natural order

[43] Olsen, *Nature and Nationalism*, 25.

are supreme and demand obedience to nature's laws, the solution to environmental problems can justify authoritarian measures. Nature, symbolising authority, sacrifice, and purity, legitimises the notion of an ethno-culturally based eco-dictatorship. Olsen puts it eloquently:

> Within a right-wing ecological framework, therefore, the key to solving environmental problems lies in a rejection of Enlightenment universalism and the recovery of the natural and rooted – that is to say, the ethnic and/or culturally pure nation. In short, within right-wing ecology our feeling of belonging to a specific place is *naturalised*, made into an ecological determinant. These views of a natural belonging and unnatural pollution run throughout right-wing ecology.[44]

It is also said that national identity would lose much of its enchantment without the mystical appeal attributed by cultural nationalism as being inherent within particular territories and landscapes. National symbols are constructed to reflect and consolidate historical continuities associated with specific territorial landscapes: natural contours, rivers, mountains, and forests are explored, mapped, lived in, and transformed into a homeland. National landscapes are thus always imagined as unique, and notions of belonging and identity within each unique national landscape are always defined in terms of what is supposedly internal and exclusive to that landscape. A nation thus comes to be embodied in nature and its several manifestations, and the nationalist in the avatar of the fundamentalist declares that such embodiment cannot be shared with non-national others. It cannot, in principle, be shaped by external forces, for only that which has been defined as prior and internal is non-polluting.

One way of explaining this "natural imperative" within nation-making myths is by looking at the influence of scriptures upon communities that have discursively constructed nations. The argument among Jews that God's gift consecrated the land of Israel for the Jewish people, a notion backed up by British and American imperial power after the First World War, came as a shot in the arm not just for the creation of Israel but for other communities which had long

[44] Ibid., 35.

maintained that their lands too be declared sacred. The River Ganga has a mythical significance no less than the River Jordan and there seemed to twentieth-century Hindus no reason why it should not be seen as sacred, and exclusively so, by Hindus. Another way is to look at the basis of human nature and allegiance to territory. A theoretical analysis, *Human Territoriality* by R.D. Sack, classifies many kinds of human orientation towards territoriality. Nationalism, according to Sack, arises from a combination of two categories: reification and displacement. This combination can result in a mystical perspective, which attributes authority to territory: "The territory is a physical manifestation of the state's authority, and yet allegiance to territory or homeland makes the territory appear as a source of authority."[45] Natural contours can also be binding, blinding, commanding, and beyond logic, eliciting both patriotism and xenophobia: "It would seem that we have here the sublime and the ridiculous. God's gift on the one hand, and the fatherland as a biological instinct, on the other."[46] Inspired by these writings, particularly of Olsen, I use the above frameworks in the following section of the chapter to further examine the conceptual evolution and programmatic ideas of Hindu nationalist ecology.

## Nation as Natural Holy Hindu Ecosystem

Forever I bow to thee, O Loving Motherland!
O Motherland of us Hindus,
Thou has brought me up in happiness.
May my life, O Great and Blessed Holy Land,
Be laid down in Thy Cause
I bow to Thee again and again. – RSS Prayer[47]

I argue that Hindu nationalist forces root themselves in a tradition of nature and nationalism and transform it into ultra-nationalism. Their ideas on the nation, its past, and its people are often grounded in ecology, making the "natural" contours of the nation seem supreme,

[45] Sack, *Human Territoriality*, 38.
[46] Ben-Israel, "Hallowed Land in the Theory", 278–94.
[47] Barthwal, *Rashtriya Swayamsewak Sangh*, 5.

and as lying far beyond the choice of an individual citizen. Because the nation has to be protected from the onslaught of others, its membership is defined not in terms of the sovereignty of individuals but in that of the natural world. Environmental protection coalesces with the nationalist imperative of preventing the nation from being "polluted". Hindu culture is valorised and equated with national culture, a process that might be called political synonymisation, i.e. the creation of a singular identity via eliding or collapsing separate concepts into each other. Such evolution of nationalism into ultra-nationalism has been noticed by some historians. The RSS' ultra-nationalism defines the belonging of people in the nation through their "natural" Hindu religion, faith, and practice which is perceived as sacred, pure, and ancient. Membership of such a nation is normally acquired at birth, and it is difficult, if not impossible, for those to be part of the nation who do not belong to it from the start. In the words of M.S. Golwalkar, one of the strongest adherents of this worldview:

> This vast land is our "motherland" – this is our deep faith and keeping this faith is a symbol of our nationalism. We all are her sons and service to her is our duty. This land has made our life possible as a nation. Thus, we have made it our natural duty to expand its name through our services . . . the Indian nation is a Hindu nation and this land is a Hindu land.[48]

Land, motherland, culture, and religion are all seen as natural, given, ecological, and organic entities. Furthermore, only those who already belong to this Hindu nation can be faithful and true nationalists: "The earth gives us all that we need. That is why we pray [to] the earth as our mother. The same sentiment is echoed by the word "motherland" . . . This is the reason why only a Hindu remains faithful to his *stree-mata*, *bhoo-mata*, and *bharat-mata*. This is a special quality or symbol of the life system of Hindus."[49]

[48] Golwalkar, *Dheyey-Drishti* (Aim-Vision), 15.

[49] RSS, *Hame Hindu*, 13. There are many writings of this kind by several ideologues and writers who belong to Hindutva organisations. For example,

Hinduism is described as a religion of nature and earth, finding "holy" places in every mountain, stream, valley, and stream: "Its roots are organic. It arises out of the soul and out of the land."[50] There is "life natural" in a Hindu ecosystem. It is thus argued that

> The Sangh has taken up this movement because it realises that conservation of nature is part of Hindus ethos. The Hindu system of worship, be it Vedic or Tantric, is essentially worship of nature. As part of "divide and digest" policy, Christian missionaries and Western sociologists called nature worship "animistic" and separated it from the Vedic system of worship.[51]

The defence of a natural holy motherland becomes a "supreme goal", the driving force behind which can come from the "amalgamation of spiritualism with the vibrating spirit of nationalism, patriotism, valor-ism and chivalry-ism." The call of the movement has been described thus: "Each should take a Solomon Vedic oath, i.e. 'I am the son of my motherland' and 'I will sacrifice myself for her' and I will fight with all my resources and even sacrifice my life for the preservation and protection of Hindu Dharma."[52]

The next step is to harness land, water, rivers, and mountains to construct a specific national identity, i.e. "Ours is a sacred nation."[53] Pandit Deendayal Upadhyaya, a famous Hindutva ideologue and leader of the Bharatiya Jana Sangh – the political party which was the

---

see K.S. Sudarshan, "The Western and the Hindu Way of Life", *Organiser*, 18 February 1996, 2, where he emphasises ecological balance as the key to Hindu philosophy. Thus, Hindus have accorded the status of mother to nature and refer to mother-nature as Bhoomimata, Gangamata, Gomata, and Tulsimata. Also see Sehgal, *Ram Arthat Rashtra*, 17–20. Here the writer argues that the Indian notion of nation has an inherent and quite important element of land, *matribhoomi*, *pitribhoomi*, *punyabhoomi*, and *nagar-nadiya-parvat*. Nature has decided the nation, from Kashmir to Kanyakumari and from Sindhu to Brahmaputra, and this is why no partition is acceptable to Indians.

[50] Swarup, *On Hinduism: Reviews*, xi.

[51] Nandakumar, *Hindutva*, 24–5.

[52] Paliwal, *Challenges Before*, 61.

[53] Nandakumar, *Hindutva*, 159.

forerunner of the BJP – visualised the unity of the nation by applying the yardstick of Indian nationalism, which is Hindu nationalism, and Indian culture which is Hindu culture, for which the rivers should be invoked: "Let us allow all other streams to merge with this mainstream Bhagirathi. Yamuna will merge with it. So will Ganga, shedding all its pollution. And one continuous Bhagirathi will flow throughout India."[54] Ashok Singhal, a leader of the VHP, frequently deployed the Ganga for the VHP's environmental campaign: "To us Bharatvasis Ganga is no river; it is a deity. Ganga is the Divine Mother in whose bosom every son of the *devbhumi* Bharat feels that indescribable spiritual experience where words fade into silence. If Bharatiya *sanskriti* could be symbolised in one word, that one word is 'Ganga'."[55] The river as personification of Hindu holiness shades into a call for cleanliness of self and country: "O Holy Mother Ganga! Yamuna! Godavari! Saraswati! Narmada! Sindhu! Kaveri! May you all be pleased to manifest in these waters, with which I shall purify myself and my country."[56] As a holy mother the river is also invoked in the fight against polluting enemies. The RSS' journals regularly publish on the might of Hindu rivers and push their power into contemporary political contexts:

> Dear Ganga, the current of the Saryu river has risen. You too must arise!
> Draw within your folds the vast pollution that has collected!!
> Come mother, come!!
> The grave of communism has been dug.
> Blood is filled with the exploitation of wealth.
> The earth is burning with Saddams.
> Come mother, come!![57]

India's glorious natural past is constructed through environmental imaginaries and the enemies of the country's past and present are

[54] Quoted in ibid., 59.

[55] Ashok Singhal, "The Tehri Dam: A Monstrosity that Would Sound the Death-knell of the Sacred Ganga", *Organiser*, 28 June 1998, 2.

[56] "O Holy Mother Ganga!", *Manthan*, vol. VI, no. 3, October 1985, 6.

[57] Chandrakant Bhardwaj, "Ganga ka Aahwan" (The Call of Ganga), *Manthan*, vol. 12, no. 5, May 1991, 72.

identified to save "the holy land": "This is the ancient land where wisdom made its home before it went into any other country, the same India whose influx of spirituality is represented, as it were, on the material plane, by rolling rivers, like oceans, where the eternal Himalayas, rising tier with their snow-caps, look, as it were, into the very mysteries of heaven."[58] This glorious past is naturally unique and pure, thus making a strong case for its conservation from alien influences: "No one can deny that India has been marked out by Nature as an indisputable geographical unit, clearly separated from the rest of Asia by outstanding natural boundaries, the mountains of the North and the seas of the South."[59] Foreign invaders – Shakas, Hoons, Yavansa, Islamic raiders, and the British – it is argued, destroyed the holy land: "Therefore, the Sangh's goal is to forge unity in the society, to consolidate and organise the Hindu *samaj* (who dedicate themselves to Bharat as their Motherland, Fatherland and Sacred land) to protect its Dharma, society and culture."[60]

The most significant threats to the environment are seen as stemming from Western values, systems, and modes of development. These can be connected to the ecologist's model of nature, because the Hindu communalist views society as a natural ecosystem in a manner analogous to the ecological perception of the natural world. This view comprises two interrelated streams: first, that while ecosystems are diverse – naturally and socially – each system possesses unique characteristics. Second, that preserving these unique characteristics is essential to the health and survival of that system. These two notions are important because they relate to a principle drawn from ecology: namely, that the introduction of a foreign species into an ecosystem threatens ecological balance. In the conservative ecological discourse of the communalist this idea is used to argue that the nation is a unique and fragile natural entity endangered by external pollutants. Diversity is valorised primarily as the existence of various ecosystems/nations, not as something desirable within each. As against

[58] Lal, *India*, 31.
[59] Ibid., 53.
[60] Barthwal, *Rashtriya Swayamsewak Sangh*, 13.

this, the social and natural health of each such entity depends on doing everything to preserve the ecological balance – the unique, pure, and holy characteristics internal to that system: "Here we must remember the facts of ecology. Nature consists of various ecosystems, each with its own characteristics, energies and interlinking factors. If we indiscriminately introduce new species from an outside ecosystem, we may not improve the integrity of the ecosystem but can cause it to collapse, compromising its immunity, integrity and balance."[61]

These broad contours of the nation as "natural ecosystem" can be seen in the Swadeshi Jagaran Manch (SJM), an organisation initiated by the RSS which makes a clear-cut distinction between two men, two worlds, and two systems when making a case for ancient Indian wisdom vis-à-vis the nation:

> Encouraged by a theology that legitimised man's dominance over nature, Western man started looking upon himself as the centre of the universe, ignoring his neighbours and his environment and the delicate balance inherent in nature. Because of this mentality, Western man started perceiving the universe as a machine and devised a philosophical justification for exploiting nature and his neighbours. This view arose out of the denial of sacredness to nature.[62]

Simultaneously, the SJM's argument goes, ancient Indian intellect, by contrast, always perceives the all-pervasive unity and oneness of creation. Hinduism's "man" is apparently forever in a relationship of mutual interaction and harmony with nature and his fellow Hindus. Ancient Indian wisdom is characterised by certain well-accepted principles of life on this earth, such as "integral relationship with nature, ruling out exploitation", and "unity underlying diversity in nature and society."[63]

In the SJM's worldview, environmental destruction, like Cerberus, comes under many heads: both capitalism and communism are forms of this monster because both have originated the same drift towards consumerism. Exploitation of the environment is seen as

[61] Nandakumar, *Hindutva*, xxiii.
[62] SJM, *Rebuilding the Nation*, 4.
[63] Ibid., 5.

inherent in both. The Akhil Bharatiya Grahak Panchayat, another outfit of the RSS, views America as the main enemy of the environment. Bindumadhav Joshi, president of the panchayat, remarks:

> With the slogan of "consumerism", America has announced "consumers of the world unite". Because of this, commodity culture has taken birth there. This is how today's situation has come about, where man exists only for the commodity. For the satisfaction of this undignified consumption, a process of merciless plunder of natural capital has been initiated. Our natural and mineral resources have now virtually ended.[64]

The West as a whole is Attila the Hun reincarnate. It blindly slaughters human beings, animals, birds, sacred cows, tribals; in its wake fall monuments, temples, homes, because "For them [Westerners], a tree is merely wood or fodder, a cow or a buffalo is just meat. Why be surprised if this consumerist view takes root everywhere – from all living and non-living organisms to human beings (and especially in women)?"[65] But, says an RSS mouthpiece, "Their mischief cannot succeed so long as Hindus continue to cherish their cultural traditional values. The intense love with which they identify themselves with the country and its cultural heritage rules out any breach in it. This realisation has prompted them to damn and denigrate Hindu pride and their glorious past and present a distorted image of Bharat before the world."[66] Plants and animals belong naturally to a particular ecosystem, and so do people: ethnic and religious groups have their specific natural spaces.[67] This is how Hindu authoritarianism defines nature and nation.

[64] Joshi, *Swadeshi*, 61–2.

[65] Kishorilal Vyas, "Paryavaran Sanrakhshan" (Environmental Protection), *Manthan*, vol. 4, October–December 1998, 59–63. This article deals in detail with the Western vs the Indian in the context of environment conservation. It concludes that our culture establishes an emotional relationship with nature, whereas Western culture is inclined to change human nature into a deformed, distorted one.

[66] "RSS Calls for Atmosphere Free of Cultural Pollution", 10.

[67] Madhok, *Rationale*, 8–9. The author, a long-standing Hindu nationalist ideologue, argues that the adoration of land is a strong rationale for the Hindu state. Hindu Bhumi, a vast and varied stretch of land, sustains the physical,

A related myth is that ancient India of a Vedic "golden" age and other such gilded periods harmonised with the countryside and the community and possessed a kind of primitive ecological wisdom. This is widely held by Hindu nationalists and occupies a very prominent place in their environmental thought. The view that their glorious past – non-industrial, rural, agricultural, pastoral – was ecologically sound, a "paradise on earth",[68] and its people paragons of ecological virtue, has been occasionally articulated in environmental thought. Kay Milton identifies at least five elements in this vision: first, in accordance with the romantic tradition of idealising the natural, the most ecologically sound ways of living are assumed to be those that conform most closely to what is seen as a "natural" existence. In turn, the most natural ways of living are assumed to be those that appear to transform the environment the least, leaving it as close as possible to its raw state. Second, because the image of primitive ecological wisdom is born out of a comparison with industrial practice, it tends to be shaped by issues of concern within industrial society. Third, proximity to industrial society has directed the spotlight towards some non-industrial societies and not others. Fourth, there is a greater respect for the indigenous peoples of the region than for inhabitants whose origins lie elsewhere. Fifth, environmental thought has focused more on the human inhabitants of certain ecosystems and not others because the ecosystems focused on have been, for various reasons, the centre of environmentalist concern.[69]

This myth of past glory is also an implicit valorisation of caste, of a relationship of individuals to society in which service to those who hold society's political, economic, and cultural strings by those who do not is part of the reason for the past having been so golden. This past becomes an image of the country in its ideal state of environmental harmony, peace, and stability, to be contrasted with

---

material, and spiritual life of Hindus, the people of Hindustan, irrespective of caste, creed, and language. Natural contours, a specific ethnicity, and religion determine motherland, fatherland, and holy land.

[68] Lal, *India*, 43.

[69] For a detailed account on the myth of primitive ecological wisdom, see Milton, *Environmentalism and Cultural Theory*, 106–41.

destruction, crisis, and depredations in the present, all perpetrated by others. In this environmental narrative, in fact, the caste system is a sustainable and ideal system within which everyone lived and worked as part of an organic community. RSS ideologues and activists reason uniquely in defence of caste:

> Hindu dharma has also been described as *varnaasrama dharma* which represents an important facet of ancient Hindu thinking. The old sages saw that men are broadly divided into four psychological types (*chaturvarna*), a very different thing from the castes-system with which it is often confused. They found that these psychological differences were natural and their variety matched the variety of man's needs.[70]

Nana Deshmukh, a prominent figure in RSS ideological circles, says:

> Bharat is primarily referred to as an agricultural country. However, before the British, the population of every village fulfilled its needs through small industries at the local level . . . In ancient times, castes were formed on the basis of industry and commerce. This system has continued for generations . . . Children were trained in their homes. There was no scope for unemployment. Daughters of the same caste came into homes as daughters-in-law. They were also trained in the same vocations. Ideally, all men and women were involved in their given trade.[71]

The village is another essential element of the Hindu idealised past. Villages, villagers, and village life, based either on Manu's philosophy or Sanatana Dharma, is seen as the simplest way of life, free of environmental destruction and socio-economic conflict. It is said: "India's village region has not been a workshop of agriculture-industry. Rather, it has been a region for the spread of *satvik* culture and values. Manu's *grihasth-ashram*, which is the best among all

[70] Swarup, *On Hinduism*, 26.

[71] Nana Deshmukh, "Parivartan ke Saath Arthik Vikas" (Economic Development along with Change), *Manthan*, vol. 16, no. 1, April–June 1995, 10. Also see Dwivedi, "Satyagraha for Conservation", 159. The author, quite sympathetic to Hindu forces, says that the Hindu caste system can be seen as a progenitor of the concept of sustainable development.

*ashrams*, can be seen in these villages . . . The vision of a village life system propounded by Maharaja Manu, the originator and founder of Indian culture and values, was the best."[72] At other times, kings and queens, rich people, sadhus and saints – the so-called ancestors of all good Hindus – are upheld as the heroes and heroines who made up this past; they made plantations, they encouraged the digging of tanks, they lit the lamp of ancient environmental conservation.[73] Next, agriculture: Hindu nationalists almost see agriculture as required less for food and wealth than for religion and culture. For a true Indian, it appears, growing food is in itself a religious act, and the Hindu farmer is really always engaged in an act of intense worship. The Dharma Sabhas – congregations of *dharmacharyas* – during a gathering to deliberate and pronounce upon the dharma of growing and sharing food, are reported to have said: "The prevalence of scarcity and hunger in India is not merely an economic failure, it is a moral failure, it is a grim pointer to our failure to protect and nourish the Sanatana Dharma . . . India's land and people are languishing as a result of our failure to remember our traditions. We have to re-anchor ourselves in Sanatana Dharma."[74]

[72] See the three-part article by Rabindranath, "Bharat mein Gramon ka Uday" (Rise of Villages in India), "Jivan-Pranali ke Nirman mein Gaon ka Yogdan" (Contribution of Villages in the Formation of Lifestyle), and "Bharatiya Krishi Padhati mein Gramon ki Bhoomika" (The Role of Villages in Indian Agricultural Methods), *Manthan*, vol. 11, no. 7, July 1991, 11–15; vol. 11, no. 8, August 1991, 17–21; vol. 11, no. 9, September 1991, 17–21, respectively. The articles extensively quote from the *Manusmriti* to illustrate that Indian villages and agriculture were self-reliant, that indigenous lifestyle was pious, pure, and in accordance with Vedic principles, that villagers led a natural life, and nature was worshipped in every village. Also see Vijayshankar, "Gramon se Nagron ki ore Badhta Palayan" (Increasing Migration from Villages to Towns), *Manthan*, vol. 18, no. 1, January–March 1997, 24. The article says Indian villages were very prosperous and self-sufficient units as a result of the good work and thoughts of Hindu saints.

[73] Vyas, "Paryavaran Sanrakhshan", 63.

[74] "Growing Food is a Religious Act: Dharma Sadas", *Organiser*, 29 December 1996, 10. Also see Rabindranath, "Bharatiya Krishi Paddhati mein Gramon ki Bhoomika" (The Role of the Village in the Indian Agricultural System), 17–21.

A superstructure of justifications for hoary tradition and belief supplements the more materialist rationalisations of caste, village, and agriculture for socio-environmental balance. The Rashtra Jagran Abhiyan (RJA), an organisation affiliated with the RSS, argues that beliefs which help in forest conservation may be blind, or may have no logical explanation, but must be pursued for conservation: "There is the law of Karma, or the concept of Sin. If one cuts a living tree, or kills an animal for no reason, one incurs sins. Whether one actually incurs sin and whether one has to get rid of this karma by toiling in hell are rational questions. But rationalism does not always work; faith achieves what rationalism can't."[75]

Such eco-naturalism is an important element in the environmental discourse of Hindu nationalists. It is entwined with the idea that the nation itself is a product of nature. This view is visible also in the concepts and language Hindu nationalists use to express social relationships as well as argue for environmental protection. Among the most telling of these concepts is the coupling of environmental protection with the protection of life *in its natural order*. By this I mean that, while defining their development strategy for a better life, Hindu nationalists not only underline human life as an expression of nature but – and this is the important point – also justify the supposed naturalness of the social order. They suggest there are certain fundamental principles of nature – such as recycling, symbiosis, antibiosis, and stability – and that all human activities, such as agriculture, industry, and social organisation, need to be based on these natural principles:

> Development needs to be defined in terms of (i) universal accessibility to health-giving food, unpolluted air and water, hygienic clothing and shelter; (ii) enhancement of the resource base while improving the yield; (iii) self-reliance – and optimum realisation of the potential – of each locale, region and nation in the perspective of better use of ecological resources; (iv) harmony between the individual, the family, and the society; (v) protection of all plant and animal species in the knowledge that each species, as an expression of life force of Nature, has a full right to existence, and protection of the inanimate environment which

[75] Rashtra Jagran Abhiyan (RJA), *Hindu Sanskriti and Environment*, Delhi, Suruchi Prakashan, 2000, 11.

provides the niche for, and supports, life; and (vi) nurture of "whole, many-sided, evenly-balanced, broad-minded men and women."[76]

Elsewhere, one Shailendranath Ghosh says that the human–nature relationship and its emphasis on the protection of life have centrally to do with the principles inherent in Sanatana Dharma, according to which man is a part of nature. Men may live in a condition of ecological safety only if they accept that state of nature.[77] A proper ecological ethic, it is argued, is the only guarantee of human survival. The natural order of itself provides the basis for recognising that the protection of nature, culture, and life are inseparable. To this end nature and the natural order should be left alone; human intervention is malign since nature has its own capacity to heal its wounds and revive its energies. Hindu culture, traditions, and *samskar*s imbibed this knowledge in the past and thus survived and sustained the natural balance over the ages.[78] The natural cycle is the key – it must not be broken, it has to be preserved: "Those who break the natural cycle – that sinner is not worthy to be alive. To maintain the natural cycle is environment conservation and environment balance."[79]

So, what happened to cause the disbalance that is modernity? This is where eco-nationalism and eco-naturalism outline the eco-enemy: immigrants, migrants, and minorities are the eco-enemy. Multiculturalism and immigration on the one hand, and environmental destruction on the other, are conjoined as the threat. To counter this threat, a new assertive, confident, patriotism is required, as well as a population free of pollution. Within this logic, multicultural society

[76] Ghosh, "Development Strategy for a Better Quality of Life", *Manthan*, vol. XI, no. 5, May 1990, 41–56.

[77] Shailendranath Ghosh, "Adhunikikaran ka Abhishap: Paryavaran-Vidhwansh" (The Curse of Modernity: Environmental Destruction), *Manthan*, vol. 18, no. 3, July–September 1997, 49–53.

[78] Vyas, "Paryavaran Sanrakhshan". He argues that protection of life is the hallmark of Indian culture and guides our relationship with nature. He explains that nature and the natural order are self-sustaining and ideal for us. Also see Ghosh, "Development Strategy for a Better Quality of Life": he says human survival at the basic level depends on an ecological ethic. This holds true for spiritual as well as material resource management.

[79] Gupta, *Paryavaran Premi Hindu*, 17.

is suspect because it stands in contrast to the ethno-cultural conception of identity. In that sense it violates the natural unity between the people of Bharat and their environs.

Much of the discussion on environmental destruction is also a discussion on migrants. It could be asserted that a vocabulary hostile to migrants and immigrants is the Hindu nationalist's ecological language. They argue for instance that the forests of the Western Ghats, in the Shimoga and Dakshina Kannada districts, have been subject to total destruction by migrant settlers from Kerala. These migrants are Syrian Christians and seen as those who have by hook or by crook occupied forests and vacant revenue lands. They are also seen as using all sorts of pressure – sheer muscle as well as political power – to occupy and retain these lands. In this they are being aided by missionaries: "The role of a Shimoga-based missionary institution, called Shantiniketan, is said to be glaringly visible in the migration of people from Kerala and their encroaching forest and vacant revenue lands."[80] The destroyers of the environment are said to get money from foreign countries, particularly the USA. Their motive is to convert Hindus into Christians. The natives have to be awakened against foreigners:

> The Awakening: The local people are slowly realising the meaning and the dangers of this illegal encroachment and deforestation. They are preparing for a struggle against this threat. The Appiko (just like the Chipko) movement, Vriksha Samrakshishi Vedik (Save the Tree Forum), Parisara Samrakshana Vedike, Hindu Jagarana Vedic, etc., are some of the organisations spearheading this people's movement. They have already held meetings, processions and *dharnas* to bring pressure on the state government to bring a halt to this dangerous trend. They have also taken up some positive projects such as "Vriksha Raksha Andolan" by planting lakhs of saplings to reinforce our vanishing forests. Educating the public is also a part of the movement.[81]

The *Organiser* outlines a supposed decline in the Hindu population. Muslims procreate at rates higher than Hindus; apparently this

[80] H.B. Mallya, "Rape of the Western Ghats", *Organiser*, 15 February 1987, 8 and 10.

[81] Ibid., 10.

has been a feature of the last forty years. This demographic catastrophe is tantamount to the destruction of natural resources: "The Muslim fundamentalists who raise a hue and cry for Muslim interests must answer why the community – an integral part of Hindusthan – fails to safeguard the national interest and depletes the nation's resources."[82]

## Brahminical Models and Nature Protection

"Old India had castes but no casteists; new India has casteists but no worthwhile castes. In old India, all people and castes united in defending their society, in defending temples, Brahmins and cows – still worthy objects of protection by a great and compassionate people and civilisation." – Ram Swarup[83]

Hindu nationalists deploy Hindu religious texts which, they argue, contain insights into nature and environmental sustainability that might be usefully translated into an environmental rhetoric for present-day India. They quote the Vedas and the Dharmasastras to demonstrate that Bharat and the Hindu religion uphold conservation as central to life systems and processes. Several articles and books advance this Hindu religion-based approach as a way of addressing India's ecological problems. Passages from the Vedas, Puranas, the Ramayana, and the Mahabharata are cited, as are Vedic hymns celebrating earth and water. The Purusa Sukta, one of the best-known hymns of the Rig Veda, proclaims a continuity between humans and the cosmos, suggesting that the gods, the heavens, and the earth itself arose from the *purusa*. This assertion of relationship carries a message of interconnectedness that can be used to advocate respect for nature and its elements. Many of the later legal books of the Brahminical tradition do in fact stipulate that trees must be protected and that water must not be defiled.[84] The common sense of these

[82] Vasudha Saini, "Hindu Population Going Down", *Organiser*, 20 July 1997, 7 and 19. A cogent rebuttal of the RSS view of declining Hindu numbers vis-à-vis Muslims is available in Datta, *Carving Blocs*.

[83] Swarup, *On Hinduism*, 30.

[84] Chapple, "Towards an Indigenous", 20–2.

texts is elevated to an environmental ethic emanating from the mouth of Hindu deities. The Vedic approach to the environment is, moreover, seen as coherent, consistent, holistic, and best suited to Indian conditions. A long article in the magazine *Manthan* titled "Environment and Vedic Heritage" starts with an exploration of a central idea in Vedic religion, which it says is nothing but a unity in numerous forms and names.[85] Diversities are resolved and reconciled through the supervening philosophy and doctrine of Vedic monotheism: "The symbolism of Fire, Light and Dawn, in the same way as the symbolism of different gods of the Vedic pantheon including Surya, Savitri, Varuna, Mitra and many others, represents and reflects the larger cosmic truth of concordance between inner and outer space and a bridge between the spiritual and the ecological."[86] The author then asserts that the Vedic hymn of the earth is unquestionably the oldest environmental invocation in world history, the most sublime, the most evocative. The earth is a "sacred space;" the Vedic vision of the world is filled with the purity of a spiritual environment as well as the sanctity of environmental spirituality and morality. All variety of faith communities in India have through the ages, it is concluded, shared the Vedic value system. To seek logic in this sequence of arguments is, naturally, off the mark, it being an aspect of divine revelation.

In another long article, Pandit Deen Dayal Upadhyaya is characterised as one of finest exponents of the Hindu vision of development – Ekatma Darshan – which is based on the "oneness" of Man and Nature: "The diversity is superficial. Because of the common *Atma*, all things naturally are cooperative and complementary. This is expressed by the word *Ekatma*."[87] Pandit Deen Dayal believed that nature has its own equilibrium, which is maintained by the natural cycle. The article then proposes that in order to attain oneness between man and nature, social and individual life based on four Purusharthas – Dharma, Artha, Kama and Moksha – is ideal: "If we link the *Purusharthas* with the *Chaturashramas* of *Brahmacharya*,

[85] L.M. Singhvi, "Environment and Vedic Heritage", *Manthan*, vol. XIX, no. 3, July-September 1998, 41–6.

[86] Ibid., 43.

[87] Muralivallabhan, "Protection of Environment", 157.

*Grahastya*, *Vanaprastha* and *Sanyasa*, the best sustainable model of an individual and social lifestyle is available."[88] The article proposes the worship of five Hindu deities – Vishnu, Devi, Shiva, Ganapathi, and Soorya – to prevent any imbalance in society and environment, and also to attain peace.

Ruling dynasties whose politics was based on Vedic texts are seen to represent the ideal political order, partly because the works of ancient poets and writers of that era reverberate with environmental consciousness. The age of Kalidasa, who flourished in the Gupta era (fourth to sixth centuries CE), was, we are told, a "golden age". Its intellectuals had proclaimed their affluent world a prototype of heaven. This found expression in art and architecture, in people's relationship with nature, and in social and religious systems.[89] Rituals and traditions came into being to ensure the right balance, making the Vedic texts the basis for desirable social prescription. Every Hindu came to perform certain rituals which could be in the form of worship, daily or occasionally.[90]

In this rhetoric of nature, culture, and naturalness, Brahminical ways of thinking and working – the karma, the vegetarianism, the rituals and chanting, the pilgrimages, the sacred places – were the key to nature protection. "A mass awakening in terms of the revival of India's old cultural values is necessary for the progress in the direction of environmental sustainability."[91]

## Hindu Nationalism and Environmental Themes post-2014

"We are an inseparable limb of Mother Nature and it is for us to make contributions for her upkeep. We must be grateful to Mother Nature." – Dr Mohanrao Bhagwat, RSS Sarsanghchalak, speaking in New Delhi, 17 September 2018.[92]

[88] Ibid., 158.

[89] S.R. Sehgal, "In Vedic Lore Ten Sons Were Equal to One Tree", *Organiser*, 29 June 1986, 9 and 11.

[90] RJA, *Hindu Sanskriti and Environment*, 10.

[91] Singh, "Ecological Cosmology", https://nenp.facebook.com/people/Sumangalam/100084819411949/.

[92] Bhagwat, *Future BHARAT*, 23.

The environmental politics of Hindu nationalism in India after 2014 has continued with much more aggression and organisation. At the same time, it has developed new themes that are entangled with its earlier activities and which are used interchangeably. RSS articles, reports, visuals, and activities bring out four ubiquitous environmental themes – the reimagination of a great Hindu Motherland; icons of a suffering Mother embodied by rivers and animals; climate change and renewable energy; and the idealisation of Prime Minister Modi as the country's – at times even the world's – environmental saviour.[93] There are significant visual representations – photos, cartoons, sketches, illustrations – of these themes. Through texts and visuals India is projected as a great ancient ecological and scientific Hindu nation, even as hatred and violence are directed against "polluted" Muslims. The ascendancy of Hindu nationalists to power has resulted in radical changes which have signalled multiple governmental "green" initiatives and brought climate change and renewable energy centre stage. These are couched on the one hand in an optic of purity and pollution as well as caste and religion, and on the other the mobilisation of corporations and mega "clean" industrial projects which are propagated in the name of the people, development, and the environment.

Current Hindu nationalist environmentalism has also found expression in a glowing portrayal of the ancient past when, we are asked to believe, science, technology, and environmental knowledge had been perfected by Vedic Hindu religion. This greatness is often

[93] In the 250 issues of *Organiser* published over 2014–19 (the first five-year rule of the BJP government) that I have examined, eighty articles and news reports are related directly (climate change and renewable energy) or indirectly (agriculture and science) to the environment. I have tried to identify definite trends that emerge from the data. This particular archive comprises the formal, regular, and most widely circulated publication of the RSS (*Organiser:* https://organiser.org/about-us/) which articulates and spread the views of the organisation among its activists and sympathisers. Claiming a readership of 500,000, and growing steadily amongst students, teachers, lawyers, doctors, chartered accountants, company executives, businessmen and other enlightened sections of the population through a wide network of RSS front organisations and agents the magazine also has a dynamic digital footprint.

contrasted with two opposites: first, a malign Western world which is awful despite being next to naught by comparison with the super-scientific and glorious Bharat of the ancient past; and second, cruel Muslim and British rulers who tried to destroy the glorious traditions of Bharatiya science and technology. This is the Hindu nationalist version of the country's "holy science", whereby science, technology, and religion are collectively harnessed and mobilised to create a new, modern, political Hindu nation.[94] The RSS calls it "Hindu Science": it is the "mother of sciences",[95] the core of which has been religion and nature. It propagates the view that the origins and global foundations of astronomy, mathematics, Arabic numerals, the decimal system, algebra, geometry, physics, chemistry, anaesthetics, vaccination, surgery, and medicine lay in ancient India. India was thus the "Preceptor of the Universe" (Jagatguru) in ancient times, and its achievements are foundational for all ages and geographies. Unfortunately, the barbaric invasions of India by Muslims who held sway for 1500 years, and the economic exploitation of Bharat by the British for 190 years, killed the goose that laid so many golden eggs: "Today's generation is faced with the challenge of reviving India's position as the Golden Bird and the *Jagatguru*."[96]

## The Great Hindu Motherland/Fatherland: Natural and Scientific

> "The motherland is not just a territorial map; she is a great spiritual being. When a Hindu offers prayers through the rituals of *sankalp*, or resolution, he does so by stating his location and thus initials his prayers with an identity, address, anthology of his ancestry, date, time, and season. In today's world, this would be coterminous to a three-dimensional GPS location. This is how Hindu traditions developed through scientific methodology."
> – Sunil Ambekar[97]

[94] Subramaniam, *Holy Science*.
[95] Lal, *India*, 102.
[96] Soni, *India's Glorious*, 14.
[97] Ambekar, *The RSS Roadmaps*, 85–6.

According to Raminder Kaur, visuals of nature and natural contours, land and landscapes, rivers, mountains, forests, people, and animals help to construct a homeland.[98] Notions of belonging and identity within a unique homeland are always defined in terms of what is supposedly internal, exclusive, religious, and cultural. Thus, a nation comes to be embodied in nature and its representations, and such embodiment can allegedly not be shared with non-national others. Environmental protection coalesces with the nationalist imperative of preventing the nation from being polluted.

The *Organiser* sees Bharat as the Motherland – "this Bharat is so carved out by Mother Nature that our sub-continent is a world of its own with an inalienable soul of the highest Everest-high esoteric wisdom, enshrined in our Vedic culture."[99] An article in the magazine visualises the Motherland – her body, arms, feet, head, and hair – with land, river, and mountain. A map of the Motherland is placed prominently in the middle of the page, where the figure of a mother is seen holding a saffron flag atop the geographically contoured body of the country. Declaring that the time has come when everybody must hail the Motherland, this article also warns of traitors and "those who aggressed this holy land and subjugated the Rashtra."[100]

Motherland is sometimes used interchangeably with Fatherland, man, *purusharthas* (manly power), and dharma. For example, one article states: "We believe in the oneness of Man and Nature. Right from the Vedic period till date the Indian life line has never deviated from this main line of thought."[101] Two visuals display a strong man holding a sapling, and the five fingers of his rising palm express five primordial elements of the universe (fire, air, space, earth, and water). The landscape is projected as being protected by the powerful arms of Man. These written texts and visuals frame the future in specifically political ways: Hindu unity, purity, integration, and balance held safely in the mighty hands of Hindu men.

[98] Kaur, "Spectacles of Nationalism", 206–41.

[99] Sadhu Prof. V Rangarajan, "Bharat as the Motherland", *Organiser*, 1 May 2016, 23.

[100] Ibid.

[101] Muralivallabhan, "Sustainable Development *Mantra*", 56–7.

This illustrates the Hindu nationalist "matrix of integration", invoking a glorious tradition of unity of nature-nation-culture while simultaneously subverting the "disintegrative" identity politics of region, language, caste, or gender which "we get to see in the post-colonial polity."[102] The nation is defined in geo-cultural units wherein the divinity and sacrality of landscapes, tradition, and culture are the most prominent aspects of Hindu *rajya* (reign). Indeed, and in contrast to post-colonial Indian states and institutions (recognised on the basis of democratic, federal, and linguistic aspirations), the RSS imagines society based on divine geography, a traditional Bharata, and various collectivities like *jati* (caste) or *sampradaya* (traditionalism) and civilising refiners. In this myth-making, Vedic and ancient Hindu India is projected as glorious and "golden" in *every* sphere, place, and space, including its village system, community, local knowledge, food, health, land, water, and forest management. Industrialisation, westernisation, and colonisation continue to be identified as enemies of the natural, harmonious, and environmentally sound system that was once Hindu society. The *Organiser* repeatedly calls for a return to the ancient natural Hindu system:

> Guruji believed that our villages had all the required trades and solutions for all. He was of the view that our villages had about 360 "*Jatis*" and each *Jati* was a profession, an expertise in an art. *Jati* was not merely a caste but a skill in a particular trade . . . Further, each profession had sub-classifications within them which in modern terms can be seen as super specialisations . . . This entire ecosystem made our villages self-sufficient.[103]

In the accompanying photo, Guruji Ravinder Sharma is seen amidst the background of a vast spread of land, squatting to make miniature idols of the Hindu gods. Caste divisions, hierarchies, and the subjugation of Dalits and low-caste people find no mention in this construction of Hinduism's "ideal" village eco-system.

At the same time, in its environmental language post-2014, Hindu nationalists have also been trying to blur the binaries between

[102] Bharadwaj, "Matrix of Integration", 9–11.
[103] Vaidyaraj, "Decolonising the Village Ecosystem", 72–3.

West and India, tradition and modernity, rural and urban. The major markers of such divisions – science, technology, industry, city, development, and globalisation – have at times been embraced in this projection. Indeed, BJP rule has also seen the RSS go through a series of modulations: modernity, development, science, and technology have resurfaced; they are now embraced and no longer rejected outright, but repackaged using nativism. The simultaneous presence of natural and scientific, past and future, described through myth and missile, creates a new hybrid Hindu world. RSS writers explain that such a world of sophisticated science and technology (including knowledge of astronomy and nuclear physics, engineering and climate change) existed in the great Hindu Motherland, which was culturally sound and environmentally sustainable; these developments, they argue, were suppressed under Muslim and colonial rule; however, they have been revived under the BJP government and must be taken further. In this changed rhetoric, Motherland and modernity strengthen each other and provide a new rationale to Hindu readers to comprehend the changing stances of the RSS and BJP.

The relevant articles in the *Organiser*, such as "A Return to India's Glorious Scientific Past",[104] "India, or More Correctly Bharat, Was Once in the Vanguard of Scientific Discoveries, Technologies, and Theories",[105] and "With Civilisation to Globalisation"[106] are eye-catching in terms of their regularity and coverage. They highlight how ancient Indian science and technology, and its modern avatars, can bring glory, pride, confidence, and power back to the Motherland.

Texts and visuals focus on taking their ancient and contemporary understanding of science to the masses to highlight that Hindus are hailing new innovations and solutions for sustainable development. For example, "Confluence in Science" is accompanied by four

[104] Alok Kumar, "A Return to India's Glorious Scientific Past", *Organiser*, 22 March 2015, 22–3.

[105] Manekar, "Confluence in Science", 34–5.

[106] Madan Diwan, "With Civilisation to Globalisation", *Organiser*, 7 October 2018, 27–8.

photographs (a minister, a child, a group of people, and another mass of people) appreciating the "true spirit of science by bringing traditional and modern stream together."

In sum, the RSS' construction of a Motherland and Fatherland – with natural, social, and economic contours – is based on a Hindu supremacist view where a majoritarian religious community presents a case for the return of a glorious scientific past, to effect which it calls for aggression, masculinity, and power in culture and religion, as well as unity and integration against enemies.

## Icons of the Mother: River and Cow

"Today there is a need to scream into the ears of our sleeping *dharmacharyaas* to awaken them and appeal to them to go to every nook and corner of the country spreading the cult of worship of the Motherland Bharatavarsha, who is the Mother of all our gods, goddesses, saints, sages, sanyasins and of our *sampradayas* and consecrating temples dedicated to Her."
– Sadhu Prof. V. Rangarajan[107]

The RSS' devotion to Motherland/Fatherland, and its provocative declarations of men's history and power to defend her, extend to visualising rivers and places, animals and forests, as icons of Mother. In metaphorical representations by Hindu nationalism in North India, the female body and the many faces of the Mother – motherland, mother tongue, motherhood – have served as the most universal and potent symbols of imagining the nation.[108] Consequently, the icon of Mother India enables Hindu nationalist parties to make specific claims regarding ownership of land, the exercise of sovereignty over it, and the legitimacy of Hindu rule.[109]

The *Organiser* has regularly featured different figures of Mother India as environmental icons since 2014. On the one hand, the BJP in power has driven the RSS to reimagine the physical body of the nation as a river (Mother Ganga, Narmada, Sarasvati), and on

[107] Rangarajan, "Bharat as the Motherland", 22.
[108] Gupta, "The Icon of Mother", 4291–9.
[109] Ramaswamy, "Maps and Mother Goddesses", 97–114.

the other hand as Mother Cow. These environmental icons are described as natural, ideal, pure, and generous, living amidst danger, destruction, and pollution. The mothers that emerge from the river and the animal are Hindu culture- and religion-specific, and emblematic of passive female figures. In nationalistic politics the nation-space has been frequently conceived as a passive, vulnerable woman who enables the heroism of the active masculine man. In a new Hindu world, where many things are destabilised, the mother provides a stable, personal, emotional, and traditional setting. She touches heart and soul, as well as makes one's blood boil. What is powerful is the continued production of an active, strong, passionate, and heroic male body of environmental politics which must deal decisively with the enemies of the Mother.

Concerning "Mother Ganga", in 2014 Modi himself spoke of "feeling like a child when he returns to his mother's lap."[110] Two articles published in the *Organiser*, "Namami Gange"[111] and "Hey Gange",[112] display similar aspects of the cultural and ecological politics of the RSS around rivers. The author describes the River Ganga as "Mother Ganga", as "the heart of the world's one of the richest civilisations" (*sic*), and stresses the extent to which Indians are "emotionally attached to the river". "Hey Gange" also has a top spread of two photographs of the river, along with water, mountain, construction, and erosion, where the written text focuses on "pollution", "vigorous action against those who cause pollution", and "most strict action . . . against those who pollute the Ganga." Several researches have shown that in its campaigns the RSS constantly refers to purity and pollution, particularly cultural pollution. The image of a pure, sacred Mother Ganga descending from the heavens has been created for its "unique power of salvation", "purification", and killing of "evil spirits".[113]

Mother Ganga is suffering because of pollution and polluted people. RSS slogans like *Pukarti hai Maa, Pukarti hai Bharti, Khoon se*

[110] *Organiser*, 18 May 2014.

[111] Sudhansu R. Das, "Namami Gange", *Organiser*, 31 May 2015, 18.

[112] Sirohi, "Hey Gange", 42–3.

[113] Misra, "The Mother of All", 43–5.

*Tilak Karo aur Goliyon se Aarti!* (Mother gives a clarion call, as does Bharat, mark your forehead with blood and perform prayer with bullets!) and *Jis Desh mein Shastr aur Shaastr ki Puja Hoti Hai Woh Kabhi Parajit Nahi Hota!* (A country where weapons and scriptures are worshipped is never defeated!) help in crystallising feelings for a pure and sacred river flowing amidst an ethnically and culturally homogeneous, naturally existing nation. Hindu national identity becomes the pre-eminent sense of identity and belonging, and environmental politics is made synonymous with the protection of various elements of that identity.[114]

A campaign around "servicing Mother/Goddess Narmada" River in Madhya Pradesh, launched by the BJP government, not only focuses on pollution but builds the visual of a "cradle with natural Shivalinga from where the Narmada originates."[115] The state chief minister, Modi, RSS functionaries, and sadhus are shown performing religious rituals to purify the river. The texts are visualised in a continuum of Hindu imageries and imaginations, conveying an agressively nationalist meaning. The importance of mother rivers in the environmental politics of the Hindu Right led the *Organiser* to run a four-page photo essay on the "resurgence of Sarasvati Ethos": an endeavour "to resurrect the spiritual and cultural legacy attached to the Vedic heritage river and to restore its glory enshrined in scriptures";[116] this was in BJP-ruled Haryana. After the BJP's acquisition of power, the RSS has tried to revive the mythical River Sarasvati to bolster its idea of a golden age of Hindu India before the invasions of Muslims and Christians.[117]

Second, and along with the Mother River, the RSS constructs a Mother Cow as a maternal figure imperative for economic, environmental, political, and emotional rejuvenation of community

[114] Sharma, "Nature and Nationalism", 94–6.

[115] Kumar, "Turning the Tide", 24–5.

[116] Ajay Bharadwaj, "Resurgence of Sarasvati Ethos", *Organiser*, 12 March 2017, 30–3.

[117] Nair and Daniel, "Battling for India's Soul", https://www.reuters.com/article/us-india-rss-specialreport/special-report-battling-for-indias-soul-state-by-state-idUSKCN0S700A20151013.

and country. The cow, a sacred symbol, has long religious and cultural roots in Hindu society. There is in fact an entire "cattle complex" in which the agro-economic system, ecology, and people are closely interrelated.[118] The cow as mother has also been made a significant trope for the reassertion of religious and national identities.[119] Peter van der Veer links the Hindu love for a mother cow and the protection of her body to Brahmanical rituals, devotional religion, a nurturing mother goddess, and the usefulness of dairy products.[120] Another scholar, Christopher Pinney, highlights how in colonial India locally produced visual images for the masses played a crucial role in the organisation as well as ideology of the cow-protection agitation.[121] In these the body of the cow was invested with divinity and made a proto-nation. This new space of the "cow-nation" embodied a Hindu cosmology with the idea of sacredness inscribed onto her body.[122] This extends into cow protection as a central symbol of the preservation of nature. The RJA states:

> There are two ways to use a cow: to slaughter it and use her beef; or to milk it. Slaughtering destroys, whereas milking sustains. We can slaughter only once, but milking can continue for years. A Hindu, therefore, milks, rather than exploits Nature. Pandit Deendayal Upadhyaya, while expounding his "Integral Humanism", has said: "(True) civilisation will not thrive on exploitation of Nature, but will sustain Nature, and will, in turn, itself be nourished." Milking, rather than exploitation, should be our aim. The system should be such that the overflow from Nature is used to sustain our lives.[123]

The cow then expands into a symbol of the nation, the bovine as divine. She thereby represents motherhood to all Hindus as well as to Hindu identity and nationality.

[118] Harris, "The Cultural Ecology", 51–66.

[119] Sharma, "Cow as a Sacred National Symbol".

[120] Van der Veer, *Religious Nationalism.*

[121] Pinney, "The Nation (Un)Pictured?", 841–7; idem, "Indian Magical Realism", 221–4, 230–3.

[122] Pinney, "The Nation (Un)Pictured?", 841–7.

[123] RJA, *Hindu Sanskriti and Environment*, 9.

The BJP considers the cow an effective form of protection against environmental degradation and has made vegetarianism and cow worship a central part of its Hindu nationalist agenda. In this vision, on the patient back of the cow and its progeny rests the entire structure of Indian agriculture. Their election manifesto promises to amend Article 45 of the Constitution to cover bulls and bullocks, to prohibit all trade (state as well as private) involving the slaughter of cows, and to implement a policy of Go-Samvardhan, Goshalas, and Pinjarapoles.[124] In its 2009 and 2014 manifestos, the protection of cows and their progeny was listed under the classification "preserving our cultural heritage".[125] In the 2014 election the BJP, time and again, brought up cows in its political discourse. Narendra Modi said that those owning slaughterhouses and exporting cow meat were being given subsidies and tax breaks. The country, according to him, wanted a Green and White Revolution, but the (Congress-led) government was only interested in a Pink Revolution: "When animals are slaughtered, the colour of their flesh is pink."[126]

To be protected against enemies, the cow must be seen as Gau Mata (Mother Cow). These enemies are identified as those who butcher, sell, or eat cows: "The situation has so greatly deteriorated that on the one hand selfish businessmen are importing large quantities of beef tallow with the connivance of bureaucrats and mixing it with vegetable ghee and thus playing with the sentiments and health of the people, while on the other, taking undue advantage of a Supreme Court decision, they are exporting beef by killing healthy bullocks and cows in the name of old and infirm bullocks and cows."[127] A

[124] BJP, *Towards Ram Rajya*, 13–14.

[125] For an analysis of this, see Rao, "Saffronisation of the Holy Cow", 80–7.

[126] Quoted in Damodaran, "What Pink Revolution", *thehindubussinessline.com*, accessed on 15 February 2023.

[127] BJP Pamphlet no. 40, quoted in Ahuja, *BJP and the Indian Politics*, 10. Also see Upadhyaya, "*Political Diary*", 153. Here the RSS ideologue emphasises the socio-economic and environmental importance of cows, saying that there is a strong sentiment for the cow in India which Westerners cannot understand; only Westernised, and therefore denationalised, Indians favour the slaughter of cows. Also see Pramod Kumar, "Rajasthan Respects the Cow and the Constitution", *Organiser*, 10 September 1995, 12.

prominent RSS thinker and social worker asserts that the cow is not only to be evaluated in terms of its manifold uses, but also on the basis of its cultural, religious, and national appeal.[128]

Post-2014, Hindu nationalist cow politics has acquired an aggressive tone. Many states have imposed stringent criminal penalties, including life imprisonment, for cow slaughter. As there have been several attacks on and even lynchings of Muslims suspected of "trafficking" and transporting cows, and since virtually nothing is ever said by the BJP leadership against such attacks, the conclusion widely reached is that militant Hindu groups have been weaponised against Muslims and Dalits under the pretext of cow protection. In 2017 Raman Singh, the BJP chief minister of Chhattisgarh, declared, "We will hang those who kill cows." Vikram Saini, a BJP Member of the Legislative Assembly (MLA) from Uttar Pradesh, issued this threat: "I had promised that I will break the hands and legs of those who do not consider cows their mother and kill them." A BJP MLA from Rajasthan promised: "I will say it straight out, if you smuggle and slaughter cows, then you will be killed. The cow is our mother."[129] Between May 2015 and December 2018 Hindutva activists killed 44 people, mainly Muslims, and injured some 280 others in over 100 attacks across India over cow protection.[130] It was thus analysed that:

[128] Nana Deshmukh, "Manaviya Sanskriti ke Vikas ke liye Gau-Vans ka Sanrakshan Aavashyak" (Cow Protection is Necessary for the Progress of Human Culture), *Manthan*, vol. 18, no. 1, January–March 1997, 37–41. Various organisations working closely with the RSS repeatedly emphasise the importance of the cow in these terms, and there are a large number of publications on this. For example, see "Gau Sewa se Sampoorna Kranti" (Total Revolution by Serving the Cow), *Manthan*, vol. 19, no. 4, October–December 1998, unpaginated. Also see, Rabindranath, "Bharatiya Krishi Paddhati mein Gramon ki Bhoomika"; "Gai, Ram aur Aaj ka Hindu" (Cow, Ram and Today's Hindu), *Divya Alok*, vol. 1, no. 3, April–June 1996, 38–54.

[129] These quotes were taken from NDTV, 2018.

[130] Iain Marlow, "Cow Vigilantes Killed at Least 44 People in Three Years, Report Finds", *The Print*, 20 February 2019, https://theprint.in/india/governance/cow-vigilantes-killed- at-least-44-people-in-three-years-report-finds/195450.

> the bovine body represents Mother Cow *as* Mother India – implicitly a racially pure, "upper-caste" Hindu Mother India. The sentient, living (dairy) cow is a living embodiment of *Hindustan*, the "land of Hindus". Allowing the cow to be slaughtered amounts, in effect, to sending the Hindu cow-mother-nation herself to the abattoir.[131]

This has become a way of establishing sacred spaces via processes of sanctification and group solidarity.[132] The BJP and RSS have strengthened these planks and markers of cow-protection movements through aggressive campaigns and vigilantism.

The spread of the cow as cultural artefact is multifaceted. A large number of written texts and images saturated with Hindu idioms are devoted to her. For example, "Cow Protection: Cow is a Cultural Symbol",[133] refurbishes an earlier ubiquitous image of the cow as the being in whose body several Hindu gods reside. A calf is at her udder and a woman sits before the calf holding a bowl waiting for her turn. This woman is labelled "The Hindu". Behind the cow, above her tail, is a representation of Krishna labelled "Dharmraj", and in front of the cow, above her head, is a man with a drawn sword labelled "Kali-yug". Upper-caste Hindus expiate on the meaning of the image by identifying the swordsman as an immediate threat to the cow. The overtly Hindu symbolism of the cow is usually accompanied with images and written texts on the killing, slaughtering, and smuggling of cows, often targeting Muslims as the chief culprits – to the extent of defending their lynching by Hindutva groups. An article titled "Bring an End to Cow Slaughter" has an image of a sadhu holding a banner with the slogan "DON'T SLAUGHTER YOUR MOTHER COW" and begins thus: "Asaduddin Owaisi [a prominent Muslim leader] and so many other Muslims as well as secularists tell us that they have so-called freedom to eat whatsoever they want to eat. Yes, you have the freedom to do whatsoever you want to. But you also have the freedom to urinate. But do you pass water openly in the public?

[131] Narayanan, *Mother Cow*, 8. There are many publications that analyse the politics of Hindu nationalists on cow protection in recent times. For example, Staples, *Sacred Cows*; Ganapatye, *Who Will Bell the Cow?*; Puniyani, *Cow-Beef*.

[132] Yang, "Sacred Symbol", 576–96.

[133] Kashyap, "Cow is a Cultural Symbol", 42–3.

No [. . .] you should be aware of the environmental hazards of cow slaughter as well."[134] A suffering Mother Ganga and an endangered Mother Cow are cursed by pollution and Muslims, both urgently in need of protection through action by militant Hindu conservationists.

## Climate Change and Renewable Energy

> "My views on complementary relationship between man and nature took definite shape when I studied the *Prithvi-Sukta* of *Atharva Veda* during my college days. The sixty-three Suktas (couplets) composed thousands of years ago, contain a whole spectrum of knowledge which is now being propounded under various scientific, academic and analytical banners during discussions on global warming, damage to earth's environment and the resultant Climate Change." – Narendra Modi[135]

The links between conservatism, right-wing nationalism, xenophobia, and climate change have been much researched in the contexts of the USA and Europe. There is a significant level of denial of climate change among conservative white males in the United States,[136] and studies have shown how the growth of right-wing nationalism in Europe has contributed to an increase in climate change denial.[137] This is also linked with such right-wing parties' exclusionary sociocultural issues and institutional distrust.[138] However, researchers have also pointed out that some far-right populist parties, for instance France's Rassemblement National (RN), are adopting climate-protection policy positions, showing much more flexibility and adaptability than previously anticipated, and using these issues strategically for the benefit of their organisations.[139] Indeed, some

[134] Das, "Bring an End", 25.

[135] Modi, *Convenient Action,* 4.

[136] McCright and Dunlop, "The Denial of Climate Change", 1163–72.

[137] Ulrika Ernstrom, "Climate Change Denial Strongly Linked to Right-wing Nationalism", *Chalmers*, 2021, https://www.chalmers.se/en/departments/tme/news/pages/climate-change-denial-strongly-linked-to-right-wing-nationalism.aspx.

[138] Jylha, Strimling, and Rydgren, "Climate Change Denial", 1–15.

[139] Oswald, Fromm, and Broda, "Strategic Clustering", 185–205.

have acknowledged climate change, incorporating this into the casting of blame on immigrants and to advocate stronger borders – this has been referred to as "eco-bordering".[140]

In India, climate change has been a significant political and economic project of Hindu nationalists to propagate their vision of a "New India". They have emphasised the glory of ancient and "natural" Hindu India, condemned the West, and promoted the renewable energy sector to mitigate climate change. Such patterns of assent and action create positive channels between three core constituencies: Hindutva organisations, BJP-run states, and big industry, all working closely in championing certain kinds of climate solutions. In line with this, visuals that are abstract and scientific, photographs of natural disasters and peoples' misery, and images of dedicated organisational efforts and political leadership at local and national levels bring to the fore Hindu nationalist politics and mega-modern industrial projects.

The BJP Election Manifesto for 2014 highlighted "climate change mitigation activities" at its "centre of thoughts and actions", and promised to take initiatives like cleaner production, cleaner fuels, carbon credit, ecological audit, pollution control, green building, and environment technology. It also promised to accord renewable energy "highest priority".[141] In December 2015, the cover of the *Organiser* displayed a full-size image of the Eiffel Tower and its cover story was titled "Paris Climate 2015: Towering Task", explaining in stark terms that the issue of climate change is related to national security, terrorism, and the stability of the country. It called for Paris to be turned into "a unifying ground for the world" to tackle climate change and terrorism, which the magazine viewed as "a towering task and the role of Bharat will be critical in this process."[142]

Another article on the Paris Climate Summit called it "an attempt to save the world" from instability, insecurity, and disasters.[143] Several such articles on climate change and its impact are image-driven, exposing readers to a deluge of photos of destruction and disasters.

[140] Turner and Bailey, "Ecobordering", 110–31.

[141] Bharatiya Janata Party, https://www.bjp.org/bjp-manifesto-2014.

[142] *Organiser*, 6 December 2015.

[143] *Organiser*, 27 December 2015, 22–3.

The images are placed within an overarching story of climate disorders and threats to the country, their intention being to create fear, anxiety, and concern. Human misery, loss of lives, and displacement loom large, the fear in them being enmeshed within a series of disturbing and frightening communications about Muslims, Pakistan, China, terrorists, the killing of cows, and conversions.[144] Amidst this, calls are given to awaken the great Hindu nation to become a superpower.

These articles and images on the RSS' conceptualisation and visualisation of climate change never deal with issues like social and economic justice, climate equity, caste, gender, industry, fossil fuels, mining, large dams, nuclear projects, natural resources, displacement, development, and capitalism.[145] Interestingly, and against the backdrop of climate change, Hindu nationalists extensively focus on renewable energy and new sources of power. Alongside an immense faith in the past and future of Indian science and technology, the RSS rides on the shoulders of the Modi-led government towards "Powering Bharat",[146] and to "Energise India"[147] through a vast expansion of industry-energy endeavours led by state and private-public enterprises. Little mention is made of local, micro, decentralised, and community-initiated renewable energy. The need to transform energy production, distribution, storage, and consumption in the context of renewables is never discussed. Instead, the renewable energy sector, especially solar and wind, becomes an extension of the big corporate and capital-driven power sector, forming a nexus of specific political, economic, technological, and global bodies. The articles on renewable energy display pictures and pathways of big growth, targets, and a capacity-driven "sunrise" sector in India, and take pride in claiming that

> In the face of rising pollution, depleting natural resources and the looming threat of climate change, Renewable Energy is fast becoming a

[144] Omar, "The Muslim 'Threat'", https://www.soas.ac.uk/south-asia-institute/publications/working-papers/file152729.pdf.

[145] Bidwai, *The Politics of Climate.*

[146] *Organiser*, 6 December 2015, 12–14.

[147] *Organiser*, 19 July 2015.

> mantra across the world. Indian tradition has long recognised the energy emanating from the Surya (Sun), Varuna (Water), Vayu (Wind), and Gau (biofuel). It is therefore, befitting that India should aim to be the Clean Energy Capital of the World. And India has started working towards it, and it was clearly reflected when the Prime Minister, Narendra Modi said that "India is now thinking in Gigawatts rather than Megawatts when it comes to renewable."[148]

The high capacity and overall renewal target of 175 GW by 2022 also claimed to "set a direction and commitment to travel creating an attractive market for global investors."[149] Indeed, public-private power/coal/renewal energy companies have regularly advertised in this media, displaying their commitment for a clean and green India. Researchers have shown the convergence of neoliberalism and Hindutva, resulting in the creation of a Hindutva-ised neoliberal subjectivity.[150] It has also been pointed out how neoliberalism and Hindutva share common, deeper class interests and political goals by "articulating shared notions of a bounded, unitary and individual-based conceptions of society."[151]

The *Organiser* grants substantial space for the subject of climate change and renewable energy, and for multiple industrial and developmental protagonists who claim to follow the path of green and sustainable development. Sectors like urban development ("Smart cities: Reshaping urban life"),[152] nuclear energy ("Nuclear security summit: One hurdle down, A few to go"),[153] natural gas ("Energising pipeline diplomacy"),[154] big dams ("Sardar Sarovar project: An engineering miracle"),[155] mining ("Upscale mining"),[156] natural resources like land ("Land acquisition bill is farmer friendly"),[157] water

148 Sandeep Singh, "The Electrifying Effect", *Organiser*, 31 July 2016, 24–7.
149 *Organiser*, 2 July 2017, 29.
150 Chhachhi, "Neoliberalism, Hindutva and Gender", 50–93.
151 Gopalakrishnan, "Defining, Constructing and Policing", 2810–13.
152 *Organiser*, 14 February 2016.
153 *Organiser*, 10 July 2016.
154 *Organiser*, 10 January 2016.
155 *Organiser*, 1 October 2017.
156 *Organiser*, 8 March 2015.
157 *Organiser*, 29 March 2015.

("Mainstreaming of water transport"),[158] material infrastructure ("Mining new gains in infrastructure"),[159] and its cultural forms ("Six steps to the renaissance")[160] – together create a ground for green growth. These articles make a strong case for how Indian scientific and technological progress can better harness the potential of gas and mining, big dams and infrastructure, for the grandeur of Bharat and its modern developments. This is a "*brand new nation*: the nation revitalised and renewed as a profitable business enterprise with claims to ownership over cultural property within its territory."[161]

The visuality of renewable energy and its associated industries, in contrast to climate change imageries, offers bright photos, diagrams, and enclosures of solar panels, grid infrastructure, sunshine and wind turbines, thus providing an aesthetic composition to economic and industrial activities. Images of renewable energy are merged with engineering, science, and technology to support the text. Images are also used to demonstrate the success of such measures in transforming people, and community lives, showing big industry and capital to be right, justifiable, accessible, and acceptable. The *Organiser*'s cover story on "Energise India: To energise India promoting clean and green energy with cost effective innovations is inevitable to realise future development potential" has fifteen photos depicting people, villages, darkness, and light, agriculture, solar panel, wind turbine, city, political leader and expert; four diagrams and sketches showing waves, water, currents, and statistics; and four advertisements of power companies claiming to green the world. Renewable energy, people, corporate sector, growth, and development merge into a single natural-industrial frame.

Climate change and renewable energy have clearly emerged as new sites of environmental politics of the Hindu nationalists, both inextricably intertwined. The focus on climate change deals with its impact on human population, floods, droughts, and disasters, and the individual-organisational roles of "nationalists" and "Hindus"

[158] *Organiser*, 4 October 2015.
[159] *Organiser*, 6 August 2017
[160] *Organiser*, 18 March 2018.
[161] Kaur, *Brand New Nation*, 8.

in supporting a community in crisis. However, the RSS gives industries, scientists, and technocrats a leading role in addressing climate change, and in the same breath positions the mega renewable energy sector to address the problem. Climate change and corporate activities are twinned in its vision, made visible in its choice of images. The Modi-led Indian government becomes the key for climate change and renewable energy projects with a wider global and corporate outreach. This valorises the present regime's formation of a new Hindutva, where Hindu nationalists take economic and foreign policy projects and aspirations to be as important as their efforts in shaping cultural and religious identities along a Hindu majoritarian line.[162]

## Modi: Evolution of Environmental Legitimacy

> "Prime Minister Narendra Modi has been an efficient ambassador of ancient Indian wisdom. He always highlights the Hindu vision of nature and the principles of environment conservation in all global platforms." – J. Nandakumar[163]

Explaining the political authority of governments in South East Asia, Alagappa underscores how rationales like normative goals, performance, personal authority, and international support have been critical for their legitimation.[164] However, since legitimation on the basis of these rationales is highly contingent and subject to periodic erosion and crisis, there is always a search for a new and more durable basis of authority. In this respect, the natural environment becomes a new constituent element in the politics of right-wing leaders.

Modi as prime minister and past RSS propagandist personifies the governmentality and politicality of Hindu nationalists in relation to the environment. Indeed, in his persona as the environmental saviour of the nation, the dominant environmental themes discussed in this chapter are merged. The written texts and visuals pertaining

[162] For details, Hansen and Roy, eds, *Saffron Republic. Legitimacy.*

[163] Nandakumar, *Hindutva*, 23.

[164] Alagappa, ed., *Political Legitimacy.*

to Modi are of a strong and decisive personality whose vision is a new Bharat based on RSS ideology. Salient features of his personality and personal authority are continuously expanded to solidify the image of a supreme leader. This has been characterised as "populist-authoritarianism in India" under the "strongman" Modi who claims a legacy of the poor and the marginalised based on his past, and the power of the rich and the corporate based on his current stature.[165] In European countries "the politics of fear" has brought populist right-wing politics centre-stage, which further entrenches the social divides of nation, gender, and body.[166] In India today, the goals of environment and development are increasingly deployed to legitimise Modi and his government and to advance a Hindu nationalist agenda. Modi himself uses his image on multiple media platforms to create a positive and edifying impression about his personality, leadership, and power. Diverse images and visuals of him as strong, active, cheerful, communicative, energetic, and agile, both indoors and outdoors, have been crafted and displayed by his official and organisational networks to make him ever-visible in the Indian political landscape.

In 2014 Modi's visit to Banaras, his political constituency, and his naming of himself as the "Ganga-son" provided an interesting starting point to this brand of environmental politics. The primary metaphors in the event were Hindu religiosity, sacrality, the purity of Mother and Modi, all magnified with large visuals of him.[167] Since 2014, his environmental image has moved forward, expanded, and come to encompass many themes in the pages of the *Organiser*: for example, "It's time to deliver: Modern industry & environment friendly",[168] "Beautifying Banaras",[169] and "Clean India campaign".[170] Energy, climate change, smart-green cities and urban development have been recurrent themes for Modi since 2016. The *Organiser* has continuously published on these issues since 2014,

[165] Gudavarthy, *India after Modi*.
[166] Wodak, *The Politics of Fear*.
[167] *Organiser*, 18 May 2014.
[168] *Organiser*, 1 June 2014.
[169] *Organiser*, 8 March 2015.
[170] *Organiser*, 2 October 2016.

particularly focusing on Modi: "Narendra Modi-led Government has given a new edge to the gas pipeline diplomacy as one of the cornerstones of meeting Bharat's growing energy needs",[171] "International Solar Alliance: Let us turn to sun",[172] "PM Narendra Modi dedicates the Sardar Sarovar Dam to the Nation",[173] "Indian Prime Minister Narendra Modi and President of France Emmanuel Macron inaugurated a 75 MW solar power plant in Mirzapur".[174]

In 2019, Cyclone Fani struck Odisha and West Bengal, causing severe human and environmental damage. The *Organiser*'s cover story, "Cyclone Fani",[175] represented the disaster, climate change, and the people affected along with the work done by the RSS, through a multitude of texts and visuals. The captions of the photos read: "Odisha's spiritual city, Puri, ravaged in an unseasonal cyclone", "RSS Sahsarkaryavahk distributing relief to the cyclone affected people", "RSS workers distributing relief to Fani cyclone affected people", and "RSS swayamsevaks restoring road connectivity". Along with this, the magazine placed a long article titled "Not 'Fani' but Modi Wave Rattles Didi" – denoting Modi unsettling the West Bengal chief minister Mamata Banerjee. The article inclued a photograph of Modi – victorious and aggressive, with both his hands raised in the air – to suggest he had triumphed over the damage caused by Fani in West Bengal. The BJP has particularly concentrated on West Bengal in the past few years to spread its Hindutva politics since political control has remained elusive for them in this state.

In sum, Modi extensively uses environmental issues, especially the Ganga, the cow, climate change, and renewable energy to strengthen his political image. This knits into a composite fabric narrativising the great Motherland with the power of a strong nation and leader. Modi is shown "taking holy dips" and championing climate change, all meant as propaganda in elections for a future Bharat where the identity of Bharat itself is part of a bitter electoral battle.

[171] *Organiser*, 31 July 2016.

[172] Ibid.

[173] *Organiser*, 1 October 2017.

[174] *Organiser*, 2 September 2018.

[175] *Organiser*, 19 May 2019, 6–13.

The environmental concerns of Hindu nationalists are sometimes channelled through virtually the language used by radical environmental and social movements. Both speak of natural wealth. But Hindu nationalists argue for the exclusivity of Hindu tradition while lauding traditional agriculture, traditional industries, traditional systems of water management, and other such living technological, social, religious, and cultural traditions. Their priorities are the management of natural resources through participation by local communities with their exclusive initiatives, accountability, and trusteeship. Here the initiative by Gram Sabhas in water management is a first step. Other important features are the decisive role of and control by village communities in areas like agriculture, forests, water management, and fisheries; the fair distribution of land, keeping in view tillage capacity; an emphasis on community management of forest land and revenue land; and the share of the local community in mining and other industries in their areas. These underline the importance of harmonising Jan (people), Jal (water), Jameen (land), Jangal (forests), and Janvar (animals), with the greatest emphasis being given to agriculture and rural planning. They advocate the need for reviving and strengthening the *pani panchayat* and village traditions of forest management.[176]

In discussing the phenomenon of right-wing ecology in Germany, Jonathan Olsen argues that "the themes around which right-wing ecology are organised – eco-naturalism, eco-organicism, and eco-authoritarianism – are not often translated into concrete, specific political solutions to environmental problems. But that is hardly the point. Nature within right-wing ecology is understood as an ontological home through which a collective identity (Germanness) is defined."[177] For Hindu nationalists, nature functions in an almost identical way. The environmental ideas of Hindu nationalists – eco-nationalism, eco-primitivism, eco-naturalism, eco-enemy, Brahmanical models, and cow protection – are less concerned with outlining specific environmental policies than with defining a collective Hindu identity.

[176] SJM, *Rebuilding the Nation*, 12–19.
[177] Olsen, *Nature and Nationalism*, 51.

The RSS outfits are united in their common belief of pollution of water, air, and environment as inextricably tied to the pollution of Hindu identity: the pollution of external and internal nature thus stems from the same violation of a natural and rooted order. Accordingly, the notion of "foreign" within this discourse denotes not simply an increased number of immigrants/migrants who are destroying land and forests, but rather a nebulous alien presence that disrupts the national unity of Hindus with their specific home in nature.

Post-2014, Hindu nationalists have shown flexibility in adopting new strategies for articulating the challenge of climate change which feed into their standard environmental narratives. Some distinctive trends have emerged regarding Hindu nationalism and environmental communication in India: embracing a narrative of climate change and renewable energy; targeting Muslims as the cause of natural and social pollution; promoting a caste-based, aggressive Hindutva; and state-initiated, mass-based environmental campaigns. These invoke polarised notions of community and environment which emphasise and find justification in exclusive, violent, weaponised, and centralised resource management. Relations between environment, people, and culture have often been explained in a linear narrative by the Hindu Right: Bharat versus the West, inigenous versus foreign, Mother versus Other(s), Hindu versus Muslim, and purity versus pollution.

The RSS and the BJP have skilfully combined governmentality with politics, Hindu nationalism with environmental ideology, and green practice with corporate interests to undertake their massive organisational and political outreach activities on environmental issues. In *Environmentality: Technologies of Government and the Making of Subjects*, Agrawal describes how various strategies of power, knowledge, and statistics create particular environments as domains fit for government, and how different sets of new relations – governmentalised communities, regulatory communities, and the constitution of environmental subjects – change the politics of environment.[178] Through its written texts and images, the RSS helps in carving out

[178] Agrawal, *Environmentality.*

a distinct environmental public sphere where individuals and collectives are actively mobilised around a sectarian ecological ideology that can even justify the killing of the perceived "other" in the name of animals, food, and pollution.

The triangle of RSS, BJP, and Modi – the principal faces of contemporary Hindu nationalism in India – are resourceful and savvy in their uses of media and communication for their political and governmental agenda. At a time when the media has transformed religion and religious consciousness in South Asia,[179] the RSS has designed a regular flow, at times flooding the media with its environmental communication. The streams of organisations, activities, text and visuals discussed expand the Hindu nationalist's ideological outreach and magnify its political appeal, aiding the rise of a new, aggressive, and hyper-Hindu environmental subject which stands up for right-wing agendas and activities.

[179] Babb and Wadley, eds, *Media and the Transformation*.

# 3

# The Making of an Authority

## Anna Hazare and the Watershed Management Programme in Ralegan Siddhi

Anna Hazare's programme of watershed development in Ralegan Siddhi merits attention not only for its environmental impact but also because of its comprehensive and multifaceted nature. It gives us insights into the ways in which an individual and his organisation can play a central role in reshaping rural life. In Hazare's case the elusive but crucial element is "moral authority", which can only be effectively exercised if there is a large degree of consent and conservative or traditional respect for exemplars among those upon whom such authority is sought to be exercised. Surprisingly, accounts of this experiment, largely celebratory in nature, have not examined the ideology and politics which underpin it. I believe it is crucial, in order to understand the likely future of "green villages", to critically interrogate all that surrounds this brand of environmentalism. Therefore this chapter is focused mainly on understanding precisely how rural developmental and environmental work in the journeys of Anna Hazare and Ralegan Siddhi acquire their legitimacy and authority. In what ways are they fed by, and feed into, some of the dominant political cultures of the state? To what extent are they articulated within a coherent ideological framework? Built on such a framework, does a political theory and its practice open up or expand political conservatism?

Like the ideology and appeal of any other rural organisation or movement, those of Anna Hazare's programme are not based on a single plank. Although developmental and environmental works form the core of its ideological structure, the organisation includes other issues. At times it provides a variety of activities to its audience, but all these also eventually reinforce its principal ideological framework. An understanding of the ideological DNA of green villagers and their environmentalist fellow-travellers will give us an idea of the core elements of this endeavour and ideology which motivate villagers and environmentalists, as well as the nature of ideological perceptions and preferences among a connected set of people and organisations.

## The Historical Context of Maharashtra

Anna Hazare and Ralegan Siddhi are not a new addition to the social history of Maharashtra state. Indeed, the movement has borrowed many features from the historical evolution of the region, especially from the political culture of the state, with which it negotiates at different levels. Many factors are at play, with four being of primary importance: (i) nativism and regionalism in Maharashtrian culture and politics; (ii) the structure and nature of caste and class; (iii) the agrarian environment and the rural economy; and (iv) local environmentalism.

### *Nativism and Regionalism in Maharashtrian Culture and Politics*

In his pioneering work on the Shiv Sena in Mumbai, Dipankar Gupta gives an overview of nativism in the culture and politics of Maharashtra. He shows how the popularity and mass appeal of the Samyukta Maharashtra Samithi (SMS) and Shiv Sena were largely made possible by relying on certain dominant sentiments among Maharashtrians regarding the exclusiveness and superiority of their culture and history.[1]

[1] Gupta, *Nativism in a Metropolis*, 40–6.

Gupta says that the Maratha empire, established in the seventeenth and eighteenth centuries, created strong affinities within the population on account of a common language, race, religion, literature, and political existence. The Maratha wars against the Mughals were portrayed as a religious conflict of Hindus against Muslims, idealised as the rivalry between Shivaji and Aurangzeb, strengthening Hindu solidarity by the identification of a common enemy and the quasi-deification of heroic resistance centred in a local ruler. The Maratha empire became not only a bastion of Hinduism – the *Hindu pad padshahi* – but also a kind of last haven for the subjugated indigenous population. In the early twentieth century, initially under the leadership of Gopal Krishna Gokhale and later under Lokmanya Tilak, Maharashtrians tried to reassert themselves in the mainstream of India's national and political life by re-emphasising the high points of Maharashtrian history in the days of the *Hindu pad padshahi* and by activating pride in their culture and tradition. Tilak revived the Ganpati and Shivaji festivals and also demanded the formation of a unilingual province of Maharashtra. The SMS systematically and successfully tapped these local and regional sentiments by emphasising the cultural identity of Maharashtrians. Shivaji was especially glorified, soon being transformed into a public god, and Marathi sentiments of linguistic regionalism and parochialism were taken to new heights. Later, a few years after the unilingual state of Maharashtra was formed, there began the rise and growth of the Shiv Sena, especially in Mumbai, riding on the same sentiments and invoking once again the glorious days of Shivaji.

The legend of Shivaji is so deeply rooted in the Maharashtrian psyche that it could be asserted no other figure in Indian history has transcended his or her time to this degree. The Marathas, the ruling caste of Maharashtra, have always prided themselves on their connection with Shivaji, and the official support given by various governments to this legend has only strengthened their pride.[2] Tilak cultivated and used the Shivaji legend, with a public celebration of his birthday for the purpose of mobilising the masses in the freedom

[2] Sirsikar, "Political Culture of Maharashtra", 5–17.

struggle.[3] As James Laine puts it: "The nationalist project later appropriated Shivaji, taking his tale of Maratha *swarajya* and making it an anticipation of the independence movement. In stages, Shivaji has become a Vaishnava Varkari, a 'Maharashtrian' and finally an Indian, even a secular nationalist one . . . The nationalist must construct a romantic, nostalgic, primordialist discourse which imitates the language of local communities."[4]

The Shiv Sena and the Hindu nationalists have in the more recent past used the Shivaji legend maximally, with nostalgic references, saffron flags, and of course what they are reputed for, namely militancy. In fact, when the Shiv Sena first came to power in the state in 1995, it was at the Shivaji Park that Manohar Joshi took his oath as chief minister.[5]

Religion has also supplied a strong input within the creation of Maharashtra's cultural identity.[6] Religious festivals, especially the Ganpati festival, have been the centre around which large public gatherings have been constituted since the 1890s. Ganpati, a syncretic figure, combined elements of high Hinduism, asceticism, and wisdom with the values of village Hinduism, devotion, and pleasure. Ganpati had the potential for a political career since one part of his personality derived from Shiva, the potent warrior. Ganpati was an "overcomer of obstacles" and thus a useful symbol for a protest movement.[7] In contemporary India this kaleidoscopic event is of interest to various institutions – from political parties to the state, from media conglomerates to community organisations. This has helped the event to become a focal point for community and national identities in the making. Martial representations of Ganpati and the development of shrine tableaux which provide commentaries on issues of

[3] Johnson, *Provincial Politics*, 82, 89–91.

[4] Laine, "A Question of Maharashtrian Identity", 70.

[5] Purandare, *The Sena Story*, 7–8. During poll campaigns the Shiv Sena chief Bal Thackeray repeatedly announced that if they came to power, the swearing-in ceremony of the Shiv Sena chief minister would not be at the exclusive Raj Bhavan, it would be at Shivaji Park, under the statue of Chhatrapati Shivaji Maharaj, with the entire city invited.

[6] Kosambi, "Introduction", 4.

[7] Cashman, *The Myth of the "Lokamanya"*, 75.

broad interest, such as the freedom struggle, political corruption, and the nuclear rivalry with Pakistan, are evidence of their appeal among the populace.[8]

### *The Structure and Nature of Caste and Class*

Historically, western India under Peshwa rule was a relatively closed society in religious terms, especially in comparison with what it was under the East India Company. In pre-nineteenth-century society, upward mobility was relatively easier for individuals and even for entire castes. After the move up, these sanskritising castes frequently adopted the religious and social practices of the groups above them in the hierarchy. However, change in social status within the larger hierarchy of Hindu society was a difficult issue. The Brahmins remained firmly on the highest rung of the ladder, the Shudras on the last. British rule, instead of breaking down these inequalities, reinforced them by adding to the older religious authority of Brahmins a formidable new range of administrative and political powers.[9]

The nineteenth century also witnessed strong social movements of the lower and middle castes against upper-caste dominance. Gail Omvedt sees this as a more radical cultural revolt in Maharashtra whose basis was the *bahujan samaj* (the non-Brahmin peasant masses), with leadership being provided by certain prominent non-Brahmin intellectuals. The most influential, Jyotirao Phule (1827–90), of the *mali* (gardener) caste, formulated an ideology of genuine cultural revolt which called for the abolition of caste and the adoption of a scientific and rational outlook. Omvedt also observes that in Maharashtra the peasant and the lower- and middle-caste "masses" have a social reality and a historical tradition of their own, which is in opposition at crucial points to elite tradition (including the tradition of aristocratic non-Brahmins).[10]

The present jati pyramid of Maharashtra is composed of Brahmins, elite Marathas claiming Kshatriya ancestry; peasant Marathas

[8] Kaur, *Performative Politics.*

[9] O'Hanlon, *Caste, Conflict, and Ideology,* 4–7.

[10] Omvedt, *Cultural Revolt,* 7, 120.

(known earlier, and in some parts of Maharashtra even now, as Kunbis); artisan and service jatis (of the Shudra varna); and a number of former "untouchable" jatis technically outside the varna system, such as Mahars, who are known by the generic term "Dalits".[11] In a large majority of the state's villages, Marathas are the dominant caste. Villages with other castes in dominant positions exist, but are few in number and normally conform to the requirements of the regional Maratha dominance. In most villages Marathas constitute a very substantial portion of the total population, but only a few have wealth, power, and rank. The latter two are often the consequence of the first, but were in the past closely linked with the hereditary headmanship (*patilki*).[12] The dominance of the Marathas in the power structure is generally ascribed to their large number in the region. There are various estimates of the Maratha population: the Maratha-Kunbi cluster is reckoned to be about 50 per cent, or about 55 per cent in rural Maharashtra, this representing about 35 per cent of the state's population.[13] Thus, elite Marathas constitute the rural hegemonic class in Maharashtra. Their hegemony rests on simultaneous control over economy and culture.[14] There has come about a new kind of concentration of wealth and resources within this hegemonic high Maratha class or people. The so-called "rabi-belt" of food-grain production and regions producing cotton and sugarcane have many "co-operative kings".[15] These fractions of the hegemonic class have used the policy processes of pluralist democracy with great sophistication and to maximum advantage – even in the context of a generally stagnant economy.[16]

### *Agrarian Environment and Rural Polity*

The "agrarian environment" denotes a field of social negotiations around the environment in predominantly agrarian contexts. Agrarian affiliations affect the interactions and processes of the actors and

[11] Kosambi, "Introduction", 3.
[12] Lele, *Elite Pluralism*, 31–5.
[13] Dahiwale, "Consolidation of Maratha Dominance", 336.
[14] Lele, *Elite Pluralism and Class Rule*, 31–5.
[15] Rosenthal, "Deurbanisation, Elite Displacement", 1970.
[16] Dandekar, "Introduction".

issues involved, and, given that India is predominantly agrarian, the agrarian and the environmental are enmeshed and never autonomous. Environmental changes are connected with agrarian structures, and environmental politics is linked with the agrarian world, the locus and object of this politics.[17]

So it is partially possible to explain why Maharashtra has a distinct culture of its own on the basis of the principles of cultural ecology: the environment has played a very important role in the making of Maharashtrian culture. The region witnessed a flowering of its culture when the environment was congenial, and the quality of life deteriorated when the conditions were adverse.[18] Other than the plateau-like morphology, the shallow stream valleys, and the semi-arid monsoonal climate, the most significant environmental feature of the state is its rainfall, the year-to-year variability being very high and droughts fairly common.

For historical reasons the agrarian structure of the state varies significantly across its different regions. As in other states of the country, land reforms and agrarian changes in the state began in two phases. The first phase constituted reform measures in the period before 1965, the second phase being reform measures in the early 1970s. These measures focused on the prevention of fragmentation, the abolition of intermediaries and tenancy reforms, a ceiling on the size of landholdings, and redistribution of land to the landless. But the implementation of these was not only tardy, it also revealed many imperfections.[19] For example, in a detailed study on the distribution of government land to the poor in western Maharashtra, it was found that norms had been violated in the scarcity zone – where 79.31 per cent of the beneficiaries were not Scheduled Castes (SCs) and Scheduled Tribes (STs); similarly, in the west coastal plains 56.6 per cent of the beneficiaries were not SCs and STs. The districts where such violations were high were Kolhapur, Pune, Ahmadnagar, Sangli, and Thane, where 64 to 100 per cent of the land had been distributed to other castes.[20] The uneven regional development, the

[17] Agrawal and Sivaramakrishnan, eds, *Agrarian Environments*, 1–21.

[18] Dhavalikar, "Maharashtra Environmental", 41.

[19] Deshpande, "Land Reforms and Agrarian", 95–126.

[20] Iyer, "Distribution of Government Land", 220–44.

nexus between agriculture and industry, the emergence of a strong class of rural elites, a history of social movements with an active role played by the peasantry, and social stratification are other important characteristics of the agrarian environment and rural polity.

The co-operatives, local governments, and educational institutions are all part of the rural polity as well. In the post-Independence period the rich Marathas have dominated these. Given their power and position, they act as patrons, extending help in matters pertaining to employment and finance, securing the benefits of government programmes, and providing positions in local bodies. Those who receive help obviously feel obliged to these elites and become subservient to their leaders.[21]

### *Local Environmentalism*

Environmental issues are inextricable from local, social, and developmental problems. A village constructing its own little dam or a region struggling to reclaim wasteland are focusing on environmental issues while simultaneously engaging with local developmental issues. There has in fact been no such thing as a single perspective, or a single movement, in relation to the environment. Given the range of environments and diversity of people, there has been a corresponding multitude of issues and perspectives as well as organisational initiatives in relation to the environment. Since the 1970s, particularly, organisations, campaigns, and movements have constantly appeared in remote areas, addressing specific local environmental issues. Each movement picks up a specific problem, such as stopping or building a particular dam, or claiming rights over land in forests, or fish in the seas. Each initiative chooses its own strategy, depending upon the nature of the main issue, the socio-cultural life of the people, and the character of the local organisation. In the process, some inspiring and persuasive leaders have emerged. Many have contributed considerably to the creation of greater environmental sensitivity. Numerous NGOs have also made their

[21] Dahiwale, "Consolidation of Maratha Dominance", 336–42.

presence felt through issue-based campaigns and constructive activity. And several environmental movements have sought to associate themselves more closely with these NGOs.[22]

From the perspective of institutionalised social action, the early 1970s – the student movements, the movement led by Jayaprakash Narayan, and the state repression during the "Emergency" (1975–7) – form the springboard for a wide spectrum of social action initiatives. An unprecedented range of institutionalisation processes happened from 1975 to 1995, impacting voluntary social action initiatives which were influenced by new trends in international politics as well as the revitalised accent on the "development" of the third world. These institutional and ideological contours were also influenced by the emergence of international human rights and development organisations, and secularised groups of church and sponsorship organisations.[23] Given the inefficiency of the state to address increasing deprivation, as well as the techno-economic approach adopted by the ruling elite, the 1970s and 1980s saw the emergence of localised social action by the subaltern masses and smaller identity-based assertions for entitlements and rights within the structures of state and society.

Maharashtra too has a history of such social movements, with the rural population playing an active role. From the awakening among the rural peasantry initiated by Jyotiba Phule through the Satya Shodhak Samaj, to present-day initiatives and movements by labourers, tribals, women, and Dalits, a good base was built here for social action. From Phule to Ambedkar to Baba Amte, from the protection of sacred groves in village Gani of Shrivardhan taluka to the building of the Baliraja dam in Tandulwadi village of Sangli district, there has been much local environmentalism in Maharashtra.[24] It is in this context and the specific agrarian-environmental history of the region that the movement of Anna Hazare needs to be seen.

[22] Sharma, *Landscapes and Lives*, 1–7.

[23] Samuel, "Changing Contours", 7–8.

[24] Gadgil and Guha, *Ecology and Equity*, 57, 91.

## Ralegan Siddhi and Anna Hazare: A Profile

Ralegan Siddhi and its greatly admired leader Anna Hazare have been described thus by two prominent environmentalists, Anil Agarwal and Sunita Narain:

> In our class-ridden society, who cares for an ex-army jeep driver? And yet Kishan Baburao Hazare, now so fondly called Anna Hazare, has emerged as one of India's leading environmental warriors. His stewardship of Ralegan Siddhi, a village in Ahmadnagar district, has turned it into an environmental model. Every slope is afforested and every *nullah* bunded. The result is a green village far more capable of dealing with the area's recurrent droughts than its neighbours. A lot of money for the "environmental works" has come from the government's rural development schemes, except that Ralegan Siddhi has set its own priorities and made honest use of government money.[25]

Another study says: "It is not investment alone or the faithful implementation of government programmes that has made Ralegan an outstanding phenomenon. Social development towards an ethical and egalitarian society has preceded as well as accompanied economic development in Ralegan, giving it a special place on the development scene."[26]

Anna Hazare has his own account of his achievements:

> I was given the "Friend of the Trees" award at the hands of late Prime Minister Rajiv Gandhi in 1989 without approaching anybody or lobbying for it. Same was the case for Padmashree and Padmabhushan awards given by Rashtrapatiji, and other awards such as Krishi Bhushan, Vasantrao Naik award, Swami Vivekananda Sewa Award . . . The Central Government has coopted me as adviser in four committees without our

[25] Agarwal and Narain, "Preface", 3.

[26] Awasthi, "Rural Development", 74. Also see Lokur, *Ralegan Siddhi: Rural Tranformation*, which concludes that Ralegan Siddhi has shown that development is possible even while conserving natural resources; Bagchee and Bagchee, "Improving Rainfed Farming", 19–22; Gadgil and Guha, *Ecology and Equity*, 104; Mahapatra, "Prosperity and Beyond", 45–7.

> making any effort. The state government has also requested me to work on their committees on Water Conservation, Dry Land Development, Integration, Model Village Scheme, etc.[27]

Today Ralegan Siddhi village looks fresh and green in a district that is hilly, dry, and dusty.[28] Ahmadnagar district is situated partly in the upper Godavari basin and partly in the Bhima basin. With a total area of 17,035 sq. km, it has 776,787 households and a population of 40,40,642, out of which the rural population is 32,36,945. The SC and ST populations are 484,685 and 3,03,255, respectively.[29] Barring the district of Chanda in the Vidarbha region, Ahmadnagar is the largest district of this area of the state, occupying a somewhat central position in Maharashtra. Climatically, most of the district, barring the westernmost Akola taluka in the hilly region, receives a rainfall of 500–600 cm, but this cannot be relied upon, and so practically the whole district falls within a chronic scarcity zone in which acute shortages of food and fodder recur once every three to eight years. The climate of the district is a hot summer and general dryness much of the year. A glance at the advanced network of State Transport (ST) roads lining sugar factories surrounded by sugarcane, oil mills, engines, pumps, ginning factories, and textile centres gives an idea of the changing profile of the district.[30]

Ralegan Siddhi has a population of 2317 and comprises 434 households. The SC and ST populations are 171 and 32 respectively.[31] The caste composition of the village has always been even: except for 46 SC families, the rest are Marathas. The total geographical

[27] Hazare, *Ralegan Siddhi*, 153.

[28] I visited Ralegan Siddhi thrice: in February 1991, July 1995, and October 1999. Most of these accounts are based on my meetings and interviews during these visits. Almost all the literature and writings available on Ralegan Siddhi and Anna Hazare give detailed information on its past and present achievements.

[29] Primary Census Abstract 9, *Census of India 2001*, Office of the Registrar General, Delhi.

[30] Ahmadnagar District (Revised Edition), *Maharashtra State Gazetteers*, Government of Maharashtra, Bombay, 1976.

[31] Primary Census Abstract 9, *Census of India 2001*.

area of the village is 982.31 hectares. Landholdings are unevenly distributed. Of the 638.94 hectares of agricultural land, only 30 families have more than 4 hectares, 62 families have between 2 and 4 hectares, and the rest are either landless or have at most 1 or 2 hectares.[32] The lack of irrigation water and the low level of agricultural productivity affects everyone more or less equally. Although there are a few wells, they irrigate no more than a few hectares. With the support of working and retired jawans from the army, as well as some government employees, the village had over the years managed to survive, but only just. Its people were living on the edge, many having had to migrate for wage labour at regular intervals, especially during droughts, like the terrible one of the early 1970s which devastated the entire region. Though the village saw some government relief programmes at the time, they were poorly conceived and badly implemented. For example, the villagers say, a percolation tank was planned for the village. After many years, when it was finally constructed in 1983, it could not work because the water seeped away from the bunds.

So, under the leadership of Anna Hazare the village tried to evolve and implement a different path of watershed development. Villagers constructed storage ponds and reservoirs and *nala* bunds in a series, along the 30-to-45-metre-high hills surrounding the village. Nala bunds were of different kinds – big and small, open and underground – and extensive plantation was carved out in the spaces in between. Soon the hills and the nearby areas were all covered with bunds, trenches, nalas, and plants. Overall, 31 nala bunds were created, with a storage capacity estimated at 2,82,182 cubic metres, covering an area of 605 hectares. Four lakh trees have been planted. Significantly, most of this work has been carried out by utilising financial resources accruing to the village under the soil conservation and social forestry programmes of the government.

"Water should not be seen on the surface, it should be caught hold of and kept below": this was the guiding principle, in the words of

[32] Based on figures given by *gram sewak* K.N. Bhagat in Ralegan Siddhi in October 1999.

Anna.[33] This variety of water conservation led to many positive developments within a few years. Agricultural land increased, and so did the yield, and the groundwater level, which was 100 feet down, came up to 40–50 feet. Wells and ponds too filled up and now the village is never without water, not even in a year with no rain. Anna's success has led him to experiment with water and land in many ways: 53 small farmers with land adjacent to each other were made to join hands and dig 11 wells. They own these wells jointly, and their waters irrigate more than 100 acres of their land. In another instance, 103 farmers were convinced to form a co-operative. As they pooled their resources and produce, their input costs were reduced. Defunct percolation tanks in the village were repaired using the voluntary labour of villagers. Above all, the distribution of water among the villagers was regulated: unless all the farmers got a first round of irrigation, nobody was entitled to a second round. Those who used water for irrigation compensated, in cash or kind, the landless families that did not use irrigation water. And those who dug individual wells had to share its water with their neighbours.

*Shramshakti dwara Gramin Vikas* (Rural Development through Labour) has been Anna Hazare's slogan all these years. This is now being appropriated by the state government to design a rural development programme for the entire state. In practice, the slogan meant that within any development work programme at least two members (12 to 58 years of age) from each family in the village had to do *shramdan* (voluntary labour) for one day, once a month. If this was not possible, they had to give a day's salary to the project fund. At least fifty labourers from the village where the programme was being implemented had to guarantee to work in the project. The development work had to include forest farming, digging wells, and the construction of percolation tanks or bunds. No village could adopt any such programme without a two-thirds majority in the Gram Sabha, and with the assurance that tree-felling and free-grazing cattle would be banned in and around the village.

In the village there were also several efforts woven around the

[33] Interview with Anna Hazare in Ralegan Siddhi, 5 February 1991.

concept of dān, i.e. offering, by the villagers themselves. The school and its attached hostel building had become possible largely through such efforts. About 450 children study here till class 10, and 135 of them live in the hostel. Dropouts and rejected children were given preference during admissions, and those admitted included boys from Mumbai, Pune, and nearby areas. Students had to offer *shramdan* as part of their daily curriculum. Headmaster Thakaram Rauat spoke in detail of how the children did the cleaning up of some portion of the village for half an hour every morning. They cleaned the school latrines, and once every week the public toilets of the village. During the rains they were engaged in plantation work for days together. Dān also led to a "grain bank" in the village. When the village improved its agricultural output, most of the farmers' families, under Anna's instructions, began contributing a share of their harvest on a regular basis, and thus the grain bank came into existence. This bank was full now: in 1989–90 it even sold 100 bags of grain in the open market, the earnings from which went to the school. However, the main purpose of the bank was to provide minimum food security to needy families in the droughtprone and dry region. Those in need could get a grain loan from the bank, and in the subsequent year they had to repay the loan along with interest in the form of 10 per cent more grain.

Mobilising the villagers was an important element in Anna's strategy. He encouraged the active participation of people in the planning and decision-making processes of various programmes, so that "the village is built through the creative, productive, and innovative hard work of people themselves." There were 14 *vividh karyakari* societies in the village, dealing with forestry, water, co-operative, school, etc. Women ruled the village panchayat, so much so that all nine of its members were women. They ensured the payment of equal wages to women labourers in the village and propagated the idea of educating the village's girls. Santa Bai Maghari, *sarpanch* of the panchayat, spoke with confidence of how they were elected unopposed, according to the wishes of Anna, for he wanted women to contribute significantly to the village's development.

The face of Ralegan Siddhi has changed in many ways. The village, which had a per capita income of Rs 252 in 1976, now claims this has risen to Rs 2000. H.V. Huprikar, branch manager, Bank of Maharashtra, based in the village, says: "The village has some money now and the people are conscious of savings. The total savings with this branch of the bank is Rs 42 lakh, of which Rs 23 lakh is that of the village. Even school students have accounts under the 'minty' scheme and have deposits of nearly Rs 18,000. The recovery of crop loans in the village is about 80 per cent."[34]

The villagers have also shown an ability to learn things and manage a series of projects, artefacts, and technologies. They have successfully grafted the drip irrigation system, solar panels, and *gobar*-gas plants. Drip irrigation now covers 93 acres in the village. There are 2 bio-gas and 32 *gobar*-gas plants. Street lights with solar fittings are being managed by the locals and supplemented, if necessary, with services from agencies outside the village.

## The Meaning of Anna Hazare

A middle-aged bachelor clad in khadi, Anna Hazare lives in the village mandir, which he renovated out of his savings, after retiring from the army. "God is not in the temple and is realised through work. But the people gather at the temple, to create oneness in their task",[35] he explains. Anna Hazare is widely acknowledged to be public-spirited, honest, simple in his life-style, and self-sacrificing for the good of the community. He holds absolute power and his wish is the village's command. His power seems all-encompassing and has emerged from a long and dynamic process of interaction with his village, activists, bureaucracy, and the government. This process is characterised by projections and counter-projections of religion, culture, and tradition; by contestations of what it means to live; and by the deployment of natural and human resources, including persuasion, coercion, and, possibly, suppression.

Anna Hazare looks quite unassuming. However, among the men and women, young and old, of his village, he is seen as a man endowed with intrinsic personal qualities and exceptional powers. As he walks through the lanes of the village, women and children often

[34] Interview with H.V. Huprikar in Ralegan Siddhi, 7 February 1991.

[35] Interview with Anna Hazare.

come to touch his feet. All these years, he has lived with this image and this alone seems to suffice as the basis of his authority. He says, "If people are convinced that you are selfless and sacrificing, they are on your side."[36]

### *Belief System*

The basis for Anna's authority comes from a belief system wherein followers consider it their natural and bounden duty to obey the person exercising authority, who in turn thinks it is his natural and bounden right to rule. Thus, believing in authority and acknowledging it become crucial elements in the lives of such people. They justify their belief as rational, ultimate, and absolute. The people follow the order or structure of authority on a more stable and durable basis. Ganpat Pidi Aaauti, village *sarpanch* for four years, says: "Whatever Anna says, we do. The whole village follows his words. Anna's orders work like in the army. We all obey his orders."[37] For another villager, Lakshman Pathare, "Annajee is like God. Whatever work he will assign, I will fulfil and will never say no. Wherever he will direct, I will go. Annajee has become my nature, my habit. He is my heart."[38] Pathare Bala Sahab Ganpat, a young shopkeeper and secretary of Tarun Mandal, an organisation of young boys in the village, explains:

> When Annajee was jailed a few years ago, all the villagers went from Ralegan Siddhi to Nimani, Pune, on foot. This is called *dindi yatra*. Here, people go for *dindi yatra* for their God. We consider Annajee a god, which is why we thought it appropriate to organise a programme like this. We celebrate 15 June as the village's birthday, since it is Anna's birthday. There is a three-day festival on that occasion. We are ready to do everything he wants. If he asks me to climb to the top of a mountain and jump into a ditch, I will do it without hesitation. Annajee can say no wrong; he can do no wrong.[39]

[36] Ibid.

[37] Interview with Ganpat Pidi Aaauti in Ralegan Siddhi, 7 October 1999.

[38] Interview with Lakshman Pathare in Ralegan Siddhi, 9 October 1999.

[39] Interview with Pathare Bala Sahab Ganpat in Ralegan Siddhi, 9 October 1999.

There is thus recognition of an absolute authority locally, in several internalised ways.[40] In a village such authority stands for the shared ground of values, means, and ends that constitute an ideology, and of the system it intends to implement and achieve. These then become the structures of local governance; based on wide consensus, they can also work as normative regulations for the local society. The moral values that are internalised have a great bearing on the goals to be achieved and the means to be applied. In the case of Ralegan Siddhi they work through a central figure who strives for social unity. The common means and values are not given, they are created by the central figure. At specific moments, whenever the need arises, such a person (or a group) can also deploy environmental issues to evolve a common consensus. An environmental issue, by its sheer intensity and appeal, can become hegemonic in giving the social, political, moral, and intellectual leadership a concrete shape, create ideological unity.

Until 1975 Ralegan Siddhi was marked by poverty, unemployment, malnutrition, recurring drought, and environmental degradation. There was hardly 1 acre of irrigated land per family. The yield per acre was 3 to 4 quintals. Since sufficient water-harvesting techniques were used, the run-off carried away valuable topsoil. As a result, agricultural production could not sustain the population the whole year. Men migrated to the cities to look for jobs or worked on government employment-guarantee schemes. Their income being inadequate, villagers borrowed money from moneylenders. Family life was unstable. Children and youth lacked access to education. There was a high dropout rate and girls did not attend high school. Conflict had become a feature of every activity in the village; theft was common.[41] In this scenario, rural development work through the watershed management programme – constructing bunds of various types to catch and store rain water and thus ensure irrigation – was intended to be a unifying issue that would ease and mix the contending

[40] During my two periods of intensive fieldwork in Ralegan Siddhi, in 1991 and 1999, I gathered many similar accounts from different sets of people in the village.

[41] Lokur, *Ralegan Siddhi: Rural Transformation*, 3–4.

and conflicting elements into a common will. The Adarsh Gaon Yojana is an attempt "to motivate villagers in the selected *adarsh* (ideal) villages to integrate into their lives the principles of conservation", remarks Anna.[42]

To forge such a common will, an encompassing concept of unity becomes a crucial factor in an environmental organisation. There are many ways and expressions for the need to create such unity – it could be done either through the logic of change or through coercion. According to Anna, rural development must become a powerful instrument of national regeneration, and for this villagers have to work together with the firm conviction that "Our Village is One Family". Whatever affects one family affects the whole village, and hence all must put their shoulder to the wheel of securing the welfare of the whole community.[43] "Unity" becomes common to all interest groups and can substitute all other political institutions. Thus, in most of the villages under the programme, for the first time in years the sarpanch has been nominated through consensus. This is considered a significant step towards removing conflicts within the village and unifying it for development.[44]

History and culture become reference points in the search for the common ground of means and values. A glorified mystic past can be a powerful tool to lay the ground for norms acceptable in the present: an environmental organisation or an authority constructs a past to fulfil present needs. Cultural symbols, as given, accepted, and consensual derive their strength not only from being a part of the dominant value system but also because of their consonance with the contemporary body politic. The mystic past, the constructed culture, and the continuing present coalesce in shaping events beyond or outside the environmental domain too. Anna declares:

> In olden days, our country had a lot of wealth. We had a great civilisation. Our people were strong. Our villages were places of mutual love, affinity, and closeness. There was a lot of community work, as the

[42] Hazare, Pangare, and Lokur, *Adarsh Gaon Yojana,* 18–19.
[43] Hazare, *Ralegan Siddhi*, 48.
[44] Hazare, Pangare, and Lokur, *Adarsh Gaon Yojana*, 71.

> people used to build the temple, the school, and the tank together with their own resources. Our mythology refers to 33 crore gods. They were actually 33 crore people, with godly thinking and behaviour. Cow's milk was the main nutrient for growth at that time and this is why the cow was called the mother of 33 crore gods. Now we have lost our national culture, pride, and spirit.[45]

Symbols of the past are referred to functionally:

> Great man that he was, Chhatrapati Shivaji could have easily led a luxurious life if he had accepted being a Sardar of the Mughal kings. But he sacrificed it for the uplift and welfare of ordinary people. Today again the social and economic conditions of the common man are worsening and people are looking forward to a self-sacrificing leader like Shivaji Maharaja who will set things right.[46]

He adds: "Our history and culture is full of great women and great mothers. The great mothers have given birth to great sons like Chhatrapati Shivaji and Swami Vivekananda. Chhatrapati Shivaji's mother Jeejabai and her daughter-in-law Tararani and Rani of Jhansi are examples for present-day daughters to emulate."[47]

### *Force and Punishment*

In the process of social transformation, Anna believes, advice, persuasion, and good counsel sometimes do not work, and then one has to apply force. The fear of physical force works. However, fear cannot be used permanently, it has to be replaced by a more durable moral force. Anna says that a social worker is like a mother: no one questions the right of a mother to slap her children when they make mistakes for she nurses them too. Children recognise and accept this. Similarly, because a social worker cares for the community and

[45] Interview with Anna Hazare in Ralegan Siddhi, 9–10 October 1999.

[46] Hazare, *Ralegan Siddhi*, 40. This links to the earlier part of my chapter where I highlight the significance of Shivaji in the political and cultural milieu of Maharashtra.

[47] Interview with Anna Hazare.

selflessly works for its uplift, he can also occasionally use force. The community accepts his other roles, so it also accepts punishment from him.[48]

An environmental authority has to use force to implement its own laws, to make others trust it, and to strengthen that trust. Force can be applied in many forms, physical and social, and often just the simple persistent fear of its application suffices to regulate society. Force gives a firm grounding to socially accepted values and means, in the sense that those who dare to violate rules have to be punished. Continuous use of force is justified on the grounds that it serves a socially desirable goal and a collective will. The need for the use of force is also internalised by a large number of people, not only because it is seen as not targeting them but also because they start believing in its worth. Force becomes target-oriented, it has a goal; it becomes an integral part of an environmentally sound and socially harmonious society. Anna says:

> Continuous use of force and punishment can work as a double-edged weapon. It can also de-legitimise authority. Hence, the relationship between force, fear, and punishment on the one hand, and individual freedom and democracy on the other, needs to be addressed. But here also the prime concern remains the regulation of society. There are concerns about safeguarding individual freedoms available in a democratic system while attempting such transformation. But this concern should not mean unrestricted license as such interpretation leads to events detrimental to the interests of society and the country. There is no doubt that if misuse of personal freedom is affecting the personal freedom of others and the peace and happiness of society, it would obviously be necessary to curb such personal freedom by force as and when required. Where the persuasion of a social worker or the fear of law fail to change the thinking of society, it is necessary to employ the more effective resource of moral force of the community as a whole. Rather than physical force, the fear of being ostracised by the community is more potent. There is no ambiguity – the use of such force need not be constructed as denial or violation of personal freedom.[49]

[48] Ibid.

[49] Hazare, *Ralegan Siddhi*, 102–3.

When Anna Hazare started his work in Ralegan Siddhi, alcoholism was a serious problem among the villagers, there being a number of liquor brewing units in the village. Alongside the watershed management programme, Anna decided to first tackle alcoholism. In a meeting called by him in the village temple, it was resolved that liquor dens be closed down and alcohol be altogether banned from the village. Consequently, many brewing units voluntarily closed down after this resolve. The closure of liquor brewing units reduced alcoholism, but some villagers continued to drink. So it was decided that violators would be physically punished. Many were tied to a pole in front of the village temple and flogged. Anna believes that though flogging does not always work, it cannot be called punishment.

It is Anna who proposes flogging and fear as essential parts of a green village, but this belief seems attractive to a wide audience.

Image 1: Need of Fear

*Source*: Anna Hazare, *Ralegan Siddhi: A Veritable Transformation*, p. 93.

Even as the authority gives legitimacy to such use of force, fear makes room for itself in the social ethos and is even put on a high pedestal. It is said: "Social consciousness against drinking has been raised to such an extent that a drunken person can be brought to the centre of the village and thrashed, and no one will object."[50] Flogging and fear become a part of everyday life and belief. Not only does the authority employing it have the sanction to use it, it becomes legitimate for others to deploy it as well. Pathare Bala Sahab Ganpat's account gives an idea of this:

> Earlier there were liquor brewing units in the village. They are all closed now. Annajee gives punishment to those who take liquor. The person is tied to the pole and flogged overnight. The gram sabha has decided to form a group of twenty-five youths of the village who can also give this punishment to drunkards. Once, some people from the neighbouring village entered this village in a drunken state, saying that it was their right, it was democracy. However, the youths of the village caught hold of them and thrashed them thoroughly. Only last year, two or three villagers were caught in a drunken state. Annajee and the youths gave them the standard punishment and then handed them over to the police.[51]

The use of punishment gained expression within the ambit of law and the village's elected representatives. The vice-sarpanch of the village, Kailash Pote, says, "I was drinking. I was also tied to the pole and flogged two or three times. It is normal. Annajee will try to make you understand once or twice and, thereafter he will beat you badly."[52] The need for fear and punishment in the social organisation is pervasive. No matter what the context – public or private, social or personal – the use of force is believed to be a requirement. Anna states:

> Mere existence of a family planning law does not help; its rigid implementation is warranted. This law should be made applicable to all persons living in India, irrespective of caste or creed and if necessary by force . . . At least now political leaders of all parties should realise

[50] Rai, Mukul, Bana, and Kumar, *Call of the Commons*, 14.

[51] Interview with Pathare Bala Sahab Ganpat.

[52] Interview with Kailash Pote in Ralegan Siddhi, 8 October 1999.

> that "the party is above the individual but the country's interests should have greater priority over the interests of the party." They should unanimously pass a law permitting force for population control. We have had the practical experience of need of force while implementing family planning measures in Ralegan Siddhi and hence this conclusion![53]

### *Religion and Religious Symbols*

Religion and religious symbols are potent resources for the legitimisation of a particular regime and authority. They can be used to define and shape a community politically, and adherence to a particular regime and system of laws can be ensured through them. In a so-called environmentally sound or "ideal" village, religion becomes the vehicle for a concept of transformation and imposition. Its embodiment in a certain place and people emphasises claims to the legitimacy of that place, people, and ideology. The command–obedience relationship also gets its rationale from the belief that a specific god or temple is supreme and any decision in their precincts must be obeyed. It thus becomes a sacred duty to follow rules, to fulfil the conditions necessary for the village to remain ideal. The ideal village in this sense originates or emanates from the temple and its god, or the power of these crystallised in a prophet figure such as Anna. Not to comply with his commandments is a vice, akin to an offence committed against the divine.

It was important that Anna Hazare begin village development work along with the rebuilding of the temple which has all along been at the centre of his activities. A sense of unity and collective identity had to be achieved, and the renovation of an old and dilapidated temple out of savings from his provident fund and gratuity proved symbolically the most effective way to achieve it. Anna believes the rebuilding of the temple gave people an emotional unity, a sense of oneness, an awareness of their identity, and of an inner self interfacing with God. The village temple slowly turned into a place of village meetings, weddings, and other religious ceremonies, strengthening community and family feeling. A temple has an atmosphere of purity and sanctity. Decisions taken in a temple are believed

[53] Hazare, *Ralegan Siddhi*, 76–7.

to have the sanction of God and people are more likely to follow them, such decisions being tantamount to religious commitments.[54]

This begs the question: what is Anna's notion of religious commitment? Anna Hazare desires in himself a combination of many aspects of religion: "spirituality", or "humanity is the core of each religion". And "just as we have the concept of God within the four walls of a temple, we have to enlarge this concept to perceive our village and the country as a large temple and the inhabitants therein as almighty Gods. We must worship them as we worship God."

He asks: "what is the use of undertaking a pilgrimage if the people in our house or around us are hungry and full of sorrow?"[55]

One aspect of his religious discourse is the insistence that God is within the reach of human beings. Anna's god is not only "supreme", a "superpower" and "creator", but also a selection of earthy gods who can be called, roused, and appropriated for the needs of a village or country. According to him, Lord Rama set an example before every citizen of how to conduct everyday life. He demonstrated ideal love for parents, brothers, wife, and community. He also showed how a king, by his every thought and action, ought to look after the welfare of his subjects. But even in his time there were insolent barbarians like Ravana, as well as people like the indolent washerman who dared to doubt the chastity of Sitamai (who had been held captive by Ravana).[56] This familiarity and accessibility make it possible for Anna to call for reincarnation – a call by a legitimate authority for a familiar, earthy god: "There is need for Lord Shri Krishna to reincarnate and save the country, in the form of united strength of intellectuals of good character active in social work, economic endeavour, religious guidance, and politics."[57]

### *Rules and Codes*

Rules govern the entire social, political, and environmental life of the village, and strict adherence to these by the people make for an

[54] Interview with Anna Hazare.

[55] All expressions used by Anna Hazare in the interview.

[56] Hazare, *Ralegan Siddhi*, 43.

[57] Ibid., 158.

ideal village. These clearly defined rules and their neat execution in many spheres also contribute substantially to the creation of common means and values. It is these rules that make an authority-figure and his regime universally acceptable and recognisable. In this scenario, those who make the rules and faithfully obey them are deemed legitimate, while those who do not are rendered illegitimate and illegal. The rules are all-encompassing and exercised in the broadest possible way. This is best ensured if the rules and their adherence operate in an atmosphere of traditional patron–client relations. However, even when some of the rules are specified in a collective process and have a sound and sustainable environmental rationale, the language of their justification, or the manner of their implementation, often make them dubious.

As a social and environmental worker, Anna Hazare has been concerned with rules and norms that he considers benchmarks for an activist: "A social worker encounters people of different sexes, ages and groups. In all situations, he has to be very careful about the social norms and the rules. His work can go haywire if his mind and heart get shaky, and he is not disciplined about the rules. One has to have a very firm control on oneself."[58] This concern finds yet another expression, "It is very important that those who lead the society or the movement should possess a clean character and personality. They should also have clean ideas and clean living."[59] Anna covers much ground – from prescribing rules for a social worker to suggesting them in the context of village development work. He has a definite model for rules:

> The daily routine enforced in the army such as getting up early in the morning, the jogging and the physical training thereafter, the cleanliness of body, clothing, living quarters and the neighbourhood, etc., led to development of a disciplined life, benefits of which I am availing of even today. The habit of giving due respect and regard to seniors by age, post or competence was inculcated in us. The meticulous attention to small details such as closed up and unbroken buttons on shirts, loose shoe-laces, etc., and the system of first obeying the order and then pointing out mistakes or irregularities, if any, in the orders taught us many

[58] Interview with Anna Hazare.

[59] Interview of Anna Hazare by journalist Rajesh Kumar, 25 October 1999.

good habits. This has helped me in conducting the village development work at Ralegan Siddhi according to the rules and regulations decided by us by common consent.[60]

Others often exactly translate this language. A villager, H.Y. Mapari, who used to be in the army and whose three sons are now employed in it, says, "This village works like an army. As a commandant, Anna orders and we all follow him."[61] Similarly, 43-year-old Lakshman Pathare says, "I am an army man and my ideology is the same as Annajee. Army discipline is the ideal. Obedience is your habit there – never say no, never decline what your seniors ask you to do."[62]

Five universal rules have evolved out of the developmental experiences in Ralegan Siddhi. They are *nasbandi* (restriction in family size), *nashabandi* (ban on alcohol), *charaibandi* (ban on free grazing), *kurhabandi* (ban on tree felling), and *shramdan* (donation of voluntary labour for community welfare). It is mandatory for the villagers to take an oath to follow these rules. Through these rules alone is the integrated watershed development programme implemented in the village. There are many other such rules. For instance, if the farmers desire to keep their lands alive and useful, they must imbibe the message, "Do not use chemical fertilisers. Do not become killers of your own land. Use natural fertilisers. Protect Mother Earth."[63] Because it requires large quantities of water, the cultivation of sugarcane is banned in the village. According to a researcher, Madhukar Karr, "Anna is against sugarcane cultivation for a different reason as well. He says that the sugarcane farmers keep sitting idle. They do not work, and get involved in petty politics."[64]

A high level of adherence to many "dos" and "don'ts", both in public and private life, is central to the path of rural development in Ralegan Siddhi. Here, no shop can sell bidis or cigarettes. Film songs

[60] Hazare, *Ralegan Siddhi*, 114.

[61] Interview with H.Y. Mapari in Ralegan Siddhi, 7 October 1999.

[62] Interview with Lakshman Pathare.

[63] Hazare, *Ralegan Siddhi*, 99.

[64] Interview with Madhukar Karr in Ralegan Siddhi, 7 February 1991.

and movies are not allowed. Only religious films, like *Sant Tuka Ram*, *Sant Gyaneshwar*, etc., may be screened. Only religious songs are allowed via loudspeakers at the time of marriages. According to Kailash Pote: "Last year a villager, who is a Mahar by caste and a driver by profession, got a dish antenna installed in his house and started watching cable TV. He also asked his neighbours if they would be willing to get cable connections. Anna scolded him severely and he had to apologise."[65]

Acquiescence is the key word, assent compulsory. The regime is martial, its nearest prototype being the ancient Greek city republic of Sparta, fabled for the discipline which won it battles against forces far greater than its own. As in all such regimented arenas, in Ralegan Siddhi the fear of punishment has gradually given way to willing acceptance. The external manifestations of acceptance are dissolved by the adherent's internal belief. Such acquiescence is a kind of quietism as well, for it entails the acceptance of not simply authority but authoritarian rule, of one person's right to formulate orders and of one's unquestioning duty to follow those orders. The environmental regime in Ralegan Siddhi thrives and develops on this acceptance. It is not only crucial to the existence of the regime and its wider recognition, it is actually the basis for the creation of a set of values and means that legitimise authority. In the village it is often emphasised that the villagers themselves decide not to sell bidis and cigarettes in their shops, that they themselves do not watch films and listen to film songs. Authority has reached a kind of Hegemonic Absolute here, for coercion is no longer perceived to be coercion. Instead, it is perceived as personal desire.

This hegemonic process of acquiescence and its vocabulary are deeply Brahminical. Anna Hazare's narrative on the importance of vegetarianism is a case in point. He first contextualises the issue within Hindu philosophy, according to which the world is composed of three traits: *rajas*, *tamas*, and *satva*. Every animate or inanimate being, humans included, is dominated by one of these traits. When a baby is born, it is free from all these; it is innocent and pure of heart.

[65] Interview with Kailash Pote.

If a person, right from early childhood to his youth, is in the company of *satvaguni* people, he develops into a *satvaguni* person. *Tamoguni* company results in a *tamoguni* nature; *rajoguni* creates a *rajoguni* bent of mind.[66] Anna deliberates on how a surfeit of non-vegetarian meals has led human beings to shed their innate peacefulness and harmlessness, and to their acquisition of the aggression and cruelty of the animal kingdom; he argues that vegetarians are normally peaceful and lead a harmless life, unless provoked, and that our own saints have emphasised and propagated a vegetarian diet from ancient times. "We presented all these considerations to the people of Ralegan Siddhi," he says, "and they were influenced by this to such an extent that there is no longer anybody who eats meat and all villagers have adopted vegetarian diet."[67]

Image 2: Importance of Vegetarianism
*Source*: Anna Hazare, *Ralegan Siddhi: A Veritable Transformation*, p. 155.

[66] Hazare, *Ralegan Siddhi*, 154.

[67] Ibid., 156. Presumably no one has dared tell Anna that the most notorious monster of modern times, Hitler, was vegetarian; in any case, Anna's logic

This process found its corollary in the way Dalits were looked upon in the village and the change that was demanded of them. Anna says:

> We used to go to their area sometimes and sat in front of one house. People used to gather there, wondering how this high-caste person has come to their place. This way, a faith relationship came into being. We continued going there off and on. Sometimes we asked from them water to drink and had food together. Based on this relationship, we started telling them why people kept them at a distance and what were the reasons behind it. We said that the society condemns you because your living is dirty, your food habits are dirty, and your thinking is dirty. Therefore, you have to change. With such constant hammering, the whole village turned vegetarian. The Dalits were also made vegetarian.[68]

Rules and compliance thus find their validity in a particularly defined territory and population. Men and women, young and old, upper caste and lower, all must not only submit to rules imposed on them from above, they must also believe that these are not rules imposed but rules desired. No section of the population can be allowed to go its own way, independent of this Procrustean framework of iron rules. Children too must accept and support every such rule in order to reproduce the village's system of values. In the course of my fieldwork in Ralegan Siddhi I witnessed an everyday scene in the school campus of the village:

> It was still a couple of hours before dawn, but within the boundaries of Sri Sant Niloba Rai Vidyalaya, the hostel boys were already awake and active. They were dressed in khaki shorts and white shirts, some with Gandhi caps. They were passing in a single file on their way to work in the school's fields. Some were cleaning the schoolrooms. From the huge loudspeaker system installed in the school, popular bhajans and songs in Hindi were reaching everywhere: "*Vande Matram, Vande Matram*!", "*Sabarmati ke Sant Tune Kar Diya Kamal*". At around six o' clock in the morning I saw that the school children were marching near the main

---

would suggest that Hitler was barbaric despite his vegetarianism because he was provoked.

[68] Interview of Anna Hazare by journalist Rajesh Kumar.

chowk of the village and all were shouting slogans, *"Jai Jawan Jai Kisan"*, *"Bharat Mata ki Jai"*, *"Hum Sab Ek Hain"*.[69]

The need for a pure and healthy cultural environment is emphasised in the rules meant for schoolchildren. A strong body, *samskars*, and Indian culture are the concerns around which these rules are woven. Thakaram Rauat, principal of the school, says:

> In our secondary school, there is a five-point programme: body building, physical work, character building, knowledge development, and patriotism. Children have to get up early in the morning. They have to do body-building exercises for two and a half hours in a day. They do manual work as part of their school curriculum. Every day they sing national and patriotic songs. They take a pledge, do *surya namaskar* and chant "*Om*" for a minute. We believe that we need power and energy for all kinds of work and a sound body is the real means to achieve that.[70]

All this has a considerable bearing on the village's environmental perspective. The emphasis on accomplishment and achievement has been one of the hallmarks of environmental movements and initiatives in India. The conservation of water and forests, the sustainable use of natural resources, and the conceptualisation of people's programmes are enmeshed in the creation and consolidation of a singular moral authority, the plea for such conservation being a potent expedient to maintain power and authority. Anna Hazare firmly believes that spirituality, morality, and religion are part of a superstructure which is unsustainable without economic necessities being fulfilled, and therefore prosperity is their necessary base. He says when people were sleeping hungry in the village, nobody was ready to listen to his words. It was only after economic prosperity that they were willing to do *shramdan*. And only then could they think of morality.[71]

[69] Fieldwork in Ralegan Siddhi in February 1991 and October 1999. Also see Sharma, *Landscapes and Lives*.

[70] Interview with Thakaram Rauat in Ralegan Siddhi, 6 February 1991 and 8 October 1999.

[71] Interview with Anna Hazare.

A series of development programmes were charted out in the village. Watershed development, drinking water, agricultural production, milk production, a grain bank, social forestry, alternative energy sources, education, and an ideal village plan were a few among many that have been successfully implemented. They enhanced material welfare through an effective use of land and water resources – which were simultaneously deployed to generate or expand the base of moral authority. Anna was prepared to accomplish what had been chalked out and underline his moral vision regardless of the hostilities and opposition they evoked – even if it meant making an enemy of the government and the state, sitting on a dharna, or undertaking a "fast unto death". Indeed, it was not its land and water development programme that made Ralegan Siddhi famous all over the state in the early 1990s but Anna's massive campaign against corruption within rural development programmes.

The sense of accomplishment has found varied expression in the village. Mapari Ramdas, a villager, says, "It was difficult to even feed oneself earlier. Now those days are over. It is all because of Anna's grace that we are managing our family well."[72] For Jai Singh Mapari, the milk business is a reference point: "Within the village, we collect 2,500 litres of milk every day for sale. In 15 days, we get a payment of more than three lakh rupees. Our village has earned name and fame. Anna is being recognised everywhere in the country, and he travels extensively all over."[73] Machindra Balwant Sendge, a Dalit, has been engaged many years in his traditional occupation of making brooms and knitting ropes. He has eight acres of rocky, unproductive land, which is barely sufficient to provide fodder for his cattle. He had worked for a daily wage outside the village. However, after the village's development he has been getting enough work within the village and echoes the sentiments of many others when he says, "Anna is my God. Whenever he is in the village, I go to see him and receive his blessings. He is well known everywhere. He is from this village."[74]

[72] Interview with Mapari Ramdas in Ralegan Siddhi, 6 October 1999.

[73] Interview with Jai Singh Mapari in Ralegan Siddhi, 6 October 1999.

[74] Interview with Machindra Balwant Sendge in Ralegan Siddhi, 6 October 1999.

Sakara Bai Ganpat Gajare was a panchayat member for five years. She has a sense of satisfaction that liquor-brewing units have shut down and alcoholism has stopped, and consequently that there are no incidents of wife-beating in the village any more. However, she goes on to say: "Though we have more water, more fodder and more farming, our workload has actually increased tremendously. Even women contribute more through shramdan. We have many sewing machines in the village, but we do not have the time for any other work. Overall, therefore, we women have not achieved much."[75] These examples suggest that the sense of accomplishment, going beyond material and physical well-being, provides the moral basis for a regime.

The real and perceived feeling of continuous accomplishment in Ralegan Siddhi shows two other distinct elements. First, the village system can legitimately claim to make broader and long-term policies, covering not only the physical environment but also the social, political, and cultural life of the village. More important, achievement helps establish its own institutions, partly by justifying its own structure of governance and invalidating all others. There have been no gram panchayat elections in Ralegan Siddhi for well over two decades. No elections are allowed even to the many co-operative societies in the village that look after aspects of governance. Anna says: "Representatives to the panchayat as well as of the societies are nominated in the gram sabha. Elections were not allowed here, as they bring party politics and divide the people. Electioneering also destroys unity in the village. I have now started saying that there should be elections. However, in Ralegan Siddhi village, people are not ready for that. They have fully adjusted to the method of nominations. It has proved best for them."[76] He takes every possible opportunity to question electoral and party politics and it is his firm view that power and politics cause corruption: "Those who wish to involve themselves in our anti-corruption movement will have to take a pledge not to get involved in party politics, nor to contest elections."[77]

[75] Interview with Sakara Bai Ganpat Gajare in Ralegan Siddhi, 14 October 1999.

[76] Interview with Anna Hazare.

[77] Ibid.

There is no space or legitimacy here for the formal structures of democracy. Posters and pamphlets are not allowed during the state or national elections, nor direct election campaigning. Machindra Balwant Sendge, a villager, says: "In our village, the offices of political parties, their signboards or flags do not exist. We never allow them to exist here."[78] The virtual ban on political activities inside the village goes deeper, turning into an ideology of rejection of politics of every kind. The value of elections and voting is reduced to an enforced necessity. Another villager emphasises: "Nobody is honest or competent in politics today. Even good people become bad after entering politics. That is why we are not interested in politics. Those who work for our village and for us get our votes."[79]

### *Setting Goals*

Anna Hazare believes in setting aims and objectives for individual and society. For individuals, these can be as hard as "setting his lifetime goals", "dedicating his life entirely for his work", "doing the work in a determined way, step by step, ignoring the criticism and the opposition", "ready to face death if necessary", etc. For society, they can be as wide as "the creation of a self-reliant, self-sufficient, self-administered village", "the achievement of an ideal village", "village as the unit of planning", "watershed development", etc. The aims and objectives propounded by Anna carry present need as the context, a critique of individual and society, and precise solutions. As an ideology of developmental and environmental aims, this sketches out a structure for the future, and an ideal vision of the individual and society. It is primarily on the basis of this ideology's carrying capacity – of present needs and future ideals – that the outlined aims and objectives acquire authority. The objective is the driving force here; the means, processes, and ideas of freedom and democracy take a back seat. An environmentalist objective defines the content and form of an entire socio-political system.

[78] Interview with Machindra Balwant Sendge in Ralegan Siddhi, 6 October 1999.

[79] Interview with Pathare Bala Saheb Ganpat.

To replicate the development experiences of Ralegan Siddhi at a macro level the Government of Maharashtra launched an Adarsh Gaon Yojana in 1992. Spearheaded by Anna, this programme aimed at developing 300 villages in Maharashtra using Ralegan Siddhi as a model. The budget for each village, selected under this programme, was Rs 50 lakh. The funds provided by the government were routed through the Adarsh Gram Office, headed by Anna. The objective of the programme was to demonstrate that an individual, a family, and a village can be made self-sufficient, with sustainable use of the environment and an emphasis on conservation, being the village's hallmarks. Regarding the scheme and its implementation in present-day India, it was argued: "Today many villages are fragmented due to divided opinions. People are selfish and unprepared to think about the welfare of their neighbours. Greed for power and money, alcoholism and other vices prevent people from thinking about common welfare. Against this background, it is not easy to create ideal villages."[80] An "ideal village" and "self-reliance and self-sufficiency as stressed by Mahatma Gandhi" are ideas that have been frequently used to legitimise various programmes and policies, values and means in independent India. Anna outlines his philosophy and principles for conservation of nature and sustainable rural development in these words:

> The village needs to be united and involved in the planning process. Sparring factions and socially created barriers such as the caste system in the village usually make it difficult to implement development projects, which are meant to benefit the community as a whole. The Adarsh Gaon Yojana requires villagers to take an oath that they will follow the five principles. Shramdan is a good way of getting the villagers together to work for the welfare of their village. Shramdan transcends artificial social barriers, and fosters a feeling of unity, of working together for the common welfare of the community.[81]

This interpretation of the ideal village claims truth and perfection

[80] Hazare, Pangare, and Lokur, "Preface", in *Adarsh Gaon Yojana*, page not given.

[81] Ibid., 19–27.

for itself. It argues that its success is based on a strict adherence to its proclaimed values and principles. It claims to speak for the community as a whole, though in fact its personal and emotional appeal serves to justify the role and goal of a specific person. This personal authority, strengthened by the official sanction conferred on it, is valorised for a hegemonic end: all must accept its values and principles as the only legitimate ones. The very process of idealising and replicating an environmental model negates the possibility of holding any other version of rural development as truthful or better or correct.

At the level of ideology, the goal of creating an ideal village provides a rational relationship between the desired end and the role given to a person or group. At the level of institutions, it is the personal authority, the temple, the nominees, the committees, and the codes that provide the ideal with a support system. And a value system that denies the existence of conflict and contradiction, and fetishises "natural" harmony, feeds into the ideal.

### *Nation and Nation-Building*

Anna says: "I close this story of the village development at Ralegan Siddhi with the fervent request and hope that every village should achieve similar success and build our India into a strong, powerful nation."[82] A colourful poster with the slogan "Ideal Village, Ideal Nation" is displayed in many parts of Ralegan Siddhi.[83] The idea of a strong nation and nation-building is firmly entrenched in people's consciousness and the work they do there. Environmentally sound rural development is the effective means to make that idea a reality, and extending the ideal outwards into the nation is for Anna a matter of life and death. The meaning of such a nation took specific shape in him at the time of the Indo-China war in 1962 and crystallised during the Indo-Pak war in 1965. He is emotional when he recounts these experiences:

[82] Hazare, *Ralegan Siddhi*, 159.

[83] I saw many such in the course of my fieldwork.

> 1962 was a difficult time for our nation. China betrayed us and occupied a large portion of our territory. Our armies were suffering heavily. I wanted to do something for my country. A desire to join the army for this purpose drove me there. I was determined to live and die for the country ... In 1965, when Pakistan attacked us, my transport unit was operating in the Khemkaran sector. There was too much of a risk from the land mines laid by the enemy. One day the enemy aircraft started strafing on our convoy of 17–18 vehicles. Many jawans of our convoy were seriously injured or died. I was able to move, though a bullet grazed my head too. It was a virtual rebirth for me, and I decided to devote my life to social work after retirement.[84]

Narratives of war, army, and enemy remain core references in much of the discourse on nation and rural development in Ralegan Siddhi. This has also something to do with the fact that more than 200 people from this village are in the Indian army, and most families have at least one member employed in it.[85] However, this particular developmental discourse – in which the army, the war, and environmental engineering become one – as well as the aspects of the village consciousness that are articulated as strict codes, discipline, etc., are linked to ways in which nation and nation-building as well as the attendant culture and values, are conceptualised here: nation as ideal, nation as sufferer, nation as victim, nation as victor against the enemy. Rural development and its agents have to aid this war of the nation, for the nation, by the nation.

"National regeneration", "nation-building", "village development is the key to overall national uplift", "wholesome crop of national glory through comprehensive rural development" – these expressions of Anna and Ralegan Siddhi are not enough in themselves. They are coupled with other tasks, expressions, and appeals such as, "We have to hold the nation. Otherwise, Pakistan will grab it. That is why we consciously send our sons to the army."[86] The idea that nation-building must be the guiding principle finds other justifications: it is argued that certain greedy and corrupt people want to divide the

[84] Interview with Anna Hazare.

[85] This was highlighted in my interview with *sarpanch* Ganpat Pidi Aauti and many others in the village.

[86] Interview with H.Y. Mapari.

country: "They are in Nagaland, Manipur, Tripura, Assam, Punjab, Kashmir. Our powerful army can do many wonders. Our country can be the most prosperous and peaceful in this world."[87]

These voices can at times be stridently masculinist and assertive. For example, school pupils are taught to be nationalists. They are taught to believe in national integration. Boys in the school are put in groups named after Shivaji, Bhagat Singh, and Rajguru, names intended to arouse ideas associated with freedom and development. Images connected with women like Jhansi ki Rani are not accepted among the boys. Once, a group was named after her, but it was soon cancelled.[88] These thoughts swell into the village's rural development discourse: "The way army jawans jointly attack enemies and control them, we can similarly tackle problems here in the village."[89] And:

> If each one of us imbibes national spirit, social commitment, and works hard, something good can still be attained and the dangers currently facing the country as well as future generations could be avoided . . . Little bit of sacrifice on the part of everyone for the country and abandoning the consumerist western lifestyle has become essential . . . If these leaders devote their wealth, mind and body selflessly for the benefit of the society and the country, the general public may not have wealth but they would devote their bodies and mind equally sincerely for nation-building efforts.[90]

The case is made for a united, integrated country: "If we want to make India united and integrated, we should go deeper. If we embrace the religion of humanity, we can achieve this goal."[91]

### *Events and Incidents*

In social and political life a particular moment or an issue, an event or a series of incidents, can be taken to a climax. This heightened stage can generate deep emotions and galvanise people enormously in

[87] Interview with Lakshman Pathare.

[88] Interview with Raja Ram Shankar Gajare, an activist in the school hostel in Ralegan Siddhi, 14 October 1999.

[89] Interview with Lakshman Pathare.

[90] Hazare, *Ralegan Siddhi*, x–xi.

[91] Interview of Anna Hazare by journalist Rajesh Kumar.

support of a cause. Such instances are politically defining moments: "By its very nature, a politically defining moment has enormous moral authority that can legitimate certain causes while delegitimating others. Political institutions may be legitimated or delegitimated by these moments . . . Legitimisation based on a politically defining moment is not free of disputation and will not be durable unless, as in the case of personal authority, it is institutionalised on the basis of an ideology."[92] Anna Hazare has been able to create these politically defining moments. Some years ago, faulty transmission and low voltage caused several pump-sets to burn out. Despite repeated requests by the villagers for a sub-station, government agencies took no action. Anna went on a hunger strike and had to be hospitalised after nine days. This led to a *rasta roko andolan* by the villagers. In the police firing that ensued, four people were killed. Later, the government sanctioned money to set up a sub-station. On another occasion, the education department refused recognition to a school that the villagers had constructed. It was alleged that the education minister was penalising the villagers for not voting for him in the elections. After several futile meetings, Anna threatened to go on an indefinite hunger strike. He addressed the panchayat, "If I die, do not cremate me, but bury me under the steps of the village temple." The deeply moved and surcharged villagers *gheraoed* the *zila parishad* the next day and obtained recognition for the school. Based on this experience, Anna draws some universal and wider conclusions: 'since many administrators lack real national spirit and have rigid attitudes, it is inevitable that some of us may have to lose our lives in dealing with social problems."[93]

The anti-corruption movement was also a socially and politically defining moment for Anna. Inspired by a continuous and common set of grievances in his district, as well as in others, he decided to

[92] Alagappa, "The Bases of Legitimacy", 46–7.

[93] Hazare, *Ralegan Siddhi*, 113. This incident and some others like it were narrated in detail by Anna Hazare in February 1991. Many villagers like Jai Singh and Lakshman Pathare, whom I interviewed in October 1999, also gave an account of the incident. The book by Anna Hazare also has a detailed account of it.

take up the issue of grassroots corruption in the early 1990s. He began groundwork by writing letters to all the gram panchayats in the district and sought information on two things: first, whether the rural water-supply scheme was working in their area, and, second, details of what had been purchased under the social forestry schemes and at what rates. It was revealed through this process that the rural water scheme was not working in 165 gram panchayats and that many worthless instruments had been purchased at highly inflated rates under the social forestry scheme. As lone crusader, Anna began a silent fast in December 1990 and returned the Indira Priyadarshini Vrikshamitra Award given to him by the Government of India. He declared his intention to return his Padma Shri as well. Then came the proposal of the state government to constitute inquiry committees. Thereafter Anna broke his fast on 17 January 1991 in a meeting attended by more than 600 representatives of social and political organisations from all over the state. He put forward another demand: the formation of an inspection committee of five members – none from political parties – at the village, block, and district levels. If the government did not accept this vital demand, he said he would tour the entire state to form the committee. If no action was taken, he and his supporters would not only organise *morcha* and *gherao*, but even take the law into their own hands and beat corrupt officials out in the open.[94] Based on these series of anti-corruption movements Anna defined his political position more broadly and had it accepted through his villagers. This position again outlined his belief that anybody taking part in anti-corruption would have to take a pledge not to associate with a political party and contest elections.

### *Morality*

In relation to morality and related codes, behaviour, and practices, one observer remarks: "Anna's leadership is 'moral'. Ralegan's

[94] For details, see Mukul, "Bhrashtachar Unmulan nein Bechain Kar Diya" (Anxiety over the Elimination of Corruption) and "Shramshakti ka Pratik hai Ralegan Siddhi" (Ralegan Siddhi: A Symbol of Labour Power), both in *Navbharat Times*, Delhi, 11 February 1991, and 13 February 1991 respectively.

example has shown that moral leadership works with the people even 50 years after the death of Mahatma Gandhi. Sacrifice has always been highly valued in Hindu philosophy. It established the moral authority of a person . . . Moral leadership also has the advantage of bringing out the best in ordinary people."[95] The strong personal basis of Anna's concept of morality, which has evolved with his life experiences and personal commitments, has often been highlighted. Less observed have been his emphases on morality as a fundamental aspect of a pure and clean cultural and social environment as the basis of a strong nation and nation-building. This is a vision which comprehensively spells out the desired practices of everyday social life. "People should have good *samskar* to do service. They should believe in *nishkam karmayog*"; "It is necessary for people to retain their humanity along with prosperity"; "Prosperity and the sharing of wealth brings equity"; "Differences between the rich and the poor will remain, but the poor should get some share of the prosperity."[96] There are other moral values alongside these. For schoolchildren there is moral education and practice, which comprises elements of physical training, bodybuilding, obedience, patriotism, gender equality, national integration, the scientific temper, and sensitivity.[97] Women are expected to look after the household, but they must also look beyond and get out of the house to participate in activities intended to help neighbours, community, and country. "Woman is the Universal Mother, The Great Mother. Many such Great Mothers have given birth to Great Sons – Chhatrapati Shivaji Maharaj, Swami Vivekananda, for instance. She is also a symbol of purity, sublime as well as innate strength. She can, if she means it, make a God out of a mortal being and build a model, healthy society."[98] Morality here becomes identity, directing everyday social life in a clear hierarchical and gendered order.

Many of the problems of morality among children, the youth, and the village are outlined in relation to Western influence or a

[95] Awasthi, "Rural Development", 79.

[96] These are based on my two interviews with Anna Hazare. Many villagers and close associates of Anna substantiate these views in their own words.

[97] Based on my interview with principal Thakaram Rauat.

[98] Hazare, *Ralegan Siddhi*, 89.

modern materialist culture. "The West", "Western lifestyle", "modern development", and "invasion of Western culture" invariably signify the collapse of morality in modern India.[99] The world is now full of "indecent" cinema posters on roads, TV; videos show "undesirable" moral values; "lurid" songs blare from tape recorders and loudspeakers; "pornographic" books and magazines can be bought off roadside stalls; drunkards emerge from government-sponsored liquor shops; teachers and parents no longer act out their own precepts; all these collectively divert clean minds from clean ends.[100] "The youth of the country represent our real strength", says Anna. "The enemy is trying to spread addiction to various drugs among the young generation. It is sad that hundreds of thousands of young men in our country are falling prey to such addictions and are losing their enthusiasm and capacity to do something constructive for themselves, their families and the country."[101] The unification of anxieties under the fold of morality is a plea for the well-being of villagers in need of being saved from the scourge of modernity, but it is also quite obviously intimately associated with a precise regimen being prescribed to the nation.

### *Dalits*

In Ralegan Siddhi there are Mahars, Chamars, Matangs, Nhavis, Bharhadis, and Sutars. The first three are considered amongst the lowest in the Hindu caste structure. Barring a few STs, the rest of the villagers are Marathas.[102] Since the beginning of his work in the village, Anna has particularly emphasised the removal of untouchability, social barriers, and discriminations on caste basis against those popularly referred to as "Harijans" here. There have been many efforts on his part to do away with the ban on Harijans" entry into the temple and against allowing them to draw water from the

[99] These were invariably used by Anna Hazare, Thakaram Rauat, and Lakshman Pathare, during my long interviews and informal meetings with them.

[100] Hazare, *Ralegan Siddhi*, 69.

[101] Ibid., 96.

[102] This information was given to me in October 1999 by *gram sewak* K.N. Bhagat in Ralegan Siddhi.

same well as everyone else. The Harijans are now present in every function of the village. They are a part of the community marriage programme, alongside the other castes. They are associated with several committees formed to run village affairs, and they take active part in several village festivals. On some occasions they cook or serve food to all the villagers and even perform puja. The village once repaid a bank a loan of Rs 75,000 taken by Harijan families. Within many economic programmes Harijans have been chosen to be the first beneficiaries. The concept of "village as a joint family", or all inhabitants of the village as "almighty God", prompted villagers to give attention to the problems of Harijans.[103]

However, the Dalits themselves see it differently. Kailash Pote is a landless Chamar who pursues his traditional occupation and also works as a farm labourer. For him, the meaning of village, family, and Hinduism are expressible thus:

> We do not call Ralegan Siddhi a village. We call it a family in which Annajee is the headman and we are the people who provide service to the family. Here Hindus mean Marathas only. We Chamars and Mahars are never called Hindus. How can we claim that everybody is equal here? People who have land or jobs in the military have a different level of development. There is a lot of difference between others and me.[104]

Lakshman Dondiwa is another Dalit. In the course of an agitation for electricity in the village many years ago, he was injured when the police opened fire. He remembers how Anna took care of him like a mother. He and other members of his caste are now free from the clutches of moneylenders, and this has turned him into a devotee of Anna. However, he goes on to remark: "We have food, clothing and houses now. However, that is all. There is nothing more to it than that. Shoes are for the feet and will always be placed there. We are like the shoes. We will never be able to go ahead beyond this point. The village ethos is such."[105] Twenty-five-year-old Kailash is landless. He knows how to drive and has a driver's licence but must sur-

[103] For details, see Awasthi, "Rural Development", 79–81.

[104] Interview with Kailash Pote.

[105] Interview with Lakshman Dondiwa in Ralegan Siddhi, 15 October 1999.

vive on wage labour. He says: "I was poor before and am poor now. We were starving in the past and the situation has not changed for me. I cannot even afford to educate my children. I cannot even open my mouth. Whatever is said in this village, it has to be followed."[106]

The village includes three Matang houses. Their inhabitants are still tied to their traditional occupation, making brooms and ropes. They also work as agricultural labourers. They own some forest land, but according to them it only provides fodder for cattle. One of them says, "We get work in the village. However, it is barely enough. We need some support, work or job. Since there is no alternative, we try to be happy."[107] Mathura Dharmagadka was a vice-sarpanch until recently. During her time there was an all-women panchayat for five years. She remarks: "We women learnt how to run the panchayat and since there was no male member, we could speak freely. However, we cannot do anything about the wage difference between male and female labourers in the village. A male labourer gets Rs 50 a day, whereas it is only Rs 30 for females."[108]

Namdeo Arjun Mapari, a poor Maratha, also strikes a dissenting note. He has two acres of land, but it is mostly rocky and unproductive. He and his three sons work as agricultural labourers. He says: "We all worked for the development of the village. I did *shramdan* along with other villagers. Our village and watershed programme are world famous. However, in our land and the well there is no water. We have not benefited from all the water flowing in the village."[109]

There may be many explanations for the way Dalits are placed in Ralegan Siddhi. Within the locality and the community they are largely still tied to their traditionally ascribed status and occupation. Simultaneously, unequal possession of land and utilisation of water, exploitative labour relations and low wages, besides other forms of power, do exist and continue to work against the Dalits. The notion of Dalits as "dirty" prevails. And the village republic works in a way

[106] Interview with Kailash in Ralegan Siddhi, 15 October 1999.

[107] Interview with Machindra Balwant Sendge.

[108] Interview with Mathura Dharmagadka in Ralegan Siddhi, 6 October 1999.

[109] Interview with Namdeo Arjun Mapari in Ralegan Siddhi, 10 October 1999.

that prevents broader values and codes and rules, as well as places and performances assigned within it, from being challenged. The Dalits' own perceptions are clearly formed as much by the authoritarian discourse as by their own contesting experiences.

The idea of the integration of Dalits into an ideal village has two components in Ralegan Siddhi. The first is the assumption that they were always there to perform some duties and necessary services and that it is this usefulness that justifies their existence today. As Anna expresses it: "It was Mahatma Gandhi's vision that every village should have one Chamar, one Sunar, one Kumhar and so on. They should all do their work according to their role and occupation, and in this way a village will be self-dependent. This is what we are practising in Ralegan Siddhi."[110] The other component is hegemonic, designed to require Dalits to accept their status within the Brahminical fold. This is not only manifest in the way food or dress habits are propagated, it is clear in several direct and indirect ways too. The *Organiser*, the RSS mouthpiece, carried a series of articles on Anna Hazare and Ralegan Siddhi in which the writer expressed deep admiration for the model being followed.[111] Regarding the incorporation of Dalits he remarks:

> Anna-saheb Hajare imprinted on the minds of the villagers that, as children of the same God, any discrimination on the basis of one's birth would be reprehensible to Him . . . To start with, the young workers called a meeting of the Harijans in the village. Together they decided to bury the bitter memories of the past and start a fresh page of social equality and harmony. On their part, the Harijans decided to give up carrying of dead animals, eating their flesh and also vices like *ganja*, gambling, etc. The meeting was followed by efforts for cleanliness and sanitation in their houses and their neighbourhood and imparting of healthy samskaras to their children.[112]

[110] Interview with Anna Hazare.

[111] H.V. Seshadri, "The Village that Reminds Us of Ramarajya", *Organiser*, 8 February 1987, 6 and 10; idem, "Ralegana Sindi: A Name for Social Metamorphosis", *Organiser*, 15 February 1987, 11.

[112] H.V. Seshadri, "Ralegana Sindi: A Name for Social Metamorphosis", *Organiser*, 15 February 1987, 11.

Anna's concern for Dalits works at many levels. One is the ritual organised for the Dalits, to integrate them into a whole. Here the ritual centrality of the dominant caste is significant. These rituals also come through his totalising discourse on purity and pollution, which embrace political and economic power. Here we also see the importance of the practice of gift-giving for the cultural construction of dominance.[113] In his ethnographic history of an untouchable community, the Satnamis of Chhattisgarh, Saurabh Dube shows how a complex interplay and overlap of discourses constituted caste relations in the context of power: "The ritual hierarchy of purity and pollution and the ritual centrality of kingship and dominant caste(s) were both symbolic schemes that elaborated modes of domination and power. Defined by meanings and practices that articulated and were articulated by relations of authority, they worked together to secure the subordination of the Satnamis and other untouchable communities in Chhattisgarh."[114] In Ralegan Siddhi the position of Dalits is grounded not only in rituals and a language of integration, but also in the concept of a united family. And these are cemented by continuous references to religion, the centrality of the dominant caste, and the authority of an environmental leader.

In spite of the apparent diversities that characterise the various elements that make up Anna Hazare and Ralegan Siddhi, we find an underlying thread of unity in the ideological system of a green village. Authority and its legitimacy are the key. Not only is this authority deeply rooted in the dominant socio-political tradition of the region, it is also often blind to many basic and universal issues of rights, democracy, and justice. Personal moral authority, while contributing in harnessing water and other natural and human resources

[113] For details see Raheja, *The Poison in the Gift*, 28. She points out that the proper presentation and acceptance of dān, which ensures the well-being of the entire community, is far more important than hierarchical considerations in structuring inter-caste relationships in the village.

[114] Dube, *Untouchable Pasts*, 214–15.

to the betterment of villagers, simultaneously raises significant questions about its relationship to the making of a democratic, critical community, free from burdens of force, punishment, coercion, obligation, patronage, charity, and piety. There are other obvious limitations as well. Because a plural and democratic culture is absent, even genuinely motivated reform endeavours such as this make it difficult to imbibe, evolve, and transfer personal moral authority to independent successors and followers.

The legitimisation of moral authority is necessarily complex and variegated. This legitimisation is at times also an interactive process between the leader and the villager. Achieved as an outcome of a long journey, it is contingent, dynamic, and continuously defined. However, the basis of this ideal village is a command–obedience relationship that is seen as legitimate. It is seen as such because it is rooted in shared norms and values, in established rules and codes, in the exercise of power for the promotion of a community's common good, and in the service of the unity and integrity of nation and nation-building. In sum, the sustainable use of natural resources in the village legitimises the belief of the villagers in the moral right of their leader to issue commands, and the corresponding obligation of the people to obey his commands. Crucial to this genuine reform experiment is the absolute removal from within its precincts of many of the defining ideas of modern democracy..

## Postscript

In March 2023, during a 95-km highway journey from Pune city to Ralegan Siddhi village via Parner, there were notable changes in the urban, industrial, infrastructural, and agricultural activities in Ahmadnagar district. The route featured heavy and light motor vehicles, roadside markets, shops and restaurants, scattered buildings, industries and industrial complexes, construction activities, and labour movements, all indicating a visible transformation since the last time I travelled the same route in 2005. The entry road to Ralegan Siddhi, which was previously a single lane, was now metalled, and on both sides of the road there were cement houses, small industries, hotels, and shops in between the agricultural fields. Although the road was mostly empty, there were many human activities close to the road, and urban footprints were apparent in the countryside.

"Welcome to Ralegan Siddhi, the Ideal Village" – this was displayed on the top of the two huge cement pillars erected like a heritage open gate to the village. The place looked very fresh and new, a place now where coloured houses, roads, market, construction materials, labourers, and vehicles were visible. The village also looked environmentally green and economically prosperous.

Dairy activities, village industries, and a building of the Hind Swaraj Trust, including a museum on the Anna movement against corruption, and school campuses were looking prominent.

The village landscape has undergone significant changes. The physical appearance of the village is different, with all the buildings now made of durable materials such as brick or concrete, and some

Image 3: Ralegan Siddhi Awards Display Board.

Image 4: Greenery and warning against plucking foliage.

even with boundary walls around them. Pucca roads now connect the villages within. All houses now have access to electricity, water, cooking gas, and toilets. Mobile phones, cable TV connections, and two-wheelers are now more prevalent than before. Jai Singh Sadashiv Mapari, the village sarpanch, who was sitting in his two-storeyed pucca house that spreads over many acres of land with a boundary wall and gate, said "The village has changed in the past two decades: from the ashes to the level of prosperity never seen before. People now have money, irrigated agriculture, dairy, business, and jobs."[115] However, the architecture of the village space remains unchanged in one respect: the Dalit families of the village still live on the periphery, while the Maratha landowning families live in the centre.

### *The Meaning of Anna Hazare*

Anna Hazare, the 85-year-old pedagogue dressed in khadi attire, sat in the Hind Swaraj Trust Building surrounded by Z-security person-

[115] Interview with Jai Singh Sadashiv Mapari in Ralegan Siddhi, 23–24 March 2023.

nel, while still actively committed to protecting the environment and promoting economic development in his village. Recently, he donated a piece of his land to build a hospital and frequently visits the construction site to monitor progress. He stressed the continued importance of the several bans (*bandis*) he imposed at the start of the environmental regeneration work in the village, namely *nasbandi* (family planning), *nashabandi* (prohibition of liquor), *charaibandi* (ban on cattle grazing), and *kuladhbandi* (ban on axe-cutting of trees), along with *shramdan* (voluntary labour). He emphasised social rules as essential for environmental protection and shared an incident in which a farmer cut down some small trees without consulting village elders or the panchayat. When summoned by the panchayat and police, the farmer accepted his mistake and offered to pay a fine. However, instead of imposing a fine they directed him to plant double the number of trees he had destroyed and nurture them well. According to Anna Hazare, his personal hallmarks are selflessness, sacrifice, a pure character and culture, hard work, honesty, patience, and resistance to desire and lust. When discussing movements against corruption at the local, regional, and national levels he explained that they are an integral part of addressing pollution at multiple levels, including environmental, social, economic, and political.[116] The importance of "pure thoughts, pure morals, and untainted character" was frequently highlighted in contrast to pollution.[117] Villagers, local officials, and civil society members frequently sought out Anna Hazare for his advice and blessings. The museum on the movement against corruption, the photographs and exhibition on the village, and the literature and publicity materials primarily focused on Anna Hazare, crediting him for the success of the village, and as its sole, unique, and mass leader. The aura of his name and influence were more overwhelming than twenty years ago.

### *Belief System*

The village sarpanch, Jai Singh, proclaimed that "Anna ji is our God" and credited him with bringing glory to the village that had

[116] Interview with Anna Hazare in Ralegan Siddhi, 23–24 March 2023.
[117] Hazare, *Voice of Experience*, 8.

been celebrated throughout the country.[118] Singh also said Anna had set the present and future pathways for the village and that they must follow them. Nana Saheb Awaddi, another member of Anna's team, claimed that despite his old age Anna was still dominant and dangerous, and that young people might fear him less but would not dare disobey him.[119] The villagers' unwavering belief in Anna Hazare and their acknowledgement of his authority and governance were two crucial factors in the village's environmental and developmental progress. The sarpanch, in a command–obedience relationship with Anna, acknowledged that it was Anna who had appointed him and that he worked according to Anna's will.

As outlined earlier in this chapter, Anna Hazare wove his narratives around the themes of unity, discipline, family, service, common culture, goals, and objectives. His experiences in wars and army services provided important reference points, including the India-China war in 1962, when China suddenly attacked India, leading to the loss of many Indian soldiers and a significant amount of the country's wealth. The patriotic values of sacrificing one's life for the cause of the nation led Anna to join the army, which also laid the foundation for his lifelong social service.

During the India–Pakistan war in 1965, all of Anna's colleagues were martyred at the border of Khemkaran. This event led him to realise that God wanted him to do something for his people. Anna learned a valuable lesson from his time in the army: "Military laws, jawans fighting for their causes . . . However, one thing is for sure. If a soldier decides to overcome the challenges, the hardships turn into achievable goals." [120] Anna also spoke about the "destruction of the evil", using examples from the Hindu epics of the destruction of Raavan, the hundred Kauravas, and corrupt political figures:

> Even in this age there are Raavans in society. There are also the Duryodhans and Shakunimamas as well . . . Just as Raavan was annihilated, just as the hundred Kauravas were wiped out, the corrupt, political moneybags of today are going to be wiped out . . . Lord Shri Krishna

[118] Interview with Jai Singh.

[119] Interview with Nana Saheb Awaddi in Ralegan Siddhi, 23 March 2023.

[120] Hazare, *Voice of Experience*, 6.

has said this in the fourth chapter of Geeta. It means, for the sake of the pious and virtuous and to destroy the evil ones, I take birth in every Age.[121]

Anna's authority, based on his achievement and performance in the village, continued to have high acceptance. It was frequently employed by the villagers to explain the continued hold of Anna over them and the village. The achievements were explained not only in terms of economic performance, but also the glory he had bestowed on himself and his village in the recent past. The formation of the Shri Sant Yadavbaba Milk Co-operative was the beginning of the local dairy farming business in the village. Anna also mentioned this initiative prominently. Such effective performance was regularly deployed to regenerate his moral authority:

> The village which could supply more than 300 litres of milk, started supplying 6000 litres per day to the dairy co-operatives, amounting to two lakh rupees turnover per day. Every year, 100 to 125 trucks of onions, vegetables and papaya are sent to wholesale markets for sale. The economy of the village has changed. A village where most of its citizens would go six kilometres far for earning money; now it is not possible to find even four to five labourers for the farm fields of Ralegan Siddhi. Instead of destroying nature, we used nature's resources to transform the village.[122]

During my visit to the village it became apparent that Dalit families had not benefited from the dairy and vegetable businesses. When I spoke with some of the families, they revealed that many of them still had no land, while a few others had small plots that were not profitable for farming. Most of the Dalit families worked as agricultural labourers. As a result, most of them still fell under the category of BPL (below poverty line) families and were reliant on government welfare schemes for support. When I inquired about the poor state of the Dalit families from Nana Saheb, he acknowledged that around 10 per cent of the families in Ralegan Siddhi remained backward. However, he suggested that this was because they had taken

[121] Hazare, *My Village*, 210.
[122] Ibid., 15.

the wrong path, implying that their situation was due to their own choices rather than external factors.[123]

Anna Hazare referred to many Marathi saints – Namdeo, Tukaram, Nilobara, and Dnyaneshwar – to communicate the message of unity, service, and sacrifice. According to him, the profound thoughts of these saints can inspire and counter today's wayward society. Also, he argued that since we have now entered the orbit of science, the need of the hour is a harmonious blend of science and spirituality.

### *Economic and Normative Goals*

Anna Hazare continued to set economic goals for the villagers and these goals created the basis to build a broad set of normative goals on how to foster village unity and polity. Anna claimed authority based on the rational relationship between the goal and the main role played by him in this process. Under his leadership, the village had been able to progress through watershed management, afforestation, and soil conservation. Anna had outlined a set of future economic goals for the next twenty years: the development of dairy, village-level industries, and the marketing of these. Thus, the Maratha villagers invested heavily in dairy and local-crop-based village industries and processing units in mustard oil, groundnut oil, ghee, spices, and turmeric. A villager Rakesh Kale said that "our slogan is swadeshi and the natural products of the village can be well processed here by our small units and then marketed in the nearby districts."[124] The new economic prosperity in the village by dairy- and village-based industries was mentioned by most of the villagers. They also explained that Anna had directed them to create at least seven dairy co-operatives and other societies to run the business of milk and other processed products. He also involved the Hind Swaraj Trust, Swami Vivekananda Trust, government organisations, and various schemes to bring the necessary human expertise and financial resources to establish the enterprises. Anna himself

[123] Interview with Nana Saheb Awaddi.

[124] Interview with Rakesh Kale in Ralegan Siddhi, 24 March 2023.

explained in detail the success of these new enterprises. The new goals and tasks set by him continued to legitimise his domination in terms of his relationship to their success. He was seen as the promoter, implementer, and repository of the new knowledge in the course and goal of village development.

In Ralegan Siddhi, environmental and developmental goals were aligned with the normative goals of promoting unity and integrity in the village. Anna Hazare, the sarpanch, and the villagers interviewed believed that politics, political parties, and elections would harm the village's unity. Therefore, there had been no panchayat elections in the village, and panchayat members were selected through consensus, with Anna playing a crucial role. The village did not allow any election campaigns, including posters, pamphlets, election meetings, or rallies, and the election candidates had to come to the village without any political symbols. Anna said: "Politics is corrupt and will break the unity of the village life. Peace and harmony in the village cannot be maintained by the party-partisan politics. Environment conservation and development need complete unity amongst the villagers."[125]

### *Codes of Conduct*

Certain crucial norms, conduct, and behaviour established by Anna Hazare for the everyday social and political life of Ralegan Siddhi have been critical in the village's governance. Conformity with established rules has been commonly accepted and viewed as legitimate. A person who has acquired power by proposing and conforming to such norms remains the uncontested leader. Anna said that "social rules, discipline and control are essential in our society. They are meant to build Indian democracy. Our country is governed by the constitution and laws. However, everything cannot be run by the rule of law. People's rules are required." [126]

He emphasised the importance of "purity" in the proposed norms and behaviour for Ralegan Siddhi: "Those who dedicate their lives

[125] Interview with Anna Hazare.

[126] Ibid.

to the society need to observe some regimen. They should follow a code of conduct and have pure thoughts and their character should be taint-free."[127] Those who dedicate their lives to society should observe a code of conduct and maintain pure thoughts, with a character free of blemish.

He also recognised that pollution had two key aspects: natural and social. The village addressed natural pollution through land and forest conservation and watershed management, while social pollution caused by caste and religious divisions was being addressed through social norms. These social norms included restrictions on the sale of bidi, cigarettes, and *gutka* (a masticated tobacco product), playing only patriotic and nationalistic songs at social and other functions, prohibiting the performance of *tamasha* (a traditional folk dance in Maharashtra), which, it is alleged, contains vulgarity and immoral comments about man–woman relations, and punishment by the panchayat for those who cut plants and the branches of trees. The implementation of these norms helped to maintain social order and foster unity within the village.

### *Force and Punishment*

In Ralegan Siddhi, the use of force and punishment continued as an essential component of Anna Hazare's authority. This was applied to enforce the implementation of Anna's laws and ensure obedience to him. Physical violence, such as flogging, was seen as necessary to ensure the effectiveness of force. The legitimacy of authority and the call for public interest were used to justify the use of force, which was viewed as acceptable by the villagers. However, Sarpanch Jai Singh stated that flogging is no longer practised in the village and that persuasion and pressure are now used to address issues of alcohol consumption. If a person is caught consuming alcohol, Anna, the panchayat, and elders attempt to dissuade the person rather than resort to physical punishment.[128] Jai Singh acknowledged that some people continue to consume alcohol secretly and are punished by

[127] Hazare, *Voice of Experience*, 8.
[128] Interview with Jai Singh.

the panchayat when caught. However, this is not a frequent occurrence. Nana Saheb also expressed his views about punishment: "Anna's rule is supreme. He knows very well how to exercise his rule. Even without coercion, the compliance can be secured."[129]

In 2023, Anna Hazare's personal authority continues to be significant in Ralegan Siddhi. However, some strain is visible in his command system. Many villagers express the view that commitment to the established rules and norms showed cracks, even if the erosion in compliance and commitment had not reached a crisis point. The sarpanch noted that "not many people are available now for *shramdan*", and there was a growing concern in the village about what would happen after Anna's time. The sarpanch also added that "the future is uncertain." When asked about the future of the green, ideal village that everyone was seized of, no one had an answer. Anna himself grappled with this question of whether Ralegan Siddhi, built with so much effort, would continue to exist. He explained that with each new generation economic conditions were improving, giving rise to consumerism and enjoyment. In such a set-up, idealism had no place: "Ralegan Siddhi could sustain its ideals because of the values cultivated in the people. We would try to sustain the ideals, but we have our own doubts."[130]

[129] Interview with Nana Saheb.

[130] Anna Hazare, *My Village . . . My Place of Pilgrimage*, 157.

# 4

# Passages from Nature to Nationalism

## Sunderlal Bahuguna and the Tehri Dam Opposition in Garhwal

THE CHIPKO LEADER Sunderlal Bahuguna (1927–2021) and his long-standing opposition to the Tehri dam in Garhwal were significant within Indian environmental movements in general, and for struggles against big dams in particular. This chapter explores the shifting contours of the anti-Tehri dam movement between *c.* 1970 and 2010. It focuses on the changing declarations of environmentalists, especially Sunderlal Bahuguna, the Tehri Bandh Virodhi Sangharsh Samiti (Committee for Struggle against the Tehri Dam, henceforth TBVSS), and other leaders of the movement on the one hand, and the involvement of the VHP on the other, in their opposition to the construction of the Tehri dam, and to the damming of the River Ganga. Exploring the evocations of nature, religion, and nation in their different phases by these two groups of actors, I argue that, through a regular use of certain mythical beliefs and simplified dichotomies, there has been a sometimes inadvertent collaboration between Green and Saffron. Visions of the Ganga as holy mother, of national security and unity, and of fear and revenge criss-cross other debates over the dam – such as costs and benefits, displacement and rehabilitation – at times undermine the far more complex issues of democracy, social justice, and sustainable development. Through the regular use of these religious symbols and myths, environmental, developmental, and moral concerns became narrowly politicised, even as fundamental differences between environmental movements and authoritarian political forces were obscured.

In the long journey of opposition to the Tehri dam since the 1970s, much has been researched and written about the dam and its safety, about Sunderlal Bahuguna and the movement. However, the language and politics of the movement, its vision of the nation, its approach towards the history and culture of local society, and its alliance with certain socio-political forces have received scant attention. Least heard are the changes and shifts in the movement in one of its crucial and final phases after the 1990s. Instead, the initial versions of the movement and its concerns have been used and reused, in both environmental and developmental narratives. I focus here specifically on the later-period alterations and their implications.

## Uttarakhand: The Historical Context

According to Haripriya Rangan, the region of Uttarakhand has been bestowed with a variety of official identities and histories: the independent kingdoms of Garhwal and Kumaon; the satrap kingdoms of the Mughal empire; the western colonies of the Nepalese Gurkha kingdom; as British Garhwal and Kumaon, administrative regions of the North-West Provinces and the United Provinces of Agra and Oudh; and as eight mountain districts (five under the Garhwal Regional Commission and three under the Kumaon Regional Commission) incorporated within the Indian state of Uttar Pradesh (UP).[1] Each of these official designations has represented the efforts of administrators and political actors, past and present, to spatially demarcate the variations made to existing patterns of social networks and

[1] The Uttarakhand region embraced the eight hill districts of the state of Uttar Pradesh. These districts were Pauri, Chamoli, Tehri, Uttarkashi, and Dehradun (which constitute Uttarakhand's Garhwal region); and Almora, Pithoragarh, and Nainital (which constitute Kumaun). The new state of Uttaranchal came into existence in November 2000 and comprises thirteen districts: Almora, Nainital, Pithoragarh, Bageshwar, Champawat, Udhamsingh Nagar, Dehradun, Pauri, Tehri, Chamoli, Uttarkashi, Rudraprayag, and Haridwar.

material practices through economic conjunctures and political events.[2] Even though the opposition to the Tehri dam deals with a highly complex set of new issues and a multiplicity of stakeholders – for example, analyses of technical, social, and environmental variables; cost/benefit ratios; geology and seismicity; public-sector planners; NGOs and activists – Sunderlal Bahuguna and the TBVSS took important cues from the history of the region and dominant historical conceits in shaping their arguments and actions. There are five important historical factors to be considered here: (i) ecological and cultural underpinnings in the Garhwal region; (ii) the agrarian and rural environment; (iii) the development discourse of backwardness and progress; (iv) social movements; and (v) political changes till the 1990s.

### *Ecological and Cultural Underpinnings of the Garhwal Region*

In dealing with the cultural ecology of the Himalayas, the environmental historian Ramachandra Guha explores the ecological characteristics of mountain society in both Tehri-Garhwal and Kumaun: how the distinctive class structure meshed with other ecologically determined hallmarks of mountain society, and the close integration of agriculture with forests and pasture; how through religion, folklore, and tradition this region's village communities drew a protective ring around the forests; how ecological constraints in the region in relation to the intensification and expansion of agriculture have historically resulted in a close regulation of the common property resources so crucial for the subsistence of individual households.[3] This ecological context has many other specific dimensions. The mountainous region of Garhwal ranges in height from approximately 990 feet to more than 24,750 feet. On the basis of altitude, complexity of physiographic features, geological chronology, and structure the region can be divided from south to north into three major parallel

[2] Rangan, *Of Myths and Movements*, 184–5.

[3] Guha, *The Unquiet Woods*, 9–34.

zones or regions: the Outer Himalaya or the Sub-Himalaya or the "Siwalik" zone; the Lesser or Lower or Middle Himalaya, also known as "Himachal"; and the Greater or Inner or Main or Higher Himalaya, also known as "Himadri". All three regions can be further divided into valleys and ranges.[4]

The region has a rich Hindu history. It is said that the great philosophers of yore – spiritual souls and pilgrim forefathers, who were also ardent naturalists, voyagers, and explorers – not only made it a point to visit this sacred land at least once over their lifetime, but dotted it with religious sites and shrines so that people from far and wide, besides paying obeisance to their own deities, could also feel the varying moods of nature. The Garhwal Himalaya is often described as *devbhumi* and *tapobhumi* in the Hindu scriptures and epics.[5] It is also believed that Garhwal is the seat of the Holy Trinity – Brahma, Vishnu, and Mahesh – who, along with Lord Ganesh and Durga Ma, are known as the Panch Parmeshwar. The sacred Hemkunt Saheb, in the backdrop of the "Valley of Flowers", has become known as a place for Sikh scholars to meditate on and interpret the verses of the holy *Granth Sahib*. Besides various gurudwaras, the region is punctuated by medieval mosques and some churches. It claims to be the custodian of Badrikadham, the origin of the Ganga, and the seat of solace for both ordinary Indians and complex nonconformist *tantriks*.[6] In fact, the region has become synonymous with the idea of pilgrimage. But this pervasiveness of religion in Garhwal has also had several negative consequences: the accumulation of wealth and massive land-grabbing by high priests and caste Brahmins; the relegation of lower castes to supporting activities like cooking; landlessness among artisans and peasants; an oppressive oligarchy; and so on. Thus, religion is also held responsible for leading to an inegalitarian economic order.[7]

Apart from the venerated Ganga and Yamuna, originating in Garhwal and described in Puranic tradition, the Alaknanda, also

[4] Rawat, *History of Garhwal*, 11–12.

[5] Kandari and Gusain, "Preface".

[6] Bhatt, "And Why Not Uttarakhand/Uttaranchal", 385–9.

[7] Rawat, *History of Garhwal*, 208.

sacred to Hindus, figures prominently in religious texts. It is believed that *amrit* (nectar) – the ocean's water came down from heaven – gave rise to the sacred river, which goes through varying channels. The Alaknanda, the Vishnu Ganga, the Dhauli, the Rishi Ganga, the Girthi Ganga, the Rudri Ganga, and many more rivers and lakes are associated with religious beliefs on the Ganga's origins and purity. The Ganga is seen as a goddess who possesses the power to absorb and absolve human and worldly impurities. Cited in the *Vishnu Purana*, she washes away the impurities of the world just as she washed the foot of Lord Vishnu during her descent to earth.[8] The Bhagirathi, the other major headstream of the Ganga, is associated with King Bhagiratha, whose arduous penance secured the descent of the Ganga from the heavens to deliver his forefathers from the curse of the sage Kapil. The ascetic is said to have reduced the 60,000 sons of King Sagar to a soulless heap of ashes for having disturbed his meditations. The Yamuna is identified as the daughter of Surya, the sun god, and as a sister of Yama, the lord of death. She is one of the many consorts of Krishna, the divine flute-playing cowherd.[9] The location of many such sacred places as the founts of Hindu gods and goddesses within the region has helped identify it as vital to the Hindu mainstream. And the dominant literary language of the state, Hindi, has come to be associated with Indian nationalism. The region's contribution to national politics, the large-scale recruitment from it of jawans into the army, and a perception of them being the "defenders" of the nation's boundaries with China have all gone into the making of a specific Hindu, martial, and national ethos.[10]

### *The Agrarian and Rural Environment*

The Garhwal Himalayas present a particular agrarian and rural environment with specific agro-ecological features. Climate, altitude, and soil variations, a rugged terrain, and steep slopes are characteristic. Cultivable land is limited and the net sown area is quite small. Land is often infertile, there being severe soil erosion problems

[8] Nautiyal, "Ganga: Aakash se Sagar Tak", 131–45.
[9] Dilwali and Pant, *The Garhwal Himalayas,* 11–19.
[10] Kumar, *The Uttarakhand Movement,* 163–87.

because of steep slopes and existing cultivation practices. Based on elevation and irrigation, several farming situations or zones have been identified, such as the irrigated lower hills, the rainfed lower hills, mid hills with a south aspect, mid hills with a north aspect, high hills, and very high hills. Sixty per cent of the agricultural area is within to the mid-hills zone – the major part being rainfed – and contributes to food production for the majority of the population. The major crops grown here are rice, ragi, sawan, wheat, potato, toria, mustard rai, peas, soyabean, horse gram, and urad. The irrigated lower hills are significant for the production of rice and wheat crops; rice and wheat rotate in this zone. The high hills and very high hills zones are important for cash crops like grain amaranth, buckwheat, and rajmash.

The horticulture industry occupies an important position in the farming system of the hill areas. Apple, pear, peach, plum, apricot, cherry, and walnut are grown at elevations of 1000 to 3000 metres above sea level. Livestock is important too, linking closely with the traditional rural small-scale industry. Handicrafts, dairy farming, and the production of wool and woollen cloth are the main cottage industries. Among handicrafts there are bamboo-based objects, ropes, and toys.[11]

The agrarian and rural contexts suggest a long continuum. At the time of Independence in 1947, the major economic activities in the Garhwal Himalaya centred on subsistence agriculture, forestry, seasonal pilgrimage services, and to a slighter degree the trans-Himalayan trade. The Himalayan districts saw little economic change during the first and second national Five Year Plans (1951–5 and 1956–60), although a few community development projects aimed at providing basic infrastructure and encouraging the formation of village-level co-operatives for artisanal production were tried out in the eastern districts of the Garhwal region. The border wars between India, China, and Pakistan (1962–5) had a profound impact on the region's economy by severely limiting the trans-Himalayan trade. As more than 75 per cent of the landholdings are less than 1 hectare in size, and the scope for expanding the cultivation of commodity crops is limited, most households without access to capital

[11] Trivedi, *Autonomy of Uttarakhand*, 53–87.

or alternative employment within their localities have been reduced to subsistence cultivation. These are neither adequate nor sufficiently remunerative in Garhwal, so hillmen are forced to migrate in search of work, augmenting household incomes with their remittances. Green Revolution policies too had little impact here, geared as they were towards increasing agricultural productivity in the Indo-Gangetic plains and other grain-producing regions in India. Moreover, a succession of natural disasters in the region in 1971 and 1972 – heavy monsoons caused floods, landslides, and soil erosion – ended up damaging terraced cultivation greatly.[12]

### *The Developmental Discourse of Backwardness and Progress*

In most official discourses, the Uttarakhand of the Garhwal and Kumaon Himalaya has been seen as backward, and therefore the need for its development and progress has been a regular prescription.[13] It is often said that this ecologically and culturally rich region is one of the neglected regions of the country despite its rich natural resources. Denied economic justice, the development process here is almost as good as non-existent. Agricultural techniques and the developed variety of good seeds and fertilisers that have yielded results in the plains are unsuitable in the hills, which require a different set of techniques that have not been introduced. Industrial development too has seen negligible growth, and therefore industry is able to employ only a small percentage of the population. The infrastructure for industry is undeveloped. The region's backwardness has also been described in terms of a lack of basic amenities such as electricity, roads, bridges, credit, and marketing. Planned programmes have been marred by very long gestation periods and high costs. There is a dearth of social and public services, technical education, medical facilities, and drinking water. All this pre-empts the proper utilisation of natural resources, and the growth in horticulture, tourism, forestry, and electricity generation has been very poor.[14]

[12] Rangan, "From Chipko to Uttaranchal", 205–26.

[13] Joshi, *Uttarakhand ke Aaine Mein,* 139–43. Also see Aryal, "Angry Hills", 13.

[14] Tewari, *Unity for Identity,* 28–51.

The main instruments for encouraging the development of hilly and backward areas that have been suggested are: taking on specific projects, a central subsidy, a transport subsidy, income-tax exemption, concessional credit from national and state financial institutions, hire-purchase facilities for machinery, price preferences by the state government, lower rates for electricity, and tax exemptions and interest-free loans for specific purposes to certain categories of people.[15] In concrete terms, a Hill Development Department was created for the administrative set-up of all eight districts of the Uttarakhand region. In 1969, under the chairmanship of the chief minister, a Hill Development Council was formed. By 1974 a full-fledged separate Hill Development Department had come into being. In 1991 this department was given the name Uttaranchal Vikas Vibhag, which was changed to Uttarakhand Vikas Vibhag in 1994. From 1974 a separate sub-plan was prepared for the region.[16] Decentralised planning for development was claimed to have been initiated in the region from 1982–3. Schemes were identified for each district, for which outlays were allocated to the districts and plans formulated. Of the total sub-plan expenditure for Uttarakhand, these schemes were estimated to account for about Rs 156 crore in the year 1992–3 and Rs 178 crore during 1993–4.[17]

A number of commissions, committees, government departments, and functionaries were created in the name of development. In 1988 a commission was set up to promote the growth of small-scale industries in the hill region of UP. Two regional development centres were set up for Garhwal and Kumaon Mandal, each headed by joint secretaries. An Uttarakhand division was opened within the State Planning Institute. An ordinance in 1992 announced a separate Hill Sub-Cadre in thirty-one departments, comprising Groups B, C, and D posts. The incumbents to these posts were not to be transferred outside the hill districts, namely Almora, Chamoli, Dehradun, Nainital, Pauri Garhwal, Pithoragarh, Tehri Garhwal, and Uttar-

[15] Goyal, "Policies for Uplift", 59–64.

[16] *Development of Hill Region, Sixth Plan 1984–85*, Government of Uttar Pradesh, 28–52.

[17] *Proceedings of UP Vidhan Sabha First Session 1990*, Lucknow, Director Printing & Stationery, 40–60.

kashi. The government was empowered to determine from time to time the strength of the Hill Sub Cadre in any service.[18]

*Social Movements*

A series of social movements before and after 1947 raised issues in relation to forced labour, forests, untouchability, the exploitation of natural resources, and alcoholism. According to the well-known historian Shekhar Pathak, during colonial times Uttarakhand (1815–1947) experienced three kinds of social movements. The first comprised movements that were broad in scope, demanding improved relations between all castes and classes and general welfare. These centred around education, bonded labour, the forest, women, the welfare of tribals and craftsmen, and the construction of roads. The second type comprised movements based around particular castes or subcastes and their concerns, some of which wanted to continue with the caste dogmatism and domination that were hallmarks of the past. However, Dalits were increasingly conscious of the need to fight oppression, gain an education, form their own organisations, resulting in localised oppositional movements. The third type was connected with the activities of Christian missionaries, who were taking up education and medical treatment for the poor. Overall, these strands contributed to raising the level of education and consciousness, and also spread a nationalist awakening in hill society.[19]

Uttarakhand also shows examples of movements in the pre-Independence period of both a subaltern and elite character. Militant resistance against unpaid labour in 1878–80, 1903–4, and 1921, and organised opposition against the state acquisition of forests between 1911 and 1917, were exceptionally successful. The movement of the farmers of Ascot to claim their rights over the land and the Gari Sadak Andolan in Garhwal over the construction of motor roads were important local movements.[20] Protests against the commercial

[18] *Uttarakhand Vikas Vibhag Development 1994–95 and Programme 1995–96*, 23.

[19] Pathak, "*Uttarakhand Mein Samajik Andolanon*", *Pahar 2*, 97–111. Also see, Pathak, *Uttarakhand Mein Kuli.*

[20] Pathak and Guha, "*Sthaniya Itihaas*", 200–13.

exploitation of forests in Tehri Garhwal and Kumaun, the imposition of so-called scientific forest management, and the severe curtailment of traditional forest rights became a recurrent feature. Apart from movements such as these which occurred at regular intervals, the widespread contravention of forest laws represented the most tangible evidence of such protests.[21] In British Kumaun violent and consistent protests were organised against forest policies, culminating in 1921 with a comprehensive challenge to the *kuli begar* system and a forest management that had almost choked the administration. Between 1921 and 1942 there were numerous instances of individual defiance of forest laws, the setting of forests on fire, and attacks on forest offices.[22]

After the 1960s a new wave of social movements swept Uttarakhand. The best known was the Chipko movement of the 1970s and 1980s in the Garhwal region. Chipko meant embracing a tree to protect it from commercial felling and the movement has been written about as one of the prominent environmental movements of the world: sociologists, historians, and environmentalists still debate the fundamental characteristics of the Chipko movement.[23] That upsurge was followed in rapid succession by movements against big dams, mining, and the sale and consumption of illicit liquor. Anti-liquor movements have had a vibrant presence in the Uttarakhand region, with a massive renewal in the early 1980s with the slogan *Nasha Nahin, Rozgar Do* (Give us employment, not intoxication).[24] Then, in the early 1990s, Uttarakhand saw a surge of mass action for a new hill state of the Indian union to be carved out of UP. People protested against the deprivation and backwardness of the region and raised their voice against "stepmotherly" treatment by the state government. This movement had its own separate history of growth and development.[25]

[21] Guha, *Unquiet Woods*, 48–9.

[22] Guha, "British Kumaun", 112–30.

[23] Guha, *Unquiet Woods*; Rangan, *Of Myths and Movements*; Kunwar, ed., *Hugging the Himalayas*; Shiva, *Staying Alive*; Mukul, "Villages of Chipko Movement", 617–21.

[24] Pathak, "*Nasha ek Shadyantra Hai*", 2.

[25] Chakraborty, *A Critique of Social Movements*, 49–70.

### *Political Changes Till the 1990s*

UP played an important role in national politics and the Uttarakhand region was more or less submerged in the mainstream politics of that state. Congress, the most influential party, allowed no reference to Uttarakhand statehood, so much so that Govind Ballabh Pant, who hailed from Uttarakhand and was one of the most important Congress leaders of UP, strongly opposed the idea of the bifurcation of the state because of his feeling that "it would reduce the strength of the state in influencing the national politics of India."[26]

The 1962 war between India and China made the Indo-Tibetan border a major national security concern. In the late 1960s the Congress Party's power declined in many states, including UP, and there was an assertion of regional sentiments in Uttarakhand. Representatives of diverse peoples' organisations, individuals, and political leaders articulated the demand for separate statehood by organising fronts, forums, and demonstrations. On the eve of the 1969 general elections, the electoral alliance between the Communist Party of India (CPI) and the Bharatiya Kranti Dal (BKD) openly campaigned for separate statehood.[27] Hostilities between Hindus and Muslims in Bihar and UP caused much alarm at this time.[28] The 1977 general elections, held after the "Emergency", decimated the Congress in UP: it lost all 85 seats to the Janata–Congress for Democracy alliance.

In 1979 a regional party of the hills was founded that owed its very name and origin to the demand for Uttarakhand – the Uttarakhand Kranti Dal (UKD). The 1980s saw fresh demands being made for the formation of new states: Uttarakhand, Jharkhand, and Chhattisgarh. After the Janata Party's rout in the 1980 elections its Jana Sangh members broke away to form a party of their own, the Bharatiya Janata Party (BJP). The formation of the BJP heralded a wave of religious violence in northern and western India. There were major Hindu–Muslim riots in the UP towns of Moradabad (August 1980)

[26] Nautiyal, "Story of Statehood", 8.

[27] Chakraborty, *Critique of Social Movements,* 56–60.

[28] Guha, *India after Gandhi,* 431.

and Meerut (September–October 1982).[29] In the early 1990s, after a period of relative post-Chipko and post-anti-alcohol peace, the Kumaon and Garhwal regions saw massive unrest once more over the formation of Uttarakhand. In the middle of 1994 the movement became most vocal and visible.[30]

The great success story of Hindu nationalism and the main site of the BJP's rapid growth in the 1990s lay in UP. The Ramjanmabhoomi campaign to build a temple in Ayodhya was one of the important factors in this growth. The Ayodhya movement was not conceived for UP alone, but that is where the heart of the movement lay. The VHP launched its Ayodhya campaign in 1984 at a congregation on the banks of the Saryu – a prelude to the larger agenda of incorporating the disputed shrines issue into the main plank of communal mobilisation.[31] Religious pilgrimage and processions were the foremost instruments of socio-political mobilisation, in which the VHP made use of a repertoire of rituals and symbols, including the sacredness of the Ganga, to propagate its message of Hindu unity, with major initiatives undertaken by the VHP in the 1990s.[32] Over this time, communal and religious organisations came to exercise a new influence on everyday life. The expansion and consolidation of the BJP and its allies in UP owed a lot to events like the VHP's Ram Shila Pujans, the *shilanyas* in Ayodhya, the Rath Yatra, the Sant Sammelan, the formation of the Sri Ram Kar Seva Samiti, the Kar Seva in Ayodhya, Asthi Kalash yatras, the demolition of the Babri mosque, and the unleashing of communal violence.[33] The use of sadhus as symbols of Hindutva, and towards the invocation of religion in political mobilisation,[34] was specifically designed around a calendar

[29] Ibid., 562–5.

[30] Aryal, "Angry Hills", 10–21. Also see, Joshi, *Uttarakhand ke Aaine Mein,* 139–44.

[31] Hasan, "Community and Caste", 94–5.

[32] van der Veer, "Hindu Nationalism", 653; see also Puri, "Religion and Social Movement", 139–56.

[33] Jaffrelot, *The Hindu Nationalist,* 369–448.

[34] van Dyke, "The 1998 General Election", 105–28.

of religious festivals, the use of temple premises as organisational centres for political activism, and for the propagation of Hindu aspirations.[35] This context is important to any analysis of the changing contours of the opposition to the Tehri dam.

## Sunderlal Bahuguna and the Tehri Dam: A Profile

Sunderlal Bahuguna's opposition to the Tehri dam has been a great reference point for environmental movements in India. In his lifetime he was diversely acclaimed as the best-known Chipko leader and father-figure in that movement, freedom fighter, non-political person who struck a chord in the hearts of those disenchanted with the hypocrisy of politicians and the electoral process, true follower disciple of Mahatma Gandhi and Vinoba Bhave working for the oppressed, environmental thinker and writer, charismatic personality whose deeds were the object of wonder, gentle crusader, unobtrusive messiah, a rishi, epitome of the TBVSS, convenor of the Himalaya Bachao Andolan, and much more.[36] Bahuguna himself did much to maintain this plethora of views within Uttarakhand, India, and beyond. A prolific writer and communicator, he wrote articles, leaflets, and booklets on a wide range of environmental issues concerning Uttarakhand and the Himalayas, and on development, economics, culture, ethics, and values.[37] Villagers constantly marvelled at his remarkable physical endurance, sage-like appearance, simple living, personal asceticism, and communication skills. That he could, despite being non-political, draw the attention of the Indian government and national political leaders (including prime ministers) and make

[35] Hasan, "Community and Caste", 100–1.

[36] There are several write-ups on Sunderlal Bahuguna by writers, journalists, historians, and academics. For example, see Rigzen, ed., *Fire in the Heart,* 1997; Rangan, *Of Myths and Movements*, 27–32; Seabrook, *Victims of Development.*

[37] To name a few, Bahuguna, *Dharti ki Pukar*; idem, *Vikas aur Paryavaran*; idem, *Kate Jungle Roti Dharti*; idem, *Save Himalayas*; idem, *Tehri Dam and High Dams*; idem, *People's Programme.*

them intervene in the Tehri dam issue was seen as a big asset for the opposition.

For Bahuguna, the construction of the Tehri dam was tied to a development system based on two lies: one, that nature is a commodity; and, two, that society is only for human beings. This system he claimed was born and developed in the West, where the state had vast colonies to exploit, a low population density, and a big area. However, the application of this system to densely populated countries had created a host of problems, one of which was the crisis of the Ganga. Instead, he argued, development here needed to be based on cultural values with its objective the achievement of peace, happiness, and fulfilment instead of affluence. The production system should be decentralised and run by human, animal, bio, solar, wind, tidal, and hydel (from the run of the river) energy. This would help save the Ganga from pollution created by big industries, big dams, and thermal and nuclear power stations. It was not the dam, but the River Ganga, as seen from time immemorial, that could solve the problems of pollution and poverty in the region. Dense tree cover in its hill catchments had to be restored by reviving natural vegetation to conserve water. Trees that provided food, fodder, and fibre, besides medicinal herbs, had to be cultivated. He stressed the tradition of worshipping the Ganga, which he felt should be augmented with the backing of science.[38] The concerns against the Tehri dam, in Bahuguna's view, were extendable into a Himalayan policy, and gave birth to the Save Himalaya Movement. This movement asked for:

> A Himalayan policy in which inspiring aspects of Himalaya are maintained. The wounds of this great mountain system should be healed up. Himalaya should remain a living space for its permanent residents, spiritual seekers, pilgrims, and tourists visiting for peace and enjoying scenic beauty. Resources should be used for regional economic self-sufficiency. There should be ban on indiscriminate exploitation and export of resources, like mining, deforestation, construction of big dams, etc.

The immediate steps recommended by Bahuguna to heal the wounds caused by the Tehri dam and other such projects were

[38] Bahuguna, *Save Ganga*, 5.

(a) power generation from each and every stream and rivulet without flooding the cultivated land, forests, and habitats, and (b) maximum land use for afforestation with tree and shrub species that showed a capacity to conserve soil and water, and those that provided food, fodder, fuel, fertilisers, and fibres to make local communities self-sufficient.[39]

Bahuguna also related his opposition to the Tehri dam with the broad cultural and religious beliefs of the Hindus in the region. He said there was a legend that the waters of the Bhagirathi could be contained only with the matted locks of Lord Shiva. Villagers believe that if there was any attempt to interfere with the flow of the sacred water, the Bhagirathi would exact a terrible vengeance. The Bhagirathi had bound the whole country into one unit; the thousands of pilgrims who visited the holy shrines in Uttarakhand would be aghast if their holy river were bound down into a lake and if their places of inspiration connected with the great Vedantic saints went under water.[40] While evoking this spirituality, Bahuguna put forward an alternative agenda for action against the Tehri dam: the real spirituality for him was to see life in all living beings – in trees, in rivers, in mountains. It was what could constitute the ideal society. Spiritually informed science and technology could ensure that all living beings enjoyed their birthright by giving priority to the planting of the five Fs – food (nuts, edible seeds, oilseeds, honey), fodder, fuel, fertiliser, and fibre trees. These trees, of course, should be soil-builders and soil-improvers, those with the greatest capacity to conserve water, for soil and water are man's two basic capital resources. This would re-establish the harmonious relationship between man and Nature – the relationship of the Child with the Mother.[41]

Invoking national and historical figures like Mahatma Gandhi, Gautam Buddha, Kabir, Vinoba Bhave, and Jayaprakash Narayan in the context of the opposition to the Tehri dam, Bahuguna emphasised the joys of simple living: fulfilment could never be achieved by industrial projects, material progress, and the accumulation of wealth.

[39] Bahuguna, *Save Himalayas.*

[40] Bahuguna, *Tehri Dam and High Dams.*

[41] Bahuguna (with George James), *In Conversation.*

Our ancestors had put a limit on desires. By following their sage advice, we could bring into existence a *sanskritik samaj*. This would represent an evolution from nature to culture (*prakriti* to *sanskriti*), a long-cherished dream of humankind.[42]

### *The Evolution of the Tehri Dam*

Irrigation planning was high on the agenda of the Indian government after 1947. By 1979 the country had 1554 big dams, mostly constructed after Independence, with a financial outlay of nearly Rs 70,000 crore allocated to irrigation. Of these, UP had 84: 1 built prior to 1900, 22 over 1901–51, 49 completed over 1952–79, and 12 more under construction.[43] Among them, the Tehri dam was the most ambitious – one of the highest dams in the world, meant to harness the waters of two important Himalayan rivers, the Bhagirathi and the Bhilangana.[44] This dam takes advantage of the sheer drop in height at many points along the course of the rivers for hydel electricity generation. This is part of a larger plan, formulated for tapping the discharge of the Upper Ganga Basin, wherein some 7400 million cubic metres of water is said to be "going waste". This plan envisages three storage schemes, namely, a reservoir on the Bhagirathi at Tehri, another at Kotli Bhel a little downstream, and a third at Utyasu on the Alaknanda (the other tributary of the Ganga).

The project was conceived in 1949 by the Geological Survey of India. The Tehri site was earmarked for consideration, subject to approval if the sub-surface investigations did not reveal adverse factors. Detailed investigations were carried out only much later, in 1963. Two years later, following the visit of K.L. Rao, then union minister for irrigation and power, the site was declared selected. The dam was

[42] Bahuguna, *Dharti ki Pukar*.

[43] Singh, *Taming the Waters*, 55–99.

[44] Many reports and booklets are available, at both official and unofficial levels, which give information on the Tehri dam. For example, *Multipurpose and Hydroelectric Projects in Ganga and Yamuna Valleys, UP*, Lucknow, Irrigation Department (UP), May 1986; Sen, *Tehri Dam*; Singh, *Tehri Bandh Pariyojana ki Byatha*; Singh, *Vivad evam Tathya*.

commissioned in 1972, but work began only in 1978. The dam, finally expected to be 260.5 metres high, is intended to impound 3.22 million cubic metres of water. The reservoir extends up to 45 kilometres in the Bhagirathi valley and 25 kilometres in the Bhilangana valley, with a water spread area of 42.5 square kilometres. The reservoir is expected to irrigate 270,000 hectares of land and generate 346 MW of hydel power. The turbines in the powerhouse at Tehri have an installed capacity of 1000 MW, said to be enough to meet the peak power requirements of the UP power grid. However, peaking cannot be allowed unless fluctuations in the river discharges are balanced by some storage scheme. Therefore, a balancing reservoir at Koteshwar, 22 kilometres downstream from Tehri, was built and the dam got an additional installed capacity of 400 MW. The Tehri dam also supplies large volumes of drinking water to Delhi. The dam submergence area included Tehri town (now entirely submerged) and 23 villages in the vicinity, while 72 other villages were partially submerged. Nearly 5200 hectares of land, including 1600 hectares of cultivable land, was lost to the reservoir. About 85,000 people have been entirely or partially displaced because of the dam.[45] Irregularities, gaps, and injustices in the rehabilitation process have been reported widely by activists, organisations, and the media.[46]

## Opposition to the Tehri Dam

*Tehri bandh ki denei char:*
*atyachar, begharbar, bhrastachar, narsamhar*[47]

(The four gifts of the Tehri dam:
atrocity, displacement, corruption, and genocide)

[45] There are several reports on submergence, displacement, and rehabilitation. See Chandola, "*Dubta Hamara Sahar*", 265–8; Yadav, "Going Under", 21–4.

[46] *Tehri Bandh: Bolti Khabre/Aankre* (Tehri Dam: Revealing News/Statistics), Tehri, Matu, n.d. This is a collection of several newspaper reports and articles that expose the shortcomings and injustices of rehabilitation.

[47] Slogan written at the Tehri dam project site that I saw during my fieldwork in June 1995.

Ever flowing from Gaumukh Himalaya
O! Mother! Bhagwati your name
The saints ever chant at Gangotri
From the lotus feet of Vishnu you issue
To disappear in the forest like locks of Shiva . . .
I am your undeserving son but you are my very own Mother.[48]

The Tehri dam witnessed continuous questioning and protests of numerous kinds by various people, including Bahuguna. His mission was to stop the construction of the dam by living at the dam site and sporadically fasting against it.[49] In the wake of Chipko, this opposition coincided with a period when organised opposition to big new projects was gathering force in the early 1970s, with movements emerging independently in different parts of the country.[50] The anti-Tehri dam movement has been seen as a part of the social movements of the 1970s, adding an ecological dimension to popular oppositional movements. A series of these were transforming the passive environmental consciousness of people into organised struggles. Chipko, Tehri, Silent Valley, and the fish workers' struggles were some of the prominent environmental movements of the decade.[51] The Tehri movement was in particular seen as demonstrating the growth of grassroots mobilisation, the forging of transnational links among rapidly proliferating big-dam opponents around the world, and the growing domestic institutionalisation of globalising norms which legitimised critiques of big dams.[52] Silent Valley, Ichampalli, Koel Karo, Tehri, and Narmada became collectively synonymous with peoples' struggles at a time when all large infrastructure projects in the water and power sectors generated political

[48] This is a Ganga *stuti*, written by the famous Garhwali poet Ghanshyam Sailani. It was regularly recited at the dharna site during the agitation against the dam in 2000.

[49] For a detailed account of these many protests, petitions, committees, see Agarwal, Narain, and Sen, eds, *State of India's Environment*, 145–9. Also, *Update from Delhi*, New Delhi, Update Collective, n.d.

[50] Gadgil and Guha, *Ecology and Equity*, 72.

[51] Chakraborty, "The Silent Valley", 186.

[52] Khagram, *Dam and Development*, 43.

resistance as well as intellectual criticism over the ways resources are used and justified.[53] An unusually heavy monsoon in 1970 and a devastating flood in the Alaknanda valley, coupled with discontent against the likely impact of large dams projected for the region, became anchoring points for the Tehri dam opposition. The Vishnu Prayag Hydel Project, situated in the upper reaches of the Alaknanda river, and the barrage to be constructed between Lambagadh and Hanumanchatti to generate 262 MW of electricity, were also opposed by environmentalists such as Chandi Prasad Bhatt. Frequent landslides, the construction of roads, and earthquakes were becoming issues of concern and action in the region.[54]

In this context, the Tehri opposition tried to establish connections between ecological, social, and mythical values through scientific studies, environmental campaigns, and cultural-religious references, thus engaging a wide gamut of environmental politics. It emphasised the economic life and structure of the dam, its geology and seismicity, displacement and rehabilitation, costs and benefits. Proponents of this opposition spoke of the cultural and religious values of the Ganga and the Himalayan region. They attempted to use scientific knowledge to explain their perceptions of imaginative and emotional truths. They went on fasts, dharnas, demonstrations, and agitational programmes to focus their demands. They were speaking a language of ecological politics, the universal language of the anti-big-dam movements of the 1970s and 1980s.

However, by invoking certain metaphors, myths, emotions, and faith, and by reaching out to particular religious sections and their practices, these environmentalists came close in their worldview to Hindu nationalist forces and their communal agenda, and this happened at a crucial political juncture. In effect, the metaphor and myth acted as Trojan horses through which communal politics regularly entered and re-entered Green politics. For the anti-dam forces – and especially the face of Sunderlal Bahuguna which represented them – the politics of the anti-Tehri dam movement became a

[53] Dwivedi, *Conflict and Collective Action*, 1.

[54] Bhatt, *The Future of Large Projects*; Lok Soochna evam Sahayta Kendra, *The Calamity–Prone Central Himalayas*; Bhatt, *Meddling with Himalaya*.

"normal" collaborative relationship between the factual, environmental, natural, and sustainable on the one hand, and the religious, emotional, national, and Hindu on the other. It was this emotional and communal content, rather than any other aspect of environmentalism, which changed the form and the function of the movement against the Tehri dam in its final stage.

There are vivid accounts of the long journey of the opposition to the Tehri dam. The TBVSS was formed in the early 1970s under the presidentship of the veteran freedom fighter and local MLA Virendra Dutt Saklani. Saklani took upon himself the painstaking task of acquiring reports pertaining to the dam construction, making a thorough study of different aspects of the project, inviting acknowledged experts from the relevant disciplines to visit the project site and offer their opinions, compiling voluminous documents and petitions, and mobilising people to educate them about the risks and dangers of the project. Thus, when officers of the UP government arrived with engineers to inaugurate the construction of the first diversion tunnel of the dam in early 1978, thousands of men, women, and children blocked their way. Saklani was arrested along with many others, and the town of Tehri was converted into a police cantonment.[55]

With the active participation of anti-liquor movement activist Kadambari Devi, Sunderlal Bahuguna, and others, the Samiti collected 10,000 signatures for a petition submitted to the Parliament's Petition Committee. Those who signed the writ petition filed in the Supreme Court of India against the dam included the CPI district secretary Vidya Sagar, Samiti president Saklani, and Sunderlal Bahuguna. Later, two prominent non-governmental organisations, the Indian National Trust for Art and Cultural Heritage (INTACH) and the World Wildlife Fund-India (WWF-India), also became signatories to the writ petition. And two of the country's eminent lawyers, Soli Sorabjee and Fali Nariman, agreed to appear on behalf of INTACH and WWF-India respectively.

Through appeals to national political leaders of diverse affiliations

[55] Bahuguna, "Tehri Dam", 84–5.

and various central governments, the Samiti and Sunderlal Bahuguna forced the state to constitute several committees and managed to officially halt or slow the dam project several times. The prime minister, Indira Gandhi, took up the petition submitted to the parliament committee and set up a committee under S.K. Roy. In March 1980 the Roy committee lamented the lack of sufficient scientific data for definite conclusions on the geological and seismological aspects of building a dam. The group therefore deputed the Wadia Institute, Dehradun, the National Geophysical Research Institute, Hyderabad, and Roorkee University to conduct studies. The group was critical of the lack of attention paid to environmental considerations, and to the arbitrary ousting and dislocation of populations. There were, however, differences of opinion within the working group.

After the Roy committee submitted its report in 1986, the Ministry of Environment and Forests (MoEF) recommended abandoning the project, and the pace of work on the dam slowed. Although the project was not formally abandoned, no central funds were made available and the UP government provided only sustenance funds. However, in 1986 itself the USSR's president Mikhail Gorbachev visited Delhi and his visit paved the way for an agreement to the effect that the erstwhile USSR would underwrite Rs 1800 crore out of a total Rs 3000 crore credit. In June 1987, a collaboration agreement was signed in Moscow under which the Soviet Union was to render technical assistance in building the dam. The Tehri Hydroelectric Development Corporation, a public sector undertaking, was set up in 1988, in which the centre had a 75 per cent and the state government a 25 per cent financial commitment. In 1993 a Russian–Uzbek consortium offered to finance the project.

In light of an earthquake in 1991 in the upper Bhagirathi valley, another five-member team of earthquake experts was appointed. They overruled the Roy committee's recommendations. Consequently, the MoEF granted the project conditional clearance. Sunderlal Bahuguna alleged that certain conditions had not been fulfilled and went on a hunger strike in 1992. On the forty-fifth day of his fast the prime minister, P.V. Narasimha Rao, promised to review the project.

The same year the environment minister, Kamal Nath, told the Lok Sabha that the centre was seriously considering withdrawal of environmental clearance to the project. However, with the prime minister's go-ahead, construction work on the project resumed in 1995. After yet another long fast in January 1995 Bahuguna was promised an emergency review committee, but later arrested and taken to a hospital. Narasimha Rao's promise was never kept and the report of an expert group appointed by yet another prime minister, Deve Gowda, to examine the safety and environmental aspects of the dam never saw the light of day. Therefore, Bahuguna went on a hunger strike once again in October 1997. After fifty-six days of his fast one more prime minister, I.K. Gujral, ordered a ban on rock blasting and the movement of vehicular traffic at the dam site. In 1997 a panel headed by the economist Hanumantha Rao submitted its report on rehabilitation and suggested major changes in policy. In 1999 the Chamoli area was hit by an earthquake which once again cast doubt on the dam. A committee of secretaries was constituted: this showed a green light to the dam. In April 2001 the government came up with yet another committee, the Murli Manohar Joshi Committee, but nothing came of it.

Other than government-appointed committees and their recommendations, Sunderlal Bahuguna's fasts in 1992, 1995, 1997, and 2001 became the main rallying point for the opposition to the Tehri dam. Fasts and *vratas* were the truly *satvik* (righteous) methods to solve the complex problems of our society, which were developed by our ancestors in the course of their researches on the science of *atma gyan* (knowledge of the inner self) – this is how Bahuguna described his strategy against the dam.[56] Those involved in the struggle have had other and varying visions; the controversy, after all, involved a complex set of issues and a multiplicity of stakeholders. No wonder these stakeholders often had divergent perceptions of development, facts, problems, solutions, and costs and benefits. However, as I suggest below, these divergent positions, values, and beliefs were simplified and narrowed down – a process best personified in the words and

[56] Interview with Sunderlal Bahuguna, Tehri, 20 June 2001.

deeds of Bahuguna and the groups associated with him. This served to obscure many other fundamental arguments against the dam, even as the simplified and narrowed positions coexisted with conservative ideas and values.

### *The Ecological Discourse and the Tehri Dam*

Within the growing environmental consciousness of the 1970s an important and popular impulse was to use facts and figures, scientific methods and techniques, to challenge a project that claimed to be based on scientific calculation and assessment. The concern with reason and measurement, data and cost calculation was like a social enterprise and found expression not only in the setting up in 1978 of the TBVSS and its various campaigns, but also in studies, research papers, and articles. The Samiti and these varied expressions took upon themselves the painstaking task of making a thorough study of every aspect of the project report, visiting the project site, offering objective and scientific opinion, and compiling voluminous documents and petitions.

Through an analysis of technical, social, and environmental variables,[57] it was argued that the economic life of the dam would not exceed 61.4 years, and that it would take at least another fifty years to yield the desired outcomes, by which time the reservoir would quite possibly be substantially silted. The design of the dam was arguably unsafe and, therefore, justified the fears of local Garhwalis around Tehri of the possibility of its catastrophic collapse. While calculating the benefit–cost ratio of the irrigation component of the project, the project authorities had committed conceptual errors and the revised benefit–cost ratio was 1.28 as against 3.49 reported by the project authorities. Numerous lacunae in the project formulation were also pointed out. Renowned scientists, such as Vinod K. Gaur, asked many questions: what was the probability of an occurrence of a major earthquake, of magnitude 7.5 or greater, whose rupture zone could traverse the Tehri region during the lifetime of the dam, that

[57] Paranjpye, *Evaluating the Tehri*, 43–138.

is, over the coming ten years? What would be the effect of a large reservoir, if it were near-critically stressed, in inducing rock failure in the region? Bahuguna pleaded for the more human aspect: safeguarding the interests of people who were being uprooted and made permanent oustees. The journalist and writer Bharat Dogra spoke of data deficiency: how the absence of data on soil erosion, slope stability characteristics in the catchment, and knowledge of landslides could have serious ramifications in understanding the potential problem posed by the dam.[58] The ones most likely to ensue were identified as land alienation, destitution, inequality, forced changes in the agricultural pattern, havoc to the joint family system, the lack of village commons, and impaired educational and health facilities.[59] Beyond these there was an informed discussion on the special susceptibility of the entire Himalayan range: that the Himalayas, being the youngest mountain ranges, pose serious geological hazards for the siting of an engineering project of this scale.[60]

### *The Aesthetic Impulse*

Environmental politics against big projects is often also about the perseverance and pursuit of the "natural" and the "beautiful". Aesthetic issues revolve around the depiction of what is pristine and heavenly at the project site, and what constitutes natural and harmonious living. This has been an important part of the criticism of big dams. In Tehri both the region and the project site have been most frequently referred to as sacred, peaceful, and solitary. The Himalayan region and the Ganga, symbols of a divine force, are a thing

[58] *The Tehri Dam: A Prescription for Disaster*, New Delhi, Intach, 1987. This is a selection of writings by well-known environmentalists, scientists, academics, and journalists on the Tehri dam project. There are many more books and booklets like this. For example, a booklet, *A Note on Tehri Dam*, by S.P. Nautiyal, ex-Director General of the Geological Survey of India, published by TBVSS, suggests after a thorough study that alternative proposals should be considered. Also see Saklani, *Tehri Dam*; Dogra, *A Colossal Risk*.

[59] UP Voluntary Health Association, *Rehabilitation of Tehri Dam Oustees*, 1–13; Dogra, *Tehri Bandh Pariyojana*.

[60] Paneuli, "Tehri Bandh", 58–72. Also see Dogra, *Tehri Bandh Pariyojana*.

of beauty and points of contact with the infinite. This landscape appears on the canvas of environmentalists regularly, though it is not necessarily associated with mythical religious figures and symbols. Thus, during his "prayerful fast" against the dam in October 1997, Bahuguna concluded one of his letters with these words: "Sitting on the lap of Mother Bhagirathi with the inspiring sight of her murmuring flow, a holy dip and drinking her nectar-like water, gives me a unique pleasure. I have the desire to enjoy it until the last breath."[61]

The landscapes are also given meaning, shape, and form with reference to people. For the anti-dam activists, sublime dignity lies in local people's contact with and love of their environment. In a vivid description, Swami Chidananda Saraswati, an active figure in the anti-Tehri dam agitation and whom Bahuguna considered his mentor, explained:

> The Himalayan region is a sacred region. Here people come in contact with the Supreme. For their self-realization, for their knowledge, they come to this peaceful region . . . Himalaya is your father. You have taken birth there. You have grown up in His lap and will remain there for the whole of your life. All that you get there will be your source of livelihood. Your land, your trees and garden, all come from there.[62]

Similarly, there are examples of the beauty of the Ganga becoming a major source of protest against the dam, with pictorial and highly emotional representations of the river being also a way of presenting the politics of the anti-dam activists. According to Saklani, "Even the murmuring of the word 'Ganga' fills us with a splendid fragrance. Tides of emotion flow. From times without number, India's people have sung songs in praise of the river."[63] There are poems on her, such as: "Flowing, like a divine girl, singing songs, we see many colours, many faces of her, she continues to flow."[64]

[61] A letter by Sunderlal Bahuguna, 2 October 1997, Ganga Himalaya Kuti, Tehri. Also see Bahuguna, *The Himalayan Threat*, 1–2.

[62] Saraswati, *Himalaya ke Paryavaran*, 2–3.

[63] Saklani, *Gangajee ke Pavitra*, 1.

[64] Papne, "*Saswat Bahane Do*", 16–22.

This aesthetic impulse has echoed throughout the period of the anti-dam movement. However, it has had a marginal importance. Hindu myths and faiths have not been the central elements of this aesthetic sensibility; nature and its contours provided both confirmation and affirmation of individual and collective concerns, of the need to appreciate beauty and fight for it.

### *Creating the Past*

Myths of a glorious past were another important metaphor in the anti-Tehri dam movement. In the land of rivers and hills, a fertile, peaceful region was metaphorically carved up. The narrative oscillated between two poles: at one end, the focus was on a place of greatness and sacredness; at the other, its people, families, society, and work situations were shown to be ideal. The central importance of the past was explained in unequivocal terms. In the words of Kameshwar Prasad Bahuguna, "This is not only a question of drowning or displacing. It is a question of being attached with one's self and honour. It is a question of preserving our cultural heritage, to save the Ganga water from being poisoned. It is a question of being attached with our past."[65] This past has a long history, a history evoked beyond all sense of time and place. According to Sunderlal Bahuguna, "It has a long history. Its roots are in the forest culture of India. Our *rishi-munis* lived in ashrams within the forests. There were forests everywhere. In this environment, they got a new vision of life."[66] This history has some variations – as a place of mythical figures, as a place of healthy and happy people, as a place of one's ultimate being and living. Bahuguna narrated an idea of Garhwal about a century earlier:

> Every member of the family was busy. There was so much work related to agriculture and cattle-rearing that none in the family could sit idle. There was too much work for the menfolk. Men spent their night in thatches. In winter they had to be involved in making fences on the farm and expanding the agriculture. Life was busy, people were happy. Their

[65] Bahuguna, "*Tehri Bandh ka Virodh Kyon?*", 12.
[66] Bahuguna, "*Jeewan ki Jai*", 25–6.

world was limited to their land and cattle. Families lived with each other to make their lives happy and prosperous.[67]

Sometimes, the past has included concrete, earthy references. The past and its history become images of people's achievements:

> Tehri is no ordinary town; it is a historic town of cultural importance, which after the division of Garhwal in the early nineteenth century, became the centre of Garhwali culture. It has produced eminent Garhwali poets like Satya Sharan, Chandra Mohan Raturi and Tota Krishna Gairola, scholars like Rao Virendra Shah, art critics like Barrister Mukandilal and the famous sculptor Avtar Singh Panwar. Tehri has been the place of penance of the famous Vedantic saint Swami Ram Tirtha.[68]

In all these ways, the metaphors in the anti-dam movement have involved creating a past and its history from within the local environment. The forest, the river, the mountains become dominant in the narration and contain the possibility of varied justifications for protest. Such a past, created on the basis of local theology and myths, is then also deployed for the ecological dimensions of the movement.

### *The Tehri Dam and the Nation*

For the state and the pro-dam people, nation and nation-building were intimately related to completing the dam.[69] Ironically, for the environmentalists and the anti-dam activists national security, the national interest, and national unity are no less important. Bahuguna and other prominent anti-dam activists throughout emphasised that a safe and secure nation, free of external threat, would emerge from the water and the forests. The enemy and a threat perception occupied special places in their environmental identity. There was a recognition that these catchwords and universally acknowledged valorisations of the nation and its unity and integrity needed to be invoked to

[67] Bahuguna, "*Parvatiya Vikas aur Bhoomi*", 15–17.

[68] Bahuguna, "The Humanitarian Aspect", 36.

[69] Singh, *Vivad evam Tathya*, 61; Singh, *Tehri Bandh Pariyojana ki Bhaytha*, 14. He forcefully argues that the Tehri dam is beneficial for the nation and to stop it would adversely affect the national interest and nation-building.

impart credibility and acceptability to their environmental message. This threat perception to the nation, however, never remained fixed; it was always in a flux. Sometimes Bahuguna was worried about the whole Himalayan region:

> The threat from the Himalayas is to the security of the nation. Himalaya at one time was the abode of peace, where sages and saints did penance . . . The most expensive item of expenditure in this region is the guarding of Himalayan borders . . . China has adopted a clever strategy of defence in Tibet, adjacent to its borders with India, Bhutan, and Nepal. China has settled its soldiers, married to Tibetan women, as farmers and cattle herdsmen in this region.[70]

His worries took another shape in a memorandum to the Parliamentary Standing Committee during its visit to Tehri to evaluate the Tehri dam project: "Another threat to the safety of the dam is from the defence angle. At least three ex-Army officers, Major General Bhuvan Chandra Khanduri, ex-MP, Sri Ranjit Singh, ex-MP, and Air-Commodore R.S. Bishnoi have indicated that this dam is in the missile range of neighbouring countries."[71]

The threat perception got around. Many other social activists and concerned people and organisations started raising it. Rajendra Singh Dhotiyal, advocate and convenor of the Jan Jagaran Manch, said, "The Tehri dam can be fatal from the viewpoint of national security. The dam is at an air distance of 100 kilometres from China. If there is an Indo–China war, this dam will be the target of attack by Chinese missiles."[72] Even an extended cost-benefit appraisal of the Tehri dam found it necessary to mention this: "An important aspect of the Tehri dam is its proximity to the Chinese border. We cannot ignore the fact that at present China is an unfriendly neighbour,

[70] Bahuguna, *The Himalayan Threat*, 4.

[71] Bahuguna, *Himalayan Policy Solution*, 5. Also see Bahuguna, *Ghayal Himalaya*, 1. A known activist in the anti-Tehri dam movement, Rajeev explains how, from Kohima to Kashmir, the Himalaya is engulfed by violence. He asks how, if it continues to be wounded by internal attacks, it will withstand external attacks.

[72] Dhotiyal, *Vikas ka Pratik*, 4.

and that the Tehri dam might be an attractive target for Chinese bombers."[73]

Environmentalists argued that a dam on the Ganga-Bhagirathi constituted a kind of leave-taking from the country, a loss of national unity and integrity whereby the nation loses its character: "Bhagirathi binds the whole country into one unit";[74] "Ganga is most important from the point-of-view of national integrity, cultural unity and the oneness of India";[75] "Ganga is not only a holy river, but is most important for national integrity and for cultural unity and the oneness of our nation";[76] and so on. If the pro-dam people saw the construction of the dam as an important marker for the creation of a national landscape, the environmentalists, equally, saw the preservation of a pristine Indian ecological landscape, free of the dam, as true nationalism.

### *Holy Mother Ganga and the Tehri Dam*

The shadow of mythical accounts, traditional values, and ancient beliefs abounds in most varieties of environmental politics. There is an identification of people with plants and animals – in other contexts, the emblems of whales, seals, and pandas are common. There is also a feeling that people belong to particular places, which they express as a cosmic relatedness that runs deeper than familial and ancestral solidarity.[77] In the vocabulary of environmentalism there are always holy lands and rivers, sacred groves and forests.[78] In effect, such

[73] Paranjpye, *Evaluating the Tehri*, 10.

[74] Bahuguna, *Save Himalayas*, 34.

[75] Bahuguna, "Save Mother Ganga", 33–7.

[76] Chidananda, "An Appeal to Save", 1.

[77] It is explained in a different context that autochthonic beliefs, associated with the possessive symbolism of the cavern in the religion of palaeolithic hunter-gatherers and later with worship of the Earth Mother, led the Romans to call a bastard *terrae filius* – son of the earth – and to the widespread folk custom of giving birth on the soil: hence the expression "native soil". They also clearly share some form of psychological ancestry with the growing assertion of local, regional, and ethnic identities, the search for roots, and a sense of belonging. For details, see Nicholson-Lord, *The Greening of the Cities*, 38–55.

[78] Sacred groves are said to be one of the finest instances of traditional con-

environmentalist mythologising moves at will through a vast cultural treasure-house, its shelves loaded with beliefs and practices from the past. Here, it is apparent that what distinguishes Green from Saffron lies in the elements of the past that they choose for their mythmaking, the sorts of meanings they extract from their myths, and the political uses to which they put these myths.

What these mythologies seek to achieve is a new union between man and nature by the integration of two divergent traditions: on the one hand the technological and scientific, and on the other the mythical and imaginative. This fusion takes varied and interesting ecological forms. The Himalaya and the Ganga have a greater role in India's environmental politics of India and in the making of a national identity than any other topographical features. The Himalaya and the Ganga are physical entities, true, but they have also been culturally re-created by being endowed with a variety of meanings. In the anti-Tehri dam movement, environmentalists as well as religious leaders have opted for a Hinduised cultural representation of the Ganga and the Himalaya; this representation is dominant and has become an essential part of the movement's environmental politics and identity. Especially in the later years of the movement, anti-Tehri dam views have been constructed using Hindu imagery, often partnering Hindutva politics. Such ecological reasoning is fuzzy, going beyond logic, eliciting Hindu support, patriotism, and xenophobia.

This religio-cultural creation of the Himalaya and the Ganga is a result of the combination of several features: Hindu religious and social values; the supposed holiness and purity of the Ganga's water; the river's great economic and practical significance; the holy places, temple complexes, and *rishi-munis* at vantage points along its banks. The Ganga stems from some ancient golden period and flows into the nationalist one. The voices of Pandit Jawaharlal Nehru as well as obscure sadhus float and mingle in it. Sometimes, as in Bahu-

---

servation practices. They are identified with wild woodland spirits and deities of pre-Brahminic societies and with the gods of the Hindu pantheon. This has resulted in the installation of the idols of Hindu gods in such groves. For details, see Gadgil and Chandran, "Sacred Groves", 187.

guna's views, the main reason for the Tehri dam issue remaining unresolved is blamed on the fact that the river is viewed in isolation by the dam builders, instead of being seen in the context of the Himalaya as a mountain range – the source of economic prosperity, ecological security, and spiritual inspiration to a billion Indians.[79] Pamphleteering in the form of "Ganga Abhiyan" emphasises the rich topography of the Himalaya and the Ganga as conjoined features of a single region, offers information on the ill-effects of the dam, and denounces the dam's consequences.[80] Occasionally, we are referred to the will and testament of Jawaharlal Nehru:

> The belief among the Hindus about the holiness of the Ganga is so strong that every Hindu wishes his ashes to be immersed in it. The popular feelings about the Ganga have been very aptly put in words by Pandit Jawaharlal Nehru in his last will and testament: 'The Ganga especially, is the river of India, beloved of her people, around which are intertwined her racial memories, her hopes and fears, her songs of triumph, her victories and defeats' . . . If we leave aside the Ganga and the Himalaya, nothing will remain of the high values we cherish. All the preachers of India from Vyas Dev to Mahatma Gandhi took inspiration from the Ganga and the Himalaya. Shankaracharya, Guru Nanakdev, Tulsidas, Maharshi Dayanand and Vivekanand came in between.[81]

In Chidananda's words, "India is a holy land; and holiest of the holy and greatest of the great is the Himalaya, especially its Uttarakhand region. All our scriptures support this view. Uttarakhand is *devbhumi* (a place sanctified by Gods) and *tapobhumi* (a sacred land of penance and austerity) . . . A land of Gods, it is called. It makes its dwellers God-like."[82]

Other environmentalists deploy Hindu myths about the Ganga which integrate the identity of a river and a "Hindu" country.[83] One

[79] Bahuguna, *Himalayan Policy Solution,* 2–3.

[80] *Ganga Abhiyan*, a two-page pamphlet by TBVSS, Delhi, n.d.

[81] Bahuguna, *Save Ganga*, 1.

[82] Chidananda, "Save the Himalaya", 1.

[83] Hindu mythology has it that the Ganga, oldest daughter of Himavat (Himalayas), was brought down from the heavens in the form of a river. Because

myth goes thus: "Bhagirath, through long and arduous prayers persuaded the holy Ganga to descend from heaven, to wet the ashes of his ancestors, so that they might then ascend to eternal heaven. Lord Brahma advised Bhagirath to ask Lord Shiva to receive Ganga as she descended, because the earth could not sustain her fall."[84] Lord Shiva agreed to help bring down the holy Ganga, and by catching it in his tangled locks he saved the world from her impact. The story goes on to describe how before joining the sea the Ganga watered the mortal remains of King Sagar's 60,000 sons, liberating their souls once and forever. Another appeal makes it clear that the river is virtually the nation:

> The emotions created by her [Ganga] have integrated the nation into one. To wound this feeling would be most unfortunate for the Nation . . . We should not think of Holy Divine Mother Ganga in terms of kilowatts, in terms of hectares of irrigated land, or in terms of drinking water facility for any city . . . Ganga is not only a holy river, but is most important for national integrity and for cultural integrity and the oneness of our nation.[85]

The cultural creation that was hitherto a combination of several agencies overlapping with each other seemed to be culminating, especially in the 1990s, in a narrow, conservative environmental politics. The appeal to Hindus and their organisations became an important expression of the mood of the TBVSS – Sunderlal Bahuguna and his Himalaya Bachao Andolan – giving it an increasingly powerful political-cultural undertow. What the anti-Tehri dam agitation subscribed to was not only Hindu religious culture but also the conviction that only through the recovery of a Hindu religious platform could a successful case be made against the dam. The bond uniting

---

of its descent from the heavens, Hindus regard the Ganga as the mother of all Indian rivers and as the purest, holiest, and most sacred stream of the world, and consider that a dip in it or the imbibing of its holy water will purge their sins and ensure their soul's liberation (*moksha*).

[84] "Ganga: The Legend and the Life Line", *Himalaya: Man and Nature*, vol. XVI, no. 10, March 1993, 1.

[85] Chidananda, "An Appeal to Save", 1.

the environmental and heterogeneous coalition of religious and political concerns created the mainstream of the movement. Its targeted call was to arouse Hindus for a greater cause. The TBVSS appealed to *sadhus-sants* to stop a catastrophe:

> The foreign powers are conspiring for the Tehri dam, to end the religion and tradition of the *Bharatbhoomi* . . . Tehri dam is the murder of our culture, religion, and tradition. Whenever there has been a crisis in our religion and culture, our *rishis* and *avatars* have protected us. This is such a moment of crisis . . . It is natural that India's highly respected Jagadguru Sankaracharyas, Mahamandaleshwars and thoughtful *sadhus-sants* are worried over the direct interference in our religion by the Tehri dam . . . *Parampujya Mahamandaleshwar Swami* Sri Yogeshwar Videhi Hari Jee Maharaj, President, Kumbh Mela Sadhu Samaj, has also appealed to the *sadhus-sants* to make people conscious in this hour of terrible national problem.[86]

At the time of the Mahashivratri festival they go to *kawarias* – Hindus, who walk carrying Ganga water on their shoulders to pour it in their temple, or on Lord Shiva. The anti-Tehri activists address these travellers: "The free, holy flow of the mother Ganga is being disrupted by constructing the Tehri dam and by establishing the industries. Is it not your pious, Hindu duty to oppose it? Awake devotees, it is the call of your God! Fulfil your duty to Mother Ganga! Never leave the opportunity to serve your God, your religion and your Mother Ganga!"[87] A booklet, prepared and distributed by a social activist, says: "Atheists, anti-religious people and anti-social elements are exploiting the Ganga and the Tehri dam is a classic example of all this . . . The Tehri dam will make it impossible for Hindus and

[86] All quotes in this para have been taken from a pamphlet entitled *Tehri Bandh dwara Sarvanash ko Rokane ke liye Pujya Sadhu-Santo ka Aahwan* (A Call by Honoured Sadhus-Sants to Stop Destruction by the Tehri Dam), published by TBVSS. The pamphlet is released in the name of Virendra Dutta Saklani, President, Tehri, TBVSS, n.d.

[87] *Kawarion se Appeal*, a pamphlet released jointly by the TBVSS and Shiv Kawar Sangh, Meerut, n.d. Another pamphlet of similar nature, titled *Dekh Raha hai Aaj Himalaya Ganga ke Rakhwalon ko* (The Himalaya is Watching Today the Saviours of Ganga), was also released by the Tehri, TBVSS, n.d.

# टिहरी बांध द्वारा सर्वनाश को रोकने के लिए पूज्य साधु-संतों का आह्वान

परमपूज्य महामंडलेश्वर स्वामी श्री सोमेश्वर गिरि हरि जी महाराज, माघ कुम्भ मेला साधु समाज ... ने टिहरी बांध क्षेत्र का निरीक्षण करने तथा संबन्धित लोगों से चर्चा के उपरान्त पूज्य साधु-संतों से प्रार्थना की कि वे देश को टिहरी बांध के सर्वनाश से बचाने के लिए सर्वसाधारण को जागृत करें।

**विदेशी ऋण**

सर्वपूज्य गंगा माता को श्री भगीरथ जी अथक त्याग, तप से इस पावन भूमि पर लाये परन्तु विदेशी कुचेष्टा से भारत भूमि से धर्म एवं परम्परा समाप्त करने के लिए टिहरी बांध का षड़यन्त्र चल रहा है। वर्तमान सरकार उपरोक्त षड़यन्त्र में फंस कर, विकास की आड़ में जनता को धोखा देकर देश को विदेशी ऋण में डुबो रही है। बताया जा रहा है कि ४ अरब रुपया व्यय हो चुका है, जिसमें से वास्तविक व्यय बहुत कम तथा अधिकांश व्यर्थ बरबाद हुआ है। अनुमानतः अभी ४६ अरब रुपया और व्यय होगा, जिसपर भारत को प्रतिवर्ष करोड़ों रुपया केवल ब्याज के रूप में देना होगा। "बीत गयी सो बीत गयी, अब राख रही को" कहावत के अनुसार देश की शेष बची राशि सुरक्षित रखना ही बुद्धिमानी है।

**देश एवं परम्परा की हत्या—**

स्वामी जी ने कहा कि यह समझ में नहीं आता कि सरकार देश, विदेश के वैज्ञानिकों, स्वतन्त्रता सेनानियों एवं विद्वान विचारशील सज्जनों की मान्यता को ठुकराते हुये टिहरी बांध बनाकर धर्म, संस्कृति एवं परम्परा की हत्या करने पर क्यों तुली है। जब-२ धर्म एवं परम्परा पर संकट आया तब-तब भारत के पूज्य अवतारों तथा ऋषियों ने सदा सुरक्षा की। यह भी एक ऐसी ही घड़ी है।

**बांध तोड़ने एवं टूटने की सम्भावना—**

टिहरी बांध को तोड़ने एवं अकस्मात टूटने की सम्भावना निराधार नहीं है। इस क्षेत्र की पहाड़ियां कच्ची होने से समय-समय टूट-टूट कर भागीरथी में गिरती रही हैं। इस भू-स्खलन तथा वैज्ञानिकों के अनुसार बांध क्षेत्र की भूकम्पीय पहाड़ियों में बड़ी-बड़ी दरारें होने से इतने बड़े जलाशय का भार सहन न कर अथवा भूकम्प के झटके से बांध अकस्मात टूट सकता है।

**धर्म में हस्तक्षेप—**

भारत के सर्वपूज्य जगद्गुरु शंकराचार्यों, महामण्डलेश्वरों एवं विचारशील साधु सन्तों का धर्म में इस कोटि हस्तक्षेप से चिन्तित होना स्वाभाविक है। इस बांध से १—गंगोत्री-यमुनोत्री आदि चारों धामों की धार्मिक यात्रायें बन्द होंगी २—श्री गंगाजी का पावन जल रुका रहने से प्रदूषित होगा। ३—गंगोत्री से लेकर गंगासागर तक के सभी तीर्थों, मन्दिरों एवं घाटों की अत्यधिक क्षति होने से धर्म, संस्कृति एवं परम्परा के स्रोत समाप्त होंगे। परम पूज्य श्री रामतीर्थ जी महाराज के स्मारक डूब जायेंगे। ४—वन्य पशु, पेड़-पौधे तथा जड़ी-बूटियां नष्ट होंगी। ५—अकस्मात् बांध टूटने या तोड़े जाने से देवप्रयाग, ऋषिकेश, मुनि-की-रेती, एवं हरिद्वार आदि तीर्थ अविलम्ब डूबेंगे तथा देश के बहुत बड़े भाग में भयंकर नाश होगा।

अतएव स्वामी जी ने पूज्य साधु-संतों से विनम्र प्रार्थना की है कि वे इस भयंकर राष्ट्रीय समस्या के लिए सर्व साधारण जनता को जागृत करें। तथा इस विनाशकारी बांध को बन्द कराने व भगवती भागीरथी की गरिमा व पवित्रता को अक्षुण रखने के लिये हर सम्भव प्रयत्न करें।

विनीत :

**(विरेन्द्र दत्त सकलानी)**
*अध्यक्ष*
*टिहरी बांध विरोधी संघर्ष समिति*
*टिहरी, गढ़वाल*

**टिहरी बांध विरोधी संघर्ष समिति द्वारा प्रचारित।**

*अरुण प्रिंटर्स, घनसाली रोड, टिहरी से मुद्रित।*

Image 3: TBVSS's Appeal to Sadhus-Sants to Stop the Tehri Dam Construction

**कावड़ियों से अपील**

प्यारे शिव भक्तों,

आप जानते हैं हम अपने पुरखों की शान्ति के लिए तथा उनके प्रति कृतज्ञता प्रकट करने हेतु भागीरथी का पवित्र जल अपने इष्ट देव भगवान शंकर को अर्पण करते हैं। हम धरती माँ का स्पर्श करते हुए बाबा की भक्ति में मस्त बोल बम्ब-बोल बम्ब का जप घोष करते हुए गंगा जल को लाते हैं।

हम नहीं जानते कि आज इसी जल को कितना प्रदूषित किया जा रहा है। जिस जल के प्रति सभी प्राणी इतनी अधिक श्रद्धा भावना रखते हैं। जिस गंगा का ब्रह्मा जी के कमण्डल में निवास था। राजा भागीरथ ने उसे धरती पर उतारने के लिए कठोर तपस्या की, बांबा भोले ने गंगा जी का वेग धरती पर अपनी जटाओं में संभाला और हिमालय से सागर तक भागीरथ गंगा को लेकर गये। आज उसी गंगा मैया को टिहरी बांध में बांधकर और कारखाने लगाकर उसकी अविरल पवित्र धारा को रोका व प्रदूषित किया जा रहा है। क्या इसके प्रति हमारा कोई कर्त्तव्य नहीं? अपने बाबा की आवाज है, भक्तों उठो ! गंगा मैया की सेवा में जुटो ! बाबा की भक्ति तथा गंगा मैया की सेवा का मौका मत छोड़ो।

यह हमारी परीक्षा का समय है। आओ हम गंगा मैया की पवित्रता बनाये रखेन के लिए एक जुट होकर सेवा करे। गंगा की पवित्र धारा को टिहरी बांध या अन्य बांध-बांधकर नहीं रोकने दें तथा गंगा मैया में कोई गन्दगी न डालें। ऐसा संकल्प लेने के लिए महाशिव रात्रि 25 फरवरी को "पूरा महादेव" पर एक बड़ा सम्मेलन होगा जिसमें सभी भाई-बहिन शामिल होवें।

**समय : 25 फरवरी दोपहर 12 बजे से सायं 6 बजे तक**

**"कैसे हो गंगा का रक्षण"**

**सम्मेलन**

दोपहर **12** से सायं **6** बजे तक

*विनीत :*
**शिव कावड़ संघ**
शिव मन्दिर, ग्राम-पौ० डौला
मेरठ (उत्तर-प्रदेश)

*सम्मेलन स्थल :*
**पूरा महादेवजी का मन्दिर**
वाथा बालेनी
जिला मेरठ

Image 4: TBVSS' appeal to *Kawarias*.

the religious people to see the Ganga. The Hindus will not be able to perform the last rites of their ancestors."[88]

Sometimes popular stereotypes of the Muslim community are invoked to distinguish purity from pollutants. At the time of one of his fasts against the dam in 1996, Bahuguna is quoted thus in a report: "Sample the story narrated by Bahuguna at one of his evening ser-

[88] Raturi, *Sri Ganga Jee ka Mahatya*, 1–2.

mons. The environmentalist said Muslim emperor Aurangzeb refused water to his dying father, but 'we Hindus' even offer water to the dead. The analogy by this 'Gandhian' stunned two local Muslim women who silently walked out of the meeting even as the audience, including some VHP activists, burst into an applause."[89] In a conversation he is reported as saying, "The Hindus are praiseworthy. They give water to their dead. Oh Muslim! Are you so cruel that you cannot give water to your own father in jail?"[90] There is also an attempt to widen the political terrain of Hinduism in other ways:

> We should take initiatives for the preservation and beautification of Rameshwaram, Kanchi, Vraja (Mathura-Vrindavan), Kashi and Haridwar, to place an ideal before the entire Hindu community . . . To embrace the Vedic system of water conservation, according to our *tirth* tradition, can only ensure pure and pious water to all the Indians . . . To re-establish the land's productivity, we must immediately implement the Vedic system of undisrupted flow of pious rivers.[91]

### *A Thing to Fear*

Fears over the safety, geology, seismicity, hydrology, and other life and death risks involved in the construction of the dam are based on a comprehensive technical analysis of the project. The literature published by the TBVSS, Sunderlal Bahuguna, and others of this camp is full of references to this aspect. It is said that the mountains on which the Tehri dam is being built are criss-crossed with geological faults, that the region is seismically too active to situate such a large dam, that the dam is not designed to withstand the intensity of earthquakes which may strike the region, that such a high-risk project can place at great risk many cities and their population downstream of the dam: "Should the Tehri dam ever collapse, the 700 billion gallons of water in the reservoir would crash down the river, towards the holy cities of Rishikesh and Haridwar, 50 miles or so away.

[89] Radhika, "Bahuguna Plays the Hindu Card", 7.

[90] Bahuguna (with George James), *In Conversation*, 3.

[91] A joint communique by the Rashtriya Tirth Chetna Sangh and TBVSS, 1996, 1–2.

The two cities have a combined population of 200,000, although on any given day 10,000 or more Hindu pilgrims are there too. Presumably, the flood would kill many people who had not already been killed by the quake itself."[92]

The basis of these fears is marked by a transition in the later period of the anti-dam movement, when there are wild imaginings and paranoia over the dam. Not geology, seismicity, hydrology, or earthquakes, but the Ganga turning into a *jheel* captures the mood. Contact with the dam is contact with the worst social values. Family, morality, and the dignity of women are all now endangered. Fear becomes an environmental metaphor for the propagation of certain images and values. For Swami Chidananda Saraswati, saving the Ganga from the dam is like "saving [it] from Ravan", for "It [the dam] is a big giant, Ravan, who is going to eat us all."[93] There are new reasons for opposition to the dam: "Now the question arises: what if Ganga is turned into an artificial lake? What will be its impact on Ganga *jal*?"[94] To this "The answer is obvious. The purity of Ganga *jal* and her greatness will be destroyed."[95] The tone of the opposition is new and changing: "Will people of India, who chant the victory of Mother Ganga, silently and helplessly, like impotents, watch this horrible act?"[96] A consumer-centred culture will replace Hindu culture: this is yet another fear. "Since ancient times, the Himalayan region has been calling upon peoples' consciousness for spiritual progress and cultural and natural beauty . . . The big dam will add to the growth

[92] Svitil, "The Coming Himalayan Catastrophe", 1–4. Also see, Khattri, "Perceptions of Seismic Hazard", 1–4; *Tehri Bandh? Vastvikta*, a booklet by Delhi Forum, 6–10, n.d.; Sen, *Tehri Dam*, 9–31.

[93] Saraswati, *Ganga Maiya ko Bachana Hai*, 2. Also see Saraswati, *Himalaya ke Paryavan*, 7. Here it says that, since the Himalaya and the Ganga are incarnations of Krishna, the construction of the Tehri dam implies hostility to Krishna.

[94] The fear of the Ganga turning into a lake is repeatedly mentioned by Sunderlal Bahuguna and others. See Bahuguna, "*Tehri Dam: Ab Tak*", 34. Also, BJP Rajya Sabha MP Trilokinath Chaturvedi said this in his speech in parliament. Saklani, *Gangajee ke Pavitra Jal*, 4–5.

[95] Ibid., 14.

[96] Ibid., 15.

of a particular tourism that induces consumerism. This will harm natural beauty and morality. Especially liquor and its attraction will hurt family life and the dignity of women."[97]

## The RSS, the VHP, and the Tehri Dam

A notable feature of the RSS' and VHP's activities in the 1980s and 1990s was their active campaign against the Tehri dam and their subsequent alliance with Bahuguna. The latter also joined a delegation of the VHP against the Tehri dam in early 2000 and at times positively evoked the VHP president Ashok Singhal's pledge to stop the murder of the Ganga by halting the Tehri dam.[98] The campaign was a mixture of Hindu faith and emotion, mythical beliefs and metaphors, concerns of national unity and integrity, constructions of a glorious past and a threatened present, and culminated in a clarion call to all Hindus. Many references from the anti-Tehri dam movement have been culled to create not so much a fearful or threatened as an aggressive Hindu identity. In this version the Himalaya and Ganga's landscapes are haunted not only by an aggressive China but also by a Muslim Pakistan, a communist Russia, and a conspiring West that make war against Hindu Bharat and its culture. Myths about the Holy Mother Ganga take many forms, from the holiest and most motherly to the crisis-ridden maiden crying for help.

For Hindu nationalists the Ganga and the Tehri dam are conscious political constructions which embody beliefs, values, and information, and which influence events, behaviour, and perceptions. Their projections cover a wide field, from simple religious texts to imaginative accounts, from the river in danger to a community and country in danger. This school holds that holiness and the sacred must be obeyed as absolute commands beyond history and ideology. "To understand Ganga, we need such minds and hearts that consider

[97] "*13 April 1995 ko Tehri Garhwal ke Pratinidhiyo ki Baithak Mein Parit Prastav*", *Himalaya: Man and Nature*, vol. XVIII, no. 4, April–June 1995, 36. This worry is expressed in several writings. For example, see Sunderlal Bahuguna, untitled speech in *Ganga Sandesh*, Tehri, 17. Also, Saklani, "*Bhoomika*", 1.

[98] Bahuguna, *Vikas aur Paryavaran*, 33.

mythology more credible than history."[99] Articles on the Ganga's pollution, purification, and cleanliness and the threat to these from the Tehri dam proliferate in various publications of the Hindu Right. "Somebody must tell the Prime Minister of India that it is not enough to smear *bhasma* (ashes) on his forehead to show his religiosity and that he will gain greater status by cleaning up Ganga *mata* (Mother Ganga)."[100] There is a comprehensive detailing of promises made to the agitationists by successive governments and government-appointed committees, and a history of how they have been violated.[101]

When the VHP journeyed through this realm, it marked the anti-dam politics with its usual brand of aggression. Ashok Singhal, leader of the VHP, was militant on the subject:

> To us *Bharatvasis*, Ganga is no river; it is a deity . . . The human monsters that conceived the 'damming' of the holy Ganga have displayed a monumental insensitivity to the very soul of Bharat. The VHP had launched Ganga *yatras* to every village and city of this vast country . . . The intensity of love and faith with which Ganga *jal* was revered during the *yatras* by every son and daughter of this soil transcending all barriers of caste, creed and religion is our precious treasure . . . The enemies of Hindu heritage and Hindu *sanskriti* seem determined to destroy the Ganga in the name of progress, disguised in the garb of the Tehri dam.[102]

The rhetoric was more than sufficiently supplemented by activities on the ground. In 1995 the VHP organised a pilgrimage, the Ekatmata Yatra. Branches of the pilgrimage started at Rameshwaram and Kanyakumari in Tamil Nadu, Pashupatinath in Nepal, Gangasagar in West Bengal, Somnath in Gujarat, Parashuram Kund in Arunachal Pradesh, Amritsar in Punjab, Mahavirji in Rajasthan, and

[99] Mishra, *Desh Dharma aur Sahitya*, 81.

[100] M.V. Kamath, "The Polluted Ganga", *Organiser*, Delhi, 22 September 1996, 6.

[101] Pramod Kumar, "Tehri Dam: Tinkering at the Ganga", *Organiser*, 24 September 1995, 7.

[102] Ashok Singhal, "The Tehri Dam: A Monstrosity that Would Sound the Death-Knell of the Sacred Ganga", *Organiser*, 28 June 1998, 7–8.

Haridwar in Uttar Pradesh, and they all converged in Nagpur, Maharashtra. The aim was to teach Indians the joint importance of Mother India, Mother Cow, and Mother Ganga. The movement's leaders claimed that the pilgrimage would bring unity to a Hindu community that had "fallen asleep"; it would remind Hindus of the importance of the cow for agriculture and of the Ganga for the advent of Hindu civilisation. They linked these goals to their 1984 promise to destroy the mosques in Ayodhya and Kashi and the *idgah* in Mathura. In Haridwar, at the beginning of one part of the Ekatmata Yatra, leaders of the VHP gathered with swamis, shankaracharyas, and members of parliament on Har ki Pauri ghat to inaugurate the event. Afterwards, pilgrims and tourists who had gathered to watch the puja took darshan of these "spiritual" leaders. In the ensuing pujas these leaders spoke more about decimating Islam than saving the Ganga.[103]

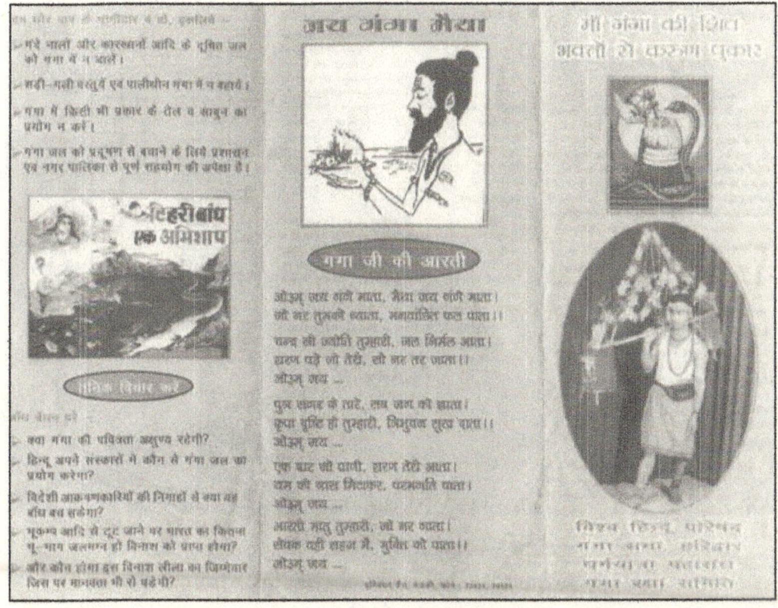


Image 5: A Pamphlet by the VHP, Ganga Sabha Haridwar, Dharmyatra Mahasangh, and Ganga Raksha Samiti Against the Tehri Dam.

[103] Alley, "Separate Domains", 372–3.

The VHP, Bajrang Dal, Ganga Sabha, Dharmayatra Mahasangh, and Ganga Raksha Samiti also carried out a series of programmes in UP, Delhi, and the contiguous states against the Tehri dam, arguing the dam would destroy Hindu pilgrimages and the holy bits of the river where Hindus immersed the ashes of their dead.[104]

### *The VHP, the Ganga Raksha Yatra, and the Tehri Dam*

The VHP's mobilisation against the construction of the Tehri dam reached its peak in the year 2000, when, on 19 October at the Ramlila Grounds in Delhi, hundreds of its activists and sadhus began

Image 6: VHP's Week-Long Protest Against the Dam at Ramlila Grounds, Delhi, October 2000. Photograph by the Author.

[104] With the stated objective of acquainting the people with the dangers of polluting the Ganga and opposing the construction of the Tehri dam, the VHP, Calcutta, organised the Ganga Sanrakshan Jagaran Yatra in the first week of November 1997. The Yatra started off at Calcutta and culminated in

a week-long dharna in makeshift tents. A *sadhvi* called upon the gathering to be prepared for any sacrifice in the name of Mother Ganga: "The Tehri dam is being constructed to imprison the Ganga forever. This is an organised conspiracy to demolish our religion and culture. The way we had to demolish Babri mosque at our own risk, we have to get ready now for the demolition of the Tehri dam."[105] This event had been preceded by a week-long dharna from 15 October 2000 at Tehri Garhwal under the banner of the VHP and its front organisation, the Ganga Raksha Samiti, where Ashok Singhal had threatened to launch an Ayodhya-type movement if the government did not stop construction of the dam. Bahuguna had joined the meeting.[106]

The most ambitious of these activities was the Sri Ganga Raksha Yatra, carried out from 26 to 31 July 2000.[107] A few hundred sadhus arrived at the VIP ghat in Har ki Pauri, Haridwar, carrying their burden of water pots, tridents, and cloth bags as close as possible to the small-built stage. On one side flowed the Ganga. Soon after the arrival of Ashok Singhal and prominent *sants* and *mahants* like Kaushal Kishore Das, Ramvilas Vedanti, Mahamandaleshwar Bhakti Hari, Swami Vishwamitranand, and Kalyananand, Hindu rituals involving worship of the river were done. The six-day-long Sri Ganga Raksha Yatra, from Haridwar to Delhi, via Bahdarabad, Roorkee, Purkajee, Muzaffarnagar, Khatauli, Modipuram, Meerut, and a number of villages and *kasbas* took off from here with slogans such as *Bharat Mata ki Jai, Sri Ram Janmabhoomi ki Jai, Kasi Vishwanath ki Jai*! *Sri Ram Jai Ram Jai Jai Ram*! *Jaikara Hai Veer Bajrange, Har-Har Mahadeo!*

Three well-carved *raths*, carrying an idol of Mother Ganga and an earthen pot of immortal Ganga water called *amrit kalash*, led the

---

Allahabad, UP. For details see, "Ban Construction of Tehri Dam: Ashok Singhal", *Organiser*, 2 November 1997, 8.

[105] Ramlila Grounds, Delhi, 19 October 2000.

[106] Meeting at Tehri, 15 October 2000. See Sharma, "Nature and Nationalism".

[107] I was present throughout the yatra, 26–31 July 2000. See Sharma, "Down with the Dam".

Image 7: Ashok Singhal at Har ki Pauri, Haridwar, 26 July 2000.
Photograph by the Author.

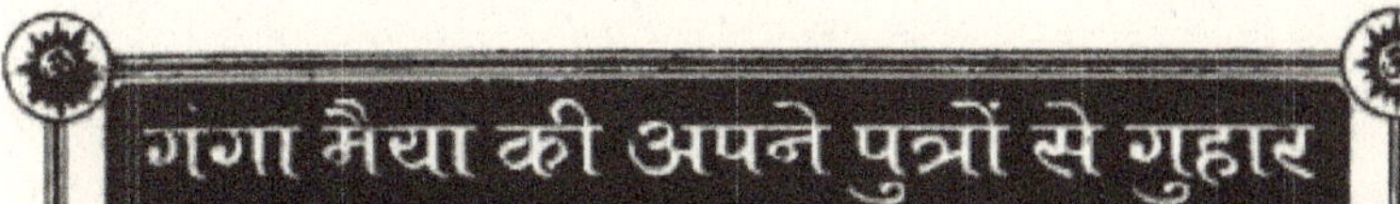

गंगा मैया की अपने पुत्रों से गुहार

मेरे प्यारे पुत्रों !

प्रभु तुम्हें सद्बुद्धि प्रदान करें !

हाँ तो, इस पृथ्वी पर आने से पूर्व सृष्टिकर्ता ने मुझे वचन दिया था कि पृथ्वी पर मेरी रक्षा मेरे भक्त और संत करेंगे आज उसका समय आ गया है।

टिहरी बाँध के रूप में मुझे बंदी बनाया जा रहा है। 42 वर्ग किलोमीटर की बाँध रूपी उस झील में मैं बरसाती पानी के साथ रहने के लिए बाध्य की जाऊँगी। बरसाती जल की मात्रा कितनी होगी, इस तथ्य का आश्वासन आज कोई भी वैज्ञानिक देने को तैयार नहीं। यह भी हो सकता है कि आपके पावन तीर्थ ऋषिकेश और हरिद्वार आदि स्थानों पर मेरा जल मात्र 20 प्रतिशत ही रह जाये और तुम्हारी माँ गंगा की स्वयं को स्वयं ही पावन करने की क्षमता समाप्त हो जायेगी और तब मृत्यु को प्राप्त करने वाले अपने प्रिय जनों के मुख में गंगाजल डालकर उसकी मुक्ति की कामना भी तुम न कर सकोगे क्योंकि वह गंगा जल होगा ही नहीं वह तो 80 प्रतिशत बरसाती पानी होगा।

**एक याद**

इस संकटकाल में मुझे अपने सुपुत्र पं. मदनमोहन मालवीय की बहुत याद आ रही है, जिसने ब्रिटिश शासकों के द्वारा मुझे हरिद्वार में बाँधने के दुस्साहस को अपने अपूर्व साहस से विफल कर दिया था और हरिद्वार हरि का द्वार ही बना रहा।

**लज्जा की बात**

आज मुझे यह कहते लज्जा आ रही है कि तुम स्वतन्त्र हो और मेरे पुत्र होने का दावा भी करते हो। भागीरथ के वंशज और गंगा पुत्र भीष्म होने का तुम्हें गौरव भी प्राप्त है फिर भी तुम्हारे ही सामने कुछ [illegible] के द्वारा देश की समृद्धि और धर्मनिरपेक्षता के नाम पर मुझे बंदी बनाया जा रहा है। धिक्कार है तुम्हारे पौरुषत्व को। मेरे पुत्र [illegible] कलंकित न करो।

**[illegible]बाड़ियों से**

प्रिय शिव एवं गंगा भक्तो! बाँध की त्रासदी तो है ही, मैं तो तुम्हारे कर्मों से दुखी हूँ काश तुमने उपरोक्त सब तथ्यों पर ध्यान दिया होता, मेरे किनारों पर खड़े कारखानों पर एक दृष्टि डाली होती तो मेरे तन को विषैला करने के महापाप से तुम बच जाते।

**सावधान**

मेरे पुत्रों और शत्रुओं सावधान! मैं अपने पुत्रों को उनकी लापरवाही के लिये, शत्रुओं को उनकी दुष्टता के लिए सावधान कर रही हूँ। मैं जानती हूँ कि लापरवाही और दुष्टता में कोई अन्तर नहीं होता दोनों ही विनाश का कारण बनती है। अतः मैं समय रहते सावधान कर रही हूँ कि यदि मैंने अपना विकराल रूप धारण कर लिया तो सर्वनाश निश्चित है। बाँध के टूटने पर हरिद्वार तक 800 फुट तथा मेरठ तक 700 फुट ऊँची मेरी लहरें तुम्हारे घरबार, मठ मन्दिर, गुरुद्वारे सभी कुछ बहा ले जायेंगी। एक प्रकार से प्रलय होकर सभी कुछ समाप्त हो जायेगा। तुम्हारा भूत–भविष्य और वर्तमान सब कुछ नष्ट हो जायेगा। तुम्हारी अपनी पहचान ही नष्ट हो जायेगी क्योंकि भारत और भारतीयों की पहचान मुझसे है मेरे पुत्रों! मुझसे अर्थात् गंगा से।

**एक सद्प्रयास**

मेरे संत पुत्रों ने मेरी व्यथा को समझकर 15 जून एवं 27 जून 2000 को हरिद्वार में संतों की दो विशाल सभाओं में एक संकल्प लिया है कि वे 26 जुलाई को हरिद्वार से एक विराट संत यात्रा निकालेंगे। यह रुड़की, मुजफ्फरनगर, खतौली, मेरठ, गाजियाबाद आदि स्थानों पर जन जागरण हेतु विशाल धर्म सभायें करती हुई दिनांक 31 जुलाई को चाँदनी चौक, दिल्ली में विराट धर्म सम्मेलन में परिवर्तित हो जायेगी। तदुपरांत संतों का एक प्रतिनिधि मण्डल राष्ट्रपति एवं प्रधानमंत्री से मिलेगा।

यह शुभ संदेश मेरे मन में आशा की किरण जगाता है। सजग रहते चेतो मेरे पुत्रों चेतो। ध्यान रहे मैं रही तो तुम रहोगे। अतः मेरा प्रवाह अबाध गति से चलता रहे इसी में सबका कल्याण है। शिवशुभम्!

तुम्हारी माँ गंगा

मुद्रक : [illegible] प्रिन्टिंग प्रेस, रुड़की, फोन : 72424, 79124

Image 8: Pamphlet in the name of Mother Ganga, declaring the yatra from 26 to 31 July, released by the VHP.

caravan of over two-dozen vehicles in the Ganga Raksha Yatra and its regional editions. The route is closed to vehicular traffic in this season, but the caravan took it and passed through thousands of devotee *kanwarias*. The caravan had a huge loudspeaker system that incessantly blared out popular Hindi bhajans. These performances and

Image 9: Idol of Mother Ganga with "Amrit Kalash" at the Ganga Raksha Yatra.
Photograph by the Author.

processes of ritualisation continued all along the yatra, blurring the boundaries between a few hundred VHP *sadhus-sants* primarily from Uttar Pradesh and thousands of pilgrims across the country. The yatra thus broadened its canvas and strengthened its appeal. No wonder Ashok Singhal could say at a meeting in the Sanatam Dharma Prakashchand Girls College, Roorkee: "I am here not to talk about the seismicity of the dam, or the cost-benefit of the project. I am talking about Gangatva. Gangatva is Hindutva. Hindutva is Rashtratva."

The Raksha Yatra for the Holy Hindu Ganga was intended to purvey information, beliefs, and values which would influence events not just pertaining to the environment, but others more local. For Ram Vilas Vedanti, a *mahant* from Ayodhya, the prime minister, Atal Bihari Vajpayee, was like Ram and the *sadhus-sants* in the yatra were like his Lakshman. He addressed a meeting in a village temple at Budhana on 28 July: "It was after Sri Ram's victory over Sri Lanka and his coronation that Lakshman came to worship his brother. The guard informed Lord Ram, but Ram forgot who Lakshman was. After being reminded of his brother, he came down from his throne to receive him. Our Vajpayee will do the same thing with us *sadhus*." It occasionally came down to specifics – a particular state, a territory, and certain societies. In an evening meeting at Roorkee, Singhal made a special and detailed announcement of how the UP chief minister had repealed the UP Religious Act; how he came a long way to Haridwar to reassure the sadhus; how some of them had dared to doubt the integrity of the RSS and decided against participation in the yatra.

Environmental myths continued being created around the Ganga and the Tehri dam, combining facts and fancies. Singhal said on the first day of the yatra: "After the construction of the Tehri dam, the Ganga will become a rainy river. In places of pilgrimage like Haridwar and Rishikesh, the rain water will fill the course of the river Ganga and only 20 per cent will be the original Ganga water. The Ganga will not remain the same and her capacity for self-purification will be finished." In the following days, through the public announcement system of the rath, and from several renowned speakers, we heard of the Ganga turning into a small drain, even a tank. The question was not only "is it true?" but also "whose truth is it?" The myths were portrayed in specific texts of Sri Ram, which provided a ready-made source for the production of a particular national ethos and social metaphors. Swami Chinmayanand, a BJP MP, said: "In his journey through Ganga, Lord Sri Ram decided to bow down before Nishad. He could have made a bridge over it, as he did in the case of a sea." And then added conclusively, "Only those who understand the issue of faith in Ram can understand the faith in Ganga." For Jeeveshwar Mishra, Convenor, Ganga Raksha Yatra, the reservoir of the dam was being built over the place where Hanuman had got life-giving herbs for the dying Lakshman. Another, Vedanti, said in a meeting at Khatauli: "In case of the Tehri dam being damaged, from Gangotri to Gangasagar more than 1000 cities, including Calcutta, Patna, Kanpur, will be drowned completely in 700 feet water." The fear also reflected concern for the many *maths* and ashrams that were making huge sums of money in places of pilgrimage. As Swami Chinmayanand expressed it: "Ganga flow ensures enormous cash flow in our *ashrams* of Haridwar-Rishikesh. If something goes wrong to this flow here, the money flow will dry out."

Ashok Singhal, Kalayanand, Kaushal Kishore and almost everyone else said that the Tehri dam was a conspiracy of the West in general and communist Russia in particular to destroy Hindu culture and India. The logic was simple: first, the dam would be built, and then it would be destroyed either by an earthquake or by a bomb installed by an ISI agent (of Pakistan), thereby wiping out Hindu religious places and people. To stop this conspiracy, the Tehri dam had to be stopped. And the way to stop it recalled the Ram Janmabhoomi Movement and the destruction of the Babri mosque. "The way we decided to demolish the mosque and build a temple there, we are now deciding to stop the dam," announced a local VHP leader in Roorkee. This was supplemented by wall-writings of the Bajrang Dal, here and there, near the locations of meetings. In Roorkee, for example, a graffiti went: *Pukarti hai Maa, Pukarti hai Bharti, Khoon se Tilak Karo, Goliyon se Aarti!* (This is the call of our Mother, the call of Bharat, mark your forehead with blood and worship with bullets). In Bahdarabad: *Jis Desh mein Shastr aur Shaastr ki Puja*

*Hoti Hai, Woh Kabhi Parajit Nahi Hota!* (Where arms and religious scriptures are worshipped, a country is never defeated).

The yatras tried to bind Hindus while sidelining Muslims. In response to a question about the presence of a sizeable Muslim population along the yatra route, and their likely response to a Hinduised campaign, Maha Mandaleshwar Swami Bhakt Hari, a prominent figure of the campaign, said, "Ganga is our mother. How can they accompany us, who do not consider Ganga their mother? They are unworthy, bad sons. Even then, Ganga blesses them equally." Thus, within the VHP campaign, feelings for the river Ganga crystallised around the form of an ethnically and culturally homogeneous, naturally existing nation. Hindu national identity gave the pre-eminent sense of belonging, and environmental politics was made synonymous with protecting elements of that identity. There were repeated and sympathetic references to Sunderlal Bahuguna during the yatra – not a populist attempt to jump on Bahuguna's bandwagon but rather an effort to make common cause with a particular form of environmentalism in India. Thus, Singhal and others of his ilk repeatedly said they had the support of the existing environmental protests and personalities.

The opposition to the Tehri dam was not just a simple disagreement about questions of viability and non-viability, costs and benefits, and displacement or resettlement. Like Chipko, it struck right at the heart of philosophical, cultural, religious, political, and moral debates around contemporary development efforts. However, the increasing references and emphasis by prominent environmental activists and groups to the purity and holiness of the Ganga, the evocation of Hindu myths and ideas of cultural pollution, and the raising of fears and conspiracies became a breeding ground for conservatism. The Hindu Right too moved beyond its familiar extremist milieu and made common cause with Green issues, in the process gaining for itself a certain credibility.[108] In this process the issue of the Tehri dam

108 Sharma, "Saffronizing Green".

became the means for combining sacredness with impulse, the gravity of high politics with the solemnity of daily worship, and nature with nationalism. River water was transformed into a political, moral, and emotional idea.

This collaboration, sometimes inadvertent, between the activities and views of environmental activists and Hindu nationalists raises larger questions on certain facets and ideologies of the Hindu Right and environmental movements in India. It would be a crude simplification to see the VHP's engagement with the issue of a dam – an environmental question – as merely a simple political attempt to harness votes in favour of the BJP. After all, it is not at the level of direct political or electoral success that we count the influence of the VHP, but rather at the level of political-environmental discourse; it was actually their comfort with a stream of environmental discourse that needs to be taken into account. The issues of dam, displacement, and resettlement are, first and foremost, political issues. No doubt important economic, ecological, cultural, legal, administrative and other issues were also involved, but, ultimately, seeing the whole course of events surrounding the Tehri dam, it can be said that political battles and persuasion between the contending parties determined the fate of the project. Though there were divergent interactions and contests, the dominant political discourse of Hindu nationalists was seen to possess the power to absorb, co-opt, and alter the views and values of an environmental movement, which in turn contained the seeds of conservatism. In sum, the myth of the Ganga, having been seen to embody Hindu beliefs, was perfectly deployed by Hindu nationalism to influence large sections of the Hindu masses. The essential purpose was to connect the Ganga to an idea of the Hindu community, and this community to a Hindu nation. Green politics was thereby effectively made Saffron.

# 5

# Environmentalism and Revivalism

## The Vrindavan Forest Revival and Conservation Project in Mathura

THE VRINDAVAN FOREST REVIVAL PROJECT, or the Vrindavan Conservation Project, of the World Wide Fund for Nature (WWF) reveals certain processes of religious revivalism in environmental politics. Here, particular religious symbols and places become embedded with the idea and practice of environmentalism in particular cultural and social settings, which in turn become allied with a sectarian Hindu politics. By focusing on understandings of a place, and of the deity Krishna by environmental organisations and activists in Vrindavan in the 1990s, I look at how, through environmentalism, Hindu politics finds a fertile ground in a region. As we have seen in the earlier chapters, environmentalism within one variety of Hindu community is never simply an expression of established religious or cultural paradigms. It is also a product of the encounter between popular understandings of place, existing environmental narratives and created versions, religious cults, ideas of masculinity, and perspectives deployed to construct and narrate a political vision of the past and history. Although referred through religion and culture, the place and the central figure on whom people are focused (earlier Anna Hazare and Sunderlal Bahuguna; here Lord Krishna) are not static but are historically constructed and open to continuous change and manipulation.

## Vrindavan, Mathura, Krishna: The Background

Vrindavan, a town located in the cultural and linguistic region of Braj, situated on the banks of the river Yamuna in present-day Uttar Pradesh (UP), has a special, mystic place for Hindus in India. The Braj-bhoomi is considered sacred, various locations and places within it having been associated with the activities of Lord Krishna. It is said that "The associations are in fact so strong and specific, that they create a sense of immediacy which blurs the distinctions between myth, legend and history."[1] The *Mathura Gazetteer*, published in 1911, suggests that Vrindavan was constituted as a municipality in 1866. The population was 20,350 in 1872. In 1901 it was 22,717 and, classified by religion, there were 21,088 Hindus, 1409 Muslims, 156 Christians, 40 Jains, and 24 of unspecified religion. There were no manufacturers in the city, but the city had a police station, a post office, a registration office, a dispensary, a primary school and a middle school for boys, and a school for girls. There were within the limits of Vrindavan municipality about 1000 temples and 32 ghats.[2]

The district gazetteer also indicates that most people in Vrindavan generally saw themselves fitting into one of the traditional varna categories: Brahman, Kshatriya, Vaishya, or Shudra. The famous district memoir of Mathura, written by F.S. Growse, also found

> Brinda-ban . . . a rich and prosperous municipality, and for several centuries past one of the most holy places of the Hindus . . . the word Brinda-ban derived from an obvious physical feature, and when first attached to the spot signified no more than the "tulsi grove", *brinda* and *tulsi* being synonymous terms, used indifferently to denote the sacred aromatic herb known to botanists *ocymum sanctum*. But this explanation is far too simple to find favour with the more modern and extravagant school of Vaishnava sectaries.[3]

While detailing the diversity of impact of Vaishnava reformers in Vrindavan, the memoir also marks the particularly deep influence of

[1] Ravindran and Team, *Vrindavan*, 3.

[2] Drake-Brockman, ed. and comp., *Mathura: A Gazetteer*, 241–50.

[3] Growse, *Mathura: A District Memoir*, 184–6.

Chaitanya and Bengali Vaishnavas here.[4] Several religious and literary texts, like the Rigveda and the Vaishnava Puranas – especially the *Harivamsha Vishnu*, *Brahma*, *Padma*, and *Brahmavaivarta Puranas*, and most popularly, *Bhagavata-Purana* – are said to provide a repertoire of sources for the images of Vrindavan and Krishna.[5] It is believed that the Vrindavan area saw the entire sequence of Indian civilisation in northern India, from the Aryan conquerors to the Maurya, Kushan, and Gupta empires, to the Turkish and Afghan invasions, to Mughal dominance and British rule. It also had its share of foreign visitors. Thus, "while Mathura has historically been the political seat of the district that bears its name, at least since the construction of its first temples in the sixteenth century, most inhabitants of the region have considered Vrindavan to be its cultural centre."[6]

Presently, Vrindavan city comes within Mathura district and *tehsil*. It is part of the Mathura assembly and parliamentary constituencies. According to the 2001 census, Vrindavan is spread over 2.25 square kilometres, has 10,086 households with a population of 56,692. The religion-wise break-up of the population is 93.32% (52,906) Hindus, 6.37% (3613) Muslims, 0.03% (15) Sikhs, 0.07% (38) Christians, 0.04% (23) Jains, and 0.02% (10) Buddhists. Among the Hindus, the population of Scheduled Castes is 4967 (8.76%).[7] Most people of Vrindavan make their livelihood either directly or indirectly from the pilgrimage trade. The pilgrimage complex has continued to expand, best exemplified by the big temple of Krishna-Balram constructed by the International Society for Krishna Consciousness (ISKCON) in 1975, whose priests and staffs are mainly American and European devotees.

Mathura is recognised as one of Hinduism's seven sacred cities.

[4] Ibid., 184–98. It is said that Chaitanya's disciples were the first temple builders in Vrindavan. The special tenet of Bengali Vaishnavas is the all-sufficiency of faith in the divine Krishna, such faith being adequately expressed by the mere repetition of his name, without added prayer or devotion. Chaitanya's life and doctrines are recorded in a voluminous Bengali work entitled *Chaitanya Charitamrita*, composed by one of his disciples, Krishna Das.

[5] Brahmacari, *The Complete Guide to Vrndavana*, 7–10.

[6] Brooks, *The Hare Krishnas in India*, 27–55.

[7] Seshagiri, ed., *Encyclopaedia of Cities*, 1439–41.

For more than a millennium and a half before the medieval period, the place had been an important centre simultaneously of three religious systems: the Brahminical, the Jain, and the Buddhist. Subsequently, it became a stronghold of the Krishna-bhakti cult. It is believed that Krishna was born in the city of Mathura and passed his early life in its neighbourhood. Many of the important places in the district are associated with one or other story connected with the Krishna legend.[8] It is called the centre of Vraj, the original region of the cowherd god-cum-epic hero Krishna, whose lively *lilas* enthral and evoke devotion, resulting in the production of voluminous devotional texts and scores of songs through the ages. Exquisite artefacts from Mathura's past – its stone sculptures and terracotta figures, its stupa fragments and temples – excite many lovers of early Indian art.[9]

The historical evidence also points to a much more heterogeneous composition of social groups in Mathura.[10] Pilgrims come here throughout the year to bathe in the Yamuna and visit temples, particularly the one on Krishna's believed birth-site, and the Dwarkadhish temple. The latter is the largest *pusthi marg* temple in the town. It is dedicated to Krishna as Dwarkadhish (Lord of Dwarka). Many come for the annual Braj *chaurasi kos parikrama* (a 160-mile circumambulation around the land of Braj), a 40-day pilgrimage, visiting many of the places where Krishna performed his miraculous *lilas* as a child.[11] It is also a centre of popular Vaishnava sects, such as the Gaudiya Sampradaya, which attracts followers from Bengal. There are in addition a few establishments of the Ramanandi orders, whose members are primarily devotees of Ram.[12] The old part of the city is constructed on a hilly area on the banks of the River Yamuna. It is constituted by a complicated labyrinth of very narrow alleys which lead to ghats. This area of the city was traditionally divided into 110 *mohallas*.[13] Today, the neighbourhoods still remain an important focus of many

[8] Bhatt, ed., *The Encyclopaedic District Gazetteers*, 821–3.
[9] Chattopadhyaya, "Foreword", vii–viii.
[10] Singh, *Mathura*, 120–49.
[11] Lynch, "The Mastram", 99–116.
[12] Burghart, "The Founding of the Ramanandi Sect", 121–9.
[13] Growse, *Mathura Memoir*, 271.

cultural and religious activities. Certain neighbourhoods are largely constituted of Muslims. An estimated 20 per cent of Mathura city's population is Muslim. According to the 2001 census, the total population of Mathura city is 302,770.

The regions of Mathura and Vrindavan have proved to be deeply symbolic. They have served an ideological purpose, imprinting a culturally constructed identity in the post-colonial polity of UP. After Independence, two of the prominent colonial names changed were Ganges to "Ganga" and Muttra to "Mathura". In the course of debates on the reorganisation of UP in the 1950s, it was argued that the elements of unity in the state were far more important than the differences. The holy cities of Ayodhya, Mathura, Vrindavan, Kashi, Haridwar, and Prayag were said to be the repositories of spiritual influence, providing homogeneity and oneness on a higher plane.[14] The overwhelmingly Hindu character of the city makes Mathura an important site for Hindu nationalist leaders. Hindu religious imagery, in particular of Krishna, is deployed to forge and popularise Hindu political agendas and attract support for rallies where "activists publicise Hindu nationalist ideology and organise support for the movement".[15] In 1998, for instance, the shankaracharyas of Dwarka, Badrikashram, and Puri came together for the first time, after a 22-day-long festival at Vrindavan, to call for unifying Hinduism.[16]

Historically, it has become usual to speak of three Krishnas, although each melts into the others. There is Krishna, the chief of the Yadavas, who served as Arjuna's charioteer in the Bharata epic. There is Krishna, the god incarnate, the instructor of Arjuna and, through him, of all mankind, who appears not in the old epic but in the Mahabharata. Then there is Krishna of Gokula, the god brought up among cowherds, the mischievous child, the endearing lover, the eternal paradox of flesh and spirit.[17] There is Krishna the warrior, the struggling hero of the Mahabharata. One of its parts, the Bhagavad Gita, is believed to be the utterance of Krishna himself.[18]

[14] Kudaisya, *Region, Nation, "Heartland"*, 341–99.

[15] McKean, *Divine Enterprise*, 43.

[16] *The Hindu*, 25 November 1998.

[17] Ingalls, "Foreword", v.

[18] Hiltebeitel, "Empire, Invasion, and India's National Epics", 387–421.

It is the image of Krishna as the rigorous, moral, military, and masculine adviser of Arjuna in the Bhagavad Gita that welcomes pilgrims into the Krishnajanmabhoomi complex. This area was constructed in the late 1950s. It stands opposite the Shahi mosque, which was allegedly constructed in the seventeenth century on the ruins of a Krishna nativity temple, the Kesava Deo temple. Hindu nationalist narratives tell the story of how a series of Muslim invaders, concluding with Aurangzeb, demolished the Kesava Deo temple and built a mosque in its place. Hindu nationalists believe that Krishna was born 3500 years ago in a prison cell where his parents were held captive by the tyrannical king Kansa. This cell is supposed to be located under the present mosque. Today, against the rear wall of the mosque is an underground chamber which is said to represent the cell in which Krishna was born.[19]

In 1984 the VHP decided to "liberate" three temple sites in North India: Mathura, Varanasi, and Ayodhya. Although the Sangh Parivar chose to focus its initial efforts on the Ramjanmabhoomi in Ayodhya, it has since taken up the liberation of Krishna's birthplace. In particular, on the yearly occasion of Krishna's birthday celebrations (Janmashtami) and the anniversary of the demolition of the Babri Masjid in Ayodhya, it has organised demonstrations and protests on this issue.[20] The Krishnajanmabhoomi problem has also been raised in pre-election campaigning, in an attempt to mobilise the Yadav community in UP. The BJP employed this strategy in 1996. According to a Hindu activist, "Though Lord Krishna cannot be compared with Lord Ram as a role model of the Hindu way of life, and though (the) Mathura deity does not have as much popular appeal as Ram, we (the VHP) had thought it would generate enthusiasm at least among the Yadav community in UP who consider Krishna as their ancestor."[21]

The 1980s saw the most crucial phase in the transformation of UP politics. Four factors dominated the process of change: the aliena-

[19] Michelutti, *The Vernacularisation of Democracy*, 44–7.

[20] *The Hindustan Times*, 22 August 1995; *Frontline*, 8 September 1995; *The Economic Times*, 20 August 1996; *The Indian Express*, 13 August 1998; *The Hindustan Times*, 15 August 2000.

[21] Ramakrishnan, "Saffron Offensive", 4–16.

tion of rural producers, the discontent of marginal groups in rural society, the growing confidence of the backward castes, and the challenge of communalism. Widespread social and economic disaffection was manifest in two ways: by the decline of the Congress as the principal actor in UP politics; and ineptitude in managing social diversity, increasing the political salience of communal strategies. The social and political changes have been most marked in western UP.[22] The underlying caste and community dynamics of UP in general and western UP in particular has enabled ruling class parties to exploit caste and community appeals to their advantage.[23] From the 1950s on, communal riots have regularly recurred in Mathura city. The city was under curfew in December 1992, August 2000, and March 2002. In all these instances, Muslim–Hindu or Christian–Hindu tensions were the cause. In fact, Hindu nationalist and anti-Muslim rhetoric is present in the everyday life of Mathura's residents.

There is a permanent military command, "the black cat", whose duty is to protect the temple and the mosque twenty-four hours a day.[24] Electorally, throughout the 1990s the BJP was in control of Mathura. They won the 1991, 1996, 1998, and 1999 Lok Sabha elections and dominated in the five Vidhan Sabha constituencies in the 1996 state elections. In several parliamentary and assembly elections after 2000, the BJP started losing, and other parties like the Congress, the Bahujan Samaj Party, and the Rashtriya Lok Dal claimed some seats.

### *Vrindavan and its Environmental Problems*

Present-day Vrindavan is besieged by a number of environmental problems. The population growth of Vrindavan town has not only been fast, its distribution has remained uneven. A large number of pilgrims – two to three million by different estimates – visit it every year. Activities connected with construction, transport, real estate, and the market are widespread and visible. "Welcome to this holy land of

[22] Hasan, "Party Politics and Communal", 59.

[23] Hasan, *Dominance and Mobilisation,* 12–23.

[24] Michelutti, *Vernacularisation of Democracy*, 47.

Lord Krishna. Holy forest plots for sale. Freehold residential complex in very peaceful and tranquil atmosphere", reads the hoarding of a real estate developer in Vrindavan. According to *State of the Environment: Vrindavan*, sponsored by WWF-India, spiralling population densities and poor sanitation and civic facilities, alongside real-estate speculation, remain the root cause of several environmental problems in the city.[25] Temple trusts, ashrams, and land dealers have interests in common: together they own 70 per cent of the urban land. The lack of adequate drinking water is acute in Vrindavan and the area's ground aquifers are polluted daily because pathetic sanitary conditions and inadequate solid-waste disposal leach untreated pathogens into the substrata, contaminating the underground water that is meant to serve the town. Choked sewers, overflowing drains, and garbage dumps are everywhere in sight. The outlets of individual toilets and septic tanks are illegally linked to overflowing sewer lines or directly joined to open drains. The water table is falling by as much as five feet a year, and the quality of the available water is deteriorating. The Yamuna is also heavily polluted by industrial runoff from factories upriver and from sewage, some of which comes from Vrindavan. Raw sewage flows over the *parikrama* pilgrimage path and discharges directly into the Yamuna. The problem is so serious that the Government of India has declared the Yamuna's water unfit for drinking and bathing.[26]

Many have spoken of Vrindavan's environmental problems. One account says that the town has become badly deforested and the area is rapidly turning into a desert such as is to be found just to the west, in Rajasthan. Criticism of this variety has prompted many organisations and individuals to initiate rectificatory programmes in Vrindavan. According to one report, past attempts at protecting the identity and environment of Vrindavan go back to 1880, when the district magistrate, F.S. Growse, tried to restore the ancient Brahma Kund. In 1958 Shri Kanhaiya Lal Gupta, a member of the legislative assembly, made efforts to bring the river back to Vrindavan's ghats but official apathy let him down. In 1969 Shri K.P. Ramanuja Das, a

[25] Singh and Vir, *State of the Environment*, 1–23.
[26] Sullivan, "Theology and Ecology", 252–3.

"saint" from Govardhan, formed the Braj Sanskriti Sanrakshan Samiti (Braj Cultural Conservation Committee). After a few months this became dormant. In 1980 the Sri Vrindavan Swaroputthan Paribhavna (Movement for the Restoration of Vrindavan's Identity) was set up; this too was not able to achieve the desired results. INTACH made a cleansing plan in 1984 but it petered out. The UP government set up the Vraja Bhumi Conservation and Development Committee in 1984 with the chief minister as chairperson and various senior government babus as members. The committee met once in 1985 but has been defunct ever since. In 1985 attempts to hand over the entire solid waste disposal system to Sulabh International were stalled by the Jal Nigam (State Water Corporation). In 1986 AFRO was involved in social forestry and the management of water resources. They gave up because of the apathy of the district authorities. In 1987 a national seminar was organised by a historian, Professor Krishna Dutt Bajpai, on "Sri Krishna in Epochal Vraja and Indian Culture", and its report was published.[27]

## Vrindavan Forest Revival and Conservation Project: An Account

The Vrindavan Forest Revival Project started as a small environmental effort by those who cared for Lord Krishna and his land. It is said that Ranchor Prime, an English member of ISKCON, who was familiar with the situation in Vrindavan, conceived a plan – with Swami Sewak Sharan "Hit Kinkar" of the Movement for Ecological Restoration of Vrindavan and a long-time resident of the area – to plant trees along the eleven-kilometre *parikrama path* that encircles the town. Ranchor Prime prepared a report for the WWF.

Established in 1961, the WWF is one of the largest international conservation organisations, its work focused around biodiversity and habitat conservation.[28] The organisation highlights the ecological value of cultures and religious traditions while funding such projects. It provided initial funding for three years to the Vrindavan

[27] The People's Commission on Environment and Development, *Report of Twenty Fifth Public Hearing*, 4–5.

[28] For details, see WWF website www.panda.org.

project, to run from mid-1991 through mid-1994, some $40,000 per year. ISKCON donated 1.5 acres of land adjacent to the pilgrimage path for a nursery to raise some 10,000 trees of local origin to be planted in the succeeding months.[29]

Ranchor Prime was a major influence from the outset in this Vrindavan Forest Revival Project. He has been an advisor to the WWF on religion and conservation, and a disciple of Bhaktivedanta Swami, taking on the name Ranchor Das. He joined the London Radha Krishna temple during the 1970s and pioneered a Hare Krishna centre in Manchester. He also built and managed a new Radha Krishna temple in the West End of London. The Vrindavan project was formally initiated on 21 November 1991, the festival day of Vrinda Devi, goddess of the local flora. A pledge was taken: "The forest of Vrindavan is the sacred playground of Radha and Krishna. However, we, the people of this region, have cut its tree, polluted its Yamuna River, and spoilt its sacred dust with our rubbish and sewage. I pledge that from now on I will do all within my power to protect Vrindavan from further destruction and to restore it to its original beauty."[30]

Other official accounts available on the rationale of this project complement each other. WWF-India sees Vrindavan and its programme as "A Symbol of Regeneration" and "an effort to involve Hindus in conserving their environment". It adds:

> Although Krishna is the symbol of environmental purity and beauty, his holy land, like many of India's sacred places, has become a symbol of neglect and decline . . . WWF-India wants pilgrims to see Vrindavan's environment restored and cared for, and the original Hindu traditions of cleanliness and respect for nature being practised in this great holy place of India. This will demonstrate that these traditions need not just be something of the past.[31]

Vrindavan's "strategic position" also had an important bearing on its selection: "Vrindavan lies at the focus of Braj, which has been

[29] WWF-India, *Vrindavan Forest (Brochure 1)*; Prime, *Hinduism and Ecology*, 104–18.

[30] WWF-India, *Vrindavan Forest (Brochure 1)*.

[31] Ibid. *(Brochure 2)*.

worshipped for thousands of years as the sacred land of Krishna. Braj is inside the 'golden triangle' between Delhi, Agra, and Jaipur. Mathura, Krishna's birthplace five miles south-west of Vrindavan, is one of India's oldest cities."[32]

The symbol of a *parikrama path* was especially chosen and explained in detail:

> WWF-India has chosen Vrindavan's *parikrama path* as a symbol around which to focus its conservation efforts. Every sacred Hindu site has a *parikrama path*: a pilgrim route that encircles it. The performance of *parikrama*, or walking around a holy place, is one of the most powerful ways of honouring it. Serious pilgrims to Vrindavan all do *parikrama*, usually in groups. Residents sometimes take vows to do *parikrama* every day, every week, every month or on special holy days. Sometimes thousands do it at one time. The eleven-kilometre walk passes mostly through sand and loose earth, and the bare footprints of walkers are left imprinted on the path. Over thousands of years, it has become hallowed ground. It is nothing less than a living temple. However, the twentieth century has taken its toll on the *parikrama path*.[33]

Stage One of the project was to encourage community involvement so that the trees planted would be protected. Stage Two included further planting along the entire pathway and continuing outreach efforts to involve the populace. Assorted eyesores and environmental problems were to be dealt with along the way: "A solution to the problems of Vrindavan's inadequate sewerage system is badly needed: at present untreated sewage discharges into the Yamuna river through unsightly open ditches which pass alongside the parikrama path, adding to the already high degree of pollution in the river and forcing pilgrims to bathe in contaminated water. WWF-India is seeking a solution to this as it spoils the aesthetic image and spiritual atmosphere of Vrindavan."[34]

In 1994 the Vrindavan Forest Revival Project was renamed the Vrindavan Conservation Project. This was not simply a change of name:

[32] Ibid.

[33] Ibid.

[34] Ibid.

from now on the project became more ambitious and wide-ranging. Its project-in-charge in Delhi outlined the change:

> The project was now envisaged to include other religious places of Braj, like Barsana, Nandgaon, Sunrakh, Mathura and its temple, in its area of operation. It was also thought to involve increasingly religious people and their organisations, ashrams and trusts in the work. We realised that the time had come to broadly mobilise peoples' specific faith, leaning and spiritual belief for the protection of the holy place and its environment.[35]

Widening its influence in this phase, the project could now boast of its links with many layers of society. It could also rightly claim to understand the existing socio-political currents. According to a WWF-India brochure:

> A movement has been started successfully by WWF-India. Strong linkages have been formed. An Advisory Group of 11 leading citizens is now advising the project and establishing crucial linkages within Vrindavan's intricate religious, political, and social structure. Local groups such as neighbourhood associations and citizen NGOs such as the Bal Vikas Manch (Child Development Forum) and Vrindavan Vikas Parishad (Vrindavan Development Association) have undertaken joint work programmes and created joint charters to support the project activities. A youth group has helped WWF in promotion campaigns and plantation programmes along with other youth bodies such as the NSS and Scouts. International well-wishers such as "Friends of Vrindavan" (UK) are also very supportive of the programme.[36]

The programmes of the WWF Vrindavan Conservation Project were manifold and widespread, including plantation, nature clubs, community awareness, education, citizen's action, river watch, and protection of sacred groves. It maintained ten nurseries in schools, temples, ashrams, and villages. Trees were planted along the *parikrama path*, on roadsides, in public spaces, ashrams, temples, and schools. Its educational activities ranged from cultural programmes,

[35] Interview with Anup Sharma, project-in-charge in Delhi, Delhi, WWF–India, 12 August 1999. The project officer in Vrindavan coincidentally also has the same name, only spelt a little differently – Anoop Sharma.

[36] WWF–India, *Vrindavan Conservation Project (Brochure)*, Delhi, 1995.

like dramas, folk dances and songs, to poster making, field trips, teacher training seminars, public hearings, and meetings. A variety of community awareness activities like environmental rallies, *raslilas*, environmental dramas, art exhibitions, video shows, and prayer lectures were held.[37] Sacred-grove projects were under way in several places of Vraja like Ral, Baelvan, Basanti, Narakund, and Manasarovar. Simultaneously, cleanliness drives were organised in temple complexes, largely involving the sweepers of the Braj area. In all such activities of the project, along with the WWF, various others, namely the Friends of Vrindavan, ISKCON, Sanskar Bharti, VHP, and Braj Rakshak Sena, were the formal or informal partners at different points of time.

Though it is difficult to assess the impact of the project because of its geographical spread and unevenness, WWF-India reported that from mid 1993 through mid 1994 that "cultural activities by children were an important instrument for influencing parents and community," which incorporated folk dramas on Krishna and Radha's love for the environment.[38] The report went on to state that at the end of three years of work, the programme had successfully "evoked the people's collective religious conscience; previously they had no answer to the drastic decline in their environment, and the quiet abandonment of religious conservation practice is now being slowly reversed."[39] The WWF further argued that it was because of their Vrindavan project that the UP government had decided to include traditional religious views of nature into their official school curriculum.[40]

Thus, in the recently dominant environmental narratives and projects on Vrindavan, the place and its richness were out there, in the heart of North India, awaiting environmental discovery, and would provide an antidote to the poisons of pollution and other forms of degradation. The place and its mythology had been constructed as a hybrid of Braj/Vrindavan/Hindu and provided with a new sacred identity with which to legitimise ecological cleansing. This process

[37] For details, see, Friends of Vrindavan, *1998 Newsletter*, London, 13.

[38] WWF–India, *Reviving the Sacred Forests,* 6.

[39] Ibid., 7.

[40] WWF–India, *Vrindavan Conservation Project (Brochure).*

of transformation and identity layering has, as we shall see, been a conscious and oft-repeated "discovery" and reformulation of a specific past. The attempt has been to arrive at a set of Hindu traditions, symbols, and ways of life that can be used in relation to or towards the modification of existing socio-political realities.

## Hindu Environmental Utopias and Dystopias

The most tangible expression of religious ecology is the veneration of nature. Various dimensions of the natural world are designated sacred and viewed with deep respect on account of their assumed holiness.[41] The concept of sacred groves in India is said to have its roots in prehistoric times, stretching back to the time before the Vedas. This notion of holiness was apparently extended by Vedic migrants to specific species and based on a holistic ecological philosophy. Different offshoots of Hinduism further refined and concretised the concept.[42] A religious or cultural sense of place allowed people to articulate seemingly diverse concerns.[43] In the case of Vrindavan, the imagery of a sacred environment flows from a single historical narrative of a city, cast broadly in the Hindu mould. Simultaneously, these environmental narratives capture some important features of Hindu political identity and community. Such descriptions are constructed and reconstructed in diverse fields of activity, leading to a subtle and constant interplay between sectarian Hindu politics and the environment.

Most environmental narratives on Vrindavan create a utopia which has no real existence. The constructed utopia is very much an imagined space. In this utopian narration, flowers always bloom in

[41] Park, *Sacred Worlds,* 246–85.

[42] Ramakrishnan, "Conserving the Sacred", 239–51. Also see Chandran and Hughes, "The Sacred Groves of South India", 413–27. Vraja's forests are also called sacred groves, and are filled with divine and magical symbols of Krishna. For details, see Dasa, "Protecting Vraja's Sacred", 45–9.

[43] For details, see Hays, *Beauty, Health, and Permanence,* 529. He shows how the sense of a place can be used for different purposes: for the defence of home and community, for the protection of natural environments, and for a pleasant and healthy workplace.

Vrindavan and its groves are inhabited with various kinds of "decorated" deer. The birds here are always chirping, the peacocks dancing, the bees humming, the cuckoos singing five kinds of tune. The lakes are surrounded by green grass and various kinds of lotus flowers bloom in them. The breeze carries the aromatic pollen of these flowers and when particles of water from the waves of the Yamuna, the lakes, and the waterfalls touch the bodies of local inhabitants, they at once experience a cooling effect. The many waterfalls are always merrily pouring, their sound so sweet that it even muffles the cacophony of crickets. The water flows all over, making the forest green and beautiful.[44] Environmental narratives of this saccharine variety also show faith in the sacredness of the totality: all trees, birds, and beasts are pious living entities born in the transcendental abode of Vrindavana to give pleasure to the Lord and His eternal associates, the boy-cowherds.[45] Examples of soothing narratives offering images of complete environmental and spiritual salvation abound in the region.

Creating a place environmentally also simultaneously involves a defence of the customs, traditions, and values of that place. So the references to Vrindavan and Brajmandala cover ground which goes beyond environmental regeneration: in order to understand the significance of local forests, we must understand customs that were prevalent in ancient Braj. Norms practised in ancient times must be outlined so that we truly understand the principles and rules of present-day society.[46] A history comes into being: the Braj region was attacked by outsiders during the Middle Ages. Muslim invaders plundered and ravaged Mathura. As a result, many pilgrim places disappeared and many of the area's norms and traditions passed into oblivion.[47] In the same breath it is concluded that "Vrindaban is a unified symbolic entity with no demarcation between sacred and secular components as found in most other pilgrimage towns. It is a singular sacred space, perceived by pilgrims as the place of Krishna's activities or *lilas*."[48]

[44] Ibid., 1.

[45] Swami, *Appreciating Sri Vrndavana,* 18–19.

[46] Banwari, *Pancavati,* 65–6.

[47] Ibid., 66.

[48] Ibid., 56.

### *The Politics of Place: Power to Imagination*

Environmental practice is sometimes animated less by concern for an all-encompassing whole than by the desire to defend a specific and particularly valued place.[49] It has been argued that the symbol of place politics is the colour green. Place politics is based on the control of land, space, and nature.[50] A certain attachment to special places, sites, landscapes, and environmental projects is an important strategy in the struggle against environmental destruction, displacement, and pollution.

However, what goes unnoticed in the above view is the fact that the appeal to protect a particular place often also contributes to a fresh creation of its specific political identity, and that this new identity may have a colour quite other than green. The historian of place and nature Simon Schama has persuasively argued that inherited landscape myths and memories share two common characteristics: their surprising endurance through time, and their power to shape contemporary meanings and institutions.[51] He shows that landscapes are imagined as unique, and that notions of belonging and identity associated with them are perceived as internal and exclusive. Place politics and its imagery can thus become powerful elements in environmental narratives because they include a propensity to combine geographical belonging with complex stories of extraordinary characters and religious-cultural symbols. The place empowers those who belong to it, those whose being and living are mapped by it.

The imagination of sacred places can also be rendered clouded and ambiguous.[52] It can refer to a supreme or ultimate subject – for

[49] For details, see Torgerson, "Images of Place in Green Politics", 186–203. He argues how in practice the ecological sensibility of the green movement is not only concerned with nature in general but also attuned to a defence of place.

[50] O'Connor, *Natural Causes*, 296.

[51] Schama, *Landscape and Memory*, 15.

[52] Keulartz, "Engineering the Environment", 83–102. He uses these terms to explain the politics of nature development in the Netherlands, which is no longer meant to protect and conserve existing nature but produce new nature.

example, to primeval nature. Such ambivalence can give place imagination a new form of political strength, allowing it to become a *cause célèbre*. It is this ambivalence, and not just the actual programmes and campaigns of afforestation and cleanliness, which have become the core form and function of the Vrindavan Project. For a larger picture of the project and its relationship with sectarian Hindu politics, one needs to look at precisely what meanings the project has endowed to this selected "place". How these connotations have been articulated in the deeper layers of power and politics also requires scrutiny, since it is in these layers that the outlines of the project become clear.

During colonial times Mathura district was known as Muttra. In 1803 it was included within British territory, and in 1832 the city of Mathura became a local administrative and government unit. It was part of the North-West Provinces, Agra Division, and then from 1877 it was part of the United Provinces of Agra and Oudh. In 1950 it became part of the new state of UP. However, in the mythical and religious universe, Vrindavan, Mathura, and the surrounding areas of Braj harbour a unique and different history. Braj refers less to an area or region with clearly defined boundaries, as the country where Krishna grazed his cattle and where all the sacred places associated with his childhood can be located. This mythical and religious perspective is followed up in the continuous efforts of environmentalists towards developing an expanding sacred geography for their conservation project – a region which is governed by the Supreme, a region where the social and political should be based on the *Manusmriti*, a region where the human self has to merge with a divine system. It is here that Vrindavan becomes Brajbhoomi, which can then be transformed into a call for the protection of the centre of ancient Indian culture. The transformation of region into sacred ecological location is accomplished by the mystification and Hinduisation of the region. In many of the descriptions, Vrindavan is equal to Vraj, and Vraj could be anything and everything. Traditionally, it seems to have been believed that Brajmandala was spread over an area of 84 *kosa*, that is, about 168 miles. Even today, this area of 84 *kosa* has great significance, despite the Braj region having spread much beyond these bounds and the population of the people speaking Braj having spread over a much larger area.[53] Imagining and extending the sacred boundaries of Vrindavan and Mathura sometimes involves wonderful narrative deviousness in the construction of an origin myth:

> Information about places like Brajmandala kept travelling from one place to the other through persons engaged in transactions . . . The town of Madurai in Tamilnadu constitutes a very obvious example of this. The town's real name is Madhura. For a short time when there were agitations against Sanskrit and the northern culture, people started saying that the Tamil Madhura had nothing to do with the Mathura of Brajmandala. But slowly these misunderstandings are being clarified . . . The Mathura of Brajmandala is also Madhura and the reason for the change in the nomenclature is that, in the course of time, Madhura was distorted to Mathura just as Tamil Madhura has changed to Madurai. The cultural and spiritual centres of the North like Mathura and Ayodhya have always been regarded and emulated as models, and there is nothing surprising in this. We find Mathura and Ayodhya being established not only in different parts of India but also in different regions of the world.[54]

The Vrindavan Project's relationship with Krishna's birthplace, a site heavily politicised by the Hindu Right, becomes a natural reference, as explained in "Restoring the Forests of Krishna" by Ranchor Prime: "Vrindavan lies at the focus of Vraj, the region where Lord Krishna lived. The whole region has been worshipped for thousands of years. It falls just inside the 'golden triangle', stretching from Delhi south to Agra and west to Jaipur in Rajasthan, which was the setting for many of the events recorded in the Mahabharata, the epic history of ancient India. Mathura, Krishna's birthplace, seven miles southwest of Vrindavan, is one of India's oldest cities."[55] Sewak Sharan, a

[53] WWF–India and Vrindavan Conservation Project, *Invitation*, circulated in Vrindavan, 29 March 1997, 67.

[54] Ibid., 75.

[55] Prime, *Hinduism and Ecology*, 105.

leading participant in the WWF-India project, says: "Sri Vrindavan area is not a small place and a city. It is an ancient place of worship – a temple of worship. For the integrity of Indian spirituality and culture, it is necessary to protect its original nature and environment – the Krishna, the Mathura, the birth place – in its entirety."[56] It is thus that a "new" Vrindavan emerges in the project period. Sewak Sharan further observes:

> The sylvan resort of Radha and Krishna is the foremost centre for understanding the synergy between man, nature and spiritualism. Linked to such deep spiritual and religious traditions, this sacred place is not a township but a *van mandir* (forest-temple). Restoring the splendour of Vrindavan's sacred ecology and its ancient cultural and religious identity is essential in the interests of mankind. Till about 1800 AD, Vrindavan's environment was serene and peaceful.[57]

Along with this synergy, Sewak Sharan adds: "Since childhood, Vrindavan gives a different kind of religious samskar. It is the samskar of being different and unique, being conscious of cleanliness and purity and living harmoniously with nature. We know God and nature are the same. God is behind nature's wisdom and natural wisdom is superior to human wisdom. The basic principle of environment conservation is not to break the cycle of nature."[58]

A place is turned into a central command area, a vital nerve system for its believers. Contested histories are homogenised to become a major reference point for future revival. These acquire an unquestionable authority. Friends of Vrindavan is a registered charity. It has British and Indian trustees, with offices in London and Vrindavan. It works in partnership with the WWF-India and the Alliance of Religions and Conservation. Michael Duffy of this organisation says in

[56] WWF–India, *Brij Vrindavan Sanrakshan* (Protection of Brij Vrindavan), background paper of a conference on the same subject in Vrindavan, 8 April 1998, n.p.

[57] "Sewak Sharan 'Hit Kinkar'", "Conservation of Vrindavan's Identity", in The People's Commission on Environment and Development, *Report of Twenty Fifth Public Hearing*, 3.

[58] Interview with Swami Sewak Sharan in Vrindavan, 30 August 1999.

Vrindavan: "Vrindavan is one of the world's richest, living and pristine culture. It is like Rome and Jerusalem and is, in fact, better than them. It is the homeland of Krishna, the cradle of India's past and the key to her future. It is a focus for understanding sacred values and sacred cultural traditions. It is a place for unconditional love, service and sacrifice."[59] Place imagery also becomes necessary because of its usefulness in combining geographical belonging with varied narratives of human exploits and cultural-political groups. Anoop Sharma of Vrindavan says: "Vrindavan symbolises the close proximity of Hindu religion with environment. Here, Hindu religion, Hindu organisations and the environment can always go together. That is why the Vrindavan Forest Revival Project was inaugurated on *devothan ekadasmi* in 1991 and Rajmata Gayatri Devi of Jaipur *gharana* was called for the inauguration."[60] At the same time: "Indian culture is a Vedic culture and Vedic culture is a forest-based culture. This Vedic culture has been expressed by Krishna through his birth and through various messages in Vrindavan and Braj. Even today, Braj consciousness is the only way to save world environment and to construct human culture."[61]

New political moves too come into play. Srivatsa Goswami of the Sri Chaitanya Prema Sansthana and a leading member of the advisory committee of the WWF project from its beginning, visualises a new power relation flowing from the glory of Vrindavan: "Vrindavan and Krishna show the power of religion. Religion is the dark horse all over the world. Religious power runs supreme over economic power and the power of the bureaucracy. Humanity and its various facets drive through this power. Power and Politics are two legs on which our culture stands. We have to streamline the religious power through many of these works."[62] Such moves to extend the boundaries of Krishna and Vrindavan through the conservation project also suggest that the existing environmental boundaries are not seen as sufficiently

[59] Interview with Michael Duffy of Friends of Vrindavan, in Vrindavan, 28 August 1999.

[60] Interview with Anoop Sharma (in Vrindavan), Project Officer, Vrindavan Conservation Project, 24 August 1999.

[61] Interview with Anup Sharma in Delhi, 12 August 1999.

[62] Interview with Srivatsa Goswami in Vrindavan, 27 August 1999.

## ब्रज रक्षक सेना

चौरासी कोस ब्रजमंडल क्षेत्र के संरक्षण एवं संवर्धन के लिए समर्पित [illegible]

ब्रजवासियों का संगठन

लक्ष्य

1. चौरासी कोस ब्रजमंडल क्षेत्र को श्रीवैंकटेश्वर बालाजी व वैष्णव देवी [illegible] की तरह सुंदर, सुव्यवस्थित व सुविधासंपन्न क्षेत्र बनाने का प्रयास करना।
2. चौरासी कोस ब्रजमंडल क्षेत्र में आने वाली प्राकृतिक व सांस्कृतिक धरोहर का विनाश रोकना और उनके संरक्षण के लिए सार्वजनिक सहयोग से [illegible] तैयार करना।
3. चौरासी कोस ब्रजमंडल क्षेत्र में आपसी रंजिश और फिजूल की हिंसा में लिप्त युवा ऊर्जा को इस क्षेत्र में अव्यवस्था फैलाने वालों के विरुद्ध [illegible] प्रयास करना।
4. चौरासी कोस ब्रजमंडल क्षेत्र के बहुसंख्यक कृषक व [illegible] के लिए सम्मानपूर्ण जीवन जीने योग्य हालात पैदा करना।
5. चौरासी कोस ब्रजमंडल क्षेत्र की युवा शक्ति को सफेदपोश [illegible] बाबूगिरी के मोह से मुक्त करा कर आर्थिक स्वावलंबन के लिए प्रेरित करना और उसका माहौल तैयार करना।
6. ऐसे हालात पैदा करना कि व्यापारी व औद्योगिक वर्ग बिना भय के [illegible] ईमानदारी से जी सकें।
7. चौरासी कोस ब्रजमंडल क्षेत्र के हर वर्ग को यह अहसास दिलाना कि हमारे ब्रजमंडल के हालात सुधारने कोई पाकिस्तानी या चीनी नहीं आएगा [illegible] ही कुछ करना होगा। ताकि हमारी संताने सुख से जी सकें।
8. चौरासी कोस ब्रजमंडल क्षेत्र में निष्ठा से भजन करने वाले साधु [illegible] और वैष्णवों को सताने वालों को सही रास्ते पर लाना।
9. चौरासी कोस ब्रजमंडल क्षेत्र में तीर्थ यात्रा या पर्यटन के लिए आने [illegible] की सुख–सुविधाओं की माकूल व्यवस्था करना। साथ ही उन्हें [illegible] तन, मन और धन से कारसेवा करने के लिए प्रेरित करना।

**सैनिक कौन बन सकता है ?**

हर वह ब्रजवासी जो अपनी मातृभूमि से प्यार करता है। जो अपने दैनिक [illegible] के अतिरिक्त चौरासी कोस ब्रजमंडल क्षेत्र के लिए भी अपनी क्षमता [illegible] शक्ति, बुद्धि व साधन देने को तैयार है। जो सेना के अनुशासन में रह कर [illegible] तैयार है। जो यह मानता है कि कर्म में ही उसका अधिकार है, फल [illegible] नहीं। जो दूसरों को सुधारने के साथ स्वयं भी सुधरने को तैयार है

Image 10: A Pamphlet of Braj Rakshak Sena.

ध्वज : केसरिया ध्वज
समूहगान : नृसिंह आरती
आध्यात्मिक ग्रंथ : भगवत् गीता
शुल्क : कृष्णभक्ति

शपथ : हर सैनिक निम्न शपथ लेगा;

*"मैं स्वेच्छा से ब्रज रक्षक सेना का सैनिक बन रहा हूं। मैं ब्रज रक्षक सेना के उद्देश्यों की प्राप्ति के लिए समर्पित हूं। इन्हें प्राप्त करने के लिए मैं कोई भी त्याग करने को तैयार हूं।*

*मैं पैसे या पद के लालच से विचलित हुए बगैर पूरी निष्ठा से चौरासी कोस ब्रजमंडल क्षेत्र की सेवा करूंगा।*

*मैं सेना के सभी नियमों व अपने सेना नायकों के संगठन संबंधी सभी आदेशों का पालन करूंगा।*

*मैं जाति, धर्म, भाषा, क्षेत्र, लिंग व संप्रदाय के भेद से ऊपर उठकर हर मानव के कल्याण के लिए कार्य करूंगा।*

*मैं अपने जीवन से हर किस्म के नशे, व्यभिचार व जुआखोरी जैसे व्यसनों का (यदि है तो) यथाशीघ्र परित्याग करने का प्रयास करूंगा।*

*यदि अपरिहार्य न हो तो मैं जीव हत्या पर आधारित तामसी भोजन का भी परित्याग करूंगा।*

*मैं भारत की महान् संस्कृति के प्रति आस्थावन रहते हुए अपने जीवन में इसका यथा संभव पालन करूंगा।*

*मैं अपने परिवार व समाज के बुजुर्गों का सम्मान करूंगा।*

*मैं परमपिता परमेश्वर से, इस तपोभूमि पर तप करने वाले ऋषि–मुनियों से व राष्ट्र के प्रति जीवन बलिदान करने वाले शहीदों से विनम्रतापूर्वक अपनी दुर्बलताओं को स्वीकार करता हूं। वे मुझे सिंह सा पौरूष, बगुले सा ध्यान, काक सी चेष्टा, श्वान सी निद्रा व राष्ट्रभक्ति देने की कृपा करें।"*

Image 11: Oath Taken by Members of the Braj Rakshak Sena.

conducive; they need to be re-situated according to the political configurations of a place. This finds resonance in the voices of Hindu sectarian politics: "Vrindavan conservation is not only about Vrindavan, but also about the way we see Mathura, the birthplace of Krishna and the whole region. For us, the conservation is an effort to restore the ancient temples, forests, rivers, and fruits to our Hindu devotees."[63] The VHP decided to constitute a Braj Rakshak Sena in the same period. The area of concern for this Sena became the Chaurasi Kos Brajmandal Chetra. One of its main aims was "to stop the destruction of the environmental and cultural tradition of the region and to mobilise people for the conservation."[64]

### *Krishna as Environmentalist*

Krishna, one of the greatest figures in Hindu mythology, has been much afflicted by the vicissitudes of history.[65] Various texts dealing with him emphasise one or other aspect of his character, these being often the products of widely separated eras. As such, his life story has also assumed a new tinge under the influence of political, social, and religious upheaval.[66] A range of factors lie behind his various transformations and dilations – sectarian rivalries, the impact of Bhakti doctrines, the reworkings of symbolism, mythological assimilations, changed political environments, and upsurges of anti-Brahminism.[67] Viewing the Krishna myth in a colonial context, Sudipta Kaviraj argues that the novelist Bankimchandra Chattopadhyay's Krishna ought to be seen as a Sorelian myth, an ideal condensation of energies, a focus of "national-popular" mobilisation by the unremitting use of metaphors and myths. Here, Krishna is transformed from a lovable popular figure of eroticism, excess, transgression, and playfulness to a classic figure – calm, poised, rational, perfect, irreproachable. From a god of playful villagers and their folk festivals and a god who has helped them sort out small and everyday problems, he has been transformed into the supreme deity of a dependent nation, the god who helped them cross, nullify, reject, and transcend the historic indignity of subjection.[68] Krishna can thus be reinvented quite quickly by the requirements

[63] Interview with Ram Swarup Sharma in Vrindavan, 18 August 1999.

[64] VHP, *Braj Rakshak Sena* (Braj Protection Army), pamphlet distributed in Vrindavan, n.d.

[65] Chaitanya, *The Betrayal of Krishna,* 15–45.

[66] Goswami, *Krsna-Katha,* 20–35.

[67] Goswami, *The Krsna Legend,* 1–8.

[68] Kaviraj, *The Myth of Praxis,* 55–89.

of historical circumstance; an intelligentsia, it is apparent, can manufacture a classic tradition for itself in a matter of a few years when there is an audience willing, receptive, and hungry for a new messiah. What matters in this invention of tradition, far from its non-existence and non-continuity in real history, is its convincing appearance of the contrary – of having always being there.[69]

Of the many descriptions that flow into the Krishna story as it swells over to the environmentalists, we also see an environmentalist Krishna created by romanticised poetic narrations and arguments. These usually follow a simple and uncomplicated formula: environmental motives are added on to his life and deeds. It is stated that Vrindavan and its surroundings resound with the tales of "Sri Krsna". Most of these tales are descriptions of various lilas of "Sri Krsna" amidst nature and have environmental, spiritual, and philosophical undercurrents.[70] This is not a single voice, nor an individual's creation. Through a series of writings and speeches by environmentalists it becomes the collective argument with many outlines and manifestations. Sometimes, at the heart of it stand Sri Krishna and Radha Rani, the eternal pair representing *purusha* and *prakriti*, dual aspects of the primal force that permeates the universe. In their love and dalliance we find a powerful symbol of divine beauty and power, and into their dance we are drawn not only by cowherd youths and maidens but also by cows, birds, rivers, and plants.[71]

At other times, Krishna is Destroyer of Evil and Protector of the Weak. The killing of Kansa is the principal event in projecting this aspect, with other less important events – like Kalia Mardana, Pootana Moksha, and the slaying of the Horse Demon Keshi – are built up through various stages of his life. Each of these events has a specific geographic association with Brajbhoomi, with Mathura, apart from being the place of Krishna's miraculous birth, playing a central role as the venue of the killing of Kansa. This image is complemented by his personality as the *sarathi* (charioteer) who guides people through

[69] Kaviraj, *The Unhappy Consciousness*, 73.

[70] Banwari, *Pancavati*, xv.

[71] Singh, "Foreword", vii.

worldly crises by outlining the canons of relationship between man and the cosmos, and who propounds *dharma yudha* for self-preservation. This aspect of Krishna is developed through the central event of Geethopadesha, which remains at a conceptual, classical, and metaphysical level, and geographically outside Brajbhoomi, in Kurukshetra.[72]

The ideal of an environmental god and his absoluteness is often emphasised. Krishna here represents the supreme ideal who can give unity to religion and tradition, past and present, "the symbol of environmental purity and beauty",[73] the ultimate environmentalist who held up Gowardhan for everyone, the great role model for present times.[74] At the heart of this adoration of an environmentalist Krishna is Krishna's land, the Hindu's Jerusalem and Mecca: "Krishna is the key to the world. His land has a power like Jerusalem and Mecca. Krishna emphasised water harvesting and the way people could adapt to their landscape."[75] He can simultaneously serve as an icon for all time. Srivatsa Goswami says:

> Vrindavan is sending us a message today, a message it has been sending out down the corridors of time for thousands of years. It is that, to keep the flame of environmental conservation alive in human consciousness, we need an icon. Krishna loved the *tamal* tree, He considered *Kadamba* unique. Mango groves were His favourite places. These became a part of the environmental iconography, a part of the message that had gone forth from the groves here for ages and were nurtured by our sages. Vrindavan evolved as a centre of celebration of divine presence and consciousness amidst Nature's splendour.[76]

After the initial environmental celebrations are over, a systematic manipulation of Krishna's figure is apparent: there is a constant

[72] Ravindran and Team, *Vrindavan*, 3.

[73] WWF–India, *Vrindavan Forest Revival (Brochure 2)*.

[74] Interview with Michael Duffy in Vrindavan, 29 August 1999.

[75] Interview with Robyn Beeche of Friends of Vrindavan, in Vrindavan, 27 August 1999.

[76] The People's Commission on Environment and Development, *Report of Twenty Fifth Public Hearing*, 2.

shifting of his centre of activity from that of a lover, to an erotic environmentalist, to a killer-purifier. In Sewak Sharan's view, his environmentalist and heroic-political virtues fuse:

> In ancient times, Krishna came to undo some evils of Brajbhoomi. Kansa and his terror were the greatest evil, as he was the enemy of Braj. Krishna destroyed the evil by environmental methods: by blocking the supply of vegetables, fruits, and milk, and by killing all the messengers of Kansa who came to terrorise the people. We have to again arouse Krishna to eliminate present-day evils; we have to kill the enemies. Krishna also emphasised the importance of physical strength and He never used any weapon other than *lathi*s. To fight out the perpetuators of pollution in Vrindavan, we also need to be physically strong and mentally clean.[77]

Ranchor Prime affirms this ideal: "Krishna overcomes the demon Kaliya, who was poisoning the Yamuna, with the result that trees and animals were dying. Krishna wrestled with the demon and subdued it, saving the region from the effects of poisoned water. This is the image of Krishna as an environmentalist."[78]

Statements of the wars fought by Krishna against Jarasamdh, Srgala, Hamsa, Angas, Vangas, Kalingas, Karusas, and Vatsyas, the weapons he used in these battles – the *cakra* (discus), the bow, the *kaumodki gada* (mace) – and the death of various asuras or demons at his hands appear as regular reference points in the conservation efforts of such environmentalists. The asuras destroyed by Lord Krishna represent wicked people. These evil asuras symbolise the nation's external and internal enemies today as well. Krishna is in this sense our eternal weapon against all enemies, including those in Vrindavan now.[79] This is the forging of a mythical context which explains why the Vrindavan Conservation Project and the WWF-India organised a *kalidahan lila* at Rang Mandir, Vrindavan, on 5 June 1997 – World Environment Day.[80]

[77] Interview with Swami Sewak Sharan in Vrindavan, 30 August 1999.
[78] Dasa, "Reviving the Forests", 31.
[79] Interview with Anoop Sharma in Vrindavan, 24 August 1999.
[80] WWF–India and Vrindavan Conservation Project, *Invitation*.

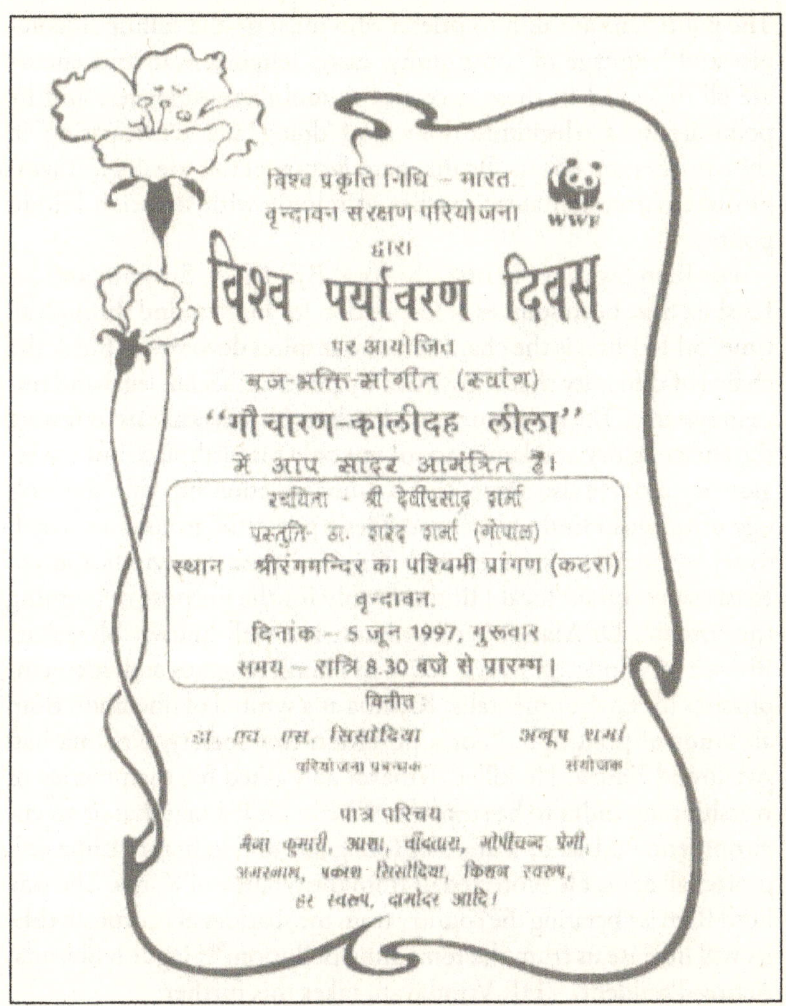


Image 12: Poster for Kalidahan Lila, organised by Vrindavan Conservation Project and WWF-India.

Local Hindu political leaders are enabled by all this to come into the picture and present themselves as committed to the cause of environmental conservation in Vrindavan. Their commitments are couched in a political language centred on Krishna the warrior who needs to be called upon to restore the ancient glory of Hindu society.

The politicians are akin to priests who must do the calling. Ideologies and language of community, caste, religion, war, and enemy are all deployed in these speeches to mobilise audiences, and by political parties to legitimise this way of "doing" and "participating" in the conservation efforts. By the manufacture of this ideological symbiosis, environmentalism meshes seamlessly with sectarian Hindu politics.

For Ram Swarup Sharma, the local BJP MLA, Sri Ram and Sri Krishna have been sources of inspiration for humankind through all time. Sri Krishna is the character who inspires devotees to break the chains of difficulty shackling them by political, social, legal and human systems. The environmental Krishna, he says, calls us to restore the ancient glory and landscape of not only his birthplace but the region beyond. He also argues that Krishna's relationship with the ecology of various Hindu places provides a powerful ground on which to achieve victory over enemies.[81] This environmental vindication of Krishna by certain local Hindus is only for the purpose of blaming the "other". Dr Manoj Mohan Shastri, a well-known Bhagavat-Bhusan in Vrindavan who is active in Hindu religious activities, emphasises the environmentalist Krishna as a symbol of liberation from all kinds of pollution: "For a pollution-free society, Krishna had swallowed Kaliya. He killed Trinavat and asked for the practice of worshipping Indra to be stopped. Whether it is a material or an environmental crisis, or a crisis of foreigners and kafirs, Krishna will protect all of us. He protected us from the tyranny of Kansa. The way Lord Ram is liberating the country from the shackles of misrule, Krishna will liberate us from the remaining pollution."[82] Jagdish Sharma, Acting-President, VHP, Vrindavan, takes this further:

> In Vrindavan, everybody sees Krishna as a great social and political reformer. He was the one who lifted the Govardhan hills, who built a dam with just the flick of a finger. Only an extremely strong person like him could decide to destroy a genealogy. He was an icon whose one call was the last word for the people. Nobody is more prudent than Him; nobody

[81] Interview with Ram Swarup Sharma in Vrindavan, 18 August 1999.
[82] Interview with Dr Manoj Mohan Shastri in Vrindavan, 30 August 1999.

> is as great a warrior as He. His different images are one, and are complementary with each other. There is no contradiction between Krishna as a lover, a warrior, and an environmentalist. Even God Ram had to bear weapons, but Krishna could do whatever He wanted to even without weapons. We need icons like Krishna to solve all the problems of Hindu society in this region. His image of immense power and force is needed today to strike fear in the hearts of opponents.[83]

Krishna here is a continuously conscious construction and reconstruction, instrumental for beliefs, values, and information needed for specific politico-environmental ends. The dominant imagery of his power works primarily through the transformation of meanings, semantic extensions, and analogical (ab)uses. The narratives encompass varied fields of activities and are targeted to influence events, behaviour, and perceptions well beyond any specific environmental arena.

### *Religious and Social Mappings through Environmental Ills*

Given the varying cosmologies and changing symbolisms associated with Vrindavan and Krishna, we can look also at the deployment of environment and conservation as the context through which cultural constructions of "good" and "bad" in terms of gender, family, and social systems are created and recreated. The environment and conservation project in Vrindavan draws on and brings together two sets of overlapping concepts: environmental "goods" and "bads", and their social mappings and performances.

Caste comes into the picture in relation to the sewage system in Vrindavan. It is said that before 1970 the traditional latrine method was in vogue here, by which the waste was supposedly recycled into the fields as fertiliser. It goes without saying that to make this possible Dalits had to carry "night soil" (human excreta) on their heads and perform other related cleaning-up jobs. The modern sewage system was designed after 1970 to treat the sewage – so that it could

[83] Interview with Jagdish Sharma, Acting President, VHP, in Vrindavan, 2 August 1999.

be safely dumped into the River Yamuna. However, the main line, which would have connected toilets all over the town, was never completed and the treatment plant never saw the light of day. Consequently, sewage is everywhere in the city, overflowing into the streets, gathering in low spots, dumped into the river. Ranchor Prime argues that the traditional method of waste disposal should return. When making his case, he goes to the *Manusmriti*: "One should not cause urine, stool or mucus to enter water. Anything mixed with these unholy substances, or with blood or poison, should never be thrown into water."[84] He accuses Indians of becoming enamoured with new Western technology and applying the technology inappropriately, in the process forgetting their ancient and time-tested technology appropriate to the situation and therefore ignoring venerable injunctions such as those found in *Manusmriti*.[85] He points out underlying causes for the widespread abandoning of traditional Hindu values and technology, citing centuries of Muslim and British rule as detrimental to traditional Hindu culture and practice:

> For 800 years Muslims ruled from Delhi. The whole surrounding region, including Vrindavan, bears the deep impression of this rule, which did nothing to foster Hindu culture, and at times bitterly suppressed it. Then the British, with their more subtle form of tyranny, made Hindus second-class citizens in their own land. The effect of this subjugation has been to drain the enterprising spirit, the self-determination and inner resourcefulness from a people who had their affairs run for them by outsiders for longer than most nations or cultures have endured.[86]

Meat-eating is identified as a serious ecological problem. And again the *Manusmriti* is cited as prohibiting the eating of meat because the butcher, vendor, cook, and consumer are all murderers and have to reap bad karmic consequences.[87]

In a background paper prepared by the WWF for a workshop to analyse and plan Vrindavan's conservation, it was said that Radha

[84] Prime, *Hinduism and Ecology*, 109–12.
[85] Ibid.
[86] Ibid., 112.
[87] Ibid., 102.

and Krishna fought against urban culture and established a human–nature harmony in the form of a village system. From their childhood, they launched a campaign for the re-establishment of spiritual, natural, social, and economic values in society.[88] These values are

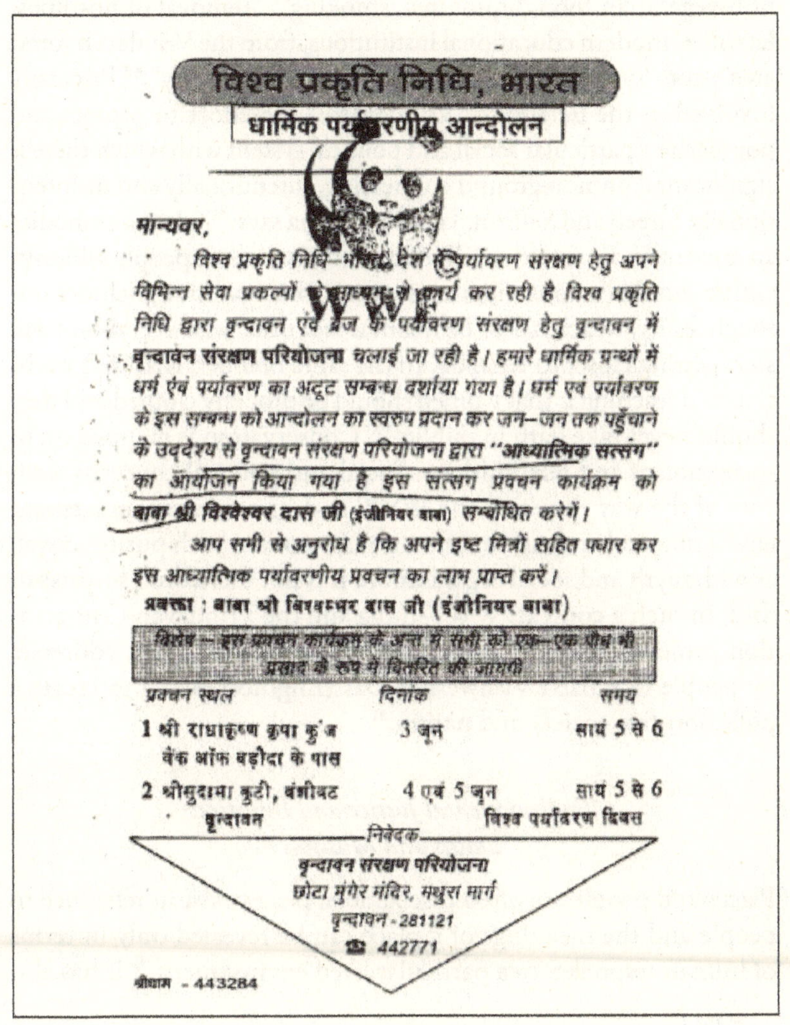

विश्व प्रकृति निधि, भारत

धार्मिक पर्यावरणीय आन्दोलन

WWF

मान्यवर,

विश्व प्रकृति निधि–भारत, देश में पर्यावरण संरक्षण हेतु अपने विभिन्न सेवा प्रकल्पों के माध्यम से कार्य कर रही है विश्व प्रकृति निधि द्वारा वृन्दावन एंवं ब्रज के पर्यावरण संरक्षण हेतु वृन्दावन में **वृन्दावन संरक्षण परियोजना** चलाई जा रही है। हमारे धार्मिक ग्रन्थों में धर्म एंवं पर्यावरण का अटूट सम्बन्ध दर्शाया गया है। धर्म एवं पर्यावरण के इस सम्बन्ध को आन्दोलन का स्वरुप प्रदान कर जन–जन तक पहुँचाने के उद्देश्य से वृन्दावन संरक्षण परियोजना द्वारा **"आध्यात्मिक सत्संग"** का आयोजन किया गया है इस सत्सग प्रवचन कार्यक्रम को **बाबा श्री विश्वेश्वर दास जी** (इंजीनियर बाबा) सम्बोधित करेगें।

आप सभी से अनुरोध है कि अपने इष्ट मित्रों सहित पधार कर इस आध्यात्मिक पर्यावरणीय प्रवचन का लाभ प्राप्त करें।

**प्रवक्ता : बाबा श्री विश्वम्भर दास जी (इंजीनियर बाबा)**

विशेष – इस प्रवचन कार्यक्रम के अन्त में सभी को एक–एक पौधा भी प्रसाद के रूप में वितरित की जायेगी

| प्रवचन स्थल | दिनांक | समय |
|---|---|---|
| 1 श्री राधाकृष्ण कृपा कुंज<br>बैंक ऑफ बड़ौदा के पास | 3 जून | सायं 5 से 6 |
| 2 श्रीसुदामा कुटी, वंशीवट<br>वृन्दावन | 4 एवं 5 जून | सायं 5 से 6<br>विश्व पर्यावरण दिवस |

निवेदक

वृन्दावन संरक्षण परियोजना
छोटा मुंगेर मंदिर, मथुरा मार्ग
वृन्दावन - 281121
☎ 442771

श्रीधाम - 443284

Image 13: *Satsang* Organised by WWF-India.

[88] WWF–India, *Brij Vrindavan Sanrakshan* (Brij Vrindavan Conservation).

also listed in the background paper and include the following: "pure married life is the basis of a strong and organised human society"; and "separate lust from love making". The solutions suggested to various problems include "restriction on electricity"; "total ban on non-vegetarian food, liquor, tea, smoking"; "removal of hospitals, factories, modern educational institutions, from the Vrindavan forest area"; and "system to guarantee cleanliness and purity".[89] Primarily involved in the defence of Vrindavan is the effort to protect and popularise a particular social and political system with which there is significant common ground connecting, intentionally and unintentionally, Green and Saffron. Jagdish Sharma says: "Krishna embodies an ancient Vedic tradition. That tradition is to serve people selflessly, which should be continued at any cost. That tradition includes untouchability, which has to be maintained; otherwise everybody will start getting closer to Krishna. In the same manner, Krishna's tradition and teaching is that women should be properly clothed and they should never take bath in public."[90] Conservation is mapped on to social norms and relationships. Social and political concerns seem part of the way in which the WWF and its associates understand environmental and cultural situations, resonant with purity, as well as with myth and social organisation. It is not therefore a surprise to find, in such a context, WWF-India and the Vrindavan Conservation project frequently organising *satsang* and religious addresses by people like Baba Vishweshar Das (Engineer Baba) to create a pollution-free society and nation.[91]

### *Environmental Justice and Injustice: Dalits and Muslims*

Places and people are often inseparable: places exist in reference to people and the meanings of a place can be revealed only in terms of human responses to a particular lived environment.[92] It has also

[89] Ibid.

[90] Interview with Jagdish Sharma in Vrindavan, 2 August 1999.

[91] WWF–India and Vrindavan Conservation Project, *Invitation.*

[92] Violich, "Towards Revealing the Sense", 113.

been said that the use of the word "place" highlights concerns about the interaction between people and environments which creates particular places.[93] Two points here complement each other: first, that places are created; and, second, that they are created through an interaction between people and environments.

Vrindavan has sizeable Dalit and Muslim populations even in the area covered by the WWF project. The Dalits here are mainly Chamar, Balmiki, Kori, Khatik, and Dhobi. They too are inseparable from the place and the project. If we wish to accept that they also have a sense of place, with a capacity for memory, experience, intentionality, and a sense of attachment to and identification with cultural values, we have to be prepared for an entirely different picture of the Vrindavan project – their picture.

It has been claimed that although varna categories are recognised in Vrindavan, they are not the primary concerns of the city. Vrindavan has not been seen as a place where normal social considerations are in effect, and perceptions of caste and hierarchy are stated to considerably differ here from what is generally accepted within the Indian situation. It is the opinion of the majority of Vrindavan residents, including most Brahmins, that a person's status in the town can properly be determined only by the quality of his devotion to Krishna. In effect, broadly, the structure of hierarchy in Vrindavan is not based upon a Brahmin/non-Brahmin opposition, but rather on a devotee/non-devotee one.[94]

However, at the heart of Vrindavan lies Kishorepura Valmiki *basti*, where Chowdhary Bhagwan Das Balmiki's family has been living for three generations. He claims that the famous Banke Bihari Mandir was built by the labour of his ancestors:

> Since my childhood, I never ever felt anything special about Krishna and his land. It is being said that His supposed birth in Vrindavan itself has a special significance. However, how is this meaningful if we continue to be called *bhangi*, *chura* or *balmiki*. We have no role in the creation of Krishna and any related activities. We are only involved in

[93] The journal *Ethics, Place and Environment*, University of London, UK, explains the use of the word "place" in its title in this way.

[94] Brooks, *Hare Krishnas in India*, 68–71.

cleaning up the dirt here and that gives us our bread. We are not considered a part of Hindu society, we cannot enter the temples, we cannot put up our kiosks to sell foodstuffs, we are not allowed to open juice shops, we cannot even rent out a place.[95]

Bhagwan was a part of the cleanliness and conservation drive of Friends of Vrindavan, a partner organisation of the WWF. He narrates his experience:

The cleanliness drive was launched at six temple points. The 100-metre diameter of Banke Bihari Mandir was the starting place. However, the priests and the Krishna *bhakts* there bitterly objected to our presence even 100 metres away, as according to them we *bhangis* were polluting the people, their ways and the *mandir*. The drive was stopped after their objection, when they started quarrelling.[96] In this environment, we do not want to live with Krishna, never mind the conservation in His name. Our condition is pathetic here. Wherever we get love and livelihood, we are ready to go there.[97]

Charandas Jatav claims to be an *asli brajwasi* (authentic resident of Braj) as his family's seventh generation is at present in Vrindavan. His family received some temple land to build their house a long time ago. He says: "We do not belong to Krishna. Thus, we do not believe in Him. We have this painful experience that however much we live with feelings of love and cooperation, we can never be incorporated into the Krishna fold. Brajbhoomi is for Brahmins. Neither forest destruction nor pollution, but the three Bs – Brahmins, Babajees and Bandars – are the real culprits for the problems of Vrindavan."[98] Charandas has seen the WWF working near

[95] Interview with Chowdhary Bhagwan Das Balmiki in Vrindavan, 18 August 1999. In the course of twenty interviews with Dalits in Kishorepura, Khusurpura, Gandhinagar, Ganj Mohalla, Bagh Mohalla, and Gopinath Mohalla of Vrindavan, I could gather similar feelings with varied expressions and examples.

[96] For details, see *Amar Ujala*, Agra, 27 June 1997, which reported that the Valmikis were assaulted while they were cleaning the area near the temple.

[97] Interview with Chowdhary Bhagwan Das Balmiki in Vrindavan, 18 August 1999.

[98] Interview with Charandas Jatav in Vrindavan, 18 August 1999.

his colony. He continues: "Plantation came here, but soon the plants dried up as there was nobody to water them. We were never a part of the Vrindavan Conservation Programme, as we were never considered a part of Krishna. We want to be away from the Krishna land, and are ready to live in the forests if that can give us a livelihood with dignity."[99] Hari Mohan Balmiki narrates a different experience: "After taking a bath, when I pray to the sun, I often remember Krishna, along with Brahma, Vishnu and Mahesh. I am also human. After work, I would also like to go to a Krishna temple and listen to Krishna *bhajans*, but I cannot do this. Even when I take a proper bath and dress up in clean clothes, I am not allowed in the temple and the *parikrama* area. I am completely defeated here."[100]

It thus appears that far from being a binding factor in Vrindavan conservation, Krishna seems an entity that is claimed by a few to the exclusion of many. In fact, Krishna is at one level one of the symbols of discord and resistance, the adoption of his image leading to the exclusion of certain groups from the conservation project. The Muslims of Vrindavan voice a similar feeling. Noor Mohammad, an ex-corporator, says: "We have been living in this Krishna area for the last five generations. Krishna has been always a living factor here, but never a factor to rally around a certain section of the community for a specific purpose. The use of Krishna for the forest revival has no appeal to us and, in any case, that was never the intention. We are completely excluded."[101] Another Muslim resident of Vrindavan, Saiyed Ahmed, says: "Krishna has come here in many forms in the aftermath of the Ram Janmabhoomi movement. The sense of belonging to Krishna suddenly gets exposed to its connections to a particular politics. In this situation, how can one believe in the new, coming imageries?"[102] And it is not only the Dalits and the Muslims who feel excluded: some of the people associated with the project assume that these same communities are a threat to the environment, and therefore lack what might be called "ecological legitimacy".[103]

[99] Ibid.

[100] Interview with Hari Mohan Balmiki in Vrindavan, 19 August 1999.

[101] Interview with Noor Mohammad in Vrindavan, 10 August 1999.

[102] Interview with Saiyed Ahmed in Vrindavan, 10 August 1999.

[103] Ecological legitimacy is associated with environmental stewardship or

Thus, it is said: "Muslims are also one of the main sources of pollution and environmental degradation of Vrindavan. They kill cows. They produce so much of waste in their living. They cross their boundaries."[104]

On a different plane, Dalits are largely seen as "performing objects" in a romanticised way, located in a place to do certain duties. One environmentalist says: "*Sewa* and *sewak*, these two things are understood by everybody in Brajbhoomi. Unconditional love and sacrifice are a hallmark here. The only people who are the true *sewaks* are Balmikis and in our environmental drive, we are trying to demonstrate this on a wider scale."[105] One gets an echo of this in Rakesh Das, a Balmiki, and many other Balmikis who work with Michael Duffy in Friends of Vrindavan. Says 32-year-old Rakesh: "We are *sewaks*. Service – cleaning up the dirt – is our sacred duty, so that Krishnabhakts do not feel the dirt. We try hard to be faithful to our service. Wherever the bhakts put their feet, we wish to clean that area."[106]

Ecological legitimacy may be drawn from different sources and crafted in various ways. One source is to see one's own community and religion as inherently more sensitive to nature than others, whether or not this is in fact true. Thus the Congress politician Karan Singh, in his inaugural address at the 25th Public Hearing on Environment and Development in Vrindavan, on 16 September 1995, said: "The Hindu tradition of reverence for nature and all forms of life represents a powerful force that needs to be revived in our contemporary context."[107] In similar vein, Sri Chaitanya Prema Sansthana, WWF-India, and the Alliance of Religions and Conservation, UK, organised a national programme "to elevate and maintain the contributions of faiths on issues concerning land and conserva-

---

the practice of caring for the land in a sustainable manner. For a detailed discussion, see Zimmerer, "Social Erosion and Social (Dis)courses".

[104] Interview with Jagdish Sharma in Vrindavan, 2 August 1999.

[105] Interview with Michael Duffy in Vrindavan, 28 August 1999.

[106] Interview with Rakesh Das in Vrindavan, 10 August 1999.

[107] The People's Commission on Environment and Development, *Report of Twenty Fifth Public Hearing*, 1.

tion."[108] Such discourses take further shape, in that they not only regard the characteristics of Hindus as unitary, fixed, and eternal, but use these to characterise the "other". Devendra Sharma, Project Officer (Education), WWF-India, claims: "When we tried to integrate religion and environment in Vrindavan, we found that the Hindus had a big heart. They were willing to accommodate any and everything, whereas this was not observed in the other community. A Muslim in Vrindavan will never go to the Banke Bihari Mandir, but a Hindu will go to a mosque."[109]

In the Hindu mythical and cultural universe, Krishna, Vrindavan, Mathura, and the surrounding areas have a unique place. A complex history has been developing through the dynamics of culture, religion, democracy, politics, and the colonial and post-colonial state. This background contributes a great deal to the environmental project in Vrindavan. Environmentalists have used a ready treasure of cultural resources to facilitate their ideas and actions: they understand, interpret, and manipulate the place and the religion through the lens of a particular Hindu resource and the practices of caste and hierarchy. The emphasis on particular religious cults and symbols, Hindu pasts and traditions, Muslim invaders and British rule seem to have had an affinity with dominant understandings of Vrindavan's culture, community, and past. The character of Krishna and the place of Mathura and Vrindavan, with its elastic and borderless ritual status, have helped these environmentalists to define and redefine their works and words according to their Hindu and elite character. They have, on the one hand, transformed diversified understandings, knowledge, myths, epics, and religious histories into a fixed story, using them to promote a homogeneous and exclusive Hindu community. On the other hand, they have used and manipulated at their convenience the various faces of Krishna, offered by religious texts, cultural beliefs, and contemporary needs. By closely linking Krishna and Mathura to wider political contexts,

[108] Sri Chaitanya Prema Sansthana, *Invitation Letter*, 27 July 1997.

[109] Interview with Devendra Sharma in Vrindavan, 29 August 1999.

environmental rhetoric here has shown an affinity to contemporary Hindu political interests, often creating a common language.

Hindu sectarian politics has had an equally important effect on environmental religious discourse. Its politics has affected the ways in which religious and ecological cults are represented, places and regions identified, and programmes developed. Some of these changes are internalised by the environmental groups in their everyday life. The process of religious revivalism through environmentalism and vice-versa seamlessly emphasises upper-caste Hindu traditions of cleanliness and purity, Vedic culture, sacredness, faith and samskar, the *Manusmriti*, the varna system, the strong and organised family, and "pure" married life. Its language stresses the idioms of mandir, war, enemies, and Muslim invaders. In the Vrindavan environmental project Green and Saffron seem to have found a common language, symbolic meanings, and place affinities.

## Postscript

In October 2023 I travelled to Vrindavan after more than twenty years. The place had a significant city look: new, big, and modern buildings; wider roads, now with concrete; thriving markets; a large number of restaurants and hotels; travel and tour shops; polluting public and private vehicles; and a bustling human population and animals, especially cows and dogs, all around. The place was equally vibrant with sadhus, temples, worship, devotional songs on Radha–Krishna magnified through mikes and loudspeakers, and Hindu devotees on the roads and lanes, either going to or coming back from temples. The famous temples and religious centres, such as the Banke Bihari and ISKCON temples, were heavily packed with visitors, devotees, and tourists. The temples were surrounded by makeshift shops, retailers, and agents selling religious goods, all promising to make worship swift and easy.

### *Vrindavan and Its Environmental Problems*

During my fieldwork everyone spoke of the acute and escalating environmental problems in Vrindavan, which had also led to various conflicts and interventions by the High Court and National Green Tribunals. The city's narratives always revolved around the prevalence of Radha–Krishna in every particle of Vrindavan, but the everyday life of the place was marked at every turn by rampant "illegality", "encroachment and construction", and "commercialisation". While sitting and interacting in the office of *Vrindavan Today*,[110] an initiative launched in 2010 to support activities aimed at preserving the Braj–Vrindavan ecology, I was provided with documents and publications explaining some of the major present-day environmental problems. They described how the overall forest cover in Mathura district is on the decline. Mathura district boasts nearly 1400 hectares of reserved and protected forest land. However, hundreds of old trees have been cut down for infrastructure projects. For instance, trees were felled to widen the Mathura–Vrindavan and Chhatikara–Vrindavan roads and to reinforce the Parikrama Marg. These actions were even contested in the Allahabad High Court and the Supreme Court. In fact, on the state government's plea, the Supreme Court granted permission to fell 318 trees for the expansion of the Mathura–Vrindavan Road. Compensatory tree plantation efforts are struggling, both in terms of the survival rates of the newly planted trees and the remoteness of the forest locations where they are typically planted, thus failing to effectively sustain Vrindavan's green cover.

Vrindavan faces a severe water shortage every year, to the extent that water tankers must be deployed in the city each summer. The depletion of groundwater reserves in Vrindavan is alarming and largely attributed to the sheet piling carried out in the Yamuna River as part of the Yamuna Riverfront Development Project. The 30-metre thick metal sheet has separated the ground from the river, making it challenging for the groundwater table to replenish itself. The Yamuna River is highly polluted, with the Kosi drain carrying substantial sewage into the river still active, in addition to over thirty-five smaller drains. This problem intensifies during the rainy season when the drains overflow. The *kunds* (ponds) in Vrindavan are in a state of

[110] I visited the office of *Vrindavan Today* in Vrindavan on 11 October 2023.

disrepair. I visited, for instance, the purportedly sacred Govind Kund adjacent to the Garud Govind temple – it has been transformed into a veritable dumping ground, stripped of water and overwhelmed by unsightly mounds of waste and sewage, exuding a noxious odour. I was told that in 2021 Vrindavan's air quality deteriorated to such an extent that it earned the dubious distinction of being the most polluted city in Uttar Pradesh and one of the ten most polluted cities in the country. The primary culprits of chronic air pollution are vehicular emissions, waste disposal, and the burning of agricultural stubble.

Rampant encroachment and construction were evident on the Yamuna riverbed, along with cemented platforms and concretisation of the riverfronts which have significantly reduced the width of the Yamuna and dried it up. According to *Vrindavan Today*, "In reality, river front development schemes are more about money and real estate than river restoration. The river banks are heavily concretised to provide spaces for social and public infrastructure such as car parking, plaza, walkways, restaurants, theme parks and gardens."[111] As a result, due to petitions filed by activists and with support from *Vrindavan Today*, the Allahabad High Court and the National Green Tribunal have halted the construction of the Ardha Chandrakar Pul (half-circular bridge) and issued orders for the deconcretisation of the Yamuna plains and the trees there.

### *Vrindavan Forest Revival and Conservation Project*

The Vrindavan Forest Revival and Conservation Project, launched by WWF-India, is no longer operational. In the early 2000s the project was concluded, and all project activities terminated. I was unable to find any WWF-India representatives in Vrindavan. Nevertheless, during a candid conversation with Jagannath Poddar,[112] who was actively involved with the project at the time and now serves as the Director of Friends of Vrindavan (a former project partner) and

[111] Poddar, *Vrindavan Today,* 4.
[112] Interview with Jagannath Poddar in Vrindavan, 11 October 2023.

*Vrindavan Today*, I gained some insights into the conclusion of the WWF project. The project had significant components that aimed to promote the Hindu religion with ecological sensibility by reimagining Krishna as an environmentalist and depicting Vrindavan as a sacred realm encompassing forests, wildlife, rivers, ponds, and pious Hindus. Nevertheless, within the politically charged situation of the state and the nation, this religious ecology had adopted communal and conservative forms, leading to the organisation of numerous "negative" activities. The project had local partner organisations tasked with two primary activities: making the city clean and undertaking afforestation works. Initially, both activities were carried out successfully. However, the areas that were cleaned quickly became dirty again, and the afforestation initiative was ultimately unsuccessful due to a lack of local participation. The project had multiple points of conflict within it, encompassing disputes between outside experts and professionals and local partners and activists, conflicts between religious and Hindutva organisations, and tensions between sadhus and sanitation workers. These differences also led to disruptions in the execution of periodic activities, ultimately contributing to the project's demise. However, in my interactions with various individuals in Vrindavan currently involved in social, political, and environmental initiatives, I could distinctly observe certain aspects of the interrelationship between the Green and Saffron politics stemming from the WWF project.

### *The Politics of Place and Krishna*

Vrindavan reverberated with the intensity of the temple–mosque dispute, which revolves around Mathura's Krishna Janmabhoomi. Since 2014, and especially after the Supreme Court's verdict in the Babri Masjid–Ram Janmabhoomi dispute in 2019, the RSS family, including the chief minister of Uttar Pradesh, Yogi Adityanath, have directed their attention towards this site and the specific controversy. This renewed focus has infused the cultural, environmental, and social essence of the location with fresh energy, often aligning directly or indirectly with the RSS' agenda.

During interviews with several individuals in Vrindavan, Mathura, and Gokul I encountered positive narratives about recent legal and political developments aimed at reclaiming the birthplace of Lord Krishna, the Krishna Janmabhoomi temple complex, from the occupation of the Shahi Idgah mosque. I was informed that since 2020 at least a dozen cases have been filed in the courts of Mathura regarding the Sri Krishna Janmabhoomi issue, with the intention of removing the mosque. One of the multiple petitions submitted to the court has requested excavation of the disputed site under the court's supervision. Another application has sought the involvement of the Archaeological Survey of India team to investigate the existence of "Hindu temple signs" within the Shahi Idgah Masjid. Yet another petition has asked the court to issue directives for the installation of CCTV cameras inside the mosque to protect the "temple signs" present there. Furthermore, the court has been urged to pass an order to restrict entry into the Shahi Idgah mosque, permitting only those who reside on its premises.

Mahanidhi Madan Gopal Das, who has had a long association with Vrindavan and has also published extensively, characterises the place as possessing "unique and unlimited powers." He asserts that anyone who "glorifies", "visits", "lives in", or "desires" Vrindavan can acquire extraordinary abilities to sanctify both themselves and the place. The priests at the Banke Bihari temple emphasise that Vrindavan constitutes an integral part of the sacred geography within the state of Uttar Pradesh, along with Banaras, Ayodhya, and Mathura and maintain that Hindus today are resolute in building a continuum of pure ecology.

"Krishna is the first environmentalist of the world," claims Jagannath Poddar. However, the portrayal of Krishna continues to be painted with images of war, enemies, killing, and victory. Near the Sakshi Gopal temple, I met a group of sadhus who referred me to Swami Prabhupada's teachings on Krishna: Krishna is present everywhere to protect people in dangerous situations. If you are a true Hindu devotee, Krishna will immediately come to your aid against the demons. The demon Hiranyakasipu challenged his son, the devoted Prahlada, by asking, "Where is your God? You say

He is everywhere. Is He in this column of my palace? You believe your God is there? Very well, I will kill Him." Hiranyakasipu then broke the column, and at that moment Krishna emerged from the column in His form as Nrsimhadeva, half-man and half-lion, and vanquished the demon. This is the warrior Krishna.

I visited the office of the Braj Foundation in Vrindavan,[113] which has undertaken the restoration of traditional ponds, lakes, forests, and religious routes. For their efforts they acknowledged the "mercy" of Narendra Modi and the BJP MP Hema Malini. I also went to witness the restoration of Davanal Kund, a project initiated by another organisation, the Datri Foundation, in collaboration with the Friends of Vrindavan. Srivatsa Goswami, who presided over the event celebrating the restoration of the kund, remarked, "Sri Krishna eliminated scores of demons in His lifetime, but He did not kill Kaliya, the serpent of pollution living in the Yamuna. Instead, Krishna merely contained him and ordered Kaliya to dwell in the depths of the ocean." The story I was told about Davanal (the forest fire) once again revolves around the battle: wicked Kansa, who set the forest ablaze to kill Krishna and his associates. Krishna, in turn, swallowed the devastating forest fire to save the people.

### *Religious and Social Mappings through Environmental Ills*

In my interviews with activists of the RSS, VHP, and BJP, as well as various religious and some civil society organisations in Vrindavan, issues such as cow killing, animal slaughterhouses, and deforestation were consistently identified as major environmental concerns for the city. Moreover, Muslims were often perceived as the primary contributors to environmental pollution. There was a prevailing belief that "Hindus are inherently environmentalists" and that Hindu ecology was under threat.

During an extensive group conversation with activists from the RSS, VHP, and BJP in Govardhan Nagar, Mathura, Gautam

[113] I visited the office of the Braj Foundation in Vrindavan on 13 October 2023.

Hindustani (Khandelwal) highlighted the fact that Hindus have a long-standing tradition of performing pujas to specific trees and revering rivers as a maternal figure. Their reverence for nature is deeply ingrained. However, he suggested that under the influence of Westernisation and urbanisation, combined with the increasing Muslim population, the environment was deteriorating. Muslims were often attributed with activities such as tree felling in Vrindavan–Mathura, cow and animal slaughter, the operation of slaughterhouses, and primary responsibility for polluting the Yamuna.[114]

Vijay Raghav from the VHP emphasised that solving the environmental issues in Vrindavan could be achieved by focusing on the cessation of cow killing and the closure of slaughterhouses. The Muslims, being meat-eaters, were also held accountable for the decreasing numbers of birds and animals, including peacocks and parrots, in Vrindavan.[115] Some RSS activists even suggested measures such as disenfranchising the Muslim population as a means of tackling environmental and social problems in the country.

I visited the expansive premises of ISKCON in Vrindavan. Among the various books prominently displayed in their shop was one titled *India – A World Leader in Cow Killing and Beef Export: An Italian Did It in 10 Years, What the British Could Not Do in 200 Years and the Muslims in 800 Years*.[116] The book claims that after 2004, when a particular political party came to power, the government decided "to accord highest priority to beef consumption and export, making it "truly national initiative".[117] The book recounts the history of Maharaja Parikshit, who, while on his expedition to conquer the world, encountered the embodiment of Kali-yuga, a being lower in stature than a Shudra, disguised as a king and was cruel to the legs of a cow and bull. The king promptly apprehended him to administer suitable punishment. The book subsequently concludes with the words of Srila Prabhupada: "The age of Kali means mismanagement and quarrel. And the root cause of all mismanagement and

[114] Interview with Gautam Hindustani in Mathura, 14 October 2023.

[115] Interview with Vijay Raghav in Mathura, 14 October 2023.

[116] I visited ISKCON, Vrindavan Complex, on 12 October 2023.

[117] Dasa, *India – A World Leader in Cow Killing and Beef Export*, 6.

quarrel is that worthless men with the modes of lower-class men, who have no higher ambition in life, come to the helm of the state management. Such men at the post of a king are sure to first hurt the cow and the brahminical culture, thereby pushing all society towards hell."[118]

Another book on display is titled *As Long As We Have Slaughterhouses, We'll Have Wars.* It delves into the intricate connections between diet and aggression, as well as diet and crime. It discusses topics such as Al-Qaeda militants rejecting vegetarian food, the existence of slaughterhouses, the rise in crime rates, and the correlation between meat consumption and warfare. In addition, there is another book that suggests using cow dung as a practical solution to address global warming and climate change.

I departed from Vrindavan and Mathura with Jagannath Poddar's words echoing in my mind – that religion has overshadowed ecology and spirituality in Vrindavan, and that environmental and civil society organisations have become convenient instruments for the RSS and the BJP government.

[118] Ibid., 45.

6

# Modi, the "Solar Superman"

## Hindutva, Climate Change, and Renewable Energy

IN OCTOBER 2018 Prime Minister Narendra Modi was awarded the United Nations Champions of the Earth Award for Policy Leadership. During the presentation, United Nations Secretary General Antonio Guterres remarked that Modi embodies the genuine essence of climate leadership – he "recognises that climate change poses a direct existential threat to us all," and "knows what we need to do to avert catastrophe." Guterres also highlighted Modi's understanding of the "enormous benefits of climate action." Modi was acknowledged as the representative of an extraordinary legacy of Indian civilisation, philosophy, culture, Vedas, and Mahatma Gandhi, whose example of "bold environmental leadership" should be followed by the world. "This example must come to fruition, that other leaders must look at what is happening in India and must do the same – of course with different circumstances in different countries – to make sure that we are able to win the race against climate change . . ."[1] This perception marked out the centrality of India as an area of change and even as an actor on global environmental change. Beyond that it lauded the executive head of government in terms not used for any head of government by the UN on the climate-change front.

In 2021 Dr Arunabha Ghosh, a renowned climate expert and the

[1] Antonio Guterres, "Remarks on Presenting Champion of the Earth Award to Prime Minister Narendra Modi of India", *United Nations*, https://www.un.org/sg/en/content/sg/speeches/2018-10-03/champion-earth-award-narendra-modi-india-remarks, 3 October 2018.

founder of a prominent Indian non-governmental organisation dedicated to environmental and energy issues, portrayed Modi as a "climate leader". According to him, during the opening day of the UN climate conference in Glasgow (COP 26), Prime Minister Modi made a resounding declaration in favour of low-carbon development. He pledged to achieve net-zero greenhouse gas emissions by 2070 and substantiated this commitment with robust short-term goals. This transformative announcement had far-reaching implications, not only for India and the global environment but also for investors, technology developers, and climate negotiations.[2] Modi was described as "a global environmental leader" who presented the concept of *panchamrit* (five nectars), to mitigate the effects of climate change.[3]

Modi has referred to climate change and renewable energy on numerous occasions, at both national and international events that cover a wide spectrum of the subject: "Climate change is a major global challenge";[4] "Climate change must be fought not in silos but in an integrated, comprehensive and holistic way";[5] "Calls for international cooperation";[6] "Common but differential responsibilities";[7] "Importance of climate justice and equity";[8] "India's culture of climate-friendly sustainable practices";[9] "Solution to global warming lies in

[2] Arunabha Ghosh, "A Climate Leader", *Indian Express*, 5 November 2021, https://indianexpress.com/article/opinion/columns/india-cop26-un-climate-change-7607694/.

[3] Chinoy, "Modi Global Leader", 232–52.

[4] "Climate Change is a Major Global Challenge: PM Narendra Modi at Inauguration of India Pavilion at COP21 in Paris", https://www.narendramodi.in/pmsaddress-at-the-inauguration-of-the-indianpavilionat-cop21-paris.

[5] "India Exceeding Paris Targets, But Climate Change Must Not be Fought in Silos: PM Modi at G20", *The Times of India*, 22 November 2020.

[6] "India on Track to Exceed Paris Agreement Targets: PM Modi", *Bussinessline*, 12 December 2020.

[7] Narendra Modi, "Statement to the 69th Session of the United Nations General Assembly", 27 September 2014, https://www.un.org/en/ga/69/meetings/gadebate/pdf/IN_en.pdf.

[8] "PM Narendra Modi's Book About India's Efforts to Mitigate Climate Change", *Indian-Asian News Service*, 10 December 2015.

[9] "Climate Change is a Major Global Challenge: PM Narendra Modi at

India's unique tradition and practice of worshipping nature";[10] "Yoga as an answer to climate change";[11] "Saffron revolution";[12] "India to take lead in the pressing global problem of climate change";[13] "Acutely conscious and aware of his responsibility to help guide the world towards a deal on curbing greenhouse gases";[14] "One World One Sun One Grid";[15] "Lifestyle-focused solutions for climate change";[16] "10-points action plan for clean energy";[17] "Affordable renewable energy and energy access to all";[18] and "India will achieve net zero by 2070".[19]

---

Inauguration of India Pavilion at COP21 in Paris", https://www.narendramodi.in/pmsaddress-at-the-inauguration-of-the-indianpavilionat-cop21-paris.

[10] "India Will Set Climate Change Conference Agenda", *Indian Express*, 14 April 2015, http://indian-express.com/article/india/india-others/india-will-set-climate-change-conference-agenda-narendra-modi/.

[11] Narendra Modi, "Statement to the 69th Session of the United Nations General Assembly", 27 September 2014, https://www.un.org/en/ga/69/meetings/gadebate/pdf/IN_en.pdf.

[12] "Narendra Modi Gives Mantra to Take on China", *The Times of India*, 9 June 2014, https://timesofindia.indiatimes.com/india/narendra-modi-gives-mantra-to-take-on china/articleshow/36265685.cms.

[13] "Prime Minister Modi Says India Must Lead on Climate Change", *The Washington Post*, 14 April 2015.

[14] "India Pledges to Fight Climate Change but Falls Short of Stating Emissions Cap", *The Guardian*, 8 May 2015.

[15] "About OSOWOG Initiative", *International Solar Alliance*, https://isolaralliance.org/work/osowog/.

[16] "NITI Aayog, "LIFE: Lifestyle for Environment", https://www.niti.gov.in/life.

[17] "International Solar Alliance Summit: PM Modi Lays Down 10-point Action Plan for Clean Energy", *Indian Express*, 11 March, 2018, https://indianexpress.com/article/india/international-solar-alliance-summit-pm-modi-lays-down-10-point-action-plan-for-clean-energy-5093843/.

[18] "Prime Minister Narendra Modi Pushes for Affordable Renewable Energy for All", *NDTV*, 15 February 2015, https://www.ndtv.com/india-news/prime-minister-narendra-modi-pushes-for-affordable-renewable-energy-for-all-739783.

[19] "COP26: India PM Narendra Modi Pledges Net Zero by 2070", *BBC*, 2 November 2021, https://www.bbc.com/news/world-asia-india-59125143.

During election campaigns and BJP meetings, Modi has actively associated climate change and renewable energy with his political agenda. In the significant national election campaign trails of 2014 he consistently linked the revered colour of Hindus and the BJP to his energy politics: "The time has come for a saffron revolution, and saffron is the colour of energy."[20] Furthermore, it was during the BJP National Council Meeting in 2016 that Modi made a momentous announcement regarding the Government of India's decision to ratify the Paris Climate Change Agreement.[21]

Thus, Modi is widely portrayed as a prominent climate leader in both his own narratives and in the acknowledgments of others. His approach to climate change and energy encompasses various aspects, including international diplomacy, global climate negotiations, investment and economic growth, modernisation, scientific and technological developments, domestic audiences, and individual image-building. It is clear that, unlike certain strands of right-wing ecological politics which deny climate change, Hindu nationalist politics and Modi have used climate change and renewable energy as effective political tools, both in India and abroad, to enhance their public image and expand political influence. Remarkably, environmental organisations and the broader climate politics landscape in the country have paid scant attention to this particular facet of Hindu nationalist environmental politics.

Looking at these contexts, this chapter aims to cover the history of Hindu nationalist politics on climate change and renewable energy. It is possible to do so via a focus on Modi's long-term work within the political and governmental spheres, and by examining how Hindu nationalist ideologies and leaders are closely involved with climate politics. I carefully consider the literature produced and activities undertaken by RSS ideologues and organisations after the 2000s

[20] Rupa Subramanya, "Is India Ready to Be a Solar Power Leader?", *Foreign Policy*, 1 July 2015, https://foreignpolicy.com/2015/07/01/india-modi-bjp-energy-solar-softbank/.

[21] "India to Ratify Paris Climate Change Agreement on Oct 2: PM Modi", *Rediff News*, 26 September 2016, https://www.rediff.com/money/report/india-to-ratify-paris-climate-change-agreement-on-oct-2-pm-modi/20160926.htm.

with a view to charting the continuities and changes in Hindu nationalist politics. I have several questions to answer: What are the main areas characterising the climate politics of a Hindu nationalist leader? How do some key cultural and political ideas of nature and nation – such as a natural, powerful, pollution-free country – feature in such politics? How does the conception of Bharat as an ancient, glorious leader – *jagatguru* – play at the international level? How can climate change be utilised to build the popularity and legitimacy of an authoritarian leader and his regime?

I will expand my analysis by exploring new aspects of Hindu nationalism within the realms of climate change and energy. Within this context, the authority and influence of Prime Minister Modi hold a prominent position in shaping climate change policies and renewable-energy initiatives. His leadership is often portrayed as that of a "strong", "determined", and "heroic" figure. Moreover, Hindu nationalism places great emphasis on the concept of "national power", projecting India as a globally significant, civilisational, and powerful nation that leads the world. Under Modi's leadership and his Hindu nationalist party there is a heightened reliance on the politics and new governance of science and technology, as well as consent and coercion to establish their climate agenda.

The dominance of Modi as a strong-man figure in India's climate change and renewable-energy political discussions and policy-making has been remarkable. His personal authority in this domain has been so influential that the Indian government reconstituted the Prime Minister's Council on Climate Change in 2014, comprising the relevant ministries and independent experts, with the aim of realising the country's climate change objectives. The council held its inaugural meeting in January 2015 but has not convened again since then.[22] India's climate policy has been primarily linked to Modi, and, to some extent, become synonymous with the idea of Indian climate leadership.[23] The prevalence of an unquestioning and saffron civil

[22] Akshit Sangomla, "PM's Climate Change Council Has Not Met in Almost 7 Years", *Down to Earth*, 25 November 2021, https://www.downtoearth.org.in/news/climate-change/pm-s-climate-change-council-has-not-met-in-almost-7-years-80369.

[23] Hakala, "India and the Global".

society in contemporary India contributes to the effective dissemination of the leader's perspectives and narratives.

In the political landscape following 2014 and the rise of Modi, the scope for social movements and people's organisations in the field of climate change and renewable energy has significantly diminished.[24] It is also being observed that right-wing agendas – economic, political, and religious – have threatened the fight against climate change and there is no political space for critical NGOs and civil society organisations.[25] Through much of India's modern history, a diverse range of issue-based groups and movements have advocated for alternative and decentralised energy systems, particularly in response to anti-nuclear and anti-large-dam movements, which also advocated the adoption of decentralised renewable-energy systems.[26] However, the climate and energy policies under a Modi-centric approach, heavily influenced by big industry, infrastructure, and capital, have fundamentally altered the national discourse. This has resulted in a paradoxical situation: on the one hand, civil society organisations have aligned themselves with Modi's agenda, while on the other the RSS-BJP have co-opted the space traditionally occupied by social movements, calling for the transformation of renewable energy "into a popular movement" while simultaneously adhering to Modi's ideology.[27]

The interaction between nature, nationness, and nationalism and the appropriation of nature by politics in asserting identity, interest, and rights has been thoroughly examined.[28] The study of nature and its history in Asian and African societies during the imperial era and

[24] There are reports of police cases and arrests of climate activists associated with environmental groups like Fridays for Future, Extinction Rebellion and Greenpeace. For details: Joanna Slater and Niha Masih, "In India, a Climate Activist's Arrest Shows Shrinking Space for Dissent", *The Washington Post*, 18 February 2021, https://www.washingtonpost.com/world/asia_pacific/india-modi-dissent/2021/02/17/b6ab6ec8-7059-11eb-8651-6d3091eac63f_story.html.

[25] Agrawal, "Regaining Control Over Climate", 136–47.

[26] Bidwai, *The Politics of Climate*.

[27] Bharatiya Janata Party, *Sankalpit Bharat, Sakshat Bharat: Sankalp Patra, Lok Sabha 2019*, https://www.bjp.org/manifesto2019.

[28] Cederlof and Sivaramakrishnan, eds, *Ecological Nationalisms*.

in the time of independent nation-states has revealed both shifts and continuities, highlighting the significant role played by political, economic, and cultural processes in the consolidation and legitimisation of nation-states.[29] The situational and adaptive plasticity of nationalism, exemplified by its ability to adapt to changing circumstances, particularly in the time of climate change, has been elucidated using the concepts of "resource nationalism" and "green nationalism". These terms describe nationalist ideologies and practices that impede the global transition towards sustainable energy sources, thereby hindering progress in combating climate change.[30] Moreover, examining the interrelationship between environment, technology, science, race, caste, and gender has shed light on the impact of climate change and environmental transformations on peoples such as Blacks, Dalits, and women. This analysis has emphasised the importance of considering identity issues, bodily interconnectedness, and the complex interplay between nature and cultures.[31] However, there is a dearth of research examining the facets of Hindu nationalism that intersect with the contemporary green identity embodied by Modi, particularly within the context of climate change and energy.

## Modi: Political Legitimacy through Climate Change and Renewable Energy

Modi's roles as an RSS *pracharak*, a BJP leader, and head of both the BJP-led Gujarat state and Indian government have been extensively researched.[32] He has garnered immense popularity both within India and on a global scale. His communication skills, coupled with his efforts in foreign diplomacy, have earned widespread acclaim and admiration. Since assuming office as prime minister in 2014, he has

[29] Rangarajan, *Nature and Nation*.

[30] Conversi, "The Ultimate Challenge", 625–36.

[31] Among many others read Driscoll, "Black Weather", 1–9; Bullard and Wright, eds, *Race, Place and Environmental*; Sharma, *Caste & Nature*; Buckingham and Masson, eds, *Understanding Climate Change*.

[32] Read for example Marino, *Narendra Modi*; Menon, *Modi Demystified*; Mahurkar, *Centrestage*.

taken up the plank of climate change and renewable energy within the realm of foreign policy.[33] His legitimacy encompasses various elements, including the Hindu nationalist party and ideology, political and governmental power, personality and performance, and the consent of the people. However, it is important to note that "legitimacy is a complex, dynamic, variegated feature and a matter of degree rather than a simple dichotomy of legitimacy/illegitimacy."[34] The elements of legitimacy are always subject to change. Legitimacy is a contested concept, and there are instances where a legitimacy crisis arises, impacting the consent element. Consequently, rulers and governments strive to establish new elements to maintain their legitimacy. When regimes seek to sustain their rule over a given population during periods of change and crisis, they consider factors that are both widely acceptable to the people and effective practically within a specific historical context. These considerations become essential in order to preserve the legitimacy and ensure the stability of the authority.[35]

In the case of Modi, the question of legitimacy, or lack of it, became evident during various periods of his rule when he attempted to cultivate climate change and renewable energy as crucial components to build consent, confirmation, and consensus among influential stakeholders such as elite groups, media, civil society, and the international community. These entities possess greater resources and influence, and Modi sought their support to garner peoples' consent with a multiplier effect, thereby addressing the legitimacy crisis.[36] He assumed the role of chief minister of Gujarat state towards the end of 2001, a period when the BJP government in the state was plagued by corruption, inadequate administration, misuse of authority, and a poor response to the Bhuj earthquake. The construction of the Sardar Sarovar Dam,

[33] Read for example Mohan, *Modi's World*; Karnad, *Staggering Forward*; Chaulia, *Modi Doctrine*.

[34] Alagappa, ed., *Political Legitimacy*, 25.

[35] For discussions on legitimation of rulers of all kinds, read Barker, *Legitimating Identities*.

[36] For more discussion on many individuals and groups with different levels of engagements, values, intensities, and weight for the legitimation of power, read Denitch, ed., *Legitimation of Regimes*.

one of the largest in the world, became the centre of controversy, and of protests on its environmental impact and human displacement, in which the role of the Gujarat government was criticised. This situation led to a challenge against the incumbent government's legitimacy and its right to rule. Furthermore, during Modi's tenure as chief minister Gujarat experienced intense communal riots in 2002, resulting in the death, injury, and disappearance of thousands of individuals, mostly Muslims. The complicity of the chief minister and the state government in these attacks – either their perceived failure to take significant action to suppress the violence or, in some cases, allegations that they planned and carried out the attacks on the Muslim community – created huge challenges in terms of political legitimacy for Modi.[37]

After 2002, the Hindu nationalist leader embarked on a new path to legitimacy, positioning himself as a development icon, using the narrative of the "Gujarat model of development".[38] He emphasised the significance of climate change and renewable energy to portray himself as a modern leader capable of establishing shared norms and values through broader consensus. He published a book on climate change titled *Convenient Action: Gujarat's Response to Challenges of Climate Change*,[39] which was widely publicised and received national and international acclaim.[40] For Chief Minister Modi and his government, the normative goals shifted from the rule of law, security,

[37] There are numerous books, articles, and reports on Gujarat riots. To name a few: Deshpande, *Gujarat Riots*; Ayyub, *Gujarat Files*; Mitta, *The Fiction of Fact-Finding*; Lokhande, *Communal Violence*.

[38] Gujarat model of development refers to the period from 2001 to 2014 when Modi was the chief minister of the state. The high rate of growth, investment, and infrastructure development marked this model. The government performed poorly in education, health, environment, and employment for the people. For discussion, read Jaffrelot, "What 'Gujarat Model'", 820–38; Muraleedharan, "Narendra Modi's 'Gujarat Model'", 129–51.

[39] Modi, *ConvenientAction.* https://cdn.narendramodi.in/ebooks/convenient_action/files/assets/common/downloads/publication.pdf.

[40] The book was an explicit response to former US Vice President Al Gore's film "An Inconvenient Truth", which, according to some analysts, showed the desire for an international audience. The book was released in a highly publicised event, in the presence of several well-known individuals including the former

communal harmony, respect for rights, and the just exercise of governmental power. He now developed a narrative about how the massive exploitation of mother earth "promote[s] selfishness, instincts of violence, jealousy – inimical to human development,"[41] and how "time is running out with each passing month, year and decade" in addressing climate change.[42] The focus was now on creating solar cities and renewable-energy hubs and ensuring substantial investments from major corporations and round-the-clock power supply. Modi established a Climate Change Department in his government and headed it, along with other key departments of Industry and Mines, Science and Technology, Information and Broadcasting, and Ports. It was announced that "Gujarat is the first and only state in India, the first in Asia, and fourth in the world to form an independent department for climate change."[43] He initiated the creation of the largest solar park in Asia and made a commitment to make the cities of the state fully solar-powered.[44] He inaugurated Gujarat's "dream solar project" atop the Narmada branch canal, showcasing "*jal* and *urja shakti*" (power from water and the sun).[45] Modi claimed that Gujarat, under his leadership, had taken the front seat in the global fight against climate change.[46]

---

president of India, Dr A.P.J. Abdul Kalam, and the chairman of the Intergovernmental Panel on Climate Change (IPCC), Nobel Laureate R.K. Pachauri. See Express News Service, "Modi's Book Gets Rave Reviews from Kalam, Pachauri", *Indian Express*, 22 December 2010, https://indianexpress.com/article/cities/ahmedabad/modi-s-book-gets-rave-reviews-from-k0alam-p/.

[41] Modi, *Convenient Action*, 12.

[42] Ibid., 227.

[43] Climate Change Department, Government of Gujarat, https://ccd.gujarat.gov.in/

[44] Narendra Modi, "Gujarat Solar Park to be Developed as Swarnim Surya Teerth", 30 December 2010, https://www.narendramodi.in/gujarat-solar-park-to-be-developed-as-swarnim-surya-teerth-3778.

[45] "First of Its Kind: Gujarat's Dream Solar Project", *Firstpost*, 26 April 2012, https://www.firstpost.com/india/first-of-its-kind-gujarats-dream-solar-project-289214.html.

[46] Narendra Modi, "Gujarat Takes Front Seat in the Global Fight Against Climate Change", 11 December 2009, https://www.narendramodi.in/od/gujarat-takes-front-seat-in-the-global-fight-against-climate-change-3439.

A hardcore Hindu nationalist leader consciously carved out a new basis of acceptance through climate change and renewable energy, particularly at a time when his political legitimacy was weak and contested. Subsequently, dominant groups began to embrace Modi as "the visionary leader" who has "shown a definite path and determined strategy to meet the challenges of climate change."[47] It was said that Gujarat had shown the way by extensively focusing on renewable energy, and that the "Gujarat model" has proven to be a "champion of climate change".[48] Civil society organisations came forward to support Modi's "concern on the issue of climate crisis" and appreciated his writing on this subject.[49] He earned electoral dividends through solar initiatives.[50] In these ways, the articulation of a common concern emerged, one that was seemingly non-partisan and non-communal, focused on the progress of an entire society.

It is important to note that this development was the result of a political strategy in which Modi played a key role. He proudly claimed that the environmental and climate mitigation/adaptation initiatives begun under him in Gujarat were inspired by his experience of "having been an ardent follower . . . of a nationalistic ideology" which should be followed by modern knowledge actors, "including scholars, researchers, scientists, leaders and policy planners."[51]

When Modi became prime minister in 2014 he focused on strengthening his political legitimacy through a wide range of rationalisations and goals. Notably, from the beginning of his tenure, climate change and renewable energy featured prominently in his

[47] Howard, "Forward", 2.

[48] Sarthak Karol, "Narendra Modi's Climate Policy and India's Role in COP 21, December, Paris 2015", *Manupatra Articles*, 16 January 2018, https://articles.manupatra.com/article-details/Narendra-Modi-s-Climate-Policy-and-India-s-role-in-COP21-December-Paris-2015.

[49] Coalition of Organisations and Networks on Climate Change, "Urgent Action Needed to Operationalize Equity in the Context of Climate Change", 10 November 2014.

[50] Chaudhuri, "Fragmented and Fitful", 39–41.

[51] Modi, *Convenient Action*, 13.

political and governmental activities. He changed India's Ministry of Environment and Forests into the Ministry of Environment, Forests and Climate Change. He formed a high-level panel "for Integrated Development of Power, Coal and Renewable Energy". In late 2014 the Modi government announced a five-fold increase in India's solar electricity target, up from 20 gigawatts to 100 gigawatts by 2022. His cabinet approved an "ultra-mega" solar park in Gujarat. In the midst of the 2015 Paris climate negotiations, India announced it would form and host an International Solar Alliance (ISA) with the Government of France to boost the diffusion of solar technology around the world. Modi played an active role in the UNFCCC (CoP), as well as launched several bilateral relations on climate change and renewable energy. The Indian government policy push on climate change and renewable energy went beyond techno-economic considerations. It had political and ideational aims. Thus, it was observed that

> the solar push has both a domestic facing and international component. Domestically, solar enhanced the Modi and the ruling party brand and helped shape elite and mass opinion of Modi as a modern development-oriented leader. Internationally, solar was seen as a way to win plaudits in Washington, connect India to Obama's ambitious climate goals, and an easier area for gains compared to trade, where concessions are harder . . . The agency of Prime Minister Modi was crucial in centring solar in his push to sharpen and deepen his narrative.[52]

Climate change became an arena where a complex and dynamic interplay unfolded among the government, elite groups, politically

[52] A research study conducted twenty-three elite interviews with former and current Indian government officials, think-tank researchers, consultants, private sector executives, Indian media, and two U.S. officials, to evaluate nine possible drivers behind the Indian government's policy push on solar going beyond the techno-economic emphasis on declining panel prices. Based on the interviews and a review of other observable implications of the various drivers, the study identified four chief political drivers: domestic politics, global pressure and partnerships, attracting investment, and energy sovereignty. For details, see Shidore and Busby, "What Explains India's Embrace", 1179–89.

significant publics, international support, and foreign diplomacy, contributing to the cultivation of an aura around Modi's personality and performance. The contemporary global significance of climate change and India's role in addressing it played a vital part in shaping the international discourse that legitimised Modi's actions in the energy and environment sector. He garnered considerable international attention and appreciation, further solidifying his standing as a decisive leader with credibility on issues related to climate change and sustainability.

The framing of climate change and energy can have variables; it can manifest different ideologies and the worldviews of several interest groups that also influence the discourse among strategic groups – and between these groups and people – in their endeavour to control the narrative. Climate change and renewable energy have proven to be "good" domestic politics for Modi and his Hindu nationalist agenda. At the same time, his regime has made concerted efforts to mobilise the support of international actors to shape the domestic discourse. The salience of international legitimacy has also been evident from the efforts of Modi and his foreign policy to secure international support for his causes. It is not a mere coincidence that several significant Indian initiatives pertaining to climate change and renewable energy were initially introduced by Modi on foreign soil. Thus, it is important to get the "international" into the discussion.

## International Support and Political Legitimacy

> Narendra Modi is a force of nature. There is infinite energy and boundless enthusiasm in India's fourteenth prime minister who strives relentlessly for taking India forward in economic development and modernisation . . . Standing tall amidst the varied realms of policies which have undergone a distinct "Modi-fication" is foreign affairs.
> – "A Foreign Policy Revelation", Sreeram Chaulia, 2016[53]

International development and considerations have played a significant role in the legitimation of power and in shaping interactions

[53] Chaulia, *Modi Doctrine,* 15.

between rulers and the ruled. As highlighted by Muthiah Alagappa, gaining acceptance from the international community, or from the superpowers, along with accessing the resources of international organisations bestows a prestige that can enhance the capacity of a state. This increased capacity empowers leaders and their governments to solidify their domestic support base. "Non-recognition not only reduces the standing of the incumbent government and its capacity; it also enhances the status of rival claimants to power."[54] However, it has also been emphasised that international dimensions play only a contributory role in domestic legitimation. Modi, since his time as chief minister of Gujarat, has worked extensively to seek international support for his activities on climate change and renewable energy. In his book he states: "My effort is to take help of all available expertise within the country and also to network with international organizations."[55] Modi and the Gujarat government reached out to the World Bank, GIZ, BMZ, Clinton Foundation, Rockefeller Foundation, and several foreign countries for collaborations on climate-change projects. This led to many state-level initiatives: for example, the Rockefeller Foundation initiated "Asian Cities Climate Change Resilience Network" (ACCCRN) which was meant "to develop implementation proposals that are owned by a city-level advisory body comprising of stakeholders drawn from key organizations including the Municipal Corporation, Development Authority, Private Sector, Academia, Community-based organisations."[56] Other than material and economic benefits, these collaborations were able to build a common community around environment policy and politics.[57]

In his capacity as prime minister, Modi has dedicated substantial time and effort to shaping India's foreign policy and extending its

[54] Alagappa, ed., *Political Legitimacy*, 49.

[55] Modi, *Convenient Action*, 4.

[56] ACCCRN, "Surat City Resilience Strategy", https://www.acccrn.net/country/india.

[57] For details about international collaboration on climate change and renewable energy in Gujarat state under the Modi regime, see Venkatasubramanian, "Examining the Politics", 2016.

global influence. His international presence has been pronounced since 2014, as he has actively sought leadership roles in various bilateral and multilateral forums. Scholars attribute this proactive engagement to Modi's personal ambition for international statesmanship.[58] Unsurprisingly, the construction and advancement of the "Brand Modi" image have also drawn heavily from his foreign policy. This image portrays him as a dynamic, energetic, proactive, and visionary leader, among other attributes. The interaction between foreign and domestic realms has been evident in multiple domains. Modi's foreign-policy decisions have been closely interwoven with domestic political considerations, giving rise to a clear confluence between these two facets.

Modi himself has often articulated his vision of foreign policy: increasing India's economic profile in the newer, untapped markets of the world, enhancing its security in a difficult neighbourhood, and building the country into a leading global power and net-security provider.[59] Many experts have also researched Modi-centric India's foreign policies. According to the security analyst Bharat Karnad, Modi's foreign policy has been a "mix of personalized diplomacy, showmanship and bonhomie with foreign leaders." Its organising principle is the concept of India as "leading power" and "*vishwaguru*", drawing on the country's economic and cultural resources.[60] Modi has been seen as "a bundle of energy and a breath of fresh air for Indian diplomacy", a man who has surprised the nation and the world with his enthusiasm for rejuvenating India's foreign policy. "Modi had brought forth a phase of 'breakthrough diplomacy'."[61] The prime minister's "bold decisions" in authorising surgical strikes against Pakistan and tackling China have been described as decisive for securing India.[62] It is

[58] Pathak and Parris, "India's Diplomatic Discourse", 1–28.

[50] "PM Narendra Modi Talks of Foreign Policy Goals with Indian Envoys", *Times of India*, 7 May 2017, http://timesofindia.indiatimes.com/india/pm-narendramodi-talks-of-foreign-policy-goals-with-indian-envoys/articleshow/58555674.cms.

[60] Karnad, *Staggering Forward*.

[61] Mohan, *Modi's World*.

[62] Gokhale, *Securing India*.

also said that Modi's arrival at the helm of foreign affairs, and thus Indian diplomacy getting into the mould of a "leading power", have effectively challenged China.[63] Ian Hall argues that Modi has linked the Hindu nationalist ideology with Indian foreign policy, and that "as part of Modi's wider project of building a 'New India,' his government attempted to reground key elements of Indian foreign policy in Hindu nationalist ideology, to recast the language of international relations in its distinctive idiom, and redirect Indian diplomacy in ways that better fitted its political agenda."[64]

In this context, it is certainly noteworthy that Modi's foreign policy has strategically employed climate change and renewable energy as pivotal tools serving a dual purpose: first, enhancing his stature as a prominent global leader for climate action, and second, fulfilling his administration's aspirations of establishing India as a potent and esteemed global force, in line with ensuring "Bharat's rise as a strong and respected world power."[65] Thus, it was pointed out that Modi's foreign policy has a more obvious connection to Hindu nationalist ideas in two areas: in the treatment of climate change and the global environment, and in the role that religion and spirituality should play in mitigating international and civil conflict, including terrorism.[66]

A specific focus on climate change came along with other global diplomatic issues like terrorism, war, reforms in the United Nations, the G-20, the global economic and trade systems, and bilateral-multilateral agreements. Modi's image was enhanced for taking up "bold", "out of the box", and "dynamic" steps on climate change, and the acceptability of his government gained greater currency internationally. Climate change and renewable energy at times also became a glue for investment and trade agreements in energy and related sectors where

[63] Sigdel, *India in the Era.*

[64] Hall, *Modi and the Reinvention.*

[65] BJP, "Resolution on Foreign Policy Passed in BJP National Executive Meeting at Bengaluru (Karnataka)", 3 April 2015, www.bjp.org/en/mediaresources/press-releases/resolution-on-foreign-policy-passed-in-bjpnational-executive-meeting-at-bengaluru-karnataka.

[66] Hall, "Narendra Modi", 113–31.

private and multinational companies and big capital gained prominent roles.

There have been multiple instances of Modi's leadership on the global stage concerning climate change and renewable energy. I will focus on a few examples to underscore how climate change has been strategically utilised to advance political objectives.

A significant milestone was observed during Modi's visit to the United States in 2014, shortly after assuming office. A key aspect of this visit was the emphasis on showcasing Modi's image through engagement with climate change and renewable energy. Modi portrayed himself as a leader attuned to environmental concerns, intertwining this stance with the timeless principles of Hindu traditions. He also accentuated the need for integrating contemporary technologies, major industries, and substantial capital to effectively address climate change. Subsequently, this trajectory in Modi's foreign policy approach to climate change and renewable energy has persisted consistently over the years.

During his speech at the 69th session of the United Nations General Assembly on 27 September 2014, Modi covered a wide range of topics, including economic development, poverty alleviation, security, Pakistan, terrorism, UN reforms, clean energy, technology, and more. However, he dedicated considerable attention to discussing the concept of fostering "a more habitable and sustainable world" and the principle of "common but differentiated responsibilities". Within the same context, he also referred to "India's ancient wisdom", highlighting how the reverence for nature forms "an integral part of spiritualism", and how the abundance of nature is regarded as "sacred". Subsequently, he seamlessly intertwined India's tradition of yoga with the discourse on climate change. Shortly thereafter, the Government of India embarked on a path of international diplomacy, championing the cause of the International Yoga Day. This involved presenting a unified front composed of Modi, yoga, and Indian traditions, positioning them collectively as a viable solution to the array of modern global climate challenges.

The Ministry of External Affairs stated in a public diplomacy publication: "Perhaps witnessing the potential of this billion dollar brand of India can bring to the world, Indian Prime Minister Mr Narendra Modi called for observing an International Yoga Day at the UN General Assembly, describing the ancient science as India's gift to the world."[67]

Modi and Obama, after their meeting on 30 September 2014, issued a "US-India Joint Statement" which had a detailed section on "climate change and energy" (other sections were Economic Growth, Defense and Homeland Security Cooperation, High Technology, Space and Health Cooperation, and Global Issues and Regional Consultations). The statement charted out economic, social, and technological pathways for a US–India Partnership to Advance Clean Energy (PACE), New Energy Smart Cities Partnership, the formation of a Clean Energy Finance Forum to promote investment and trade in clean energy projects, boosting US renewable energy exports to India, etc. – to address climate change bilaterally and globally.[68] In various instances, the theme of climate change and renewable energy has appeared prominently, evident in notable occasions such as the inaugural collaborative article authored by Modi and Obama, Modi's statements following his bilateral discussions with Obama, and his interactions with chief executives from around the world.[69]

This foreign policy approach, with climate change as a key theme, gained momentum in 2015, during an international event – the 21st session of the United Nations Climate Change Conference of the

[67] The Ministry of External Affairs, *Yoga in India*, 2014, 36.

[68] "U.S.–India Joint Statement", The White House, 30 September 2014, https://obamawhitehouse.archives.gov/the-press-office/2014/09/30/us-India-joint-statement.

[69] Narendra Modi and Barack Obama, "A Renewed U.S.–India Partnership for the 21st Century", *The Washington Post*, 30 September 2014, https://www.washingtonpost.com/opinions/narendra-modi-and-barack-obama-a-us-india-partnership-for-the-21st-century/2014/09/29/dac66812-4824-11e4-891d-713f052086a0_story.html; "Remarks by President Obama and Prime Minister Narendra Modi of India After Bilateral Meeting", The White House, 30 September 2014, https://obamawhitehouse.archives.gov/the-press-office/2014/09/30/remarks-president-obama-and-prime-minister-narendra-modi-india-after-bil.

Parties (COP 21) held in Paris. Modi's presence here was extensively highlighted as he projected himself on the global stage. His official website documented a range of aspects:

> Prime Minister Narendra Modi attended Conference of the Parties (COP21) in Paris on November 30th. Shri Modi joined several world leaders in COP21 under the United Nations Framework Convention on Climate Change (UNFCCC); PM Modi inaugurated India Pavilion showcasing India's harmony with nature, environment, and commitment to mitigate climate change; PM Modi and French President Francois Hollande jointly unveiled the International Solar Alliance; the PM also attended "Mission Innovation" hosted by President of the United States; and Shri Narendra Modi also held extensive deliberations with several leaders on sidelines of COP21.[70]

At the launch of the ISA, a platform "for increased deployment of solar energy technologies as a means for bringing energy access, ensuring energy security, and driving energy transition in its member countries", Modi spoke about climate change, the carbon footprint, clean energy, the convergence between economy, ecology and energy, research and innovation, and investments in the solar sector. He also recalled ancient Indian civilisation's relevance for climate change: "In the Indian tradition, Sun is the source of all forms of energy. As Rig Veda says, Sun God is the Soul of all beings, moving and non-moving. Many in India begin their day with a prayer to the Sun."[71] At the founding conference of the ISA at Delhi in March 2018 he was emphatic about India's leadership role in bringing about a solar revolution in the entire world as well as in expanding renewable energy, relating accounts of ancient Indian philosophy, the Vedas, and Hindu saints.[72]

[70] Narendra Modi, https://www.narendramodi.in/.

[71] Narendra Modi, "Let us Turn to the Sun to Power Our Future", 30 November 2015, https://www.narendramodi.in/pm-modi-at-the-launch-of-international-solar-alliance-385253.

[72] English Translation of Prime Minister's Speech at Founding Conference of International Solar Alliance, 11 March 2018, https://mea.gov.in/Speeches-Statements.htm?dtl/29602.

At the 26th session of the United Nations Climate Change Conference of the Parties (COP 21) in Glasgow, UK, Modi once again raised the bar of his foreign policy diplomacy and made several announcements, some of them outlined for the first time, to demonstrate his government's commitment on climate change and renewable energy. He announced five nectar elements, *panchamrit*, to deal with climate challenges (India will take its non-fossil energy capacity to 500 GW by 2030, India will meet 50 per cent of its energy requirements from renewable energy by 2030, India will reduce the total projected carbon emissions by 1 billion tonnes from now till 2030, by 2030 India will reduce the carbon intensity of its economy by more than 45 per cent, and by the year 2070 India will achieve the target of Net Zero).[73] He addressed the Cop 26 Leaders' Summit. Alongside the British prime minister Boris Johnson he launched Green Grids Initiative – One Sun, One World, One Grid – to build a global green-energy grid. He recalled the great Indian nation and traditions and religious Hindu texts like the *Suryopanishad* to connect humankind with the sun and nature.

Foreign policy is defined as a sum total of state policy influenced by geography and external threats; pursuit of geopolitical and economic interests; pragmatism, power, domination, responses to other states, and much more. The links between foreign policy, political regimes, domestic politics, ideologies, and leadership have also been analysed theoretically and empirically.[74] Diplomacy as an important tool of foreign policy is manifested through alliances, trade, agreements, and exchanges. In the recent past, climate diplomacy has also emerged as an important arena in the foreign policy of nation-states, individually and collectively.[75] India's foreign-policy position on climate change and renewable energy under Modi is a new development

[73] National Statement by Prime Minister Shri Narendra Modi at COP26 Summit in Glasgow, 2 November 2021, https://www.mea.gov.in/Speeches Statements.htm?dtl/34466/National+Statement+by+Prime+Minister+Shri+Narendra+Modi+at+COP26+Summit+in+Glasgow.

[74] Hagan, "Regime Type". https://doi.org/10.1093/acrefore/9780190846626.013.415; Keller, "Leadership Style".

[75] Tanzler and Carius, "Beyond International Climate", 259–74.

within the framework of how a Hindu nationalist regime and leader extol the country as a world leader (of Hinduism and ancient wisdom-based climate consciousness or of renewable energy), with the leader of one nation projecting himself as a world climate leader. A foreign policy focusing on climate justice, technology transfer, renewables, and the economy blends with Hindu nationalist ideas of cultural India as a world leader, with the supreme wisdom of the Vedas and "Vedic periods". Thus, the RSS also hailed the view that "India armed with ISA under its belt is situated advantageously to play a leadership role in the negotiations on climate change by using ISA as a pivot to take the developing, LDC and SIDS countries under its fold and strengthening its bargaining power at the high table."[76] This kind of hype successfully obliterates the attention of critics on India's dismal track record on environmental issues since 2014.[77]

To understand Modi's narratives comprehensively we need to look at the post-2014 activities of the RSS, the foundational organisation of the Sangh Parivar. In fact, the RSS and BJP regularly follow up rigorously to consolidate Modi's image domestically as a statesman who has wide acceptance amongst leaders of the developed world on critical issues like climate change. This has once again received much traction among climate and energy experts and civil society organisations in India and abroad.[78]

[76] Shashanka Shekhar Panda, "International Solar Alliance: The Saffron Supergrid Superpower", *Organiser*, 10 January 2022, https://organiser.org/2022/01/10/14606/bharat/international-solar-alliance-the-saffron-supergrid-superpower/.

[77] We are not dealing with this subject. However, there are several articles and commentaries on environmental issues under the Modi regime. For details: Dutta and Nielsen, "Autocratic Environmental Governance", 70–80; Menon, "Narratives of Natural Resource".

[78] There are several articles hailing Modi and his leadership on addressing climate-change issues in India, and also demonstrating to the world the ways forward. For example, a research article outlines how at COP 21 in Paris, Prime Minister Modi made active efforts to position India as a country that was fully aware of its global responsibilities on this issue and how he himself played a direct role in making and approving the political judgement calls, trade-offs, and compromises that were observed in the lead up to, at, and following CoP: Sengupta, "India's Engagement in Global Climate", 114–41.

## The Sangh Parivar, Climate Change, and Renewable Energy

Hindu nationalist politics in India is now increasingly represented by the RSS, which consists of a wide variety of organisations, including the BJP (political party), Akhil Bharatiya Vidyarthi Parishad (students), Bharatiya Mazdoor Sangh (labour), Bharatiya Kisan Sangh (farmers), Vishva Hindu Parishad (the Ram temple and the Hindu religion), Bharatiya Itihas Sankalan Yojana (history), Akhil Bharatiya Vanvasi Kalyan Ashram (tribals), Swadeshi Jagaran Manch (economy), and more than forty sectoral groups focusing on children, women, advocates, cow protection, social service, village development, consumers, health, sports, co-operatives, literature, education, border areas, doctors, ex-servicemen, teacher, artists, and scientists. Characterised as "dynamic power-houses", these offshoots of the RSS collectively work with systems of regular co-ordination as well as with relative autonomy "to organise the entire Hindu society", "to attain the "Param Vaibhav [pinnacle of glory] of the Hindu Rashtra", and the "cultural rejuvenation and re-assertion of Hindu values such as reverence for men and nature" so that the "twenty-first century will be a century dominated by Hindutva."[79]

Recent scholarship on the RSS and its affiliates has focused on its organisational architecture and everyday activities in India and overseas, threads of Hindu nationalist ideologies, mass mobilisation and violence, policy perspectives and RSS–BJP relations, economic views, Muslims, cow protection, *ghar wapasi* (lit.: "homecoming"; idiomatically signifying reconversion to Hinduism), and the Ram temple in Ayodhya. Such research has highlighted "the growing involvement of the *parivar* in public policy" and shown how there has been a much closer co-ordination between the RSS and the BJP on critical policy issues under the Modi regime than under the 1998–2004 Vajpayee-era coalition government.[80] Another study on the "cultural entrenchment" of RSS-affiliated organisations has emphasised the importance of the "locality" and its multiple dynamics: first, at

[79] Rashtriya Swayamsevak Sangh, "Vision and Mission", https://www.rss.org//Encyc/2015/3/13/Vision-and-Mission.html.

[80] Andersen and Damle, *Messengers of Hindu Nationalism*.

the local-regional level, in discourses to a specific cultural and artistic programme; second, in relation to people operating in a more or less organised way in religious groups and associations; and third, in relation to people resisting militant Hinduism but paradoxically, and even inadvertently, adopting some aspects of its rhetoric.[81]

The history of the RSS has been revisited through the critique of M.S. Golwalkar's *Bunch of Thoughts*, the main ideological treatise of the organisation outlining the roots of its cultural nationalism, including the author's anti-modern views and anti-democratic objectives, in a work which is unapologetically casteist and deeply patriarchal.[82] The ideologies of some icons of the RSS – Keshav Baliram Hedgewar, Vinayak Damodar Savarkar, Madhav Sadashiv Golwalkar, Syama Prasad Mookerjee, Deendayal Upadhyaya, Balasaheb Deoras, Vijaya Raje Scindia, Atal Bihari Vajpayee, Lal Krishna Advani, Ashok Singhal, and Bal Thackeray – have been examined to understand the developments of Indian right-wing politics.[83] The role and representation of and by women within the Hindu-Hindutva discourse of the RSS and its women's wing, the Rashtriya Sevika Samiti, have been analysed to demonstrate that even when "women and men struggle for what they collectively call a 'Hindu Nation' they do not necessarily have the same entity in mind."[84] The interrogation of the RSS' humanitarian activities, particularly in the realm of disasters and conflict situations, has revealed that *seva* (service) is a political exercise – "a creative strategy to advance the idea of building a strong Hindu Rashtra."[85] However, none of the recent studies have acknowledged a crucial development: the Sangh Parivar's incorporation of climate change and energy issues into their Hindutva agenda, thereby magnifying the narratives of the Modi-led government.

Within the domain of climate change and renewable energy, the RSS draws upon references from ancient mythology and science and

[81] Berti, Jaoul, Kanungo, eds, *Cultural Entrenchment of Hindutva.*

[82] Kasbe, *Decoding the RSS.*

[83] Mukhopadhyay, *The RSS.*

[84] Bacchetta, *Gender in the Hindu Nation*, 4.

[85] Bhattacharjee, *Disaster Relief and the RSS*, 2.

employs them politically to support their concept of a Hindu Rashtra. In this context, a new understanding of history, culture, knowledge, physics, chemistry, engineering, technology, mathematics, geology, and geography is established, reflecting the ideological perspective of Hindutva. These narratives intertwine with the day-to-day politics of the Sangh Parivar, Modi, and the BJP government. They not only align themselves with big industry and capital but also assert their position as a *jagatguru* based on the claims of Hindu supremacy in a supposedly glorious past. It is often asserted that Hindu thoughts have been supreme, that they have survived at least since 3000 BCE in the face of the theism and human supremicism of the Judaeo-Christian and Islamic traditions. The Hindu tradition is apparently the only tradition that subscribes to the unity of life and to psychic attachment and affinity with nature in different forms at various levels, through a variety of pure rituals and sacrifices.[86] The RSS' Sumangalam campaign, which was launched to address climate change, explains that according to Indian knowledge traditions the entire universe is made of five elements, i.e. Space, Air, Fire, Water, and Earth. Collectively these five elements are called the Pancha Mahabhoot. If these elements are balanced and exist in their pure form, human life becomes blissful, meaningful, and fulfilling. The Indian concept of Pancha Mahabhoot, according to this view, was once common to and accepted by all the civilisations of the ancient world. It was "the key by which all the secrets of the world were explored, comprehended, and explained." On the one hand, this concept explained the principles of Ayurveda, and on the other it taught the techniques of sword and war fighting.[87] The supremacy, unity, and purity of Hindu life and thoughts run throughout the Hindu Right's conception of climate crisis which, they believe, should be addressed by restoring ancient Hindu religious philosophy, rituals, and social order, both ideologically and spatially. Worship of the deities of Pancha Mahabhoots – Vishnu, Devi, Shiva, Ganapathi, and Soorya –

[86] Singh, *Sumangalam*.

[87] Pancha Mahabhoota Organising Committee, "Introduction", https://panchmahabhoot.in/.

is meant to prevent any imbalance in the proportion of the five elements in the body as well as in society and the environment so that "shanti" is attained. "Agni-Shiva – A *Shiva Bhaktha* is supposed to check global warming and protect the planet. He should abstain from the activities that release CFCs in atmosphere that cause the warming of the planet."[88]

The RSS climate-change narrative prominently features the sun and its association with Hinduism, also reflecting the influence of Hindu nationalist culture, Hindu ecology, and a history of power that spans centuries. This narrative suggests that the idea of harnessing solar energy is deeply ingrained in Indian civilisation. Over time, this notion comes to be linked with Modi, and subsequently evolves into an anti-Muslim rhetoric: Prime Minister Modi said that "Since ancient times, different civilisations have given a special place to Sun. In the Indian tradition, Sun is the source of all forms of energy. As Rig Veda says, Sun God is the Soul of all beings, moving and non-moving. Many in India begin their day with a prayer to the Sun. Today, when the energy sources and excesses of our industrial age have put our planet in peril, the world must turn to Sun to power our future."[89]

The convergence of various elements, such as the power of sun, the leadership of Modi, the association with the state of Gujarat, and the establishment of the International Solar Alliance has played a significant role in shaping the communal history associated with Hindu nationalism. In this convergence Muslim rulers are condemned:

> Close to Vadnagar lies the ancient site of the Sun Temple of Modhera. The early Chinese traveller Hiuen Tsang (Xuan Zang) had visited the place around AD 640 and had referred to it as Anandpur. The Sun Temple is a Hindu temple dedicated to the solar deity Surya. Situated on

[88] Muralivallabhan, "Protection of Environment", 173.

[89] Press Information Bureau, "Remarks by Prime Minister Shri Narendra Modi at the Launch of the International Solar Alliance COP 21, Paris, 30 November 2015", Press Information Bureau, Government of India, 30 November 2015, https://pib.gov.in/newsite/PrintRelease.aspx?relid=132121.

the banks of the river Pushpavati, it is reckoned to have been built around 1026–27 CE during the reign of Bhima I of the Chaulukya dynasty. Like the famous Somnath temple by the sea near the port of Veraval in Saurashtra, the Sun Temple stands majestically on a site that had once been invaded by Mahmud of Ghazni, and was apparently built to commemorate the resistance offered by the local people to his marauding forces. Mahmud of Ghazni is long gone, reduced to dust as is the wont of even the greatest plunderers and invaders in history, but the Sun Temple continues to stand tall and provide inspiration to generations of Indians.[90]

Modi is portrayed as a recipient of divine grace and believed to possess exceptional qualities. Throughout his life, a strong Hindu background has fostered his profound connection with the sun, which is seen as a supernatural and superhuman bond. This connection is often cited as a valuable resource to support his efforts in addressing climate change and promoting renewable energy. According to one such life narrative, as a young boy practising Hinduism Modi developed a deep connection to an ancient temple dedicated to the sun god located near his home. Being a practitioner of Surya Namaskar (sun salutation), which is also represented by the corresponding yoga *asana*, the radiant sun has long held a unique and profound meaning for him. Just as it does for millions of Hindus globally, the fiery orb of the sun symbolises eternal life, energy, healing, and purity bestowed upon all living beings on earth.[91]

The discussions surrounding renewable energy, solar power, and climate change frequently reference the persona and influence of Modi, who concurrently plays the role of a prominent Hindu nationalist leader. According to the RSS perspective, Modi's initiatives in addressing climate change can be attributed to his reverence for a pre-Islamic and pre-colonial pure Hindu culture. This is personified in him as the "Solar Superman". "International Solar Alliance: The Saffron Supergird Superpower" is the title of an article published in 2022 in the *Organiser*. It narrates the history of the making of the ISA in the context of the global divisions between North and South

[90] Chinoy, *India & Mother Earth*, 27–8.

[91] Ibid., 28.

and between South and South on renewable energy and climate change. It describes the idea of ISA that has been widely and indisputably acknowledged as being the brainchild of Prime Minister Narendra Modi. Not just the ISA itself, but one of ISA's most ambitious ideas of OSOWOG (One Sun One World One Grid) was also Modi's hypothesis. "Talking to a group of people at his PM's residence at 10, Lok Kalyan Marg, New Delhi on June 8, 2014, PM Narendra Modi had first spoken about the 'Saffron Revolution'." Quick to quip that he was aware that the mere mention of the word "saffron" raises eyebrows, he further revealed that the colour "saffron" represents the energy of the Sun. The article talks of how Modi spoke of the importance of the sun in ancient, pre-colonial, pre-Islamic, Hindu traditions and repeatedly evoked the saffron-coloured imaginary that signified the rise of Hindu nationalist forces in India: "The transformative leadership of that Solar Superman started a few years ago with the declared vision of initiating a global 'saffron revolution'. The vision has led to the formation of an organisation seeking to unify the world with the ubiquitous energy of the Sun, that paints the sky saffron as it rises and sets."[92]

The Sangh's endeavours in addressing climate change are interrelated with its daily Hindutva political activities, where affiliated organisations and individual *swayamsevaks* merge their agendas of holy Hindu science and technology, the Ram temple, the motherland, and the Hindu Rashtra with the elements of water, fire, sky, and earth. By forming formal partnerships with government departments and scientific institutions associated with the government, they enhance their credibility and influence in the public domain. On 6 November 2022 the Vijnana Bharati (Vibha), a Sangh affiliate self-described as a "Swadeshi science movement", organised a conference titled Akash Tattva – Akash for Life in Dehradun, the capital of Uttarakhand state, in collaboration with the Indian Space Research Organisation (ISRO) and various departments of the science ministry. This event marked the beginning of a series of Pancha Mahabhoota conferences as part

[92] Shashanka Shekhar Panda, "International Solar Alliance: The Saffron Supergrid Superpower", *Organiser*, 10 January 2022, https://organiser.org/2022/01/10/14606/bharat/international-solar-alliance-the-saffron-supergrid-superpower/.

of the Sumangalam campaign. The objective of these conferences was to seek solutions to global warming from an "Indian perspective". RSS functionaries, BJP politicians, and scientists shared the stage, while occasional calls of "Bharat Mata Ki Jai" and "Jai Shri Ram" resounded from the audience, amidst scientific discussions on the latest research breakthroughs relating to Akash (the sky). The topics covered included the proposal for an Indian-inspired space tourism experience and the study of a cave in Tamil Nadu that could aid in weather-pattern prediction. During the inaugural address a union minister, Jitendra Singh, attributed the conceptualisation of the conference series to Suresh "Bhaiyyaji" Joshi, former general secretary of the RSS, who was also present at the inauguration. Singh highlighted the fact that India had forsaken the development of its traditional knowledge and understanding of indigenous resources while pursuing technologies and materials developed by foreigners. Suresh "Bhaiyyaji" Joshi stated that the fairy tales of yesteryears had become today's reality and emphasised the need to merge the past with modern science. Indians had been following the "wrong path" for the past seven decades and a course correction was necessary. He equated the revered saints and gurus of Hinduism with today's scientists because these sages had preserved our knowledge systems.

In his address, the ISRO chairman S. Somanath acknowledged initial scepticism within the scientific community regarding the integration of the two thought processes. He highlighted that the conference serves as a showcase of how the past can be connected to modern technology. Dr A.K. Sood, the government's principal scientific adviser, noted that Indians have been leading sustainable lifestyles for centuries, pre-dating the global popularity of such concepts. Ancient Indian and Hindu knowledge took centre stage during the event. Aakash Porwal, the founder of a Mumbai-based start-up, "Space Aura", which aims to launch space tourism for Indians by 2025, stated that the experience would be a unique fusion of space travel and Hindu culture: space tourists' one-hour stay in the stratosphere would be enhanced by ancient chants, hymns, and Ayurvedic aromas.[93]

[93] I participated in the two-day conference's opening session as an audience member and interacted with several participants. Local newspapers and television channels covered the conference extensively. For a brief report: Mohana

By referencing Hindu myths and history, ancient science and knowledge, and a divinely inspired Modi the RSS constructs a new Hindu identity based on climate change and renewable energy. The operations of the RSS also revolve around the political and governmental alliances they choose, the functions they perform, and the many connections they forge amongst themselves under the Hindu nationalist regime. Modi, the RSS and its affiliated organisations, the media and communications, and government departments are the main forces shaping this new climate and energy identity. In trying to achieve Hindu Rashtra goals, the RSS has created distinctive coalitions with environmental, scientific, business, and citizens' groups.

## Modi and the Hindu Nationalist Politics of Climate Change

Modi and his government have strategically utilised a vast array of Hindu nationalist resources to promote their particular perspective on climate change and renewable energy. However, this approach often exists with other resources derived from climate science, renewable-energy technology, industry, investment, capital, and international negotiations. Consequently, it is crucial to analyse how the Hindu nationalist political discourse manifests itself in the realm of climate change and renewable energy in everyday operations and long-term endeavours. I scrutinise Modi's speeches, writings, government activities, and policy proposals to discern how Hindu religious discourses surrounding climate change are not merely sporadic references but deeply entrenched within the larger agenda of RSS nationalist politics. These discourses also function as a source of authoritative knowledge for the government, bolstering nationalism and communal positions.

Modi's Hindu nationalist politics on climate change and renewable energy have several themes: 1. The glorification of ancient

---

Basu, "'Pancha Mahabhoota', 'Desi Space Tourism' – Wisdom Met Modern Science at Akash Tattva", *The Print*, 6 November 2022, https://theprint.in/science/pancha-mahabhoota-desi-space-tourism-how-ancient-wisdom-met-modern-science-at-akash-tattva/1200824/.

Bharat; 2. Exclusive Hindu narratives; 3. Assertion of Indian nation power and its civilisational identity as *jagatguru*; and 4. Focus on manpower and yoga. The following subsections explore the intersection of Modi's ideological themes and the RSS' politics.

### *The Glory of Ancient Bharat*

The RSS constructs a narrative of ancient India that encapsulates a vast reservoir of knowledge, wisdom, heritage, and power. From geography and environment to education and innovation, from science and technology to town planning and artistry, and from philosophy to religion, the list of India's glorious history is extensive, depicting what is often referred to as "Bharat's golden age". This rich cultural and political history has been drawn from a bewildering mass of evidence, including Vedic literary writings, cultural traditions, religious texts, and mythical accounts. These supposedly historical accounts are often juxtaposed against Muslim Mughal aggressors, shaping the narrative within that oppositional context. A prominent element in these narratives is the assertion of Hindu supremacy over all other regions, cultures, and religions.

"Bharat is the greatest land on earth, and it alone is *Karmabhoomi*, the Land of Action, while the rest are Lands of Pleasure . . . Similar sentiments are also found in Vedic, Upanishadic and Brahmanic literature, the most ancient literature in the world,"[94] says Chaman Lal, a prominent RSS leader and author of several articles and books:

> There was a time when greater India had her cultural empires in the whole of South-East Asia for fourteen centuries and Hindu and Buddhist pioneers carried the torch of religion and culture to far off South America, Mexico, Guatemala, Japan, China, Korea, Philippines in the east and to various nations in the west. About 3500 years ago Syria (ancient Surya) had an empire of the Sun and her Aryan rulers had names such as Ishwar Dutt, Vidya Dutt and Chandra Dutt. (Read "*The Bible as History*" by Werner Keller). A hundred Ayar Brahmin ruled a 2500 mile long empire in South America till 1532. (Read "Hindu America")[95]

[94] Lal, *India,* 24.
[95] Ibid., 19.

The greatness of ancient India has to be defined against "enemies". Chaman Lal emphasises that the nationalism of the Vedic Aryans was not only prayerful but also militant. They prayed not only for peace on earth and goodwill among men but also for the annihilation of enemies. "Vedic nationalists knew that preservation of nationalism meant cultivation of power in all spheres. Even while partaking of food and drink they were thinking of the national purpose to which the strength so built was to be put."[96]

Such RSS narratives strongly influenced Modi, prompting him to consistently draw upon such constructions of ancient India. In doing so, he skilfully envisions and communicates the future trajectory of the nation. In his inaugural speech to the UN General Assembly in September 2014, he emphasised the significance of "India's ancient wisdom" in shaping the country's position in global politics, particularly in addressing the complexities of conflict and environmental degradation. During the UN Convention on Climate Change in 2015 he reiterated India's commitment to environmental action, for "it is guided by the ancient belief that people and the planet are inseparable, and that human well-being and nature are indivisible." He highlighted the importance of incorporating ancient Indian sacred philosophy as a legitimate epistemology for shaping present-day climate policies.[97] This sentiment was echoed in his March 2018 speech at the opening of the International Solar Alliance, where he stressed the necessity of drawing upon "ancient philosophy" to tackle the challenge of climate change. Modi referred to the significant place assigned to the sun god in ancient India. He expressed his belief that a successful transition to solar power would fulfil the aspirations of ancient times, describing it as "the prayer of ancient ages".[98] A Hindutva intellectual later clarified that Modi's speech was an affirmation of the sun as "Brahman" – "the spiritual Supreme

[96] Ibid., 28.

[97] Narendra Modi, "PM's Statement at the United Nations Summit for the Adoption of Post-2015 Development Agenda", 25 September 2015, https://www.narendramodi.in/text-of-pm-s-statement-at-the-united-nations-summit-for-the-adoption-of-post-2015-development-agenda-332923.

[98] Government of India, "PM Modi's Speech at the Founding Conference of the International Solar Alliance", 25 March2018, https://pib.gov.in/

Being".[99] On another occasion, Modi attributed India's hesitancy in promoting its environmental wisdom to the historical legacy of being enslaved for centuries, which led to the confinement of its spiritual knowledge within books. The challenge of climate change could, he believed, only be effectively addressed if the ancient texts and traditions were put into practice.[100]

The influence of the RSS and Modi's Hindu nationalist discourse on climate change is evident in the responses of the Indian government. For example, under the UN Framework Convention on Climate Change Conference, countries, including India, adopted the INDC (Intended Nationally Determined Contributions) in which countries determine their contributions in the context of their national priorities, circumstances, and capabilities. The INDC is a primary means for governments to communicate internationally the steps they will take to address climate change in their own countries. India's INDC, submitted in 2015, articulated the glory of ancient India:

> India has a long history and tradition of harmonious co-existence between man and nature. Human beings here have regarded fauna and flora as part of their family. This is part of our heritage and manifest in our lifestyle and traditional practices. We represent a culture that calls our planet Mother Earth. As our ancient text says; "Keep pure! For the Earth is our mother! And we are her children!" The ancient Indian practice of Yoga, for example, is a system that is aimed at balancing contentment and worldly desires that helps pursue a path of moderation and a sustainable lifestyle. Environmental sustainability, which involves both intra-generational and inter-generational equity, has been the approach of Indians for very long.[101]

---

ViewVideo.aspx?V_ID=49517&MinID=1325&VPRID=42039&Day=&Month=3&Year=208.

[99] Chinoy, "Modi Global Leader", 244.

[100] Narendra Modi, "India's Cultural Heritage Holds the Answers to All Global Problems, says PM Modi", 29 October 2017, https://www.narendramodi.in/text-of-pm-modi-s-speech-at-dashamah-soundarya-lahari-parayanotsava-mahasamarpane-in-bengaluru--539503-.

[101] Government of India, "India's Intended Nationally Determined Contri-

Next, I explore how Modi's narratives of the great ancient Bharat are, in fact, an effort to construct a broader, exclusive narrative that emphasises Hindu religion and traditions as the sole foundation for addressing climate change and embracing renewable energy.

### *Exclusive Hindu Narratives*

"Hindu & Bharatiya are synonymous," says Dr Mohan Bhagwat, Sarsanghchalak (supremo) of the RSS since 2009. He adds, "When we say Bharatiya, it is not merely a geographical expression. Because, the geographical boundaries of Bharat undergo variations, when it either expands or contracts. The word Bharat represents a tendency, a nature. In short, all these words are synonymous. And Hindu is the word that clearly reflects the sum and substance of all these words."[102] According to this understanding, all those who are domiciled in Bharat, from the point of view of identity and on the basis of *rashtriyata* ("nationalness") are "inevitably Hindu". In this view, even "The tribal society is Hindu."[103]

According to the RSS, its ideologues, and front organisations, Hindu religion, culture, and tradition hold unquestionable supremacy over all others. They clearly outline their "national vision" where "Hindus are a nation, not a religious community", "the distinctive feature of our nation is Sanatana Dharma", and "Undivided India is our motherland."[104] They unequivocally state that

> Hindu culture is our national culture, Hindu society is our national society, Hindu art is our national art, Hindu literature is our national literature. Hindu history is our national history; there is no Muslim Period or British Period in this history; it is a history of continuous Hindu struggle against Muslim invaders and British colonialists. The struggle is still continuing.

---

bution: Working Towards Climate Justice", 2 October 2015, https://faolex.fao.org/docs/pdf/ind188478.pdf.

[102] Bhagwat, *Future Bharat,* 47–8.

[103] Ibid., 66.

[104] Chatterjee, *The Concept of Hindu Nation*, 44–5.

> People subscribing to the theologies of alien religions are minorities in our country, not a part of our nation. We consider these alien ideologies to be enemies of our nation. The goal is to bring our minorities back into our nation after destroying the deadly intoxication of these ideologies.[105]

Modi's *Convenient Action* serves as a compelling illustration of the emphasis on Vedic religious texts to frame climate change within the broader Hindu nationalist politics. He begins with quotes from the *Atharva Veda*: "The purity in us is due to the Earth. The Earth is my mother and I (the seer) am Her son. Cloud is my father, let that nourish us."[106] He recounts his life experiences and derives overarching conclusions from them: "I studied the *Prithvi-Sukta* of *Atharva Veda* during my college days. The sixty-three Suktas (couplets) composed thousands of years ago, contain a whole spectrum of knowledge which is now being propounded under various scientific, academic and analytical banners during discussions on global warming, damage to earth's environment and the resultant climate change."[107] He also explains how the Rig Veda has emphasised the importance of the *panch tatvas* – earth, air, water, solar energy, and sky – to underscore that the entirety of life systems on earth is based on the harmonious functioning of these five elements. "Therefore, sustainable use of these natural elements has been consistently advocated in all ancient Indian scriptures like *Rig Veda*, *Manu Smriti*, *Yagyavalkya Smriti*, etc."[108] In several other platforms, he deliberates on the potential contributions Hinduism could offer in addressing climate change.[109] He has consistently advocated for what he refers to as "lifestyle"-focused approaches derived from Hindu beliefs and

[105] Ibid., 45.

[106] Modi, *Convenient Action*, 2.

[107] Ibid., 10.

[108] Ibid., 12.

[109] Narendra Modi, "PM's Address at 'Samvaad' – Global Hindu-Buddhist Initiative on Conflict Avoidance and Environment Consciousness", 3 Sept. 2015, http://www.narendramodi.in/text-of-pm-s-address-at-samvad- global-hindu-buddhist-initiative-on-conflict-avoidance-and-environment-consciousness-290614.

practices to address climate change. These approaches encompass the promotion of vegetarianism and involve making significant policy changes in India.[110]

These exclusive Hindu accounts have become closely linked with the actions and initiatives of the Indian government. The secretary, Ministry of New and Renewable Energy, Government of India, has formally stated:

> The *Gayatri Mantra* from the ancient Rig Veda is the most revered of hymns in Hinduism – and it is dedicated to the ultimate source of energy: the sun. The government is looking to rope in an unlikely set of brand ambassadors for its ambitious solar energy program: India's godmen. The Narendra Modi government has asked spiritual leaders to install solar power units in their *ashrams,* or hermitages, and promote this renewable form of energy among millions of their followers.[111]

At COP 21 in Paris in 2015 the Government of India launched its official publication "PARAMPARA: India's Culture of Climate Friendly Sustainable Practices" which documents Hindu religious texts and traditions to solve climate challenges. The report included references to a range of "ancient" Indian practices, from air-drying clothes (instead of using electric dryers), using the sun's energy to dry spices, to the virtues of cycle rickshaws – a fossil-fuel-free mode of transport using only muscular force. Modi launched LiFE (Lifestyles for Environment) in 2022, which claims that "for centuries, ancient Indian traditions have advocated an environmentally conscious lifestyle, a life of simplicity. Three out of four *ashramas* (stages of life) – *brahmacharya* (student life), *vanaprastha* (retired life) and *sanyasa* (phase of renunciation) – emphasise leading a frugal lifestyle and practising detachment from materialism."[112]

[110] Richa Sharma, "India Should Lead Fight Against Climate Change: Modi", *New Indian Express*, 6 April 2015, https://www.newindianexpress.com/nation/2015/apr/06/India-Should-Lead-Fight-Against-Climate-Change-Modi-738888.html.

[111] Manu Balachandran, "India is Going to Use Godmen to Spread the Use of Solar Energy", *Quartz*, 13 September 2016, https://finance.yahoo.com/news/india-going-godmen-spread-solar-063214818.html.

[112] MoEFCC and UNDP, *Prayaas Se Prabhaav Tak: From Mindless Consumption to Mindful Utilization*, New Delhi: Government of India, 2022, 5.

In this discourse on climate change, ancient India is portrayed as a nation where Hindu religion, as interpreted through specific authoritative texts and practices, is the sole representative of a universal climate change sensibility. Through governmental initiatives a particular version of Hindu is officially endorsed and supported by the state, making it in effect the state-sponsored religion. This approach excludes other religions and marginalises diverse interpretations within Hinduism itself. It also creates an exclusive Hindu environmental subject in endless praise of Modi: "Modi jee, U are a Man of Action. A World Leader. Champion of the Earth. Feeling so proud that you are our Great PM ever & I want to see you again PM in 2024. Salute to U Sir. Jai Hind. Bharat Mata ki Jai."[113]

Next I address the international aspirations of Hindutva politics and explore how these aspirations are reflected in Modi's climate discourse.

### *Assertion of Indian National Power and its Civilisational Identity as Jagatguru*

The RSS has throughout been driven by a strong focus on national power. Prominent RSS figures, such as V.D. Savarkar, M.S. Golwalkar, H.V. Sheshadri, and several others believed that ancient Hindu civilisation's "golden age" was lost on account of material and moral weaknesses, leading to the subjugation of Hindus by Muslim, Christian, and British power. The RSS' mission is centred around the reconstruction of Hindu civilisation by acquiring power, eradicating the humiliation of a millennium of "foreign" rule, and disseminating the enlightening principles of Hindu religion globally. Golwalkar articulated this mission when he expressed the conviction that Hindus were a great people entrusted with a World Mission, a belief that should be ever-present in their hearts. This worldview envisions a constant struggle for kings and states and posits that genuine security can only be achieved through the establishment of *sarvabhauma* (universal empire). Beyond the goal of world conquest,

[113] Deepak Singh Bisht, "Congratulations Sir . . .", 11 December 2022, https://www.narendramodi.in/hi/social-media-corner-december-11th-2022-566393.

a more restrained conception of Hindu civilisation's scope was encapsulated in the idea of Akhand Bharat (Undivided India), which encompassed regions such as Bhutan and Nepal to the north, Myanmar to the east, and Sri Lanka to the south.[114]

Dattopant Bapurao Thengadi, a prominent ideologue of the RSS and the founder of its important front organisations such as the Swadeshi Jagaran Manch, Bharatiya Mazdoor Sangh, and Bharatiya Kisan Sangh, referred to this mission as "Param Vaibhavam" (highest glory) and raised a crucial question for proponents of the Hindu Rashtra who take pride in their glorious past: Do they possess a long-range vision of a glorious future for the world, "From sea to sea, over all land, one State?" He drew attention to Golwalkar's *Bunch of Thoughts*, a philosophical work on the RSS in which, he said, one can hear the voice of a seer articulating the "World Mission of the Hindu Rashtra." He then proclaimed:

> This is India's destination – *Param Vaibhavam.* Not the invariably transitory superpower status, but the pre-ordained *Jagad-Guru-pada.*
>
> Bharat is eminently suited to play this role – Bharat with *Sanatana Dharma* as its absolute referent and "All is One" as its ultimate realisation; its tradition of ever-changing socio-economic order in the light of the unchanging, eternal universal laws of *Dharma.*[115]

India has been projected as *jagatguru* owing to its ancient scientific traditions spanning various domains – electrical science, mechanics, mechanical science, metallurgy, aeronautics, mathematics, time, astronomy, chemistry, botany, architecture, zoology, and health. Thus, "today's generation is faced with the challenge of reviving India's position as the Golden Bird and the *Jagatguru.*"[116]

The BJP manifestos for the 2014 and 2019 elections emphasised India's significant civilisational roles in the world. The 2014 manifesto highlighted India's status as the world's oldest civilisation, with a rich history of contributions to the progress of humanity dating back several millennia before the Christian era. It acknowledged the

114 Basrur, "Modi, *Hindutva*", 7–10.
115 Thengadi, *Third Way*, 230.
116 Soni, *India's Glorious*, 14.

challenge of reigniting the spark to revive the past glory of Mother India.[117] Thereafter, Modi's foreign policy in general and climate change and renewable-energy initiatives in particular have been filled with the ideology of making Hindu Rashtra a powerhouse and its civilisational identity as *jagatguru*. Ian Hall characterises this as "Modi's vision for India as a normative power" whereby the Indian prime minister sees India as *vishwaguru* (the world's guru) to tackle pressing transnational challenges like climate change, sustainable development, terrorism, and the international power order, all the while drawing inspiration from a nineteenth-century Hindu nationalist and monk, Swami Vivekananda, famous for his ideas of an "Indian race" and a distinct "mission" for the world.[118]

In his first Independence Day speech in 2014, Modi quoted Swami Vivekananda to call for "Mother India" to act as a *vishwaguru*: "I can see before my eyes Mother India awakening once again. My Mother India would be seated as the World Guru."[119] At the inauguration of the Indian Pavilion at CoP 21 in Paris he spoke "to the world" and "to our people" that "we are a nation that must also lead in combating climate change . . . It comes from our commitment to the world. Above all, it arises, from our timeless traditions and beliefs."[120] At the Climate Adaptation Summit 2021 he emphasised "India's civilizational values" to guide the world.[121] At COP 26, he called upon the world to carry forward the concept of LiFE as a

[117] Bharatiya Janata Party, *Ek Bharat Shreshtha Bharat: Election Manifesto 2014*, New Delhi, Bharatiya Janata Party, 2014, 1.

[118] Ian Hall, "Modi's Vision for India as a Normative Power", *East Asia Forum*, 8 February 2017, https://www.eastasiaforum.org/2017/02/08/modis-vision-for-india-as-a-normative-power/. Also see Ian Hall, "Narendra Modi and India's normative power", *International Affairs* 93: 1, 2017, 113–31.

[119] "Narendra Modi's First Independence Day Speech: Full Text", *India Today*, https://www.indiatoday.in/india/story/narendra-modi-independence-day-speech-full-text-red-fort-204216-2014-08-15.

[120] "Climate Change is a Major Global Challenge: PM Narendra Modi at Inauguration of India Pavilion at COP21 in Paris", https://www.narendramodi.in/pm-s-address-at-the-inauguration-of-the-indian-pavilion-at-cop21-paris--385201.

[121] "PM Modi's Address at Climate Adaptation Summit 2021", 25 January

"campaign of Mindful and Deliberate Utilisation, instead of Mindless and Destructive Consumption."[122]

This Hindu civilisational emphasis creates a new narrative within nationalist politics, particularly for the Hindutva World Mission. It energises the domestic and international audiences of Modi and the RSS, who interpret these assertions as a resurgence of the great ancient Hindu Bharat as never before: "When India grows, the world grows; when India reforms, the world transforms."[123]

### *Focus on Manpower and Yoga*

The "biological" – the body and the workings of the body – is central to the philosophies and daily practices of Hindu nationalism. Biological metaphors and concepts litter the landscapes of the Hindu "body politic" – from metaphors of "pure" Hindu blood, blood ties, tissues, and DNA to metaphors of biological geographies, landscapes, and ecologies.[124] The idea of a militaristic and armed masculinity is deeply rooted in patriarchal conceptions of Hinduism and a biopolitical conception of the body.[125]

Thus, the RSS's *shakhas* (branches) are officially called a "man building mission" through daily routine programmes including physical exercise, singing patriotic songs in a chorus, group discussions on a varied range of subjects, and a prayer for the motherland. *Swayamsevaks* are trained in *dand* (fighting with sticks) and *niyudh* (martial

---

2021, https://www.narendramodi.in/pm-modi-s-address-at-climate-adaption-summit-2021-553541.

[122] "National Statement by Prime Minister Shri Narendra Modi at COP26 Summit in Glasgow", Ministry of External Affairs, Government of India, 2 November 2021, https://www.mea.gov.in/Speeches-Statements.htm?dtl/34466/National+Statement+by+Prime+Minister+Shri+Narendra+Modi+at+COP26+Summit+in+Glasgow#:~:text=I%20would%20like%20to%20draw,basic%20foundation%20of%20One%20World.

[123] Narendra Modi Address to the Seventy-sixth UN General Assembly, 25 September 2021, https://www.pmindia.gov.in/en/news_updates/pms-address-at-the-76th-session-of-the-united-nations-general-assembly/.

[124] Subramaniam, *Holy Science,* 11.

[125] McDonald, "Physiological Patriots?", 343–58.

art). All these physical activities serve to improve physical fitness, confidence, and the team spirit. "It is a guarantee of the unafraid movement of women and a powerful deterrent to the indecent behaviour towards them, also a powerful threat to the brutal and anti-national forces. But the most important aspect is it is a university for training the appropriate workers to be made available for the requirements of the various fields of life of the nation."[126] In a recent RSS book, concrete measures for personality building are elaborated upon – morning prayer, food, study, Surya Namaskar, yoga, sports, and festivals.[127] The checklist for an enlightened RSS family asks: Does everyone in the family follow a schedule of meditation, physical exercise, and yoga every day? Have you had a body massage with oil before your bath at least once a week? Observed a fast at least once in a fortnight? Visited a meditation or yoga centre at least once a month?[128] The physical strength and power acquired through training, discipline, and organisation have a purpose: "Only strong will power coupled with fearlessness protects himself [*sic*] and his nation; and a Hindu is born fearless as his Atman never dies. So be brave, be fearless, be prepared for a drastic change, and be a man of dynamic heroism, take a vow to defend the nation as *the world belongs to the brave*."[129]

Since 2014, under Modi the topics of yoga, climate change, and biopolitics have gained in prominence. During his first speech to the United Nations as India's prime minister he proposed the start of an International Yoga Day:

> We talk about climate change. We talk about holistic health care. When we talk about back to basic, then on this subject, I would specially like to tell one thing to you. Yoga is an invaluable gift of our ancient tradition. Yoga embodies unity of mind and body; thought and action; restraint and fulfilment; harmony between man and nature; a holistic approach to health and well being. It is not about exercise but to discover the sense of oneness with yourself, the world and the nature.

[126] Rashtriya Swayamsevak Sangh, "Basic Facts", https://www.rss.org//Encyc/2017/6/3/basic-faq-on-rss-eng.html.

[127] *Sakha Surbhi*.

[128] *Enlightening of Family*, 66–7.

[129] Paliwal, *What Hindus Should Do*, 5.

> By changing our lifestyle and creating consciousness, it can help us deal with climate change. Let us work towards adopting an International Yoga Day.[130]

The inaugural International Yoga Day took place on 21 June 2015. Subsequently, it has grown into an annual event observed under the leadership of Modi, the Indian government, and the RSS along with its affiliates. The first Yoga Day celebrations, held in New Delhi, had the participation of over 35,000 individuals, including Modi himself. During the event he collectively performed twenty-one yoga postures for a duration of thirty-five minutes. The postures were extensively showcased and the practice has been repeated each year. The RSS' Akhil Bharatiya Pratinidhi Sabha passed a resolution in 2015: "Yoga is Bharat's civilisational contribution to the world. Derived from the root 'Yuj' – meaning union and samadhi. Yoga is not limited to physical exercise but is essentially a holistic way of life leading to the union of body mind, intellect and soul as envisaged by sages like Maharshi Patanjali."[131] Modi and the RSS have greatly promoted the internationalisation of yoga, organising massive gatherings of people, accompanied by extensive media coverage and the circulation of large images. These efforts are aimed at creating a broader audience for the ideology of Hindutva. The Modi government has created a ministry of AYUSH to mainstream Ayurveda, Yoga and Naturopathy, Unani, Siddha, and Homoeopathy, all "with a vision of reviving the profound knowledge of our ancient systems of medicine and ensuring the optimal development and propagation of the Ayush systems of healthcare."[132]

Muslims have expressed their concern over this official promotion of yoga in a nationalistic and Hindutva context under the pretext of addressing climate change. The events have, they feel, been a mix

[130] Narendra Modi, United Nations General Assembly, 27 September 2022, https://www.un.org/en/ga/69/meetings/gadebate/27sep/india.shtml.

[131] Rashtriya Swayamsevak Sangh, "ABPS Resolution: Welcoming the International Yoga Day", https://www.rss.org//Encyc/2015/3/14/rss-resolution-yoga-day-eng.html.

[132] Ministry of Ayush, "About", https://ayush.gov.in/.

of cultural nationalism, commercialisation, and subtle coercion.[133] Furthermore, questions have been raised about the validity of suggesting yoga as a solution to climate challenges: What was the need to say that yoga can help us deal with climate change? How can any fitness regimen help humanity deal with climate change? Even if yoga regulates the body system and purges the body of toxins, how can one extend this to suggest that changing our lifestyles and creating consciousness through yoga can help to deal with climate change?[134]

These doubts are irrelevant because for Modi the meaning and practice of yoga is very elastic, involving spirituality, self-care, peace, harmony, health, devotion, Indian ancient culture, and tradition. In 2017, addressing the International Yoga festival in Rishikesh, he said: "World is today threatened by challenges-terrorism, climate change." Underlining that "there should be peace among nations," he prescribed yoga as "a way to create such harmony and peace within individuals, families, societies, nations . . . Yoga expands our limited sense of self to see our families, societies and mankind as an extension of our own self . . . Yoga makes an individual a better person in thought, action, knowledge and devotion."[135] Leading the International Yoga Day celebrations in 2022 he said: "This whole universe starts from our own body and soul. The universe starts from us. And, Yoga makes us conscious of everything within us and builds a sense of awareness."[136]

Christopher Patrick Miller, specifically dealing with the topic of

[133] Jason Burke, "Modi's Plan to Change India and the World through Yoga Angers Religious Minorities", *The Guardian*, 6 June 2015, https://www.theguardian.com/world/2015/jun/06/narendra-modi-yoga-india.

[134] Sohail Hashmi, "Why on Earth Would Modi Link Yoga with Climate Change?", DailyO, 7 May 2015, https://www.dailyo.in/lifestyle/modi-ramdev-yoga-climate-change-international-day-of-yoga-un-cfc-pollution-3575.

[135] "From Terrorism to Climate Change, PM Narendra Modi Prescribes Yoga as Global Panacea", *Financial Express,* 2 March 2017, https://www.financialexpress.com/india-news/from-terrorism-to-climate-change-pm-narendra-modi-prescribes-yoga-as-global-panacea/572263/.

[136] "PM Modi Full Speech on Yoga Day 2022 at Mysuru: "Yoga is a Problem-Solver, Brings Inner Peace", *India Today*, 21 June 2022, https://www.youtube.com/watch?v=Z-TWV6mEARo.

yoga, climate change, and biopolitics under the leadership of Modi and the BJP after 2014, speaks of "the polyvalency and malleability of the word yoga itself" and the many ways by which the practice of yoga has been put to use in contemporary society to achieve specific goals. There have been numerous forms of yoga historically and in our time. Among these are itinerant warrior asceticism, which seeks to attain powers aimed at controlling others' bodies, and the promotion of karma yoga (sometimes violent) as an expression of selfless service to the Indian nation-state. Based on his research data, it is evident that Modi and the BJP's yoga discourses bear a striking resemblance to historical discourses that emphasise the objectives of cultivating positive international relations and bolstering domestic nationalist politics. Miller concludes: "Modi and the BJP capitalise on yoga's polyvalency to achieve political ends . . . yoga actually appears to be quite conducive to the right-wing BJP's economic aspirations, in so far as the two seemingly disparate versions of yoga for climate change and yoga for self-care function together to support Hindutva's neoliberal economic vision."[137]

There are several other instances of yoga being employed for various purposes simultaneously. Take, for instance, Paramhansa Yogananda, who was teaching "original Christianity", kriya-yoga, while also developing environmentally and intellectually sound spiritual communities in America. However, alongside these endeavours he "showed great admiration for Italy's fascist leader, Benito Mussolini," and "also praised Hitler and his policies."[138] Modi initially promoted yoga as a means to address climate change, but then strategically expanded its scope to gain international recognition and legitimacy for both himself and the RSS' civilisational mission.

In the realm of environmental, climate change, and energy politics, scholars have also recognised the influence of masculinity in shaping both the perception of the crisis and its potential resolution. Discussions surrounding environmental security advocate for masculine, forceful, and authoritative leadership and state-heavy measures

[137] Miller, "Soft Power and Biopower", 103–4.

[138] Neumann, *Finding God*, 172.

to tackle climate change.[139] In this context, the RSS and Modi's approach of bio-power through yoga matches with these prevailing narratives of displaying determination, hardness, and unwavering toughness characteristic of a climate leader. The notion of a strong leader and state is also deemed necessary to rescue and support the vulnerable and weak masses of people who are victims of environmental challenges.

Modi-dominated and centralised climate and energy policies are also driven by a specific alignment with corporate, technological, and political economy approaches closely integrated into the current big-capital-led modern growth strategy in the country. I will illustrate how large corporates, mega projects, modern technology, and national-international markets serve as the primary driving forces behind Modi's policies. These agents advocate for large-scale, extremely extractive, and capital-intensive projects that shape the direction of climate and energy policies in the country. I will focus on renewable energy because the Indian government has repeatedly emphasised this as the core of its climate and energy policy.

## "Techno-Corporatist" Climate Policy

> We have chosen the path of reform, perform and transform. Today the way we are making investment in Indian economy easier is unprecedented. It is the result of that investing in India, travelling to India, working in India, manufacturing in India, and exporting products and services from India to the world, everything has become much easier than earlier. We have taken the resolve to completely get rid of the era of licenses and permits. Instead of red tape we are laying the red carpet.
>
> – Narendra Modi, World Economic Forum, Davos[140]

[139] Buckingham and Masson, eds, *Understanding Climate Change*; Daggett, "Petro-masculinity", 25–44; Detraz, "Threats or Vulnerabilities?", 104–20.

[140] "Prime Minister's Statement on the Subject 'Creating a Shared Future in a Fractured World' in the World Economic Forum", 23 January 2018, https://www.mea.gov.in/Speeches-Statements.htm?dtl/29378/Prime+Ministers+Keynote+Speech+at+Plenary+Session+of+World+Economic+Forum+Davos+January+23+2018.

Climate and energy scholars describe "techno-corporatist" as a form of ecological modernisation which emphasises solving environmental issues through technical methods facilitated by the collaboration of economic, political, and scientific elites in corporatist policy-making structures. Techno-corporatism centres on technology and highly prescribed top-down approaches, aiming to present universal solutions.[141] It has also been argued that the effectiveness of renewable-energy transformations in addressing climate change depends on various factors and can be influenced by "vested interests" in the political economy. Espen Moe conducted a study on the politics of vested interests in the renewable-energy sectors of Japan, China, USA, Germany, Denmark, and Norway which highlighted two important aspects: firstly, the interconnections between technology, economics, and politics which explain the growth of renewable energy in the context of a country's underlying political economy dynamics. Secondly, the significance of placing renewables within a broader political-economy tradition that focuses on structural change, recognising renewables as just one of many industries and energy providers throughout history with transformative potential.[142] I employ these studies to elucidate the process through which Modi has orchestrated the growth of significant corporate and technological structures within the realm of renewable energy as an important strategy towards climate change which also replaced the local, decentralised, autonomous identity of renewables. Environmental and energy non-governmental organisations (NGOs) appear to be aligning their strategies with the predominant renewable-energy industries, which are collaborating with Modi's administration to establish larger-scale national or regional super-grids, as against localised energy supply. This alignment is evident in initiatives such as the "One Sun-One World-One Grid" project, championed in international climate conferences (CoPs), aiming to facilitate the creation of big transmission infrastructure capable of transmitting renewable energy across extended distances.

It is widely acknowledged that the persona of Modi amalgamated the long-standing tenets of muscular Hindu nationalism with the

[141] Toke, *Ecological Modernisation*; Carter, *The Politics of the Environment*.
[142] Moe, *Renewable Energy Transformation*.

pursuit of economic advancement, positioning economic interests as central within the political landscape. Modi's tenure as chief minister of Gujarat witnessed, in the aftermath of 2002 anti-Muslim violence, the convergence of Hindu cultural nationalism and market-oriented liberalisation. In response to the resulting tarnishing of his reputation, Modi embarked on two initiatives. The first was the *gaurav yatra* (honour journey) aimed at rallying the Gujarati Hindu base to counteract a sustained negative portrayal of the state. The second move was his transformation into the *vikas purush* (development man). This transformation extended to the realms of the economy, climate change, and renewable energy, drawing the attention of corporate entities and capital alike. This transformation also found expression in the form of a grand event called Vibrant Gujarat, a spectacle that united domestic and international corporates with the potential to infuse capital into Gujarat.[143] This was "Brand Modi", an embodiment of the entanglements between the imperatives of capitalist growth and cultural nationalism. Modi's nationalist strongman identity and pro-capital credentials are loved by capitalists. According to Ravinder Kaur,

> The main pillars of Brand Modi are his strongman image – the one who doesn't flinch in the face of opposition – and the promise of good times that is held out as an agent of economic growth and prosperity . . . By harnessing the dreams of good times to the vehicle of Hindu nationalism, Modi, a longtime RSS *pracharak*, instrumentalised the neoliberal formula of economic growth toward the making of a Hindu nation. This transition is crucial.[144]

Modi's Gujarat model concerning climate change and renewable energy discourses vividly demonstrated the dominance of government-driven techno-corporatism. During his tenure Gujarat was transformed into a prominent hub for investments in the renewable energy sector, with the label "Vibrant Gujarat"positioning the

[143] There are several publications on this subject. For details: Bunsha, "Gujarats Shame", https://frontline.thehindu.com/the-nation/article30178564.ece; Noorani, "India's Reaction", 389–400; Sud, "Constructing and Contesting", 131–48; Bobbio, "Making Gujarat Vibrant", 657–72.

[144] Kaur, *Brand New Nation,* 248.

state as a promising realm of industrial private capital, underscored by proven avenues for growth internationally. During the Vibrant Gujarat Summit, a biennial gathering organised by the government of Gujarat since 2003 to attract investors, the spotlight was on climate change and clean energy industrial projects. Numerous reports highlighted the involvement of major corporations such as the Adani Group, Azure Power, Suzlon, Trina Solar, First Solar Inc, and SunEdison. These companies signed multiple Memoranda of Understanding (MoUs) pertaining to renewable energy projects with the state government. Indian and global industrial players were granted favourable treatment, prompting them to announce substantial investment commitments. This was facilitated by subsidised and easily accessible resources such as land, water, electricity, and environmental clearances.[145] Modi recalibrated the content and language of climate change and energy with growth, production, investment, technology, and modernisation. At the inauguration of RE-Invest 2015, India's first Renewable Energy Global Investors' Meet and Expo, in New Delhi, Modi called for a jump from "Megawatts to Gigawatts" in terms of renewable energy production, and asserted that "in this age of globalisation, we have no option but to make a quantum leap in energy production."[146] In an another event, he referred to India as "the world's fastest growing large economy" and asked Indian energy companies to become multinationals creating energy corridors to the Middle East, Central Asia, and South Asia. He added: "We invite you to come and Make in India. Our constant efforts have improved India's ranking in ease of doing business. Let me assure you, our commitment is strong and our motto is to replace red tape with red carpet."[147] India's green-energy sector, he said, is like-

[145] Paul, "Vibrant Gujarat", https://www.forbesindia.com/article/checkin/vibrant-gujarat-high-on-solar-energy/39445/1.

[146] Narendra Modi, "PM's Address at the Inauguration of RE-Invest 2015", https://www.narendramodi.in/pms-address-at-the-inauguration-of-re-invest-2015-the-first-renewable-energy-global-investors-meet-and-expo-7260.

[147] "Prime Minister Modi's Energetic Speech at Petrotech-2016", *Petrotech 2016*, 5 December 2016, https://energy.economictimes.indiatimes.com/news/oil-and-gas/full-text-of-prime-minister-modis-energetic-speech-at-petrotech-2016/55806415.

ly to "generate business prospects of the order of $20 billion a year."[148] The renewable-energy sector was thus transformed into a heavy-industrial and business opportunity where the private sector gained considerable prominence, both in terms of scale and power. This shift was accompanied by the adoption of aggressive financial strategies and development mechanisms by the corporate sector.

The Modi-led government pro-actively incentivised private-sector renewal industries and developers, so much so that "private-sector developers have undertaken most of the renewable energy projects in the country." The private sector and its capital became the prime leaders of India's wind and solar sectors. They received various incentives and subsidy: the government facilitated developers by allowing Foreign Direct Investment (FDI) of up to 100 per cent through the automatic route. Inter State Transmission System (ISTS) charges and losses for inter-state sale of solar and wind power have been waived for renewable projects commissioned by 2022. Big private capital was hugely welcomed for the grid integration of large-scale renewable-energy capacity addition and the development of Green Energy Corridors. Billons of Indian rupees were allocated and released in the form of Central Financial Assistance (CFA) for the implementation of renewable-power projects in private-sector and public-private partnership.[149] International capital and finance played an important role within both governmental and business spheres. Numerous industrial conglomerates and financial enterprises from countries such as the USA, Japan, France, Australia, China, Germany, and Denmark – including notable entities like EDF, Sany, SoftBank, and the World Bank – have forged wide-ranging agreements with the Indian government and its associated agencies, pri-

[148] "Modi Sees $20 Billion Annual Investment in Green Energy Sector", *Reuters*, 26 November 2020, https://www.reuters.com/article/india-renewables-modi-idINKBN2861SV.

[149] "Modi Government Taking Several Steps to Incentivise Renewable Energy Sector: R.K. Singh", *The Economic Times*, 6 December 2019, https://economictimes.indiatimes.com/small-biz/productline/power-generation/modi-government-taking-several-steps-to-incentivise-renewable-energy-sector-r-k-singh/.

marily within the renewable-energy sector.[150] The large majority of them have been found to be "global corporations from China, Middle East, Western Europe, East and South East Asia as well as venture capitalists such as Goldman Sachs exploring the potentials of green capitalism. Some are not from the energy field and are using this opportunity to get a foot into the more attractive infrastructural investment possibilities."[151] Numerous contentious corporate transactions have come to public attention. These deals involved questionable companies and entrepreneurs who have ventured into the renewable-energy sector with the apparent aim of acquiring land and government subsidies.[152]

Several notable big Indian companies, including Adani Power, Reliance Power, and Tata Power, which have historically held significant stakes in conventional power enterprises, have directed their efforts towards capturing the emerging renewable-energy sector. Their moves aligned with the strong support provided by the Modi-led government. One of the noteworthy cases is the controversial Adani

[150] There are numerous details about these agreements. For example, "France's EDF, Japan's SoftBank Give Wings to PM Modi's Renewable Energy Dream", *Firstpost*, 20 December 2016, https://www.firstpost.com/business/frances-edf-japans-softbank-give-wings-to-pm-modis-renewable-energy-dream-3012240.html; "World Bank, India Sign Deal to Boost Solar Globally", 30 June 2016, https://www.worldbank.org/en/news/press-release/2016/06/30/world-bank-india-sign-deal-to-boost-solar-globally; "PM Modi Meets Bill Gates On Sidelines Of COP26 Climate Summit In Glasgow", *NDTV*, 3 November 2021, https://www.ndtv.com/india-news/pm-narendra-modi-meets-bill-gates-on-sidelines-of-cop26-climate-summit-in-glasgow-2597157.

[151] Arabindoo, "Renewable Energy", 2300–20.

[152] There are many reports on this issue. For example: Abdul Hafiz Lakhani, "Modi Sold Gujarat to Save His Skin", *The Milli Gazette*, 17 March 2011, https://www.milligazette.com/news/4-national/820-narendra-modi-sold-gujarat-to-save-his-skin/; Virendrasingh Ghunawat, "Not Just diamonds, Nirav Modi Was Also in Solar Power Business; Misused Bank's Money", *Business Today*, 30 April 2018, https://www.businesstoday.in/industry/banks/story/nirav-modi-pnb-fraud-diamond-merchant-solar-power-business-misused-bank-money-103921-2018-04-30.

Group, which stands out as a prime example. The Adani Group is India's largest private coal mining and thermal-power producer and has been blamed for environmental destruction, land grabs, and violations of indigenous rights. Among other companies, Adani Green Energy has emerged as a standout performer, surpassing its counterparts in various aspects. In the same vein, Azure Power, a competing entity listed on the New York Stock Exchange and valued at approximately $1.4 billion, experienced an impressive surge of nearly 130 per cent in its valuation during the year 2020. Conversely, Adani Green Energy's trajectory has been even more remarkable, with its value skyrocketing by an astounding 440 per cent. This meteoric rise has resulted in the company commanding a substantial market capitalisation of nearly $20 billion. Of particular note is Mr Adani's personal stake in the solar unit being estimated at $13.9 billion – and after accounting for liabilities this stake constitutes nearly half of his total net worth, as indicated by Bloomberg's analysis. The international investment community also demonstrated keen interest. Total SA, a prominent French energy conglomerate, declared its intention to invest $510 million in Adani Green Energy. However, a long-standing observer of the Adani Group, associated with a major US investment bank for over a decade, raised questions about the market valuation of Adani Green Energy. The concerns centred around the limited liquidity observed, with a mere $2 million worth of shares traded on a daily basis. Adani Green Energy's valuation has become a point of scrutiny, especially given its modest liquidity, coupled with the fact that the company is yet to achieve profitability. Analysts note that the company resorted to accessing international debt markets, securing $863 million in funds the previous year. This move exemplified what was seen as the Adani Group's tendency to accumulate leverage as a means to fuel expansion efforts under the banner of sustainable energy ventures.[153]

[153] There are several reports about the rise of the Adani Group under the Modi regimes and its environmental impact. For example, Aditi Roy Ghatak, "Modi and Adani: The Old Friends Laying Waste to India's Environment", *Climate Home News*, 27 June 2017, https://www.climatechangenews.com/2017/06/27/modi-adani-old-friends-laying-waste-indias-environment/;

Corporatisation within the renewable-energy sector has also taken on a distinct "people" dimension. Modi has repeatedly emphasised the emergence of substantial capital and industries in this sector, highlighting their potential to positively impact the populace. In his capacity as both prime minister and prominent political figure, he has consistently woven together themes of poverty, livelihood, justice, accessibility, and recognition, aligning them with the broader concepts of economic growth, development, security, and national identity through the avenue of the energy sector. He has articulated "affordable renewable energy for all", "accessibility to the poor and in remote areas", and "renewable energy generating millions of jobs".[154] Initiating government schemes, he has pledged to achieve "universal energy access" and "free electricity for poor" through renewable sources.[155] He has personally adopted a village within his parliamentary constituency, ensuring its illumination through solar power: this has garnered widespread publicity.[156] Hence, there exists a prevalent narrative surrounding renewable energy within the public domain which diverges notably from the overarching corporate and capital-focused narrative that is evident in practical implementation.

---

Dr Ruchira Talukdar, "Responding to India's Climate Actions and Supporting Climate Justice", *Chain Reaction*, 2021, https://search.informit.org/doi/pdf/10.3316/informit.319736119227030. Renewable energy-related information and analysis have been taken from an excellent report by Stephanie Findlay, Hudson Lockett, "'Modi's Rockefeller': Gautam Adani and the Concentration of Power in India", *Financial Times*, 12 November 2020, https://www.ft.com/content/474706d6-1243-4f1e-b365-891d4c5d528b.

[154] "Prime Minister Narendra Modi Pushes for Affordable Renewable Energy for All", *NDTV*, 15 February 2015, https://www.ndtv.com/india-news/prime-minister-narendra-modi-pushes-for-affordable-renewable-energy-for-all-739783.

[155] "Modi Promises Free Electricity for Poor Under 'Saubhagya Yojana'", *The Quint*, 8 September 2018, https://www.thequint.com/news/india/bjp-national-executive-meet-pm-modi-amit-shah.

[156] Sudhir Kumar, "After Jayapur, Solar Power to Light Up Another Village Adopted by Modi", *Hindustan Times*, 10 May 2017, https://www.hindustantimes.com/india-news/after-jayapur-solar-power-to-light-up-another-village-adopted-by-modi/story-daZqegAiih3rpaJXAHEdbK.html.

The substantial surge in renewable activities within the corporate sector, with liberal support from Modi's administration, has sparked a range of environmental concerns and conflicts. Among these, the most conspicuous revolves around the matter of land acquisition and the subsequent displacement of communities.[157] Research has demonstrated that significant expanses of land are required to accommodate large-scale solar and wind projects. Specifically, estimates range from 55,000 to 125,000 square kilometres in order to fulfil India's ambitious renewable energy goal of installing 175 gigawatts by the year 2022.[158] The target was further revised to 450 gigawatts by 2030. In 2020, the Ministry of New and Renewable Energy (MNRE) made public a concept note on "Development of wind parks/wind-solar hybrid parks" identifying about 10,800 square kilometres of land across seven states to develop wind parks or wind-solar hybrid parks. Numerous cases of protest against the acquisition of land for large corporate solar and wind projects have been documented, starting from 2014.[159] A research team identified five distinct conflicts connected to wind- and solar-park initiatives throughout India. These conflicts collectively impacted 5095 hectares of land and 2036 individuals, involving a substantial investment exceeding Rs 90.89 billion. This figure can be considered a cautious approximation, as numerous additional instances of land disputes may remain unaccounted for.[160]

In short, Modi's climate policy regarding renewable energy has revolved around encouraging corporate capitalism to invest in advanced technologies, specifically in the domains of solar and wind power. The result has been a coalescence of corporate growth and climate

[157] Mayank Aggarwal, "Land Conflicts on the Horizon as India Pursues a Clean Energy Future", *Mongabay*, 14 July 2021, https://india.mongabay.com/2021/07/land-conflicts-on-the-horizon-as-india-pursues-a-clean-energy-future.

[158] Kiesecker, *et al.*, "Renewable Energy and Land Use", 1–14.

[159] Ruchira Talukdar, "Adani, India and COP26: How to Support Climate Justice?", *Green Left*, 3 November 2021, https://www.greenleft.org.au/content/adani-india-and-cop26-how-support-climate-justice.

[160] Land Conflict Watch, "Power/Renewable Power", https://www.landconflictwatch.org/all-conflicts.

concerns. This alignment has also led to the assertion that the corporatisation of renewable energy has not only nurtured growth, it has also stimulated innovation and the creation of environmentally friendly employment opportunities. The prevailing ecological discourse, which championed small-scale technologies and decentralised power structures, and which voiced concerns over corporate expansion along with the imperative to develop renewable-energy sources, suffered a setback of considerable magnitude. This shift has carried substantial implications for the trajectory of India's future development, energy, and environmental frameworks. The Indian government presents the renewable-energy sector as a pivotal means to realise Modi's growth vision of propelling India into a $5 trillion economy by 2024–5.[161]

Most scholarly investigations into India's climate and energy policies have fallen short in capturing the significant political change introduced by Modi, a change intricately intertwined with the core principles of Hindu nationalist ideology to create a Hindu environmental subject. Central to this change is also the noteworthy evolution of the renewable-energy sector's identity, which has now undergone a substantial shift. Once characterised by a focus on environmentally conscious, local, decentralised alternatives, this sector has been radically reshaped by the support to big corporate capitalist entities.

The fluid nature of climate change and renewable-energy politics in the country has also facilitated a transformative shift in Narendra Modi's public persona. Previously perceived as an authoritarian figure aligned with majoritarian Hindu nationalist goals, Modi has successfully repositioned himself as a modern and developmental leader espousing the cause of climate change and green energy. Modi has employed a varied rhetoric on the subject. Concurrently, he has consistently woven into this aspect of governance the tenets of Hindu

[161] "How Embracing Renewable Energy Can Help India Achieve Its Target of Becoming a $5 Trillion Economy by 2024", *The Economic Times*, 18 May 2020, https://economictimes.indiatimes.com/small-biz/productline/power-generation/how-embracing-renewable-energy-can-help-india-achieve-its-target-of-becoming-a-5-trillion-economy-by-2024-25/articleshow/74668710.cms?from=mdr.

nationalist ideology. This amalgamation has involved exalting ancient Bharat, Hindutva narratives, and the idea of a Hindu civilisation which has long contained the climate solutions the world is seeking. This advocacy for climate change has served, it can be argued, as an adept diversionary tactic, allowing the deflection of attention from all criticism of Modi's performance as chief minister and prime minister.

# 7

# Historical Trajectories

## Nature for Nationalism

ECOLOGICAL DEGRADATION and pressure on renewable resources and animal life, increasing pollution, and the adverse impact of rapid industrialisation have prompted environmental initiatives, books, and reports.[1] Global warming, ozone depletion, and the emission of sulphur and nitrogen oxides that cause acid rain, often uncontained within national boundaries, have led to the realisation that the futures of North and South are inextricably linked.[2] Newspapers regularly narrate environmental horror stories, with editorials demanding a better management of natural resources. Statements from the government on the need to preserve the environment are now commonplace; state-sponsored environmental programmes have increased; there are new laws for the control of air and water pollution and the conservation of forests; and there is some praise for what India has done to save tigers. Overall, it appears that "environment is an idea whose time has come."[3]

Environmental issues began to become prominent in India from the 1970s and found expression in movements in the 1980s. The origins of such environmentalism are not, of course, so recent. Environmentalists often explain particular concerns beyond their specificities,

[1] Agarwal, *et al.*, eds, *The State of India's Environment*; idem, *The State of India's Environment Second*; Agarwal, D'Monte and Samarth, eds, *The Fight for Survival*; Arnold and Guha, eds, *Nature, Culture, Imperialism*, 17–18.

[2] Baviskar, *In the Belly*, 22–5.

[3] Agarwal, "Politics of Environment – II", 362.

within a wider time and policy framework. Articulated in varied forms, environmentalism as an ideology propounds a comprehensive vision of politics and society based on its understanding of the causes of environmental problems. This vision encompasses a critique of the modern path of development and the present exploitative relationship between human beings and nature – which took shape especially in the colonial and post-colonial eras. A deep resentment against the trajectory of modernity and a fundamental unease with the environmental consequences of modernisation's intellectual heritage is often expressed.

Examining some of the major lines of developmental and environmental arguments in India before and after Independence, and paying attention to a continuing but also changing use of nature for nationalism, are both necessary for an understanding of the contemporary convergence of Green and Saffron. Although the tradition of "nature for nationalism" was not the only form of environmental reasoning earlier, it has been one of the most visible strands, and its arguments have had a powerful resonance. We need therefore to explore the ideological continuities and discontinuities that exist between this earlier tradition and its recent editions, and to mark out the major themes and features of contemporary conservative environmentalism.

Especially important in the recent convergence of Green and Saffron is environmentalism's critique of development-induced modernisation based on the Western model. One branch of environmentalists, as we have seen, posits a particular understanding of nation and national identity. Their conception of nature as unique, given, natural, spontaneous, and pure is central to their vision, for, according to them, the destructive consequences of development are caused by a false separation of the natural and social worlds. They maintain that humans are an integral part of nature. The nation, its people, and culture are as distinctive and unique as the natural landscapes in which they are supposedly rooted. By the beginning of the 1970s the negative effects of economic and industrial policies on the Indian environment had become clear, and a model for understanding the roots of this destruction of nature was being sought.

Environmentalism seeped into political discourse at this time, when India's polity and society were in the first throes of a transition to full industrialisation, giving rise to questions of how to understand Indian identity. Varieties of environmentalism became manifest in the discourse of Hindu nationalists. Imprints of these were evident in the movement against the Tehri dam, in the activism of Sunderlal Bahuguna and Anna Hazare, and in writings by authors such as Gadgil, Banwari, and Shiva. Collectively, this environmentalism saw environmental degradation essentially as a result of the imposition of a Western, colonial civilisation over a rooted, indigenous, Indian culture. In this form of environmental critique the conservation of nature was seen as dependent on the conservation of a past, pure, ideal nation, and its ancient culture and tradition – which, it was argued, was always in accord with the laws of nature. Ideas of nation and nature intermesh so completely in this view that defending the environment from pollution is virtually the same as defending the nation, and vice versa.

In examining the main features of "nature for nationalism" or the "nature and culture" tradition on the one hand, and the ideological contours of Hindu nationalist environmental concerns on the other, the intention is not to draw a straight or unbroken line between environmentalism and Hindu nationalism. Historical realities are always more complex. There are many political, historical, and structural reasons at work in the rise of Hindu nationalists – everything cannot and should not be read back into environmental history. But neither does Hindu authoritarian ideology appear out of the blue; political explanations for the rise to prominence of Hindu nationalism do not suffice by themselves. The phenomenon of Hindutva's ascent must also be understood in relation to the ideological arsenal it draws from the language, discourse, and universes of meaning in Indian political culture.

The mapping and remapping of land, water, river, mountains, frontiers, heroes, and forefathers has been a strategy by which nationalists of all kinds – literary, philosophical, or militant – have imagined, narrated, and activated their nations, even if not always consciously.

In colonial India, environmental imagery was said to be an important means of developing a national as well as regional or religious consciousness, and in contesting British cultural and political dominance.[4] Such use of nature for nationalism has been traced back to Montesquieu, who theorised nation-building in specific physical environments, and to Rousseau's idea that "the mountains, seas and rivers form the frontiers for the nations living in Europe, and it is clear that nature itself has determined the number and greatness of nations."[5] It has also been argued that new nations, for instance Canada and South Africa, which had not existed prior to the encounter with the new physical environments that helped forge them, showed a great sensitivity to their natural environment. The process of nation-building within a certain landscape was telescoped for settlers into a lifetime's experience.[6]

The British colonial regime in India, as against settler regimes, focused its attention on exploitation of the colonised landscape's natural resources. The pattern of land use within India was organised to maximise revenue yield to the British crown, and the commodities it could produce to feed the British economy. Peasants in some regions were forced to cultivate cash crops such as cotton, jute, and indigo to service British industries. The diversity of trees in other regions was curtailed to species that would better cater to the building of British ships and laying of railway lines. In every possible way, the British wanted to shape India as a supplier of cheap raw materials and as a market for its higher-priced manufactured goods.[7]

Popular resistance to British interventions in the use and ownership of natural resources, such as tribal and peasant movements, boycott and swadeshi movements, salt satyagrahas and labour rebellions,[8] are by no means the complete story. It has been remarked that there

[4] Arnold, *Environment, Culture and European*, 185.

[5] Davies, *God's Playground I*, 523–5.

[6] Ben-Israel, "Hallowed Land", 278–94.

[7] Gadgil and Guha, *Ecology and Equity*, 9–12.

[8] Sarkar, *Modern India*.

were also forms of ideological resistance, most evident among the Indian middle class, to colonial attempts to appropriate the environment exclusively to a British agenda of "civilisation" and "progress". Indians sought, at various levels, to contest these colonial "readings" of their environment, to reject the negative images and associations that western "topicality" imposed upon them, and to assert their own identity through environmentally related symbols and values.[9]

Certain images and symbols, especially drawn from the environment, were often a powerful rallying point for an emerging sense of national identity. In this sense, Gandhi's deployment of the salt tax as the central issue in his civil disobedience campaign of 1930 was emblematic of a wider determination to contest British environmental control and exploit its symbolic as well as practical significance. Salt was somewhat exceptional in its pan-Indian significance amidst the enormous ecological diversity of the country. The landscapes, flora, and fauna of Bengal, even the food, were very different from those of Gandhi's Gujarat in the west or Tamilnadu in the extreme south. Moreover, many natural symbols in India carried a specific religious connotation and so might not be readily acceptable to followers of other faiths. However, salt brought them all together.

The notion of territoriality, a combination of many environmental elements such as the boundaries of land, sea, and river, became an important factor in this nationalism. The territorial imperative was strong and blinding, commanding allegiance, and eliciting patriotism as well as xenophobia. In relation to recurrent rebellions in the hills near the Godavari River (the erstwhile Agency Areas, now in Andhra Pradesh) from 1839 to 1924, a historian notes that:

> Territoriality and xenophobia are to be found in many, if not most, peasant struggles in India, but they are particularly acute in the risings and rebellions of the hillmen of India, where such identities and aversions are reinforced by the cohesiveness of communities that have remained relatively isolated, the limited social differentiation they often exhibit, and above all by that exceptionally sharp divide between those who live in the hills and those who inhabit the plains.[10]

[9] Arnold, *Environment, Culture and European*, 185.
[10] Arnold, "Rebellious Hillmen", 141–2.

Nationalist forces tried similarly to deploy assumptions about forest society in pre-colonial India to counter the colonial regime. A picture was forged of a past in which people had long lived in unchanging egalitarianism and harmony with nature until the British grabbed their land and turned them into an exploited and subaltern class. In this narration indigenes were seen as rooted in an ancient wisdom far superior to that of the West: the civilisation of India conserved forests while the civilisation of the West destroyed them.[11]

The colonial period thus witnessed a contemplation of the profound economic significance of natural resources. Nature was not "a mere sickly sentimentalism or the vapourings of an overheated imagination," it was in fact synonymous with "that robust and practical patriotism which was broad-based upon a reasoned appreciation and analysis of the manifold contributions made to our economic life and progress."[12] To arouse the nation, the country was seen as a bountiful woman worthy of worship, and nationalists set out to record and propagate this abundance – her gifts and treasures of agricultural wealth, the richness of her botanical and zoological sources, her vegetable and animal products, her splendid livestock, her mineral wealth, the atmospheric wealth she brought, the congenial character of her climates and seasons, her very days and nights, her human wealth and heroic sons. Questions of national identity thus became even more entangled with nature devotion, which has been referred to as "ecological nationalism". Nature devotion expressed itself in the form of national pride in order to become part of processes legitimising and consolidating the nation.[13]

The economist Sukhamoy Chakravarty said that in the early 1950s, when the planning process was initiated in India, there was

[11] Hardiman, "Power in the Forest", 89–94.

[12] Mookerji, *Nationalism in Hindu Culture*, 27–8.

[13] Cederlöf and Sivaramakrishnan, eds, *Ecological Nationalisms*, 1–40. The editors argue that in claiming nationhood and celebrating the nation, nature is appropriated in order to manifest the legitimacy of claims. However, it is fruitful to explore different ways in which ecological nationalism is expressed. There is thus a distinction between metropolitan-secular nationalism and an indigenist-regionalist appropriation of nature.

a general consensus on a "commodity-centred" approach. In essence this entailed robbing the mass of India's subsistence agriculturists of their means of production and of all guarantees afforded by the old feudal arrangements. In this development model modern enterprise and industrialisation as a project specifically of the capitalist class and the state had to be expressed, however, as the general project of the nation, and this was done in part by subsuming it within the body of a single plan for the nation, and by purging those elements that appeared as "constraints" on the particular will of the modern sector.[14] When analysing development planning in the post-colonial Indian state, Partha Chatterjee explains that whereas the political strategy of building up a mass movement against colonial rule had required the Congress to espouse Gandhi's idea of machinery, commercialisation, and centralised state power as the curses of modern civilisation thrust upon the Indian people by European colonialism, the new national state had to radically reverse this view of the national good. Planning emerged as a crucial institutional modality by which the state would determine the material allocation of productive resources within the new nation:

> The reification of the "nation" in the body of the state becomes the means for constructing this hegemonic structure, and the extent of control over the new state apparatus becomes a precondition for further capitalist development. It is by means of an interventionist state, directly entering the domain of production as mobilizer and manager of investable "national" resources that the foundations are laid for industrialization and the expansion of capital.[15]

Gadgil and Guha also describe the model of development following Independence wherein nature and natural resources were used like an offering for worship by the nation:

> State power now passed into the hands of the landowner warrior and priestly castes of the countryside and the priestly and trader castes of the cities. This alliance was committed to the ideal of halting the drain

[14] Chakravarty, *Development Planning*, 2–42.

[15] Chatterjee, *The Nation and Its Fragments*, 200–19.

> of India's resources abroad. At the same time it was eager to refashion the pattern of resource use to serve its own interests. There were obvious limitations to what could be achieved in the framework of a low-input economy, one no longer capable of yielding much of a surplus. The solution obviously lay in industrialisation; in tapping the energy of coal and petroleum, of hydroelectric power, in producing steel and cement and using the resources so generated to promote manufacture.[16]

In the specific context of forests – one of the major ecological regimes – Gadgil and Guha describe how in the late 1950s foresters advocated giving up selective felling in stands of natural forest, replacing this with an aggressive plantation forestry which called for the large-scale clear-felling of natural forests to create plantations of fast-growing exotics such as eucalyptus and tropical pine.

The environmental writer and researcher Darryl D'Monte saw in this period the rebirth of a country involving the building of dams and massive projects. He remembered Nehru's words at the opening of the Nangal canal – part of the massive Bhakra multi-purpose project in Punjab in 1954 – describing mammoth development projects as "the temples of today".[17] And then, "Visiting the gigantic Bhakra dam a few years later as a teenager and marvelling at the vast ocean-like reservoir behind the concrete barrage; as my face tingled with the fine mist rising from the waters cascading through the sluices, I was infused with an emotional upsurge, the feeling that I was witnessing the rebirth of a country that had long slumbered in the throes of its colonial past."[18]

[16] Gadgil and Guha, *Ecology and Equity*, 13.

[17] In the first flush of independence, Nehru made a bold and unequivocal assertion in 1954 in support of harnessing natural resources for modernisation and industrialisation. He said, while opening the Nangal canal, "When I walked around the site, I thought that these days, the biggest temple and mosque and gurudwara is the place where man works for the good of mankind. Which place can be greater than Bhakra Nangal, where thousands of men have worked or shed their blood and sweat and laid down their lives as well? Where can be a holier place than this; which can we regard as higher?" This statement has been mythologised and is much quoted in diverse contexts.

[18] D'Monte, *Temples or Tombs?*, 1.

In relation to tribal areas and tribal communities, the independent Indian state once again justified its appropriation of rights over natural resources in the name of the national interest. The aim of this policy, according to the Report of the National Council of Applied Economic Research, was to integrate tribal communities within the body politic of the nation: "This is sought to be achieved through raising the standard of living in the tribal areas to that in the rural areas of the country. Since the tribal areas are exceptionally backward and primitive, welfare of the people living therein is sought to be achieved through some measures of protection during the next 20 years."[19] Towards this highly acclaimed end:

> Top priority has been given to a programme of rapid industrialisation and extension of means of communication to the most interior regions in the state. Our firm view is that the development of land and agriculture alone will not be adequate for the rehabilitation of the tribal communities. Agricultural land is insufficient and cannot serve the needs of even half the tribal population of the state. Fortunately, the tribal areas of the state are rich in industrial and power potential. There is no reason why in the wider interest of the nation and in the long-term interest of the tribals themselves, industries should not be developed and localised in tribal areas.[20]

Every large project was presented as beneficial for the masses and therefore in the national interest, even though it almost always required the poor to surrender land and livelihood. The hegemonic effort emanated from the top. Suresh Sharma describes Nehru reassuring those displaced by the Rihand Dam in Singrauli in 1961: "People felt that their suffering would not be in vain. Their instinctive sense of nobility was stirred when Nehru spoke of the Nation and Development. They believed in his promise of a future of plenty to be shared by all. And they half accepted the trauma of displacement believing in the promise of irrigated fields and plentiful harvests. So often have the survivors of Rihand told us that they accepted their sufferings as sacrifice for the sake of the nation."[21]

[19] NCAER, *Socio-Economic Conditions of Primitive Tribes*, vi.

[20] Ibid. And for an analysis on the rapid exploitation of natural resources in tribal areas because of these policies, see Baviskar, *In the Belly*, 49–84.

[21] Sharma, "The Vanquished Tribal", 78. Also see Roy, "Politics of Environ-

The environmental historian Mahesh Rangarajan is another illustrious academic who shows elements of nature being used for varied and different phases of nationalism and nation-building. Tracing India's wildlife history, he points out that preserving the nation's wildlife was integral to the nationalist project to save one of its emblems, the Indian tiger. Earlier, the lion had been the subject of such symbolism. The animal was part of a national emblem which had taken shape as the Ashoka Pillar with its three lions. It then became "the national animal" of India in 1952. Its qualities were praised in terms that played on regional pride. Thus, "the coming of Independence eventually ended the era of huge shoots and trophy hunts, with the lion becoming an early emblem of the new nation's bid to break with imperial legacies."[22]

In brief, it is evident that every time some element of nature or some resource of the landscape needed either to be saved or exploited for specific ends that had been identified as necessary by private and state capitalism, this element or resource was declared "national".

## Gandhian Thought: An Environmental Grounding

Mahatma Gandhi's perceptions of environment and development are said to be the single most important influence on the environmental movement in India. From being acclaimed as "the usually acknowledged and occasionally unacknowledged patron saint of the Indian environmental movement",[23] to being called "a practising ecological *yogi*",[24] the only Indian to convert environmental and ethical principles into a political movement, Gandhi has also been considered "the only hope for humanity to effectively confront and

---

ment". Roy, a well-known environmental activist and writer, argues that the response of the state towards environmental issues and movements has been to introduce more legislation, which further centralises powers in the "national interest".

[22] Rangarajan, "From Princely Symbol", 66. Also see Rangarajan, *India's Wildlife History*, 100.

[23] Guha, "Mahatma Gandhi Environmental", 45.

[24] Khoshoo, *Mahatma Gandhi*, 1.

change the conflicts, the loss of equilibrium, the irreverence for life and the degradation of the environment which afflicts our daily lives."[25] It is also argued that Gandhi's life constituted a kind of ecological treatise and functioned much like an ecosystem. From his writings to his social practices and conduct, he can be seen as having had an ecological vision of life.[26] Politics, ethics, ecology, and religion were all indistinguishably interwoven into the fabric of his thought and social practice:

> If, for instance, his practice of observing twenty-four hours of silence on a regular basis was a mode of conserving his energy, entering into an introspective state, and listening to what he called the still voice within, it was also a way of signifying his dissent from ordinary models of communication with the British and establishing the discourse on his own terms. Similarly, Gandhi deployed fasting not only to open negotiations with the British or (more frequently) various Indian communities, but to cleanse his own body, free his mind of impure thoughts, feminise the public realm, and even to partake in the experience of deprivation from which countless millions of Indians suffered. Gandhi deplored the idea of waste, and fasting was a sure means of ascertaining the true needs of the body and preserving its ecological equanimity.[27]

It is a commonplace that Gandhi extolled the virtues of village life and condemned Western industrialisation as greed: "We must resist the superficiality of mass produced, pop culture and the way it threatens to displace local indigenous cultural production. We must abandon imitative lifestyles that seek to replicate hedonism, waste and decadence of the West."[28] He lamented the neglect of tradition, the decay of morals, and the destruction of the natural environment. Influenced by Tolstoy and Thoreau, his valorisation of the village was in many ways an idealised and romantic conception of nature as a totality which could yield a solution to civilisational crisis if man grasped and applied the lessons of nature. In particular, he empha-

[25] Singh, *Global Concern,* 245.
[26] Lal, "Too Deep Ecology", 183–212.
[27] Ibid., 199–200.
[28] Patti, "Gandhi and the Village", 52.

sised the specific historical, religious, and cultural conditions of the Indian nation which had given life to its distinct tradition and culture. His ideas and programmes were rooted in a specifically Indian village, soil, nation, and civilisation, and emblematic in his view of Indian civilisation's early ties between nature and nationalism. Gandhi's close disciple J.C. Kumarappa, who wrote a number of books in the 1930s and 1940s, attempted to formalise a "Gandhian economics" and denounced industrial civilisation. According to him, there could be no industrialisation without predation.[29] In fact, with Gandhi and Gandhian thought the "nature and nationalism" tradition acquired a more wide-ranging, recognisable, programmatic, and ecologically modern form.

Gandhi's solution was thus the unpolluted village and village life; corresponding values and lifestyles would provide an impetus for the revival of ancient life and culture in India. This ideal village would have perfect sanitation of the traditional kind, based on the local recycling of human and animal manure. Village cottages, built of materials found within a five-mile radius, would be well lit and well ventilated. The lanes and streets would be clean and free of dust. There would be adequate wells accessible equally to all. There would be places of worship, a common meeting place, a village common for grazing, a co-operative dairy, and primary and secondary schools where the main subjects would be practical crafts and village industries. The village would have its own panchayat for settling disputes. It would produce its own milk, grains, vegetables, fruit, and khadi. As Ramachandra Guha points out, many elements in this description fit well into an environmentalist's utopia: local self-reliance, a clean and hygienic environment, collective management and use of those gifts of nature so necessary for human life – water and pasture.[30] This imagery of village, village life, and ecological values was also meant to

[29] The environmental historian Ramachandra Guha believes Kumarappa has strong claims to being considered the first Gandhian environmentalist: he had begun the task of building an ecological programme on Gandhian lines, though his work is largely unhonoured and forgotten today. For details, see Guha and Martinez-Alier, *Varieties of Environmentalism,* 158–60.

[30] Guha, "Mahatma Gandhi Environmental", 50.

establish swaraj against colonial rule. The ecological merit of Gandhi's views lay in the fact that while dealing with villages, rural development, industrialisation, resource use, exploitation, and ethics, he combined these concerns with fighting colonialism and laying the basis for an alternative discourse of development. The argument for self-sufficient village life was not only an antidote to the "brute force" of capitalism but also the precondition for national, political, and economic self-rule.

Gandhism suggests that nature never fails, and the ignorance or wilful flouting of nature's law causes ills in society. According to N. Radhakrishnan:

> The ashrams or the communities Gandhi founded, both in South Africa and in India, were meaningful centres where Gandhi demonstrated with convincing success how each member of this community could live in harmony with nature. The community life Gandhi was developing consisted of manual labour, tree planting, agriculture, simple life, and crafts. In short they were attempts at self-sufficiency without invoking the blessings of the temptation from outside. While they could be described to be bold experiments, by no stretch of imagination could anyone say they were utopian ideals. The running and recurrent principle of community life was to live according to the rhythm of nature and in harmony with nature with minimum needs and not to exploit nature beyond taking what nature offers.[31]

"In nature," said Gandhi, "there is fundamental unity running through all the diversity we see about us. There is an orderliness in universe. There is an unalterable law governing everything and every being that exists or lives."[32] If nature teaches us order in chaos, unity in diversity, and shows us the image of Almighty everywhere, and if the earth is essentially one as a natural entity, then the nation itself, as well as its traditions, culture, and people, can become natural. And conversely, without nationalistic feeling for the revival of tradition and culture, there can be no effective protection of the environment.[33]

[31] Quoted in Khoshoo, *Mahatma Gandhi*, 10.

[32] Ibid., 30.

[33] These arguments have been put forward by authors like T.N. Khoshoo

Larry D. Shinn argues that in order to deduce a Gandhian ecology one must set the inner logic of non-violent truth-seeking against an Indian cosmological backdrop that asserts a homologous and interdependent relationship between humans and all other animate and inanimate aspects of creation. He cites many works to explain how subtle and all-encompassing the notion of varna is in India, which organises all aspects of creation. This pervasive pattern of ranked relationships establishes cosmological interdependencies that connect human beings to all other aspects of creation. He concludes: "While Gandhi rejected the formal social and economic distinctions of caste, he clearly accepted the traditional Indian worldview that assumes the continuity and interdependence between humans and the natural world. In any case, it is clear that Gandhi accepted a fairly traditional Hindu understanding of the integral relationship and interdependence between humans and nature, and that this understanding forms a backdrop for our understanding of Gandhian ecology."[34] There is little doubt that, with variation and modification, this variety of environmental thought has endured among discourses in India which celebrate the small, the rural, and the traditional.

## Between Hope and Resignation: Inventing National Ecology

Environmental movements and initiatives in India since the 1970s have been diverse and changeable. Chipko in 1973 was considered a landmark, an unprecedented social movement, though behind and before it lies a prehistory of environmental ideas.[35] Environmental concerns have since surfaced in sophisticated, often deeply contested, public discourses on the meanings of environmentalism. There has been no such thing as a single perspective or a single movement. Given the vast range of environments, and the diversity of the

---

and Savita Singh who have researched Gandhi's views on the environment. For details, see Khoshoo, *Mahatma Gandhi*, 30–2; Singh, *Global Concern*, 212–13.

[34] Shinn, "The Inner Logic", 222–3.

[35] Guha, *How Much Should a Person Consume?*, 35–6.

people living with, and claiming rights over, their landscapes, there has been a corresponding multitude of issues and perspectives as well as varied organisational initiatives. Differences appear within the countryside, between regions and occupational groups, between rich and poor, between upper and Dalit castes, between men and women. Each movement has fought to stop or to build a particular dam, to resist a specific displacement, to claim rights over land in a forest or fish in a sea. Each struggle has chosen its own strategy, depending upon the nature of the main issue, upon the socio-cultural life of the people, and the character of the local organisation.

Some movements, like the Narmada Bachao Andolan (Save the Narmada Movement), the struggle against the new deep-sea fishing policy by coastal fisherfolk, and the movement of tribals against mining in Orissa were able to forge broader national and international alliances. Environmental issues were often inextricably caught up with the local, social, or developmental problems of India, starkly spelling out the links between environment and livelihoods. A village constructing its own dam, or a region struggling to reclaim the wasteland, or women in the Himalayas striving for basic facilities together with their afforestation campaigns were not explicitly focusing on environmental issues. Nonetheless they were closely linked with developmental and livelihood concerns. A majority of the conflicts in the 1980s and 1990s had their origin in issues of use and control over natural resources. Who owns the land? Who has access to trees and the produce of the forests? Who may cast a net into the seas? These questions emerged in new forms, and even hitherto relatively undisputed areas like ponds and ghats, ravines and wastelands, and the sea became a bone of contention between the state and business interests on the one hand, and the rural poor on the other. There were close connections between questions of entitlement and social justice for the poor and social movements, and often these were animated by the conviction that social justice was a vital aspect of resource use. Many movements stood out for their land and water management, for successful experiments in rural development, for self-governance, for the sane propagation of everyday beliefs, practices, and cultures. Some were rooted in a critique of modern industrial society and the culture of greed and acquisition. Some were run by NGOs involved in causes as a response to concrete problems in their immediate neighbourhood. The role of the state in managing the environment also provoked strong reactions. This ethos contributed to a profound rethinking of the very idea of development. Intellectual, political, and organisational currents in the country started fashioning critiques of the industrial and economic biases of government policies, urging that there should be more decentralised, socially aware, environmentally sensitive, and altogether more human forms of development.[36] Subsequently, Indian environmental movements were also referred to as the "environmentalism of the poor". They were perceived as combining shades of both Green ecological concerns and Red class politics, though there existed complex, often contradictory associations between the Red and Green aspects of environmental movements that defied categorisation.[37] There were studies to look at the similarities and differences between the ideas of the Left and the environment movement, so that "perhaps a dialogue between the two can lead us to a viable model of alternative development and a politics that effectively challenges the threats of globalisation and Hindutva in contemporary India."[38]

Amidst these trends, a critique of colonialism and its construction of environmental history has emerged as important. Referred to as a "new traditionalist" discourse, the argument here is that ecological degradation is solely a consequence of India's colonial history and post-Independence "development" policies, which challenges peoples' enduring and longer-term relationships with their local environments. This view constructs a sharp dichotomy between India and West, indigenous and foreign, tradition and modernity. This is a specific critique of Western-oriented modernity, the idea here being that discourses of modernity, masculinity, science, and development have privileged "rational" and "objective" modes of knowing. This perspective is accompanied by an equally specific reading of Indian

[36] Sharma, *Landscapes and Lives,* 1–7.

[37] Baviskar, "Red in Tooth and Claw?", 161–78.

[38] Prasad, *Environmentalism and the Left,* 23; idem, *Against Ecological Romanticism.*

tradition: traditional ecology was balanced and harmonious and practised by self-contained communities of women, forest dwellers, and peasants who were primarily the keepers of a special conservationist ethic.[39] "Enlightenment" signalled not light but darkness, an extinction of life and life-enhancing processes, a new project of Western patriarchy. Vandana Shiva has emerged as a powerful proponent of this viewpoint. She contends that modern science and development are the endeavours of males and Western in origin, both historically and ideologically. The rise of a patriarchal science of nature took place in Europe during the fifteenth and seventeenth centuries in the shape of what is termed the scientific revolution. There is something seriously wrong with this concept of progress, for it threatens survival itself. In contrast, Shiva believes rural Indian women are embedded in nature. They have challenged the Western concept of nature as an object of exploitation and protected her as *prakriti*, the living force that supports life. They have questioned Western production for profit and capital accumulation with their own perception of production for sustenance. The everyday struggles of such women towards protecting nature take place in the cognitive and ethical context of an ancient Indian worldview in which nature is *prakriti*, a living and creative process, the feminine principle from which arises all life.[40] In *Ecofeminism*, Maria Mies and Vandana Shiva even draw a contrast between a pre-capitalist Asian society which existed in organic unity with nature, and a colonial society imposed by European imperialists which shattered this harmony and paved the way for the present social, spiritual, and ecological crisis. In India, they claim, nature was venerated as sacred, and evolution was measured in terms of the human capacity to interact in harmony with nature's rhythms and patterns.[41] This was an "agrarian myth" rooted in romanticism and conservative notions of an organic society which reinforced aspects of "peasant-ness", national identity, and culture.[42]

[39] For an elaboration and sharp critique of this perspective, see Sinha, Gururani, and Greenberg, "The 'New Traditionalist' Discourse", 65–99; Brass, "The Agrarian Myth", 201–45.

[40] Shiva, *Staying Alive*, xiv–xx.

[41] Mies and Shiva, *Ecofeminism*, 263.

[42] Brass, "The Agrarian Myth".

This was an idealist-feminist version of a widespread critique of Western science as providing the foundations for a development which was ultimately destructive. As stated by the sociologist Shiv Visvanathan: "Underlying modernity was the social contract between the nation-state and modern western science and both were engaged in a soap opera called development. The process was becoming life-threatening and even genocidal."[43] Ecology was implicated in this critique in so far as ecologists made attempts to manage nature, or change local Indian landscapes in the interests of an international environmental agenda. It was argued that India needed a local, not international, ecology that would make recommendations within the context of Indian culture and folk ways.[44] It was said that the Indic civilisation had the capacity to reverse the usual one-way procedure of enriching modern science by integrating within it significant elements from all other sciences – pre-modern, non-modern, and post-modern. Instead of using an edited version of modern science for Indian purposes, India should use an edited version of its traditional sciences for contemporary purposes.[45] Western science was part and parcel of colonialism and violence, whereas none of the alternative structures of thinking – Indian, Chinese, or tribal – had hegemonic, global ambitions of the Western kind. This made it important to understand the West's oppressive rationality and uncover its consequences for older civilisations.[46]

This was implicitly or explicitly the making of a national, Indian ecology.[47] Often the binary between Western and Indian, the opposition between modernity and tradition, was aligned with the propagation of an alternative non-modern philosophy whose roots lay in the Hindu Brahmanical scriptures, apparently exemplifying a traditional reverence for nature and life forms. If India were to abandon its pursuit of Western models of economic development, it would

[43] Visvanathan, *A Carnival for Science*, 6.

[44] Lewis, *Inventing Global Ecology*, 23–4.

[45] Nandy, *Science, Hegemony and Violence*, 1–23.

[46] Alvares, "Science, Colonialism and Violence", 68–111.

[47] Gadgil and Guha urge the environmental movements of India to present a truer picture of the India that is, and the India that should be. For details, see Gadgil and Guha, *Ecology and Equity*, 6.

only be returning to its cultural roots. National ecology was in effect, by the route formulated by this critique, a return to precolonial village society, which was perceived as the exemplar of social and ecological harmony. The ancient traditions of India that incorporated profound "ecological insight" were the destination.[48] The ideal was a timeless Ram Rajya, the Hindu contrast to Western ideologies of materialism and consumerism.

The Indian state was also paradoxically a major player in the environmental discourse of the post 1970s. Along with its developmental agenda, it showed a visible shift in using nature for building a nationalist constituency. At the first UN Conference on the Environment held at Stockholm, Sweden, in 1972, the Indian prime minister Indira Gandhi spoke on a complex set of environmental issues as a global environmental leader. Such nationalism, though exceptional, pointed to a larger trend.[49]

As part of a nationalist project to save its new-found emblem, i.e. the Indian tiger, the largest wildlife conservation project in the world, Project Tiger, was launched in 1973. Some of the nine initial tiger reserves were old princely hunting grounds, and the others had been reserved forests from British days. These were located in widely varying regions: from the mangrove jungles of the Sunderbans in the Ganga delta to the thorn forests of Ranthambhore in the northwest. One of the state's main moves was closure of forestry operations in the core conservation areas, resulting in a loss of rights and livelihood for millions of tribals and forest dwellers. The tiger was portrayed as an animal at the apex of the food chain, therefore representing the health of the land: its recovery implied all-round ecological revival. The project was expanded, lands were covered beyond those of the project, and the protected area network grew much wider. Coming out of this was "an evolving nationalistic pride",[50] a recognition from international conservation organisations such as the International Union for the Conservation of Nature and Natural Resources (IUCN) and the Worldwide Fund for Nature (WWF), who

[48] Shiva, *Staying Alive*, 57.

[49] Rangarajan, *Environmental Issues in India*, xviii–ix.

[50] Lewis, *Inventing Global Ecology*, 235–6.

work with a sense of mission at educating people and politicians about the virtues of biological conservation.[51] National pride and prestige through nature conservation acquired a kind of political consensus. Even when a non-Congress government came to power in New Delhi and in several North Indian states in 1977, the projects for wildlife protection not only continued but were expanded to new areas and species.

As part of a grand national nature project, various national laws and departments came into being in quick succession: for example the Wildlife (Protection) Act in 1972 and the Forest Conservation Act in 1980. The Department of Environment at the union government level, later upgraded to a ministry, was set up in November 1980. We observe here a certain continuity since Independence in the influence and spread of national interests through nature, with some additions. In the past, the tribal was expected to give up his land and forests so that iron mines, steel plants, and large dams could be built for the nation. This mission was now joined by projects of nature conservation, and in both the interests of the nation were elevated above those of the tribal.

Commenting on India's environmental discourse in the 1970s and 1980s through the life and works of Indira Gandhi, Mahesh Rangarajan sees the threads of broader questions of conservation and livelihoods, democracy and authoritarianism, national sovereignty and international influence in this period. The Emergency was built on notions of centralist governance with a large middle-class constituency. It had an appeal amongst advocates of conservation. One common rallying point among conservationists was the issue of state rights over forests. The Forty-second Constitutional Amendment, carried into effect in January 1977, did much to weaken the democratic edifice, but it also placed "Forests and Wildlife" on the concurrent as opposed to the state list. This meant that both the federal and state governments had jurisdiction over wildlife and forests. However, in the event of a difference, it was the union whose will would prevail. It is significant, argues Rangarajan, that even after Indira

[51] Guha, *How Much Should a Person Consume?*, 126.

Gandhi lost in March 1977, and the Janata Party came to power, it did not undo this provision. He concludes: "There was a larger drift towards centralisation and also to the accretion of the power above, but this does not deny or detract from the depth of concerns that were often ecological *and* nationalistic . . . There is little doubt that there were authoritarian elements in the projects of saving nature or remaking the environment, but the shadow cast by them was not all-encompassing."[52]

The economic crisis in India, new economic policies in the 1980s, and the neo-liberal economic reforms of the 1990s became challenging for environmental movements in India. There have been broader critical discourses amongst organisations, movements, and intellectuals about the nature and contents of these economic reforms and their impact on the various branches of society, including natural resources and the environment. Simultaneously, issues like national independence and sovereignty, self-reliance and self-government, equity and environmentally sound and sustainable development have come into sharper focus.[53]

Neo-liberal globalisation, the challenge of Hindutva, and the burgeoning ecological crisis were characterised as the three most important challenges of contemporary India. It was claimed that neo-liberal globalisation had been effectively critiqued by left scholarship since the 1990s: progressives believed that globalisation had been exposed as promoting inequality, hunger, and disease among the poor. The second challenge, that of Hindutva, was again opposed by the left and its associated organisations. However, while some groups within the left recognised certain dimensions of the third challenge, that of the ecological crisis, the larger movement by and large failed to realise its full import.[54] Pro-globalisation and neo-liberal ideologies were however seen by others in India as all-encompassing forces which nullified dignity and justice. They played a crucial role in ruining the livelihood resources of a large number of people and impairing their support base, and by marginalising the welfare state.[55]

[52] Rangarajan, "Striving for a Balance", 299–312.

[53] Mukul, *Against the Stream*, 1–3.

[54] Prasad, *Environmentalism and the Left*, 112–13.

[55] Sharma and Bharti, "In Lieu of Introduction", 5.

The opening of Indian frontiers to foreign corporations, it was shown, had given rise to manifold conflicts over resources and subsistence rights, the extraction of raw materials, alterations in eco-systems, genetic engineering, climate change and livelihood rights, environmental degradation in cities, and resource prices.[56]

Various studies tried to quantify the impact of new-liberal policies on the environment in India. The liberalisation of trade was shown to have had two consequences. First, a move towards an export-led model of growth that sacrificed natural resources to earn foreign exchange, as was especially seen in the fisheries and mining sectors. Second, a flood of consumer goods and toxic matter into India, creating serious waste disposal and health problems. The moves towards industrial and agricultural liberalisation had resulted in industries increasingly ignoring environmental standards, and state governments sacrificing natural habitats and prime arable to make way for commercial enterprises. The opening up of the economy to foreign investment had brought in companies with notorious track records on the environment, and with demands to further relax social and environmental protection measures. Privatisation had encouraged the violation or dilution of environmental standards, and the neglect of social services and goods for the poor. The opposition to much of this was stated thus:

> But the most pressing need is for environmentalists, social activists, and sensitive academics to work out an alternative strategy for the economic renewal of the country, a strategy which is socially sensitive and environmentally sustainable. Elements of such a strategy are present in the widespread mass movements built around natural resource conflicts, in the various alternative energy, agricultural projects, and industrial projects which are successfully being run by citizens groups and a handful of government agencies across the country, and in the alternative governance models which are being practiced in several areas.[57]

However, by contrast, some of the critiques of globalisation and neo-liberal economic reforms were anchored in upholding a rich and glorious Indian past, in stressing ancient tradition, culture,

[56] Sachs, "Environment, Dignity and Human Rights", 23–9.
[57] Kothari, "Environment and New Economic", 131–40.

religion, and community life. India's environmental movements and initiatives were seen as emerging out of a collective resolve to establish pristine Indian ways of life in the future. In variants of the Gandhian ideal, often in extremely retrograde ones, the Indian village was constructed as the site reinforcing community, national identity, and culture. A Green village, linked with a harmonious, non-industrial, non-urban natural community, became the repository of an immutable national identity. It was said that

> Indian villages are highly integrated; as a community, Indian villagers have been great farmers and water harvesters; villagers also relate to their overall ecosystem. The biggest problem lies in the alienation that the modern state has created amongst village communities towards their commons. Traditional systems are extremely important in this world of modern science and technology. Traditional knowledge would have to be the starting point . . . A fresh evaluation of traditional systems can also have major political and cultural repercussion . . . It would force politicians, teachers and experts to speak in the idiom of the Indian.[58]

Evidence of this tradition can apparently be found in ancient texts, inscriptions, local traditions, and archaeological remains. The Puranas, the Mahabharata, the Ramayana and various Vedic, Buddhist, and Jain texts contain several references to canals, tanks, embankments, and wells. Thus, their revival is essential today.[59]

Movements like the Narmada Bachao Andolan and the Chilka Bachao Andolan deployed a creative redefinition of human rights by closely linking the movement with the right to life and livelihood. By contrast, Hindutva has adopted a selective model of environmentalism and occluded other aspects of it. As perceptively pointed out by Jeremy Seabrook:

> When the BJP talks of the need to recuperate something of India's past, who can fail to see that the rejection of Indian tradition, skills and creativity has been a profound insult, not simply to Hindus but to all Indians? The fact that malign ideologies flourish in the presence of real evils neither condones the ideologies nor nullifies the evils. The recovery

[58] Agarwal and Narain, *Towards Green Villages,* 52.

[59] Agarwal and Narain, eds, *Dying Wisdom.* Also see Mishra, *Aaj Bhi Khare.*

of something of value from a past that is being junked does not necessarily mean that the BJP is right. For there are other noble traditions which it chooses to pass over in silence, which are in far more urgent need of rehabilitation: the practice of *ahimsa* (non-violence), of self-restraint, respect for all living things, the practice of a joyful austerity, do not belong to the zealots of millennial nostalgia . . . The West imposes its version of a modernized, industrialized humanity, so irresistible that it sweeps all before it. No wonder that people retreat to the only spaces left to them – the apparent safe haven of the past or the tarnished New Jerusalems of an impossible future.[60]

Others too have offered powerful critiques from diverse angles of these strains of nostalgia, traditionalism, and Hindu nationalism that colour environmental arguments. They have shown how such positions are susceptible to misuse by Hindutva and how they negate the very idea of modernity without answering questions such as "what type of modernity, and for whom?"[61] Others state that such romanticism often presents a singularly unidimensional view of the nation's past. Moreover, it does not enable us to generate strategies responsive to contemporary understandings of ecological stability and social justice.[62] The past, it is argued, provides neither a record of harmony and utopia nor one of despoliation of nature by people. A valorisation of tradition sits uneasily with the quest for justice.[63] Still others contend that views like these carry perceptions of an idyllic/harmonious/folkloric village existence as an unchanging/unchangeable "natural" community, and thus the repository of a similarly immutable national identity.[64] In ecological theory, "this idealisation of the 'traditional' society is strongly nationalistic; blaming all of the societies' ills on 'western' colonialism, while ignoring the deep-rooted inequities which pre-dated the colonial conquest."[65] Recently

[60] Seabrook, *Notes from Another India*, 204–5.

[61] Prasad, *Against Ecological Romanticism*, 108.

[62] Sinha, Gururani, and Greenberg, "The 'New Traditionalist' Discourse", 69.

[63] Rangarajan and Sivaramakrishnan, eds, *India's Environmental History*.

[64] Brass, "The Agrarian Myth", 205.

[65] Mukta and Hardiman, "The Political Ecology", 120–1.

Kathleen Morrison, through life histories of ancient reservoir irrigation systems in South India, has shown that there never was a golden age of Indian irrigation marked by environmental stability, egalitarian social relations, and complete community self-governance. These ancient systems never worked perfectly, and power-laden technologies had always been enmeshed with the structures of inequality. She concludes that it is not necessary to falsely valorise the past in order to critique large development projects, as such views posit an (impossible) return to a past of the imagination as a solution for the real needs of rural people.[66]

So the use and abuse of nature for nationalism has a long and complex history in India. Nature has been deployed at different points of time for diverse, multiple, and competing visions of nationalism. It has become a resource at different locations, from local to international, for articulating political and cultural aspirations, and for establishing dominance. The creation of a modern, secular nation, the imagination of an indigenous nation, or the idea of a post-development, post-globalisation nation – all have nature as an important component. These different forms of "ecological nationalism" require an analysis of power and polity.[67] With the right-wing shift in India's polity since the 1980s, certain traditions deployed to use nature for nationalism help in the articulation of a particular vision of the nation which is largely Hindu and exclusive in its rendering. It is thus imperative to offer an alternative critique of modernity and the developmental state to reveal precisely how power is exercised over nature and people.

[66] Morrison, "*Dharmic* Projects", 182–95.

[67] Cederlöf and Sivaramakrishnan, eds, *Ecological Nationalisms*.

# 8

# Features of Hindu Environmentalism

## The Convergence of Green and Saffron

THE IDEOLOGICAL POINTS of convergence between Green and Saffron have exhibited remarkable diversity and diffusion. Since 2000 these convergences have emerged through numerous environmental organisations, alongside a smaller set of organised entities of Hindu nationalists. However, following the year 2014, subsequent to the rise of the BJP and Modi to power, the larger RSS network has placed a significant emphasis on environmental issues within their organisational and political activities, aligning them with Hindu nationalist objectives. Employing a strategic political approach, these environmental issues are being introduced in various ways to appeal universally, while also being manipulated often to fulfil specific political objectives. Presently, there exists a substantial domestic constituency that aligns itself with the environmental activities of Hindu nationalist groups. Furthermore, a noticeable "saffron" civil society has emerged, endorsing the environmental discourse of the RSS family, including Modi. Thus, it becomes essential to analyse this convergence in two distinct phases: pre-2014 and post-2014. It is worth noting that while there are indeed continuities in the approach of Hindu nationalist politics towards the environment in both stages, the shift after 2014 is significant.

## Post-2000: Normalising Convergence

The convergence between the green and saffron movements has appeared most notably since 2000. The ascension of the Sangh in India's political and electoral landscape during the late 1990s and beyond established them as a potent entity within the country. Concurrently, India has witnessed the proliferation of numerous environmental groups, NGOs, movements, and grassroots initiatives. Nevertheless, it is important to note that several environmental groups in India have demonstrated ambiguity in the comprehension and presentation of their environmentalism. Many organisations claim that dominant politics and ideology are part of the problem, in their content as well as in their form.

Of course, even when environmental organisations and movements are not consciously deploying a particular political ideology and party politics, there is still a certain ideological content evident from their belief system and practices. In every environmental act a set of constitutive ideas holds people together. These beliefs are not always immediately apparent but are precisely the points of reference with which to explore the convergence between environmental thought and action on the one hand, and a political ideology and party on the other. Through an analysis of the texts and activities of Hindu authoritarian groups, along with abundant environmental literature and case studies, five principal points of convergence and reference can be identified from 2000 onwards: nationalism and ultranationalism; the yearning for a Brahmanical Hindu religion, tradition, and culture; emphasis on authority, social order, unity, and discipline; an implicit hostility towards Muslims, Dalits, and Christians; and a programmatic politics entailing communalism. Each of these sources is, or has at some time been, present in environmental discourse, and contributes therefore to its set of constitutive ideas.

As we have seen, one strand of nationalist and ultra-nationalist environmentalism in India today shows a deep distaste for Westernisation, globalisation, and industrialisation, the authoritarian ideology of this strand being marked by an often vitriolic nationalism. This nationalist fervour goes well beyond the traditional desires of nation-building, national unity, and integrity. Nationalist and ultra-nationalist environmentalism is intimately related to a valorisation by the militants of Hindu religion, culture, and tradition. The nation, in this worldview, is as natural as nature, transcending all contest and the object of unquestioning allegiance. What this kind of environmentalist most desires is an overtly nationalist state with a clear, firm, and unambiguous conception of the "national", usually Hindu, interest.

In many ways Anna Hazare set the tone for this conservative environmentalism. Nationalism has from the start been a critical facet in his personal ideological synthesis, though fused with other elements. His nationalism is a matter of life and death; it demands instinctive allegiance. The idea of nation or national interest provides him a readymade traditional point of reference for his environmental activities, even as on a political plank it leads him to attack China and Pakistan, criticise migrants in Mumbai, and endorse the political claims of Hindu nationalists in Maharashtra. This is an environmentalism that echoes belief in a national destiny and patriotic commitment expressed in the most jingoistic terms.

Similarly, opposition to the Tehri Dam evokes "the missile range of neighbouring countries" and "outside threats from the enemies". References to war and victories over these enemies provide the opportunity for self-sacrifice and a rekindling of the fading embers of Indian nationalism, alongside the call to preserve ecological aspects of the Hindu sacred. Past indignation at the demise of the nation is invoked to rediscover the nation via its victories over its many enemies – who may be found in Pakistan and China as well as in Nagaland, Manipur, Tripura, Assam, Punjab, and Kashmir. Such commitment to nationalism is inseparable from a siege mentality and the consequent advocacy of militant self-defence, and thence to the argument for a strong army and state. Both Ralegan Siddhi and opposition to the Tehri Dam are characterised by Hindu political environmentalism of this variety.

The history and life of the nation is lived largely in a freshly minted environmentalism. Here, history becomes a collection of myths, and whenever the story of our nation seems not so great, we can make it up! The work of the good environmentalist is to create and supply "good" myths, such as the idea that the nation and its sacred places, such as Vrindavan, are among the world's richest, greatest, and purest places; all dams may be equal but some dams are more equal than others, especially those that dam rivers essential to the myths of a great religion. The environmentalist's reverence for Hindu culture, religion, and tradition underpins ideas about social norms and the national interest, the emphasis being upon a pure, Brahmanical, scripted, located religious culture. Nature, within this form of conservative environmentalism, is the raw material through which a collective, singular, united Hindu religious identity is identified and created. Tradition here is much more than a matter of nostalgia or personal preference. It is an active achievement of the continuity of nation and community, the totality of practices through which the individual is able to perceive allegiance to the nation, the state, and the social order as an end. In the environmental discourses of Vrindavan and Ralegan Siddhi, tradition therefore includes all rituals, activities, and actions which serve to define the individual in a social context, as part of society. This includes, for instance, birth, marriage, entertainment, food, family life, manners, modes of dress, festivals and the like, and the prescribed ways in which such activities can be organised and carried out. In some cases, the driving force behind this traditionalism and environmentalism is an obsession with the supposed purity of the collectivity (whether defined in cultural, religious, or national terms), expressing itself in a compulsive need to safeguard village boundaries, as by regulating or prescribing religiously derived values and behaviour, as much as by expelling and exterminating those viewed as violators and outsiders.

Within this traditional environmental framework, it is the work of a Brahmin priest and his prayers to initiate the appropriate efforts of conservation and flood control, as for example in the Kosi region of Bihar. Animal sacrifice, based on a mix of Hinduism and popular belief, is seen as a critical social act within the village community. In yet other places, the *Manusmriti* is lauded as key to the traditional value system – even in relation to the "ancient and time-tested technology", namely scavenging, for the disposal of sewage and human excreta in Vrindavan. A "restriction on electricity", a "total ban on non-vegetarian food", and the "removal of hospitals, factories, and modern educational facilities from the Vrindavan forest area" are upheld as desirable. In Ralegan Siddhi the ideal woman is first the bearer of children and server of her husband's household. Beating, flogging, coercion, punishment, and undemocratic processes may all be justified in the quest for a supposedly sound ecological society. Tradition, thus, plays many roles in this convergence of Green and Saffron, making the established social division and order seem natural, as well as validating and sustaining hierarchy and the status quo.

In various parts of the world authoritarian and right-wing groups, political parties as well as environmental outfits, have similarly argued for harsh and strong solutions to overcome the environmental crisis. The Independent Ecologists of Germany (UOD) and its founder Herbert Gruhl (also the one-time founder of the German Greens) have called for a return to basic German values, with the possibility of a more ecologically conscious but also more authoritarian state. Another prominent leader of the UOD, Tilman Ziegler, has demanded a rethinking of basic democratic values, beliefs, and institutions in the wake of the coming environmental holocaust; many more like author-journalist Wolfgang Venohr have argued that when the fate of the earth hangs in the balance, freedom cannot be the highest of values and eco-dictatorship need not always be evil. At a broader level, eco-national and eco-natural prescriptions for socio-political situations are said to be crucial to environmental politics:

> The most important questions to be asked when interrogating any political theory built on a natural perspective, however, is how nature should guide politics (i.e. what one perceives the lessons from nature or ecology for society to be) and which model of nature it uses. Aside from the possibility of dangerous political instrumentalization, it obviously makes a difference whether the model of nature used in constructing and interpreting the laws of nature stresses nature's functional cooperation and variety *within* an eco-system, or whether – as in its right-wing variety – eco-systems are seen as closed systems with unique and fragile qualities . . . Right-wing ecology views nature as demonstrating qualities of authority, self-sacrifice, and purity, thus legitimating its notion of an ethno-

> culturally based eco-dictatorship. Indeed it is precisely this authoritarian model of nature that provides an ecological legitimation against Enlightenment universalism. Given a view of nature as authoritarian and demanding obedience to her laws, it is not surprising that the apocalyptic scenarios of right-wing ecology serve to justify an authoritarian state.[1]

Certainly, attempts to reinvest nature with authority and make it the source of guidelines for the construction of an ecological and ideal village, as in Ralegan Siddhi, lead also to a form of authoritarianism. The moral authority of Anna Hazare views environmental conservation and development in terms of securing a stable and continuing harmonious relationship between the governed and the governing. It seeks to portray environmental initiatives as the assurance of community and national interest based on a strong, enlightened, and beneficent leader. Such environmentalism means that there are leaders and there are those who must be led, or in other words authority and obedience. This environmentalism is not concerned with democracy and social justice but with the economic and moral wellbeing of a village community within a stable order of reciprocal rights and duties. Its keywords include unity, loyalty, and morality. It openly proclaims its disdain for democratic processes – no voting and electioneering – if not for democratic institutions themselves. The measure of wisdom of a community is the commitment it provides for an environmental leadership to assume its roles and to reap its just rewards via unity and unquestioning affirmation of the leader.

Authoritarian moralism is a clear area of convergence between Green and Saffron in India, where environmentalism allies with feudal attitudes to instil moral codes, rules, and a discipline which are hegemonically justified as vital to the life of the nation. This preference for a community of moral purpose in fact represents the imposition of a moral orthodoxy. The values and standards, rules and codes, in the environmental domains of Vrindavan and Ralegan Siddhi could have been those associated with honesty, simplicity, self-restraint, kindness, discipline, hard work, initiative, good manners, responsibility, integrity, and so on. Conservative environmentalists and political

[1] Olsen, *Nature and Nationalism*, 45–6.

groups have harnessed these for political purposes which entail adherence to strict Hindu moral certainties within a secure social order: no meat, no films, no cable TV, no singing (unless religious); yes to the *Manusmriti*, the pure married woman and family life, and traditional methods of waste disposal.

There is also a strong current of "organicism", "organic unity", and "unity of opposites" in this politico-environmental discourse. Organicism considers human society to be analogous to an organism, and individual humans to the cells of an organism. Organic unity postulates interdependent parts: a body is made up of its constituent organs, a society is made up of its constituent social roles. A common thread of discipline must prevent this unity being broken and disjointed as the entity moves forward. The unity of opposites defines a situation in which the existence or identity of a thing (or situation) depends on the coexistence of at least two conditions which are opposed yet dependent on each other, and which presuppose each other within a field of tension. Often, it is implied that one of the pairs of opposites is larger, stronger, or more powerful than the other, such that over time one of the opposed conditions prevails over the other. In environmental discourse, eco-organicism assumes an already existing latent identity between society and nature, and posits this identity for collectives and communities. Thus, nation, nation-state, culture, religion, tradition, and community are deified when they function to unify. There may be a diversity of natural and social characteristics, but within the system each distinctive part is required to perform its unique work for the general good. This logic serves the argument that Dalits, a functional part of the overarching unity of a community, village, and society, must perform as dictated by a system. Consensuality precludes challenges and obviates democracy. Dalits must internalise this hegemonic consensus brought to bear on them by the authoritarian environmental discourse; ironically, of course, even the internalisation is not enough to prevent Dalits being either pushed out of such environmental politics, or pushed to its margins.

This is not, however, to suggest an environment of hopelessness and reformist impossibility. On the contrary, Indian environmental politics was extremely heterogeneous and this heterogeneity offers arenas of hope. There were oppositions, protest groups, movements, alliances, individuals, and alternative civil society organisations. Also, environmental themes and concerns appeared across a diverse spectrum of mass-based organisations affiliated with political parties. Women's groups and movements; anti-war, anti-nuclear, and peace organisations; and non-party urban, professional, and sectoral groups also widely articulated these issues. From environmental critiques of development to recognising people's right to natural resources, from emphasising the destructive features of capitalism and modern science to addressing new environmental problems, from a commitment to Indian tradition, culture, religion, and community to dealing with issues of political participation, governance, and democratisation, environmental concerns were also articulated in rich, diverse, and substantial ways. In their practical political activities, many environmental groups and movements had been at the forefront of efforts to democratise state institutions, as well as in the creation of more democratic and accountable forms of environmental decision-making. Examples include Green efforts to open up access to information and creating more open forms of public policymaking. The anti-bureaucratic strand of environmental politics in contemporary India also called into question aspects of globalisation and the modernisation model with its corporatist overtones. The environmental movement's overarching emphasis on grassroots activism and bottom-up organisational principles also testified to the democratic credentials of much environmental political practice.

## Post-2014: Modi, Motherland, Modernisation

After 2014 the ideological and political dominance of the RSS, Narendra Modi, and the BJP has made state collaboration with various non-governmental organisations for an extensive array of environmental activities encompassing areas such as climate change and renewable energy. In their renewed role within government, Hindu nationalists have adroitly intertwined four distinct dimensions of politics: the populace, political strategies, foreign affairs, and economic interest – all contributing to the formation of their environmental framework. This transformation was steered by the leadership of Modi, the co-ordinated efforts of the RSS in mobilisation, the skilful ideological sculpting by the wider *parivar* of affiliated organisations, and the strategic partnerships with civil society entities. Through a comprehensive examination of the extensive array of political and governmental activities undertaken by the RSS, BJP, and Modi, coupled with a thorough review of their recently published materials and communication, five fundamental tenets of right-wing ecology in India have been discerned: Hindu national power; the establishment of central authority; mass mobilisation and media control; climate change and renewable energy; and a saffron civil society. These principles not only align with various environmental organisations but also resonate within the broader sphere of environmentalism.

Hindu nationalist environmentalism has placed a significant emphasis on crafting a narrative of nation-power surrounding Bharat. This narrative highlights Bharat's past glory across various dimensions of both natural and human life. It asserts that Bharat is now destined to assume a leading role as a representative of human civilisation on the global stage, particularly in the realm of environmental affairs. The past and prejudices inherent in Bharat's Hindu religion and culture are reimagined as a future-looking exercise where the essence of Hindu land, rivers, animals, food, energy, technology, and science can be revitalised and reclaimed for the future glory of the motherland. This signifies a shift from the prior phase, where the present emphasis centred on promoting the concept of Hindu nationalist environmentalism as the primary solution to environmental challenges, while also serving as a possible route to establish a Hindu Rashtra.

The RSS plays a prominent role in crafting narratives that depict a splendid and potent natural Hindu nation, one tasked with a pivotal civilisational mission. In this narrative, Bharatavarsha stands as the ancestral homeland of Hindus, a conception rooted in culture and tradition. Nature itself has bestowed the nation, enclosed by the Himalayas and the Hindu Kush, the Indian Ocean, the Arabian Sea, and the Bay of Bengal. The Hindu homeland runs unbrokenly from

Gandhar to Kamrup, and from Kashmir to Kanyakumari. Hindus have an exclusive entitlement to this land, where they have fostered their culture and civilisation, venerating it as their sacred soil for over 6000 years. The imperative is for Hindus to free their motherland from external influences and ideologies. Their responsibility extends beyond their own well-being, encompassing ideologies and systems that have afflicted them for centuries and a mission to civilise the destructive Western world.[2] It is frequently noted that Hindus have a *mangal* approach towards nature, regarding it as a divine mother and deity. Their devotions extend to the earth, cows, tulsi plants, the Ganga River, and trees. Thus, a Bharatiya and Hindu dharma-oriented approach to development in this view, must be disseminated to Western communities.[3] The RSS also calls for the revival of India's glorious ancient scientific traditions across various domains, with the aim of restoring the nation's status as the "Golden Bird" and the *jagatguru.*[4]

The image of a strong natural nation finds its embodiment in Narendra Modi, who occupies a central role in asserting Hindu national power across various environmental platforms, both within the country and on the global stage. Modi has skilfully blended the responsibilities of an RSS *pracharak*, a leader of the BJP, and the prime minister. Through a substantial reliance on ancient Hindu texts he has proclaimed India as being the vanguard of environmental leadership. He has revitalised the supposedly glorious scientific tradition of Bharat to build the foundation for launching modern mega-energy projects. By igniting a resurgence of seized and subdued Hindu pride within the homeland, he has announced the emergence of a dynamic "new India" in the realm of environmental affairs. This is also intended to teach lessons to others about the synergy of manpower, strength, and success. Transitioning from being an heir to the Hindu scientific legacy, Modi has evolved into a proponent of modern-era climate corporates and capital ventures.

[2] For details, Chatterjee, *The Concept of a Hindu Nation.*

[3] For details, Lal Gupta, *A New Paradigm Development;* Nandakumar, *Hindutva.*

[4] For details, Soni, *India's Glorious Scientific Tradition.*

Apart from these individual attributes of authority in Modi, the concept of centralisation as a broader policy and governance framework is conspicuously evident in India's renewable-energy deployment. The earlier discourse surrounding energy within the nation – shaped by the trajectories of movements against big dams and nuclear facilities – consistently advocated alternative energy-production systems. These alternatives were envisioned as small-scale, decentralised systems closely linked to local communities. The objective was to cater to local energy needs while also placing a significant emphasis on energy conservation. This conceptualisation encompassed a range of dimensions, spanning political, ecological, engineering, economic, and technological aspects. It contained ideas such as granting local populations control over environmental resources, situating electricity generation in proximity to consumption points, facilitating localised energy production managed by community actors, promoting cost-effective and suitable technologies, and enabling trading decisions through non-centralised entities. These notions aligned seamlessly with the principles underpinning renewable energy.[5]

Modi's climate policy, as this book has tried to show, has taken a divergent route. It has prioritised a centralised top-down approach primarily driven by corporate interests. Modi's "One Sun One World One Grid" initiative serves as a prominent illustration of this centralised governance framework. While on the surface it pledges to provide clean energy to fulfil global-energy requirements, in practice it has been utilised by corporations, financiers, and governments to generate profits from the energy system by establishing modern, massively interconnected global, regional, and national grids. This has also meant close collaboration with international private capital and the existing infrastructural order. Hence, the trajectory of the nation's climate and energy policy has transitioned towards an authoritarian structure characterised by the dominance of a select and influential group within both government and business domains.

There also exists a substantial restriction on the freedom to advocate alternative energy options.

[5] For details, Toke, *Ecological Modernisation and Renewable Energy*.

The convergence of green and saffron in post-2014 India refers to the organisational efforts and political strategies employed by the RSS *parivar*, in collaboration with numerous governmental and non-governmental organisations, to mobilise both the general populace and media outlets around environmental themes. These environmental activities encompass a range of actions, from individuals taking pledges to safeguard the environment on Earth Day, planting trees, and practising yoga, to addressing issues such as cow protection, vegetarianism, and the defence of the motherland.

The triangle of the RSS, the BJP, and Modi has been resourceful and conscious about the uses of media and communication for its political and governmental agenda. At a time when the media has transformed religion and religious consciousness in South Asia, the RSS has designed a regular flow and, at times, flooding of images for their environmental communication. This is what is called "the politics of new image technologies at a moment of increasingly authoritarian right-wing populism."[6] Streams of texts and visuals, social media posts and tweets, have expanded Hindu nationalism's ideological outreach and magnified its political appeal, aiding the making of a new Hindu environmental subject which stands up for right-wing agendas and activities.[7]

In sum, the convergence of the green and saffron in the post-2014 period has become evident through the growth and prominence of what I have referred to as the "saffron civil society". This is a collection of non-governmental organisations, professional groups, and experts who claim to voice the concerns of the people but whose actions largely involve uncritical endorsement of the environmental policies advocated by Modi and his administration. In contemporary India, the concept of saffron civil society is composed of two distinct streams. The first consists of organisations and groups that have been established by the Sangh *parivar*. The second involves independent entities that align themselves with the right-wing ecological standpoint.

[6] Jain, *Gods in the Time of Democracy*, 5.

[7] For details, Sharma, "Hindu Nationalism", 102–17.

Within the realm of climate change and energy, the influence of India's saffron civil society has become more pronounced. This is particularly evident as issues related to Hindu nationalism, communalism, authoritative governance, democratic freedoms, corporate interests, and modernisation have been subdued by the overarching narrative of climate change mitigation, carbon emissions regulation, and ambitious targets for renewable energy adoption. I have also suggested that despite the ideological reticence displayed by these groups, the everyday climatism of this category of civil society organisations corresponds to distinctive attributes associated with the centralised and authoritative aspects of Hindu nationalist environmentalism.

It also needs reiteration, as I have tried to do in this book, that politically ambiguous notions of environment and alternative development as politics at times fall flat in the face of ever-reappearing forms of communalism, fundamentalism, regionalism, identity, and democracy. Environmental movements in India have little political space; they are for the most part not tied to those with political power. They have not created a niche in the electoral politics of Indian democracy, and they more generally aspire to practice a different kind of politics. Thus, there is little talk of an environmental political culture and environmental political identity in India. Sometimes other factors, such as the retrograde trajectories of some prominent environmental movements, and the state's apathy and repression, have made politically committed survival difficult for environmentalists. The rise of Modi, the establishment of a BJP-led government, and the subsequent expansion of RSS activities have significantly propelled Hindu nationalist environmental politics. Within an environment characterised by political dominance and suppression, the scope for radical environmental politics has markedly diminished.

In such a scenario, the general consensus among environmental groups seems to be that they have no choice but to adopt pragmatic political paths. However practical this viewpoint, its realisation is fatal in the context of the alliance between authoritarian politics and communalism on the one hand, and environmentalism on the other. Conservative environmentalism and the convergence of Green and

Saffron is a threat not only because it is practised by some key environmentalists and organisations, but also because it is propagated and supported by the institutions of civil society and democracy. This convergence requires a degree of assent, which it is well placed to elicit; but, more importantly, it prevents the formation of a counter-environmental ideology and politics. This is the clearest conclusion that I can offer as one who has seen, first-hand, and from close quarters, some prominent and influential environmental leaders, organisations, and movements in contemporary India.

# Postscript

## RSS Shakha, Environment Day, Nature Prayers, and Threats to the Motherland

**State: Delhi; District: North West; Locality: Pitampura**

PITAMPURA, LOCATED in the North West District of the national capital Delhi, is a vibrant area that encompasses upscale residential, commercial, and retail spaces. With a population exceeding seven million people, the locality boasts of plotted houses, large malls, bustling markets, esteemed schools, technical institutions, metro stations, and district parks. This makes it a dynamic region teeming with activity. On the auspicious day of 12 April 2018, known as the Hindu New Year and also marking the birth anniversary of Dr Hedgewar, the founder of the RSS, a shakha (branch) in Pitampura is preparing for its daily evening gathering at Bharat Darshan Park. The shakha has planned group singing, the performance of physical exercises, and a discussion on the environmental challenges faced by Bharat (India). This particular shakha consists of approximately forty to fifty local men, primarily middle-aged. One *swayamsevak* (volunteer) says to me that the shakhas have received guidelines from their headquarters to include "environment" as a topic of discussion during significant days and events. As is routine in the RSS, women are not allowed to participate in these shakha gatherings.

In Pitampura the RSS organises several shakhas, such as the Madav, Shiv, Maurya, Sudershan, and Vir Vinayak shakhas. These *shakhas* convene regularly in public parks, school or college grounds, either in the mornings or evenings, for an hour or two. They serve as the basic local units of the organisation and play a crucial role in implementing RSS objectives on the ground. Over the recent past, these shakhas have observed various special events: Shivaji Day, which commemorates the establishment of Hindu rule by Shivaji nearly 350 years ago, during a time when "foreign Muslim aggressors" governed Bharat; and Dharm Sabha, a religious meeting calling for the construction of the Ram temple in Ayodhya. Additionally, they celebrate Bal Sangam, a festival dedicated to children, and Guru Purnima, a ritualistic worship of spiritual figures.

The primary objective of all these is to foster the building of a "Hindu, Hindu Rashtra, Hindu Culture because the RSS believed from the day one that this country belonged to the Hindus."[1] As stated in the RSS Annual Report 2021–2, there were 60,929 shakhas across more than 38,390 locations in March 2022. These numbers have been steadily increasing over the past decade, with a target of reaching 100,000 shakhas nationwide by 2025 (compared to 55,652 shakhas in March 2021). In addition to the daily shakhas, there are weekly *milans* (meetings) and *sangh mandlis* (gatherings) which contribute to the overall organisational activities and engagements within the RSS.

The shakha begins with the unfurling of the *bhagwa dhwaj* (saffron flag), which was initially adopted by Savarkar's Akhil Bharat Hindu Mahasabha and later embraced by the RSS. This flag is regarded as a symbol of strength and victory for Hindus. The swayamsevaks then proceed to sing the RSS prayer, which reflects upon the sacred Motherland and the pledge of Hindus to protect their Hindu land with the purity of their physical and moral character.

> Forever I bow to thee, O Loving Motherland! O Motherland of us Hindus, Thou hast brought me up in happiness. May my life, O great and blessed Holy Land, be laid down in Thy Cause. I bow to Thee again and again.
>
> We the children of the Hindu Nation bow to Thee in reverence, O Almighty God. We have girded our loins to carry on Thy work. Give

[1] Rashtriya Swayamsevak Sangh, "What is the Sakha", https://www.rss.org //Encyc/2017/6/3/basic-faq-on-rss-eng.html.

> us Thy holy blessings for its fulfilment. O Lord! Grant us such might as no power on earth can ever challenge, such purity of character as would command the respect of the whole world and such knowledge as would make easy the thorny path that we have voluntarily chosen.[2]

Prayers end with the slogans *Bharat Mata ki Jai! Bharat Mata ki Jai!* A senior *swayamsevak* addresses the shakha:

> Bharatavarsha is the ancient homeland of Hindus. No country in the world have such distinct nature and natural boundaries. It seems Mother Nature – the Supreme Being – has herself created the land of Bharatavarsha, surrounded by the Himalayas, the Hindukush, the Indian Ocean, the Arab sea and the Bay of Bengal. And the Hindus have been closely associated with their land, mountain and ocean. Hindus have lived on them, nurtured, built their culture and civilization around nature. For more than 6000 years, they regarded their nature a sacred, holy entity . . . Hindu nationhood, Hindu Rashtra, Hindutva were constructed on our unique nature treasure. However, the foreign invaders' rule for a thousand years looted our nature and destroyed natural religion and culture. We lost parts of our motherland, holy river, sacred forests and our Hindu nation is now fragmented. Our land, water, river have been polluted because of rising pollutants. At the same time, recovering our lost traditional motherland, holy nature and culture will be crucial for the protection of Indian environment.

A large calendar is prominently displayed near the saffron flag, depicting details of the sacred land of Bharat and highlighting various elements of significance, including rivers, lakes, mountains, abodes of gods, *jyotirlingas* (Shiva representations), and other natural areas that are considered ideals of the nation. Notably, on it the Indian Ocean is referred to as Hindu Mahasagar and Bharat described as the country located north of the ocean and south of the Himalaya; its inhabitants are referred to as Bharati. The calendar highlights seven rivers, seven mountains, four *kumbh* places (where purifying elixir exists), four *dhams* (pilgrimage sites), twelve *jyotirlingas*, seven heavens, and four *shankarmaths* (abodes of the Hindu sage Sankara) – all these being the primary areas where Hindus should focus

[2] My translation.

their nature-conservation efforts. As a part of their ritual, the swayamsevaks approach the calendar one by one, forming a line. With utmost reverence, they bow their heads to pay respects to these depicted images symbolising their sacred land and the natural elements associated with it.

The swayamsevaks proceed to sing another song, expressing devotion to the sacred River Ganga; the song gradually becomes a celebration of warriors, emphasising aggression and containing stern warnings to those who create obstacles. It conveys the integral connection between Hindus and their river and conveys a strong message that the enemies of the river will face elimination:

> This trickle-trickle flowing, what would the Ganga streams say?
> Flowing from age to age, this virtuous flow is ours!!
> Mixing in this stream, the ashes of the warriors' flow,
> How many sages have taken refuge in this stream
>
> Will you be able to stop this, those who erase will be erased,
> What a pebble and a stone, if it comes as an obstacle,
> The hills and mountains will collapse, the whole earth will tremble
> This virtuous flow of ours!!

The swayamsevaks enthusiastically chant *Ganga Mata ki Jai* (Victory to Mother Ganga), and some apply a *tilak* (a mark on their foreheads symbolising connection to their faith). Afterwards, they gather near the saffron flag, bowing their heads to it. They then raise their hands to their chests, signifying a solemn pledge to protect the Ganga from pollution and ensure its preservation.

The gathering proceeds with another song that highlights the timeless greatness of India and its natural wonders. The lyrics describe how the mountains, rivers, and the overall geographical features have contributed to making the nation the largest and most powerful in the world. The song says Hindu knowledge and wisdom, deeply rooted in the essence of nature and the nation, will consistently maintain India's position at the pinnacle of global prominence.

> The Himalayas will stand for the highest victory banner
> Proud point of humanity, this India will remain the biggest

> Ganga-Yamuna emerged from here, to flow as one and together,
> where nature has always had something to say to Purush,
> In that India the lovely flag of valour will always be hoisted,
> India will be the highest!!

The swayamsevaks now form a close circle, listening attentively to a speaker who basically reiterates the same message of Hindu civilisation's greatness and laments its destruction by foreign invaders, colonial rulers, and Western influences. He stresses the urgent need to regain the essence of manliness, as advocated by the founder of the organisation, Dr Hedgewar. This concept, referred to as "Man-making" (Vyakti Nirmaan), aims to cultivate the qualities and virtues necessary to revive the glory of Mother Earth and restore Hindu civilisation to its former magnificence.

The speaker goes on to the rich and ancient tradition of Indian science and technology, and to man-making by rekindling the glorious past of Bharat and making it *jagatguru*:

> Bharatiyas have always flown high. In ancient times, Hindus had the knowledge of aeronautics. *Rigveda* gave an account of a three-wheeled chariot that could fly in space. In the Puranas, we find our gods and goddesses travelling by air. In the *Ramayana*, there is reference of *Pushpak Viman*. In the *Mahabharata*, god Krishna and Jaraasandh used the planes. Even the demons had constructed cities in space that were destroyed by god Shiva. This tradition inspires us to move forward to save earth and lead the world for an all-round development in harmony with nature.

What should be done to restore the environment? First, Hindus have to be proud of being Hindu. This means being fearless in defence of Motherland and Mother Earth. Pollution – external and internal – is the most serious environmental problem which can be addressed by asking the government to take effective steps. The environment and politics should be Hinduised. Hindus must purify themselves by stopping conversions to Christianity and Islam. Foreign infiltrators into the country should be banned immediately to stop the pollution of its land, air, and water: the RSS will organise such environmental education more and more through the country.

Following this prolonged self-aggrandisement and paeans to the

Hindu nation, a song dedicated to the RSS is sung, likening the organisation to an eternal and flowing river. The lyrics portray the RSS as a relentless force continuously surging forward despite encountering obstacles such as rocks, mountains, and forests, and despite them constantly gaining momentum. Environmental imagery plays a central role in this depiction, with the natural elements symbolising a journey towards the ultimate victory of Hindus and Bharat over adversaries. The song positions the RSS as the last beacon of hope in the battle against environmental adversaries. The organisation is portrayed as natural, beautiful, and righteous, embodying the principles of environmental aesthetics and stewardship.

> The Sangh stream is flowing
> Telling the unique victory story of that Bhagirath:
> A small stream began running penetrating the wide rocks,
> She grew fearless and ripped apart thick ravines and dense forests
> She became Heaven-Ganga – a great river, taking a unique
> form and deepening . . .

The shakha concludes with repeated slogan-shouting. *Bharat Mata ki Jai!* (Victory to Mother India!), *Vande Matram!* (I bow to the Motherland!), and *Janmabhoomi-Matribhoomi-Pitribhoomi Jindabad Jindabad!* (Long live the Birthplace, Motherland, and Fatherland!). A group of swayamsevaks marches in procession around the park, holding the saffron flag high in the air – a visual representation of organisational unity and purpose.

The vignette of the RSS' beliefs, propaganda, and activities shown above can no longer be seen as isolated, autonomous, and separable from everyday life in India. Since the arrival of Modi's BJP in 2014, the rebuilding and rebranding of India as Bharat is going on all around and has, especially via the power and authority endowed on the RSS, gathered an immense momentum. I have only tried to show in this book how important one specific stream – environmental concerns – has increasingly become for the ideologically right wing and nationalistically Hindu push being given to this new idea of India.

# Glossary

| | |
|---|---|
| *Adarsh Gaon Yojana* | Ideal Village Scheme |
| *Adarsh* | Ideal |
| *Agarbatti* | Incense stick |
| *Akash* | Sky |
| *Akhil Bharatiya Prachar Pramukh* | All India Publicity Chief |
| *Amaranth* | A cash crop |
| *Arti* | Lamp ceremony performed to worship a Hindu god |
| *Asthi Kalash Yatras* | Journeys for the consignment of bone remains |
| *Asuras* | Demons |
| *Atharva Veda* | A sacred text of Hinduism, and one of the four Vedas, often called the Fourth Veda |
| *Atma* | Soul |
| *Avatars* | Descendants |
| *Babajees* | Respected religious men |
| *Bahujan* | The majority of people |
| *Balmiki* | A scheduled caste |
| *Bandars* | Monkeys |
| *Bhagavat-Bhusan* | A sacred Hindu scripture |
| *Bhakts* | Devotees |
| *Bhangi* | A scheduled caste |

| | |
|---|---|
| *Bharat Mata Ki Jai* | A slogan: "Hail Mother India" |
| *Bharatiya* | Indian |
| *Bharat-mata* | Mother India |
| *Bharatvasis* | Residents of India |
| *Bhoo-mata* | Motherland |
| *Bidis* | A twist of tobacco rolled in a tobacco leaf, to be smoked |
| *Braj Rakshak Sena* | An army to save Braj |
| *Chamar* | A scheduled caste |
| *Chandan* | Sandalwood |
| *Chipko* | To cling to; to hug |
| *Chura* | A scheduled caste |
| *Dakshina* | Donation to a Brahman for performance of religious service |
| *Deodar* | The deodar pine; cedar |
| *Devbhumi* | Divine land; the land of the gods |
| *Dharmacharyas* | Devout men of learning |
| *Dharmasastras* | Religious code of precepts in Hindu law |
| *Dharmayudha* | Righteous warfare |
| *Dharmraj* | A righteous Hindu ruler, a name in the *Mahabharata* |
| *Dhoop* | Fragrant resin |
| *Ek Bharat Shreshtha Bharat Ekatma* | One India Superior India, Unity with Oneself |
| *Ekatmata Yatra* | Journey for unity |
| *Ganga Abhiyan* | Ganga Campaign |
| *Ganga raksha yatra* | A campaign journey to save the Ganga |
| *Ganga bhakts* | Devotees of Ganga |

| | |
|---|---|
| *Gari Sadak Andolan* | Motor road movement |
| *Gayatri Mantra* | A revered mantra from the Rig Veda, dedicated to the Vedic deity |
| *Geethopadesha* | A crucial chapter of the *Mahabharata* |
| *Gharana* | Family |
| *Ghatwar* | Ferryman |
| *Gherao* | Blockade |
| *Gobar* | Cow-dung |
| *Go-samvardhan* | Cow-rearing or fostering |
| *Gram sabha* | Village council |
| *Gram sewak* | A village worker |
| *Granth Sahib* | The sacred text of the Sikhs |
| *Grihasth-ashram* | The domestic stage of life, as laid down for a Brahmin |
| *Hindu bhumi* | Hindu land |
| *Hindu Janjagriti Abhiyan* | Hindu Awareness Campaign |
| *Hindu Rashtra* | Hindu Nation |
| *Homjaap* | A fire / prayer offering |
| *Hum Sab Ek Hain* | We Are One |
| *Idgah* | A site where Eid and other Muslim devotions are held |
| *Jagatguru* | World leader |
| *Jai Jawan Jai Kisan* | Hail Soldier, Hail Farmer |
| *Jal* | Water |
| *Jameen* | Land |
| *Jan* | People |
| *Jangal* | Forest |
| *Janvar* | Animal |
| *Jati* | Caste group |
| *Jawan* | Soldier |

| | |
|---|---|
| *Jhansi ki Rani* | Queen of Jhansi |
| *Jheel* | Lake |
| *Kadamba* | A tree: *Nauclea cadamba* |
| *Kafir* | A villain |
| *Kalidahan* | The act of Kali burning |
| *Kaliyug* | The age of demon and darkness in Hindu texts and belief |
| *Kar Seva* | Voluntary Service |
| *Karma* | Person's actions in Hinduism to perpetuate transmigration and in its ethical consequences to determine the nature of the person's afterlife |
| *Kasbas* | Small towns |
| *Kawar* | A bamboo or other pole, with slings or baskets suspended at each end for carrying loads |
| *Kawarias* | Religious Hindus carrying *kawar* |
| *Kosa* | A measure of distance (approx. two miles) |
| *Krishna Janmabhoomi* | Krishna's birthplace |
| *Kuli begar* | Bonded labour |
| *Kumhar* | Potter |
| *Kushti* | Wrestling |
| *Lathis* | Sticks |
| *Lilas* | The acts of a deity (Krishna) in performances |
| *Mahant* | Head of a Hindu religious establishment |
| *Mandir* | Temple |
| *Manusmriti* | Text on Hindu ethics by Manu, considered a Hindu lawgiver. *Manusmriti* is one of 18 *smritis* |

| | |
|---|---|
| *Math* | Religious establishment |
| *Matribhoomi* | Motherland |
| *Mela* | A fair |
| *Mohallas* | Wards; localities |
| *Moksha* | Deliverance |
| *Morcha* | Entrenchment; fortification |
| *Nagar-nadiya-parvat* | City-river-mountain |
| *Nala* | Drain |
| *Namami Gange* | Government of India's programme to clean the Ganga river |
| *Nasha Nahin, Rozgar Do* | No to Alcohol, Give Us Employment |
| *Nishkam Karmayog* | Selfless performance of one's proper works |
| *Nullah* | Water channel |
| *Om* | A sacred syllable uttered or written in various Hindu contexts |
| *Panch Parmeshwar* | The five supreme gods |
| *Pani panchayat* | A water council |
| *Param Vaibhavam* | Ultimate Glory |
| *Parikrama* | Circumambulation |
| *Paryavaran Samrakshan Gatividhi* | Activities on environmental conservation |
| *Paryavaran Sanrakshan* | Environment Conservation |
| *Paryavaran* | Environment |
| *Pitribhoomi* | Fatherland |
| *Pracharak* | Propagator; an individual committed to the mission and objectives of the RSS |
| *Prakriti* | Nature |
| *Punyabhoomi* | Holy land |
| *Purusa/Purusha* | Man |

| | |
|---|---|
| *Purusharthas* | Objectives of a Hindu man's life |
| *Ragi* | Millet |
| *Rai* | Mustard seed |
| *Rajas* | The quality of activity or passion |
| *Rajmash* | A cash crop |
| *Rajya* | State |
| *Ram Janmabhoomi* | Lord Ram's birthplace |
| *Ram Shila Pujans* | Worship of Ram's stone |
| *Ramrajya* | The kingdom of Ram, the Hindu utopia |
| *Rashtriyata* | Nationality |
| *Rasta roko andolan* | Movement to block roads |
| *Rath yatra* | Chariot procession |
| *Rigveda* | The oldest Hindu text in Sanskrit consisting of hymns |
| *Rishi* | Saint |
| *Sabka Saath Sabka Vikas* | Everyone Together, Everyone Prosperous |
| *Sadhus-sants* | Holy men |
| *Sadhvi* | A chaste and saintly woman |
| *Shakha* | Branch; the basic unit of the RSS as daily get-together of workers at a fixed place and time |
| *Samaj* | Society |
| *Sampradaya* | Community |
| *Samskars* | Rites or practices enshrined and ordained in Hindu scriptures to guide an individual towards a proper sense of duty and obligation over the various stages of life |
| *Sanatana Dharma* | Orthodox Hindu belief and practice |

| | |
|---|---|
| *Sangh Parivar* | Sangh family |
| *Sanskriti* | Culture |
| *Sanskritik samaj* | Cultured society |
| *Sant sammelan* | Conference of holy men |
| *Sarkaryawah* | General Secretary; the Executive Head of the RSS who conducts Sangh affairs |
| *Sarpanch* | Head of the village council |
| *Satsang* | True company; assembly of people who listen to, talk about, and assimilate the truth |
| *Satva* | The quality of purity or goodness |
| *Satvik* | Endowed with the quality of truth |
| *Sawan* | Rainy season |
| *Setu* | Bridge |
| *Sewa* | Service |
| *Sewak* | Servant |
| *Shanthi* | Peace |
| *Shilanyas* | Laying of a foundation stone |
| *Shiv Mahapuran* | A major Hindu text in Sanskrit revolving around the god Shiva and the goddess Parvati |
| *Shiva Bhakta* | Devotees of the god Shiva |
| *Shramdan* | Donation of voluntary labour for community welfare |
| *Sri Ram Kar Seva Samiti* | Sri Ram Voluntary Service Committee |
| *Stree-mata* | Mother-woman |
| *Stupa* | A mound-like Buddhist religious monument containing Buddhist relics |
| *Sunar* | Goldsmith |
| *Surya Namaskar* | Sun-worship |

| | |
|---|---|
| *Suryopanishad* | An ancient Hindu Sanskrit text dedicated to the sun god |
| *Swarajya* | Self-rule; independence |
| *Swayamsevak* | Volunteer; RSS worker who participates regularly in RSS organisational activities |
| *Taluka* | An administrative district |
| *Tamal* | An evergreen tree |
| *Tamas* | The quality of darkness or ignorance |
| *Tantrik* | A person versed in magic ritual knowledge |
| *Tapobhoomi* | Most pious land |
| *Toria* | An oil-seed crop |
| *Urad* | A pulse |
| *Urja shakti* | Energy power |
| *Uttaranchal Vikas Vibhag* | Uttaranchal Development Department |
| *Vividh Karyakari* | Various working committees |
| *Vriksha Raksha Andolan* | A movement to save trees |
| *Zila Parishad* | District Council |

# Bibliography

Agarwal, Anil, and Narain, Sunita (eds), *Dying Wisdom: Rise, Fall and Potential of India's Traditional Water Harvesting Systems* (New Delhi, CSE, 1997).

Agarwal, Anil, and Narain, Sunita, *Towards Green Villages: A Strategy for Environmentally-sound and Participatory Rural Development* (New Delhi, CSE, 1989).

Agarwal, Anil, and Sunita Narain (eds), *The State of India's Environment 1984–85: The Second Citizens' Report* (New Delhi, Centre for Science and Environment, 1985).

Agarwal, Anil, Darryl D'Monte, and Ujwala Samarth (eds), *The Fight for Survival: People's Action for Environment* (New Delhi, Centre for Science and Environment, 1987).

Agarwal, Anil, *et al.* (eds), *The State of India's Environment, 1982: A Citizens' Report* (New Delhi, Centre for Science and Environment, 1982).

Agarwal, Anil, Sunita Narain, and Srabani Sen (eds), *The State of India's Environment, The Citizens' Fifth Report, Part I: National Overview* (New Delhi, Centre for Science and Environment, 1999).

Aggarwal, J.C., and S.P. Agrawal (eds), *Uttarakhand: Past, Present and Future* (New Delhi, Concept Publishing House, 1995).

Agrawal, Arun, and K. Sivaramakrishnan (eds), *Agrarian Environments: Resources, Representation, and Rule in India* (Durham & London, Duke University Press, 2000).

Agrawal, Arun, and K. Sivaramakrishnan (eds), *Regional Modernities: The Cultural Politics of Development* (Stanford, Stanford University Press, 2003).

Agrawal, Arun, *Environmentality: Technologies of Government and the Making of Subjects* (Durham: Duke University Press, 2005).

Agrawal, Binit, "Regaining Control over Climate Change Narrative: How to Stop Right-Wing Populism from Eroding Rule of Law in the Climate Struggles in India", *Fordham Environmental Law Review*, vol. xxxii, no. 1 (2020).

Ahuja, Gurdas M., *BJP and the Indian Politics: Policies & Programmes of the Bharatiya Janata Party* (Delhi, Ram Company, 1994).

Alagappa, Muthiah (ed.), *Political Legitimacy in Southeast Asia: The Quest for Moral Authority* (California, Stanford University Press, 1995).

Alagappa, Muthiah, "The Bases of Legitimacy", in Muthiah Alagappa (ed.), *Political Legitimacy in Southeast Asia: The Quest for Moral Authority* (California, Stanford University Press, 1995), 46–7.

Alvares, Claude, "Science, Colonialism and Violence: A Luddite View", in Ashis Nandy (ed.), *Science, Hegemony and Violence: A Requiem for Modernity* (Delhi, Oxford University Press, 1988), 68–111.

Ambedkar, Sunil, *The RSS Roadmaps for the 21st Century* (New Delhi, Rupa, 2019).

Andersen, Walter, and Shridhar D. Damle, *Messengers of Hindu Nationalism: How the RSS Reshaped India* (London, Hurst & Company, 2019).

Arabindoo, Pushpa, "Renewable Energy, Sustainability Paradox and the Post-Urban Question", *Urban Studies*, vol. 57 (11) (2020).

Arnold, David, and Ramachandra Guha (eds), *Nature, Culture, Imperialism: Essays on the Environmental History of South Asia* (Delhi, Oxford University Press, 1996).

Arnold, David, "Rebellious Hillmen: The Gudem-Rampa Risings 1839–1924", in Ranajit Guha (ed.), *Subaltern Studies I* (Delhi, Oxford University Press, 1982).

Arnold, David, *Environment, Culture and European Expansion* (Oxford, Blackwell, 1996).

Aryal, Manisha, "Angry Hills: An Uttarakhand State of Mind", *Himal*, November–December 1994.

Athawale, P. Pu., Dr Jayant Balajee, and Pu. Dr Charudutta Prabhakar Pingale, *Devnadi Ganga ki Raksha Kare*! (Raigadh, Sanatan Sanstha, 2013).

Awasthi, Ramesh, "Rural Development through People's Mobilisation: A Case Study of Ralegan Siddhi", in M.L. Dantwala, Harsh Sethi, and Pravin Visaria (eds), *Social Change through Voluntary Action* (Delhi, Sage Publications, 1998), 74.

Ayyub, Rana, *Gujarat Files: Anatomy of a Cover Up* (Mumbai: Rana Ayyub, 2016).

Babb, Lawrence A., and Susan S. Wadley (eds), *Media and the Transformation of Religion in South Asia* (Delhi: Motilal Banarsidass, 1997).

Bacchetta, Paola, *Gender in the Hindu Nation: RSS Women as Ideologues* (Delhi, Women Unlimited, 2004).

Bagchee, Aruna, and Sandeep Bagchee, "Improving Rainfed Farming Systems through Watershed Development: A Case Study of Ralegan Siddhi", Paper presented at the *Asian Farming Systems Symposium*, Bangkok, 19–22 November 1990.

Bahuguna, Kameshwar Prasad, "Tehri Bandh Ka Virodh Kyon?", *Himalaya: Man and Nature*, vol. XV, no. 7–8 (December 1991–January 1992).

Bahuguna, Rajeev Nayan, *Ghayal Himalaya Ki Pira* (Amritsar, All India Pingalwara Charitable Society, 1999).

Bahuguna, Sunderlal, "*Jeewan ki Jai, Mirtu ka Ksay*" (Hail Life, Condemn Death), in *Chipko Sandesh* (Chipko Suchana Kendra, 1989), 25–6.

Bahuguna, Sunderlal, "Parvatiya Vikas aur Bhoomi Upyog" (Hill Development and Land Utilisation), in *Chipko Sandesh*, 15–17.

Bahuguna, Sunderlal, "Save Mother Ganga", *Manthan*, vol. XVIII, no. 3, July-September 1997, 33–7.

Bahuguna, Sunderlal, "The Humanitarian Aspect", in *The Tehri Dam: A Prescription for Disaster*, 36.

Bahuguna, Sunderlal, *Dharti ki Pukar* (Delhi, 1996).

Bahuguna, Sunderlal, *Himalayan Policy Solution to Tehri Dam Problems* (Tehri, 1997).

Bahuguna, Sunderlal, *In Conversation* (Amritsar, All India Pingalwara Charitable Society, 2005).

Bahuguna, Sunderlal, *Katé Jungle Rotee Dharti* (Amritsar, All India Pingalwara Charitable Society, 1997).

Bahuguna, Sunderlal, *People's Programme for Change* (New Delhi, Intach, 1992).

Bahuguna, Sunderlal, *Save Ganga* (Tehri, Save Ganga Campaign, n.d.).

Bahuguna, Sunderlal, *Save Himalayas* (Tehri, Save Himalaya Movement, n.d.).

Bahuguna, Sunderlal, *Save Himalayas, Soil, Water and Pure Air* (Amritsar, 1995).

Bahuguna, Sunderlal, *Tehri Dam and High Dams in Himalaya* (Tehri, 1995).

Bahuguna, Sunderlal, *Tehri ka Vishal Bandh* (Tehri, Tehri Bandh Virodhi Sangharsh Samiti, n.d.).

Bahuguna, Sunderlal, *The Himalayan Threat* (Tehri, n.d.).

Bahuguna, Sunderlal, *Vikas aur Paryavaran* (Amritsar, All India Pingalwara Charitable Society, 2005).

Balasubramanian, Aditya, "A More Indian Path to Prosperity? Hindu Nationalism and Development in the Mid-Twentieth Century and Beyond", *Capitalism: A Journal of History and Economics,* vol. 3, no. 2 (Summer 2022).

Banwari, *Pancavati: Indian Approach to Environment* (Delhi, Shri Vinayaka Publications, 1992).

Barker, Rodney, *Legitimating Identities: The Self-Presentations of Rulers and Subjects* (Cambridge, Cambridge University Press, 2003).

Barthwal, Dr Harish Chandra, *Rashtriya Swayamsewak Sangh: An Introduction* (New Delhi, Suruchi Prakashan, 2019).

Basrur, Rajesh, "Modi, *Hindutva*, and Foreign Policy", *International Studies Perspectives* 20 (2019).

Basu, Amrita, and Atul Kohli (eds), *Community Conflicts and the State in India* (Delhi, Oxford University Press, 1998).

Basu, Tapan, Pradip Datta, Sumit Sarkar, Tanika Sarkar, and Sambudha Sen, *Khaki Shorts and Saffron Flags: A Critique of the Hindu Right* (Delhi, Orient Longman, 1993).

Baviskar, Amita (ed.), *Waterlines* (New Delhi, Penguin Books, 2003).

Baviskar, Amita, "Red in Tooth and Claw? Looking for Class in Struggles over Nature", in Raka Ray and Mary Fainsod Katzenstein (eds), *Social Movements in India: Poverty, Power and Politics* (Delhi, Oxford University Press, 2005), 161–78.

Baviskar, Amita, *In the Belly of the River: Tribal Conflicts over Development in the Narmada Valley* (Delhi, Oxford University Press, 1995).

Ben-Israel, Hedva, "Hallowed Land in the Theory and Practice of Modern Nationalism", in Benjamin Z. Kedar and R. J. Zwi Werblowsky (eds), *Sacred Space: Shrine, City, Land* (New York, New York University Press, 1998), 278-94.

Berti, Daniela, Nicolas Jaoul, Pralay Kanungo (eds), *Cultural Entrenchment of Hindutva: Local Mediations and Forms of Convergence* (New Delhi, Routledge, 2015).

Bhadra, Gautam, Gyan Prakash, and Susie Tharu (eds), *Subaltern Studies X* (New Delhi, Oxford University Press, 1999).

Bhagwat, Dr Mohan, *Future BHARAT: An RSS Perspective* (New Delhi, Vimarsh Prakashan, 2019).

Bhalla, A., and P.J. Bumke (eds), *Images of Rural India in the 20th Century* (New Delhi, Sterling Publishers, 1992).

Bharadwaj, Ajay, "Resurgence of Sarasvati Ethos", *Organiser*, 12 March 2017.

Bharadwaj, Shankara, "Matrix of Integration", *Organiser*, 13 May 2018.

Bharatiya Janata Party, *Ek Bharat Shreshtha Bharat: Election Manifesto 2014* (New Delhi, Bharatiya Janata Party, 2014).

Bharatiya Janata Party, *Election Manifesto 1998*, https://library.bjp.org/jspui/bitstream/123456789/241/1/BJP%20ELECTION%20MANIFESTO%201998.pdf.

Bharatiya Janata Party, *Sankalpit Bharat, Sakshat Bharat: Sankalp Patra, Lok Sabha 2019*, https://www.bjp.org/manifesto2019.

Bharatiya Janata Party, *Towards Ram Rajya: Mid-Term Poll to Lok Sabha, May 1991 – Our Commitments* (Delhi, BJP, 1991).

Bharatiya Janata Party, *Election Manifesto 1998* (Delhi, 1998).

Bhatt, Anil, "And Why Not Uttarakhand/Uttaranchal", in J.C. Aggarwal and S.P. Agrawal (eds), *Uttarakhand: Past, Present and Future* (New Delhi, Concept Publishing House, 1995), 385–9.

Bhatt, Chandi Prasad, *Meddling with Himalaya-based on Incomplete Knowledge and Unfound Belief – Disastrous* (Chamoli, n.d.).

Bhatt, Chandi Prasad, *The Calamity-Prone Central Himalayas* (Chamoli, Lok Soochna Evam Sahayta Kendra, 1998).

Bhatt, Chandi Prasad, *The Future of Large Projects in the Himalaya* (Nainital, Pahar, 1992).

Bhatt, S.C. (ed.), *The Encyclopaedic District Gazetteers of India: Central Zone (Vol. 6)* (New Delhi, Gyan Publishing House, 1997).

Bhattacharjee, Malini, *Disaster Relief and the RSS: Resurrecting "Religion" through Humanitarianism* (Delhi, Sage, 2019).

Bidwai, Praful, *The Politics of Climate Change and the Global Crisis: Mortgaging our Future* (Hyderabad, Orient Blackswan, 2012).

Bobbio, Tommaso, "Making Gujarat Vibrant: *Hindutva*, Development and the Rise of Subnationalism in India", *Third World Quarterly* 33, no. 4 (2012).

Bookchin, M. Bookchin, "A Green Course", *Resurgence*, vol. 115.

Brahma Kumaris World Spiritual University, *Science, Spirituality, Ethics and Environment* (Mount Abu, 1991).

Brahmacari, Rajasekhara Dasa, *The Complete Guide to Vrndavana: India's Most Holy City Of Over 5000 Temples* (n.p., Vedanta Vision Publications, n.d.).

Bramwell, Anna, *Blood and Soil: Richard Walther Darré and Hitler's "Green Party"* (Buckinghamshire, The Kensal Press, 1985).

Bramwell, Anna, *Ecology in the Twentieth Century: A History* (New Haven, Yale University Press, 1989).

Brass, Paul, *Ethnicity and Nationalism: Theory and Comparison* (Delhi, Sage, 1991).

Brass, Tom, "The Agrarian Myth, the 'New' Populism and the 'New' Right", *The Journal of Peasant Studies,* vol. 24, no. 4 (July 1997), 201–45.

Brooks, Charles R., *The Hare Krishnas in India* (New Jersey, Princeton University Press, 1989).

Buckingham, Susan, and Virginie Le Masson (eds), *Understanding Climate Change through Gender Relations* (New York, Routledge, 2019).

Bullard, Robert D., and Beverly Wright (eds), *Race, Place and Environmental Justice after Hurricane Katrina* (Boulder, Westview Press, 2009).

Burghart, R., "The Founding of the Ramanandi Sect", *Ethnohistory,* vol. 25, no. 2 (1978).

Carter, Neil, *The Politics of the Environment – Ideas, Activism, Policy* (Cambridge, Cambridge University Press, 2001).

Cashman, Richard, *The Myth of the "Lokamanya": Tilak and Mass Politics in Maharashtra* (Berkeley, University of California Press, 1975).

Cederlöf, Gunnel, and K. Sivaramakrishnan (eds), *Ecological Nationalisms: Nature, Livelihoods, and Identities in South Asia* (Delhi, Permanent Black, 2005).

Chaitanya, Krishna, *The Betrayal of Krishna: Vicissitudes of a Great Myth* (Delhi, Clarion Books, n.d.).

Chakraborty, Somen, "The Silent Valley Movement", in Sebasti L. Raj and Arundhati Roy Choudhury (eds), *Contemporary Social Movements in India: Achievements and Hurdles* (New Delhi, Indian Social Institute, 1998).

Chakraborty, Somen, *A Critique of Social Movements in India: Experiences of Chipko, Uttarakhand and Fishworkers' Movement* (New Delhi, Indian Social Institute, 1999).

Chakravarty, Sukhamoy, *Development Planning: The Indian Experience* (Oxford, Clarendon Press, 1987).

Chandola, Harishchandra, "*Dubta Hamara Sahar*" (Our City is Drowning), *Pahar*, no. 12, 265–8.

Chandran, M.D. Subash, and J. Donald Hughes, "The Sacred Groves of South India: Ecology, Traditional Communities and Religious Change, *Social Compass*, vol. 44, no. 3 (1997).

Chapple, Christopher Key, and Mary Evelyn Tucker (eds), *Hinduism and Ecology: The Intersection of Earth, Sky, and Water* (Delhi, 2000).

Chatterjee, Abhas, *The Concept of Hindu Nation* (New Delhi, Voice of India, 2018).

Chatterjee, Partha, *The Nation and Its Fragments: Colonial and Postcolonial Histories* (Delhi, Oxford University Press, 1994).

Chattopadhyaya, B.D, "Foreword", in Vijaya Laxmi Singh, *Mathura: The Settlement Pattern and Cultural Profile of an Early Historial City* (New Delhi, Sandeep Prakashan, 2005), vii–viii.

Chaube, Shibani Kinkar, and Bidyut Chakraborty (eds), *Social Movements in Contemporary India* (Calcutta, K.P. Bagchi & Co., 1999).

Chaudhuri, Pramit Pal, "Fragmented and Fitful: India's Energy Diplomacy", *Oxford Energy Forum*, Issue 99 (February 2015).

Chaulia, Sreeram, *Modi Doctrine: The Foreign Policy of India's Prime Minister* (New Delhi, Bloomsbury, 2016).

Chhachhi, Amrita, "Neoliberalism, Hindutva and Gender: Convergence and Contradictions in the Provision of Welfare", *Feminist Dissent* 5 (2020).

Chhatre, Ashwini, and V.K. Saberwal, *Democratising Nature: Politics, Conservation and Development in India* (Delhi, Oxford University Press, 2006).

Chidananda, Swami, "An Appeal to Save the Holy Ganga", *Himalaya: Man and Nature*, vol. XV, no. 4 (September 1991).

Chidananda, Swami, "Save The Himalaya", *Bhagirathi ki Pukar*, vol. 7, no. 2 (February 1997).

Chinoy, Sujan R., *India & Mother Earth* (New Delhi, Dr Syama Prasad Mookerjee Research Foundation, 2021).

Chinoy, Sujan, "Modi as a Global Environment Leader", in Sujan Chinoy, Vijay Chauthaiwale, and Uttam Kumar Sinha (eds), *Modi Shaping a Global Order in Flux* (New Delhi, Wisdom Tree, 2023), 232–52.

Chinoy, Sujan, Vijay Chauthaiwale, and Uttam Kumar Sinha (eds), *Modi Shaping a Global Order in Flux* (New Delhi, Wisdom Tree, 2023).

Conversi, Daniele, "The Ultimate Challenge: Nationalism and Climate Change", *Nationalities Paper*, vol. 48 (4) (2020).

Corcoran, Maura, *Vrindavana in Vaisnava Literature: History, Mythology, Symbolism* (New Delhi and Vrindaban, WWF, 1995).

Cottlieb, Roger S. (ed.), *This Sacred Earth: Religion, Nature, Environment* (London, Routledge, 1996).

D. Alley, Kelly, "Separate Domains: Hinduism, Politics and Environmental Pollution", in Christopher Key Chapple and Mary Evelyn Tucker (eds), *Hinduism and Ecology: The Intersection of Earth, Sky and Water* (New Delhi, Oxford University Press, 2000), 372–3.

D'Monte, Darryl, *Temples or Tombs! Industry Versus Environment: Three*

*Controversies* (New Delhi, Centre for Science and Environment, 1985).

Daggett, Cara, "Petro-masculinity: Fossil Fuels and Authoritarian Desire", *Millennium: Journal of International Studies* 47 (1) (2018).

Dahiwale, S.M., "Consolidation of Maratha Dominance in Maharashtra", *Economic and Political Weekly* (11 February 1995).

Dandekar, V.M., "Introduction", in S.H. Deshpande (ed.), *Economy of Maharashtra* (Poona, Samaj Prabodhan Sanstha, 1973).

Dantwala, M.L., Harsh Sethi, and Pravin Visaria (eds), *Social Change through Voluntary Action* (New Delhi, Sage Publications, 1998).

Das, Nishant, "Bring an End to Cow Slaughter", *Organiser*, 20 September 2015.

Das, Sudhansu R, "Namami Gange", *Organiser*, 31 May 2015.

Das, Veena (ed.), *Mirrors of Violence: Communities, Riots and Survivors in South Asia* (Delhi, Oxford University Press, 1990).

Dasa, Ranchor, "Protecting Vraja's Sacred Groves", *Back to Godhead: The Magazine of the Hare Krishna Movement* (September–October 1998).

Dasa, Ranchor, "Reviving the Forests of Vrindavan", *Back to Godhead*, vol. 26, no. 5 (September–October 1992).

Dasa, Dr Sahadeva, *As Long As We have Slaughterhouses, We'll Have Wars* (Delhi, Golden Age Media, 2014).

Dasa, Dr Sahadeva, *India – A World Leader in Cow Killing and Beef Export* (Delhi, Golden Age Media, 2013).

Dasa, Dr Sahadeva, *Cow Dung A Down-To-Earth Solution to Global Warming and Climate Change* (Delhi, Golden Age Media, 2014).

Datta, P. K, *Carving Blocs: Communal Ideology in Early Twentieth-century Bengal* (Delhi, Oxford University Press, 1999).

Davies, N., *God's Playground, A History of Poland, Volume I: The Origins to 1795* (Oxford Clarendon Press, 1982).

Davis, Richard (ed.), *Picturing the Nation: Iconographies of Modern India* (Delhi, Orient Longman, 2007).

Denitch, Bogdan Denis (ed.), *Legitimation of Regimes: International Framework for Analysis* (Beverly Hills, Sage, 1979).

Deshpande, M.D., *Gujarat Riots: The True Story: The Truth of the 2002 Riots* (Bloomington, Patridge Publishing India, 2014).

Deshpande, R.S., "Land Reforms and Agrarian Structure in Maharashtra", in Ghanshyam Shah and D.C. Shah (eds), *Land Reforms in India, Volume 8, Performance and Challenges in Gujarat and Maharashtra* (Delhi, Sage Publications, 2002), 95–126.

Deshpande, S.H. (ed.), *Economy of Maharashtra* (Poona, Samaj Prabodhan Sanstha, 1973).

Detraz, Nicole, "Threats or Vulnerabilities? Assessing the Link between Climate Change and Security", *Global Environmental Politics*, 11 (3) (2011).

Dhavalikar, M.K., "Maharashtra: Environmental and Historical Process", in A.R. Kulkarni and N.K. Wagle (eds), *Region, Nationality and Religion*, 41.

Dhotiyal, Rajendra Singh, *Vikas ka Pratik Tehri Bandh?: Kuch Prashna – Jabab Deshhit Mei Abhisth* (Tehri, n.d.).

Dilwali, Ashok, and Pushpesh Pant, *The Garhwal Himalayas: Ramparts of Heaven* (New Delhi, Lustre Press, 1987).

*Divya Alok, A Journal* (1995, 1996).

Diwan, Madan, "With Civilisation to Globalisation", *Organiser*, 7 October 2018.

Dogra, Bharat, *A Colossal Risk: Social, Ecological and Safety Aspects of Tehri Dam (and Other Large Dam Projects in Himalayan Region)* (New Delhi, Social Change Papers, 1990).

Dogra, Bharat, *Tehri Bandh Pariyojana: Vikas Chahiye, Vinash Nahin* (New Delhi, Social Change Papers, 1990).

Drake-Brockman, D.L. (ed. and comp.), *Mathura: A Gazetteer* (Delhi, Usha Publications, 1984 [1911]).

Driscoll, Mark, "Black Weather, Whites Climate", *Cultural Dynamics*, vol. 33, no. 3 (2021).

Dube, Saurabh, *Untouchable Pasts: Religion, Identity and Power among a Central Indian Community, 1780–1950* (Albany, State University of New York Press, 1998).

Dutta, Anwesha, and Kenneth Bo Nielsen, "Autocratic Environmental Governance in India" in Sten Widmalm (ed.), *Handbook of Autocratization in South Asia* (London, Routledge, 2022).

Dwivedi, O.P., "Satyagraha for Conservation: Awakening the Spirit of Hinduism", in Roger S. Cottlieb (ed.), *This Sacred Earth: Religion, Nature, Environment* (London, Routledge, 1996), 159.

Dwivedi, Ranjit, *Conflict and Collective Action: The Sardar Sarovar Project in India* (London, Routledge, 2006).

*Enlightening of Family (Parivar Prabodhan)* (New Delhi: Suruchi Prakashan, 2018).

Ernstrom, Ulrika, "Climate Change Denial Strongly Linked to Right-wing Nationalism", *Chalmers* (2021), https://www.chalmers.se/en/departments/tme/news/pages/climate-change-denial-strongly-linked-to-right-wing-nationalism.aspx.

Fernandes, Walter, Geeta Menon, and Philip Viegas, *Forests, Environment and Tribal Economy: Deforestation, Impoverishment and Marginalisation in Orissa* (Delhi, Indian Social Institute, 1988).

Fischer, Frank, and Maarten A. Hajer (eds), *Living With Nature: Environmental Politics as Cultural Discourse* (London, Oxford University Press, 1999).

Forchtner, Bernhard (ed.), *The Far Right and the Environment: Politics, Discourse and Communication* (London, Routledge, 2020).

Frei, Norbert, *National Socialist Rule in Germany* (Oxford, 1993).

Freitag, Sandria B., *Collective Action and Community: Public Arenas and the Emergence of Communalism in Colonial North India* (Berkeley and Los Angeles, University of California Press, 1989).

Friends of Vrindavan, *1998 Newsletter* (London, 1998).

Gadgil, Madhav, and M.D. Subash Chandran, "Sacred Groves", in Geeti Sen (ed.), *Indigenous Vision: Peoples of India – Attitudes to the Environment* (Delhi, Sage & IIC, 1992), 187.

Gadgil, Madhav, and Ramachandra Guha, *Ecology and Equity: The Use and Abuse of Nature in Contemporary India* (Delhi, Penguin Books, 1995).

Ganapatye, Shruti, *Who Will Bell the Cow? Beef Ban: Decoding its Cultural, Social, and Economic Aspects in India* (Chennai, Notion Press, 2022).

Gandhi, M.K., *The Village Reconstruction* (Bombay, Bhartiya Vidya Bhavan, 1966).

Gandhi, M.K., *Hind Swaraj* (Ahmedabad, 1938).

Ghosh, Rajeshwari (ed.), *In Quest of a Secular Symbol: Ayodhya and After* (Indian Ocean Centre and South Asian Research Unit, Cutin University of Technology, 1996).

Gokhale, Nitin A., *Securing India the Modi Way: Pathankot, Surgical Strikes and More* (New Delhi, Bloomsbury, 2017).

Golwalkar, Madhavrao Sadashivrao, *Dhyey-Drishti* (Delhi, Suruchi Prakashan, 1997).

Gopalakrishnan, Shankar, "Defining, Constructing and Policing a 'New India': Relationship between Neoliberalism and Hindutva", *Economic and Political Weekly* 41(26) (2006).

Goswami, Asha, *Krsna-Katha and Allied Matters* (Delhi, Y.R. Publications, 1984).

Goswami, Asha, *The Krsna Legend: A New Perspective* (Delhi, Y.R. Publications, 2001).

Goswami, Manu, *Producing India: From Colonial Economy to National Space* (Chicago, University of Chicago Press, 2003).

Government of India, "India's Intended Nationally Determined Contribution: Working Towards Climate Justice", 2 October 2015, https://faolex.fao.org/docs/pdf/ind188478.pdf.

Government of Uttar Pradesh, *Sixth Plan* (Lucknow, 1984–5).

Goyal, S.K., "Policies for Uplift of the Hilly and Backward Districts in India: A Critique", in T.S. Papola, B.K. Joshi, H.S. Verma, and R.C. Sinha (eds), *Development of Hill Areas: Issues and Approaches* (Bombay, Himalaya Publishing House, 1983), 59–64.

Growse, F.S., *Mathura: A District Memoir* (New Delhi, Asian Educational Services, 1979 [1882]).

Gudavarthy, Ajay, *India after Modi: Populism and the Right* (Delhi, Bloomsbury, 2019).

Guha, Ramachandra, "Mahatma Gandhi and the Environmental Movement in India", *Capitalism Nature Socialism*, vol. 6, no. 3 (September 1995).

Guha, Ramachandra, and Juan Martinez-Alier, *Varieties of Environmentalism: Essays North and South* (Delhi, Oxford University Press, 1997).

Guha, Ramachandra, *How Much Should a Person Consume? Thinking Through the Environment* (Delhi, Permanent Black, 2006).

Guha, Ramachandra, *India after Gandhi: The History of the World's Largest Democracy* (Delhi, Picador, 2007).

Guha, Ramachandra, *The Unquiet Woods: Ecological Change and Peasant Resistance in the Himalaya* (1989, rpnt Ranikhet, Permanent Black, 2010).

Guha, Ramchandra (ed.), *Social Ecology* (Delhi, Oxford University Press, 1994).

Gupta, Akhil, *Postcolonial Developments: Agriculture in the Making of Modern India* (Durham, Duke University Press, 1998).

Gupta, Bajranglal, *Paryavaran Premi Hindu Drishti* (Delhi, Suruchi Prakashan, 2020).

Gupta, Charu, "The Icon of Mother in Late Colonial North India: 'Bharat Mata', 'Matri Bhasha' and 'Gau Mata'", *Economic and Political Weekly*, vol. 36, no. 45 (2001).

Gupta, Dipankar, *Nativism in a Metropolis: The Shiv Sena in Bombay* (Delhi, Manohar, 1982).

Gupta, Krishna Murthi, and B.P. Nautiyal (eds), *Ganga: Ek Prakritik tatha Sanskritik Dharohar* (New Delhi, Himalaya Seva Sangh, 1991).

Hagan, Joe D., "Regime Type, Foreign Policy, and International Relations", *International Studies*, https://doi.org/10.1093/acrefore/9780190846626.013.415.

Hakala, Emma, "India and the Global Geoeconomics of Climate Change: Gains from Cooperation?" *Observer Research Foundation*, Issue 291 (May 2019).

Hall, Ian, "Modi's Vision for India as a Normative Power", *East Asia Forum*, 8 February 2017, https://www.eastasiaforum.org/2017/02/08/modis-vision-for-india-as-a-normative-power/.

Hall, Ian, "Narendra Modi and India's Normative Power", *International Affairs* 93 (1) (2017).

Hall, Ian, *Modi and the Reinvention of Indian Foreign Policy* (UK, Bristol University Press, 2019).

Hansen, Thomas Blom, *The Saffron Wave: Democracy and Hindu Nationalism in Modern India* (Delhi, Oxford University Press, 1999).

Hansen,Thomas Blom, and Srirupa Roy (eds), *Saffron Republic: Hindu Nationalism and State Power in India* (Cambridge, Cambridge University Press, 2022).

Hardiman, David, "Power in the Forest: The Dangs, 1820–1940", in David Arnold and David Hardiman (eds), *Subaltern Studies VIII* (Delhi, Oxford University Press, 1994).

Harris, Marvin, "The Cultural Ecology of India's Sacred Cattle", *Current Anthropology*, 7(1) (1966).

Hasan, Zoya, "Community and Caste in Post-Congress Politics in Uttar Pradesh", in Amrita Basu and Atul Kohli (eds), *Community Conflicts and the State in India* (Delhi, Oxford University Press, 1998).

Hasan, Zoya, "Party Politics and Communal Mobilization in Uttar Pradesh", in Rajeshwari Ghosh (ed.), *In Quest of a Secular Symbol: Ayodhya and After* (Cutin University of Technology, Indian Ocean Centre and South Asian Research Unit, 1996), 59.

Hasan, Zoya, *Dominance and Mobilisation: Rural Politics in Western Uttar Pradesh 1930–1980* (New Delhi, Sage Publications, 1980).

Hay, P.R., "Ecological Values and Western Political Traditions: From Anarchism to Fascism", *Politics*, vol. 8, no. 2 (1988).

Hays, Samuel P., *Beauty, Health, and Permanence: Environmental Politics in the United States, 1955–1985* (Cambridge, Cambridge University Press, 1987).

Hazare, Anna, Ganesh Pangare, and Vasudha Lokur, *Adarsh Gaon Yojana: Government Participation in a People's Programme* (Pune, Hind Swaraj Trust, 1996).

Hazare, Anna, *Ralegan Siddhi: A Veritable Transformation* (Ahmednagar, Ralegan Siddhi Pariwar Prakashan, 1997).

Hazare, Anna, *My Village . . . My Place of Pilgrimage* (Ahmednagar, Swami Vivekanand Krutadnyata Nidhi, 2011).

Hazare, Anna, *Voice of Experience* (Ralegan Siddhi, Swami Vivekanand Gratitude Trust, n.d.).

Hiltebeitel, A., "Empire, Invasion, and India's National Epics", *International Journal of Hindu Studies*, vol. 2, no. 3 (1998).

Howard, Steve, "Foreword" in Narendra Modi, *Convenient Action*, 2.

Ingalls, Daniel H.H., "Foreword", in Milton Singer (ed.), *Krishna: Myths, Rites, and Attitudes* (Honolulu, East-West Centre Press, 1966), v.

Iyer, K. Gopal, "Distribution of Government Land in Western India", in G. Shah and D.C. Shah (eds), *Land Reforms in India, Volume 8*, 220–44.

Jaffrelot, Christophe, *Modi's India: Hindu Nationalism and the Rise of Ethnic Democracy* (Princeton & Oxford, Princeton University Press, 2019).

Jaffrelot, Christophe, "What 'Gujarat Model'? – Growth without Development – and with Socio-Political Polarisation", *South Asia*, vol. 38, issue 4 (2016).

Jaffrelot, Christophe, *The Hindu Nationalist Movement in India* (New York, Columbia University Press, 1993).

Jaffrelot, Christophe, *The Hindu Nationalist Movement in Indian Politics* (New York, Columbia University Press, 1996).

Jain, Kajri, *Gods in the Time of Democracy* (Durham: Duke University Press, 2021).

Jalais, Annu, *The Forest of Tigers, People, Politics and Environment in the Sundarbans* (London, Routledge, 2009).

Jayawardena, Kumari, and Malathi de Alwis (eds), *Embodied Violence: Communalising Women's Sexuality in South Asia* (Delhi, Kali for Women, 1996).

Jeffery, Partricia, and Amrita Basu (eds), *Resisting the Sacred and the Secular: Women's Activism and Politicised Religion in South Asia* (Delhi, Kali for Women, 1999).

Johnson, Gordon, *Provincial Politics and Indian Nationalism* (Cambridge, Cambridge University Press, 1973).

Johnson, S., *Caring for the Environment* (London, Conservative Political Centre and European Democratic Group, 1981).

Joshi, Bindumadhav, *Swadeshi* (Pune, Akhil Bhartiya Grahak Panchayat Prakashan, 1992).

Joshi, Purunchandra, *Uttarakhand ke Aaine Mein Humara Samaj* (Delhi, Rajkamal Prakashan, 2003).

Jylha, Kirsti M., Pontus Strimling, and Jens Rydgren, "Climate Change Denial among Radical Right-Wing Supporters", *Sustainability*, 12 (2020).

Kandari, O.P., and O.P. Gusain (eds), *Garhwal Himalaya: Nature, Culture and Society* (Garhwal, TransMedia, 2001).

Karnad, Bharat, *Staggering Forward: Narendra Modi and India's Global Ambition* (Delhi, Penguin Books, 2018).

Karol, Sarthak, "Narendra Modi's Climate Policy and India's Role in COP 21, December, Paris 2015", *Manupatra Articles*, 16 January 2018, https://articles.manupatra.com/article-details/Narendra-Modi-s-Climate-Policy-and-India-s-role-in-COP21-December-Paris-2015.

Kasbe, Raosaheb, *Decoding the RSS: Its Tradition and Politics* (New Delhi, Left Word Books, 2019).

Kashyap, Shaan, "Cow is a Cultural Symbol", *Organiser*, 13 August 2017.

Kaur, Indrajit, *Ek Vaigyanic Anusandhan: Gangajal ki Mahatta* (Amritsar, All India Pingalwara Society, 2000).

Kaur, Raminder, "Spectacles of Nationalism in the Ganapati *Utsav* of Maharashtra", in Richard Davis (ed.), *Picturing the Nation: Iconographies of Modern India* (Delhi, Orient Longman, 2007).

Kaur, Raminder, *Performative Politics and the Cultures of Hinduism: Public Uses of Religion in Western India* (Delhi, Permanent Black, 2003).

Kaur, Ravinder, *Brand New Nation: Capitalist Dreams and Nationalist Designs in Twenty-First-Century India* (Stanford, Stanford University Press, 2020).

Kaviraj, Sudipta, *The Myth of Praxis: The Construction of the Figure of Krishna in "Krishnacaritra"* (New Delhi, Nehru Memorial Museum and Library, 1987).

Kaviraj, Sudipta, *The Unhappy Consciousness: Bankimchandra Chattopadhyay and the Formation of Nationalist Discourse in India* (Delhi, Oxford University Press, 1995).

Kedar, Benjamin Z., and R.J. Zwi Werblowsky (eds), *Sacred Space: Shrine, City, Land* (New York, New York University Press, 1998).

Kedouri, Elie, *Nationalism* (Oxford, Blackwell, 1993).

Keller, Jonathan W., "Leadership Style, Regime Type, and Foreign Policy Crisis Behavior: A Contingent Monadic Peace?", *International Studies*, vol. 49, no. 2 (2005).

Keulartz, Jozef, "Engineering the Environment: The Politics of 'Nature Development'", in F. Fischer and M. Hajer (eds), *Living With Nature*, 83–102.

Khagram, Sanjeev, *Dam and Development: Transnational Struggles for Water and Power* (New Delhi, Oxford University Press, 2005).

Khattri, K.N., "Perceptions of Seismic Hazard for the Tehri Dam", *Bhagirathi ki Pukar,* vol. 6, no. 2 (February 1996).

Khoshoo, T.N., *Mahatma Gandhi: An Apostle of Applied Human Ecology* (New Delhi, Tata Energy Research Institute, 1995).

Kiesecker, Joseph, et al., "Renewable Energy and Land Use in India: A Vision to Facilitate Sustainable Development", *Sustainability* 12 (1), 2020, 1–14.

Kosambi, Meera (ed.), *Intersections: Socio-Cultural Trends in Maharashtra* (Delhi, Orient Longman, 2000).

Kothari, Ashish, "Environment and New Economic Policy", in Alternative Survey Group, *Alternative Economic Survey 1995–96* (New Delhi, Delhi Science Forum, 1996), 131–40.

Kothari, Ashish, Neema Pathak, R.V. Anuradha, and Bansure Taneja (eds), *Communities and Conservation: Natural Resource Management in South and Central Asia* (New Delhi, Sage Publications, 1998).

Kudaisya, Gyanesh, *Region, Nation, "Heartland": Uttar Pradesh in India's Body Politic* (New Delhi, Sage Publications, 2006).

Kulkarni, A.R., and N.K. Wagle (eds), *Region, Nationality and Religion* (Mumbai, Popular Prakashan, 1999).

Kumar, Alok, "A Return to India's Glorious Scientific Past", *Organiser,* 22 March 2015.

Kumar, Pradeep, *The Uttarakhand Movement: Construction of a Regional Identity* (New Delhi, Kanishka Publishers, 2000).

Kumar, Pramod, "Turning the Tide", *Organiser,* 26 February 2017.

Kunwar, Shishupal Singh (ed.), *Hugging the Himalayas: The Chipko Experience* (Gopeshwar, Dasholi Gram Swarajya Mandal, 1988).

Lal Gupta, Bajrang, *A New Paradigm of Development: Sumangalam* (Delhi, Gyan Publishing House, 2018).

Lal, Chaman, *India: Mother of Us All* (Delhi, Suruchi Prakashan, 2018).

Lal, Sheo Kumar (ed.), *Gandhiji and Village* (Delhi, 1981).

Lal, Vinay, "Too Deep for Deep Ecology: Gandhi and the Ecological Vision of Life", in Christopher Key Chapple and Mary Evelyn Tucker (eds), *Hinduism and Ecology: The Intersection of Earth, Sky, and Water* (Delhi, Oxford University Press, 2000), 183–212.

Lapid, Yosef, and Friedrich Kratochwil (eds), *The Return of Culture and Identity to International Relations Theory* (Lynne Reinner, 1995).

Lele, Jayant, *Elite Pluralism and Class Rule: Political Development in Maharashtra* (Bombay, Popular Prakashan, 1982).

Lewis, Michael, *Inventing Global Ecology: Tracking the Biodiversity Ideal in India 1945–1997* (Delhi, Orient Longman, 2003), 23–4.

Lokhande, Sanjeevini Badigar, *Communal Violence, Forced Migration and the State: Gujarat Since 2002* (Cambridge, Cambridge University Press, 2016).

Lokur, Vasudha, *Ralegan Siddhi: Rural Transformation through People's Participation* (New Delhi, CAPART, n.d.).

Lubarda, Balša, *Far-Right Ecologism. Environmental Politics and the Far Right in Hungary and Poland* (London and New York, Routledge, 2024).

Lynch, O.M., "The Mastram: Emotion and Person among Mathura's Chaubes", in O.M. Lynch (ed.), *Divine Passions: The Social Construction of Emotion in India* (Berkeley, University of California Press, 1990), 99–116.

Lynch, O.M. (ed.), *Divine Passions: The Social Construction of Emotion in India* (Berkeley, University of California Press, 1990).

Madhok, Balraj, *Rationale of Hindu State* (Delhi, Indian Book Gallery, 1982).

Mahapatra, Richard, "Prosperity and Beyond", *Down to Earth*, vol. 9, no. 10, 15 October 2000, 45–7.

*Maharashtra State Gazetteers* (Bombay, Government of Maharashtra, 1976).

Mahurkar, Uday, *Centrestage: Inside the Narendra Modi Model of Governance* (Gurugram, Random House India, 2014).

Malhotra, Kailash, *The State of India's Environment 1984–85: The Second Citizen's Report* (New Delhi, Centre for Science and Environment, 1985), 162.

Manekar, Sameer, "Confluence in Science", *Organiser*, 23 May 2017.

*Manthan* (Delhi, Deendayal Research Institute, 1985, 1986, 1987, 1988, 1989, 1990, 1991, 1991, 1992, 1993, 1994, 1995, 1996, 1997, 1998, 1999, 2000).

Marino, Andy, *Narendra Modi: A Political Biography* (Gurugram, HarperCollins, 2014).

Marty, Martin, and R. Scott Appleby (eds), *Accounting for Fundamentalism: The Dynamic Characteristics of Movements* (Chicago, University of Chicago Press, 1994).

McCright, Aaron M., and Riley E. Dunlop, "The Denial of Climate Change Among Conservative White Males in the United States", *Global Environmental Change*, 21 (4) (2011).

McDonald, Ian, "Physiological Patriots? The Politics of Physical Culture and Hindu Nationalism in India", *International Review for the Sociology of Sport* 34 (4) (1999).

McDowall, Anna, and Arvind Sharma (eds), *Vignettes Of Vrindavan* (New Delhi, Books and Books, 1987).

McKean, L., *Divine Enterprise: Gurus and the Hindu Nationalist Movement* (Chicago, Chicago University Press, 1996).

Mehta, Nalin, *The New BJP: Modi and the Making of the World's Largest Political Party* (Chennai, Westland, 2022).

Menon, Manju, "Narratives of Natural Resource Corruption and Environmental Regulatory Reforms in India", *Economic and Political Weekly*, vol. 56, issue 52 (2021).

Menon, Ramesh, *Modi Demystified: The Making of a Prime Minister* (Gurugram: HarperCollins, 2014).

Michelutti, Lucia, *The Vernacularisation of Democracy: Politics, Caste and Religion in India* (New Delhi, Routledge, 2008).

Mies, Maria, and Vandana Shiva, *Ecofeminism* (London, Zed Books, 1993).

Miller, Christopher Patrick, "Soft Power and Biopower: Narendra Modi's 'Double Discourse' Concerning Yoga for Climate Change and Self-Care", *Journal of Dharma Studies*, 3 (1) (2020)

Milton, Kay, *Environmentalism and Cultural Theory: Exploring the Role of Anthropology in Environmental Discourse* (London, Routledge, 1996).

Ministry of Environment and Forests, *125 Days of New Government: New Programmes and Initiatives* (Delhi, n.d.).

Mishra, Anupam, *Aaj Bhi Khare Hain Talaab* (New Delhi, Gandhi Shanti Pratisthan, 1993).

Mishra, Vidya Niwas, *Desh Dharma aur Sahitya* (Delhi, Radha Krishna Prakashan, 1992).

Misra, N., "The Mother of all Rivers", *Organiser*, 24 February 2019.

Mitta, Manoj, *The Fiction of Fact-Finding: Modi and Godhra* (Noida, HarperCollins, 2014).

Modi, Narendra, *Convenient Action: Gujarat's Response to Challenges of Climate Change* (Delhi, Macmillan Publishers, 2011).

Moe, Espen, *Renewable Energy Transformation or Fossil Fuel Backlash: Vested Interests in the Political Economy* (Hampshire, Palgrave Macmillan, 2015).

MoEFCC and UNDP, *Prayaas Se Prabhaav Tak: From Mindless Consumption to Mindful Utilization* (New Delhi, Government of India, 2022).

Mohan, C. Raja, *Modi's World: Expanding India's Sphere of Influence* (Noida, HarperCollins, 2015).

Mookerji, Radha Kumud, *Nationalism in Hindu Culture* (Delhi, S. Chand & Co., 1957).

Morrison, Kathleen D., "*Dharmic* Projects, Imperial Reservoirs, and New Temples of India: An Historical Perspective on Dams in India", *Conservation and Society*, vol. 8, no. 3 (2010), 182–95.

Mukhopadhyay, Nilanjan, *The RSS: Icons of the Indian Right* (Chennai, Westland Publications, 2019).

Mukta, Parita, and David Hardiman, "The Political Ecology of Nostalgia", *Capitalism, Nature, Socialism*, vol. 11, no. 1, March 2000, 120–1.

Mukul, "Threat of Mega Projects: Struggles of Two Himalayan Villages", *Economic and Political Weekly* (4 April 1992).

Mukul, "Villages of Chipko Movement", *Economic and Political Weekly* (10 April 1993).

Mukul, *Against the Stream: India's Economic Crisis and Workers' Alternatives* (Delhi, Progressive Printers, 1992).

Muraleedharan, Sruthi, "Narendra Modi's 'Gujarat Model': Re-moulding Development in the Service of Religious Nationalism", *Commonwealth & Comparative Politics* 61: 2 (2023).

Muralivallabhan, T.V., "Protection of Environment and Promotion of Development: The Hindu Wisdom of Sustainable Development", *National Security*, vol. 5, no. 2 (2022).

Muralivallabhan, T.V., "Sustainable Development *Mantra*", *Organiser*, 10 April 2016.

Nair, Rupam Jain, and Frank Jack Daniel, "Battling for India's Soul, State by State", *Reuters*, 13 October 2015, https://www.reuters.com/article/us-india-rss-specialreport/special-report-battling-for-indias-soul-state-by-state-idUSKCN0S700A20151013.

Nandakumar, J., *Hindutva for the Changing Times* (New Delhi, Indus Scrolls Press, 2019).

Nandy, Ashis (ed.), *Science, Hegemony and Violence: A Requiem for Modernity* (Delhi, Oxford University Press, 1988).

Nandy, Ashis, "Introduction: Science as a Reason of State", in Ashis Nandy (ed.), *Science, Hegemony and Violence: A Requiem for Modernity* (Delhi, Oxford University Press, 1990), 1–23.

Narayan, Badri, *Republic of Hindutva: How the Sangh is Reshaping Indian Democracy* (Delhi, Penguin Books, 2021).

Narayanan, Yamini, *Mother Cow, Mother India: A Multispecies Politics of Dairy in India* (California, Stanford University Press, 2023).

Nautiyal, Suresh, "Story of Statehood", *The Sunday Observer*, 29 September 1994.

NCAER (National Council of Applied Economic Research), *Socio-Economic Conditions of Primitive Tribes in Madhya Pradesh* (New Delhi, NCAER, 1963).

Negi, Poonam, "*Gomti Sanrakhshan Abhiyan*", *Panchjanya*, 10 June 2018, 18–21.

Nelson, Lance E. (ed.), *Purifying the Earthly Body of God: Religion and Ecology in Hindu India* (Albany, State University of New York Press, 1998).

Neumann, David, *Finding God through Yoga: Paramahansa Yogananda and Modern American Religion in a Global Age* (Chapel Hill, University of North Carolina Press, 2019).

New Delhi, *Census of India 2001* (Office of the Registrar General, n.d.).

Nicholson-Lord, David, *The Greening of the Cities* (London & New York, Routledge & Kegan Paul, 1987).

Noorani, A.G., "India's Reaction to the International Concern over Gujarat", in Siddharth Varadarajan (ed.), *Gujarat: The Making of a Tragedy* (Delhi: Penguin, 2003), 389–400.

O'Connor, James, *Natural Causes: Essays in Ecological Marxism* (New York, The Guilford Press, 1998).

O'Hanlon, Rosalind, *Caste, Conflict and Ideology: Mahatma Jotirao Phule and Low Caste Protest in Nineteenth-Century Western India* (1985, rpnt Ranikhet, Permanent Black, 2010).

Olsen, Jonathan, *Nature and Nationalism: Right-Wing Ecology and the Politics of Identity in Contemporary Germany* (London, Macmillan, 1990).

Omar, Mohammad, "The Muslim 'Threat' in Right Wing Narratives: A Critical Discourse Analysis", SSAI Working Paper Series (2021), https://www.soas.ac.uk/south-asia-institute/publications/working-papers/file152729.pdf.

Omvedt, Gail, *Cultural Revolt in a Colonial Society: The Non Brahman Movement in Western India: 1873 to 1930* (Bombay, Scientific Socialist Education Trust, 1976).

*Organiser*, a weekly of the Rastriya Swayamsevak Sangh (Delhi, 1980, 1981, 1982, 1983, 1984, 1985, 1986, 1987, 1988, 1989, 1990, 1991, 1992, 1993, 1994, 1995, 1996, 1997, 1998, 1999, 2000, 2013, 2014, 2015, 2016, 2017, 2018, 2019, 2020, 2021, 2022).

Oswald, Michael T., Meike Fromm, and Elena Broda, "Strategic Clustering in Right-wing-populist 'Green Policies' in Germany and France", *Zeitschirft für Vergleichende Politikwissenschaft*, 15 (2021).

Paliwal, Prof. K.V., *Challenges Before the Hindus* (Delhi, Suruchi Prakashan, 2014).

Paliwal, Prof. K.V., *What Hindus Should Do* (New Delhi, Suruchi Prakashan, 2015).

Palshikar, Suhas, "Towards Hegemony", *Economic and Political Weekly*, 53, no. 33, 18 August 2018.

Panda, Shashanka Shekhar, "International Solar Alliance: The Saffron Supergrid Superpower", *Organiser*, 10 January 2022.

Pandey, Gyanendra, *The Construction of Communalism in Colonial North India* (Delhi, Oxford University Press, 1990).

Paneuli, Virendra, "*Tehri Bandh: Lagat-Munafe tatha Punarwaas-Muawze ki Asliyat*" (Tehri Dam: The Reality of Cost-Benefits and Rehabilitation-Compensation), *Pahar*, no. 2, 58–72.

Papne, Trilokchand, "*Saswat Bahane Do*" (Let it Flow Eternal)", in Virendra Dutta Saklani, *Gangajee ke Pavitra Jal* (Tehri, 1980), 16–22.

Papola, T.S., B.K. Joshi, H.S. Verma, and R.C. Sinha (eds), *Development of Hill Areas: Issues and Approaches* (Bombay, Himalaya Publishing House, 1983).

Paranjpye, Vijay, *Evaluating the Tehri Dam: An Extended Cost Benefit Appraisal* (New Delhi, Indian National Trust For Art And Cultural Heritage, 1988).

Park, Chris C., *Sacred Worlds: An Introduction to Geography and Religion* (London, Routledge, 1994).

Pathak, Shekhar (ed.), *Pahar, Vols 1, 2, 3–4, 12* (Delhi, 1983, 1986, 1989, and 2008, respectively).

Pathak, Shekhar, and Ramachandra Guha, "*Sthaniya Itihaas, Jan Itihaas ya Rashtriya Itihaas*" (Local History: Peoples' History or National History), *Pahar*, no. 3–4, 200–13.

Pathak, Shekhar, *Nasha ek shadyantra hai: Uttarakhand mei chal rahe "nasha nahin rozgar do aandolan" ka pristha-bhoomi kei saath varnan-vishleshan* (Nainital, Pahar Pustika 1, 1985).

Pathak, Shekhar, *Uttarakhand mein Kuli Begar Pratha* (Delhi, Radhakrishna Prakashan, 1987).

Pathak, Swapna, and Christie Parris, "India's Diplomatic Discourse and Development Dilemma in the International Climate Change Regime", *India Review*, vol. 1, issue 1 (2021).

Patti, D. Ramachandran, "Gandhi and the Village", in Sheo Kumar Lal (ed.), *Gandhiji and Village* (Delhi, 1981), 52.

Peet, Richard, and Michael Watts (eds), *Liberation Ecologies: Environment, Development, Social Movements* (London, Routledge, 1996).

People's Commission on Environment and Development, *The Report of*

*Twenty Fifth Public Hearing on Environment and Development* (Vrindavan, 1995).

Pinney, Christopher, "Indian Magical Realism: Notes on Popular Visual Culture", in Gautam Bhadra, Gyan Prakash, and Susie Tharu (eds), *Subaltern Studies X* (Delhi, Oxford University Press, 1999).

Pinney, Christopher, "The Nation (Un) Pictured? Chromolithography and 'Popular' Politics in India, 1878–1995", *Critical Inquiry*, vol. 23 (Summer 1997).

Poddar, Jagannath, "From the Editor's Desk", *Vrindavan Today*, vol. 5, issue 7 (July 2023).

Prabhu, Nagesh, *Middle Class, Media and Modi: The Making of a New Electoral Politics* (New Delhi, Sage, 2020).

Prasad, Archana, *Against Ecological Romanticism: Verrier Elwin and the Making of an Anti-Modern Tribal Identity* (Delhi, Three Essays Collective, 2003).

Prasad, Archana, *Environmentalism and the Left: Contemporary Debates and Future Agendas in the Tribal Areas* (Delhi, Left Word Books, 2004), 23.

Prime, Ranchor, *Hinduism and Ecology: Seeds of Truth* (London, Cassell, 1992).

Puniyani, Ram, *Cow-Beef and Indian Politics* (Thiruvananthapuram, Mythri Books, 2018).

Purandare, Vaibhav, *The Sena Story* (Mumbai, Business Publications Inc., 1999).

Puri, Geeta, "Religion and Social Movement: The Case of Vishva Hindu Parishad", in Shibani Kinkar Chaube and Bidyut Chakraborty (eds), *Social Movements in Contemporary India* (Calcutta, K.P. Bagchi & Company, 1999).

Radhika, V., "Bahuguna Plays the Hindu Card to Widen Support Base", *Pioneer*, Delhi, 12 June 1996, 7.

Raheja, Gloria Goodwin, *The Poison in the Gift: Ritual, Presentation & the Dominant Caste in a North Indian Village* (Chicago, University of Chicago Press, 1988).

Rai, Usha, Mukul, Sarosh Bana, and Dinesh Kumar, *Call of the Commons: People vs Corruption* (New Delhi, Centre for Science and Environment, 1991).

Raj, Sebasti L., and Arundhati Roy Choudhury (ed.), *Contemporary Social Movements in India: Achievements and Hurdles* (New Delhi, Indian Social Institute, 1998).

Ramakrishnan, P.S., "Conserving the Sacred: Ecological and Policy Implications", in Ashish Kothari, Neema Pathak, R.V. Anuradha, and Bansure Taneja (eds), *Communities and Conservation: Natural Resource Management in South and Central Asia* (New Delhi, Sage Publications, 1998), 239–51.

Ramakrishnan, Venkitesh, "Saffron Offensive: 'Liberation Theology' of a Different Kind", *Frontline* (8 September 1995).

Ramaswamy, Sumathi, "Maps and Mother Goddesses in Modern India", *Imago Mundi*, 53 (2001).

Rangan, Haripriya, "From Chipko to Uttaranchal: Development, Environment, and Social Protest in the Garhwal Himalayas, India", in Richard Peet and Michael Watts (eds), *Liberation Ecologies: Environment, Development, Social Movements* (London and New York, Routledge, 1996), 205–26.

Rangan, Haripriya, *Of Myths and Movements: Rewriting Chipko into Himalayan History* (London, Verso, 2000).

Rangarajan, Mahesh, and K. Sivaramakrishnan (eds), *India's Environmental History: Colonialism, Modernity and the Nation* (Ranikhet, Permanent Black, 2011).

Rangarajan, Mahesh, "Striving for a Balance: Nature, Power, Science and India's Indira Gandhi, 1917–1984", *Conservation and Society*, vol. 7, no. 4 (2009), pp. 299–312.

Rangarajan, Mahesh, *From Princely Symbol to Conservation Icon: A Political History of the Lion in India* (New Delhi, NMML, 1999).

Rangarajan, Mahesh, *India's Wildlife History* (Delhi, Permanent Black, 2001).

Rangarajan, Mahesh, *Nature and Nation: Essays on Environmental History* (Delhi, Permanent Black, 2015).

Rangarajan, Sadhu Prof. V., "Bharat as the Motherland", *Organiser*, 1 May 2016.

Rao, Smitha, "Saffronisation of the Holy Cow: Unearthing Silent Communalism", *Economic and Political Weekly*, vol. XLVI, no. 15 (2011).

Rao, T. Shivaji, *Tehri Dam is a Time Bomb* (Visakhapatnam, n.d.).

Rashtriya Jagran Abhiyan, *Hindu Samskriti and Environment* (Delhi, Suruchi Prakashan, 2000).

Rashtriya Swayamsevak Sangh, "Basic Facts", https://www.rss.org//Encyc/2017/6/3/basic-faq-on-rss-eng.html.

Rashtriya Swayamsevak Sangh, "Vision and Mission", https://www.rss.org//Encyc/2015/3/13/Vision-and-Mission.html.

Rastriya Swayamsevak Sangh, *Desh Ki Chinta* (Delhi, 1988).

Rastriya Swayamsevak Sangh, Uttar Pradesh, *Hame Hindu Hone Ka Garwa Hai: Kya* (n.p., n.d.).

Raturi, Prabhudayal, *Sri Ganga Jee ka Mahatva* (Tehri, n.d.).

Ravindran, K.T., and Team, *Vrindavan: Restoration of Keshi & Pandawala Ghats* (Delhi, Intach, 1988).

Rawat, Ajay S., *History of Garhwal 1358–1947* (New Delhi, Indus Publishing Company, 1989).

Rehman, Mujibur (ed.), *Rise of Saffron Power: Reflections on Indian Politics* (Abingdon, Routledge, 2019).

Rigzen, Tenzin (ed.), *Fire in the Heart: Firewood on the Back: Writings on and by Himalayan Crusader Sunderlal Bahuguna* (Tehri, Parvatiya Navjeevan Mandal, 1997).

Rosenthal, D.B., "Deurbanization, Elite Displacement and Political Change in India", *Comparative Politics*, vol. 2, no. 2 (1970).

Roy, Dunu, "Politics of Environment", in A. Agarwal, *et al.* (eds), *The State of India's Environment, 1984–85.*

Roy, Ramashray, and Paul Wallace (eds), *Indian Politics and the 1998 Election: Regionalism, Hindutva and State Politics* (New Delhi, Sage, 1999).

Sachs, Wolfgang, "Environment, Dignity and Human Rights", in Mukul Sharma and Sana Das (eds), *Defining Dignity* (Delhi: World Dignity Forum, 2005), 23–9.

Sack, R.D., *Human Territoriality* (London, Cambridge University Press, 1986).

*Sakha Surbhi* (New Delhi: Suruchi Prakashan, 2017).

Saklani, Virendra Dutta, "*Bhoomika*", in Sunderlal Bahuguna, *Tehri ka Vishal Bandh* (Tehri's Huge Dam) (Tehri, TBVSS, n.d.), 1.

Saklani, Virendra Dutta (ed.), *Gangajee ke Pavitra Jal ko Apavitra karne Ki Yojana* (Tehri, 1980).

Saklani, Virendra Dutta, *Tehri Dam: A Dangerous Venture* (Tehri Garhwal, Tehri Bandh Virodhi Sangharsh Samiti, 1980).

Samuel, John (ed.), *Social Action: An Indian Panorama* (Delhi, Vani, 2000).

Sapre, Sadanand Damodar, *Param Vaibhav ke Path Par* (Delhi, Suruchi Prakashan, 1999).

Saraswati, Swami Chidananda, *Ganga Maiya ko Bachana Hai* (Tehri, TBVSS, 1989).

Saraswati, Swami Chidananda, *Himalaya ke Paryavaran ki Raksha Kijiye* (Tehri, TBVSS, n.d.).

Sardesai, Rajdeep, *How Modi Won India* (Noida, HarperCollins, 2020).

Sarkar, Sumit, *Modern India 1885–1947* (Delhi, Macmillan India, 1983).

Sarkar, Tanika and Urvashi Butalia (eds), *Women and the Hindu Right: A Collection of Essays* (Delhi, Kali for Women, 1995).

Sarkar, Tanika, "The Woman as Communal Subject: Rashtrasevika Samiti and Ram Janmabhoomi Movement", *Economic and Political Weekly*, vol. 26, no. 35 (21 August 1991), 2059.

Schama, Simon, *Landscape and Memory* (London, HarperCollins, 1995).

Seabrook, Jeremy, *Notes from Another India* (London, Pluto Press, 1995).

Seabrook, Jeremy, *Victims of Development: Resistance and Alternatives* (London, Verso, 1993).

Seamon, Donald, and Robert Mugerauer (eds), *Dwelling, Place and Environment: Towards a Phenomenology of Person and World* (New York, Columbia University Press, 1989).

Sehgal, Narendra, *Ram arthat Rashtra* (Delhi, Utpal Prakashan, 1995).

Sen, Geeti (ed.), *Indigenous Vision: Peoples of India, Attitudes to the Environment* (Delhi, Sage, 1992).

Sen, Rahul, *Tehri Dam: A Fact Sheet* (New Delhi, South-South Solidarity, 1995).

Sengupta, Sandeep, "India's Engagement in Global Climate Negotiations from Rio to Paris", in Navroz K. Dubash (ed.), *India in a Warming World: Integrating Climate Change and Development* (New Delhi, Oxford University Press, 2019).

Seshadri, H.V., "Thinking Workers and Working Thinkers: That's What We Need", *Manthan*, vol. v, no. 4, November 1984, 13.

Seshagiri, N. (chief ed.), *Encyclopaedia of Cities and Towns in India Vol IX (Uttar Pradesh) Part II* (New Delhi, Gyan Publishing House, 2008).

Shah, Ghanshyam, and D.C. Shah (eds), *Land Reforms in India, Volume 8, Performance and Challenges in Gujarat And Maharashtra* (New Delhi, Sage Publications, 2002).

Sharma, Ishaan, "Cow as a Sacred National Symbol: (Un)Making of the Idea of India", unpublished paper (2018).

Sharma, Mukul, and Ashok Bharti, "In Lieu of Introduction", in Mukul Sharma and Sana Das (eds), *Defining Dignity: An Anthology of Dreams, Hopes and Struggles* (Delhi: World Dignity Forum, 2005), 5.

Sharma, Mukul, and Sana Das (eds), *Defining Dignity* (Delhi: World Dignity Forum, 2005).

Sharma, Mukul, "Down with the Dam", *The Express Magazine* (20 August 2000, Delhi).

Sharma, Mukul, "Nature and Nationalism", *Frontline* (16 February 2001).

Sharma, Mukul, "Saffronising Green", *Seminar*, no. 516, August 2002.

Sharma, Mukul, *Caste & Nature: Dalits and Indian Environmental Politics* (Delhi, Oxford University Press, 2017).

Sharma, Mukul, *Landscapes and Lives: Environmental Dispatches on Rural India* (New Delhi, Oxford University Press, 2001).

Sharma, Suresh, "The Vanquished Tribal World of Shifting Cultivation", in A. Bhalla and P.J. Bumke (eds), *Images of Rural India in the 20th Century* (New Delhi, Sterling Publishers, 1992), 78.

Shidore, Sarang, Joshua W. Busby, "What Explains India's Embrace of Solar? State-led Energy Transition in a Developmental Polity", *Energy Policy* 129 (2019).

Shinn, Larry D., "The Inner Logic of Gandhian Ecology", in C.K. Chapple and M.E. Tucker (eds), *Hinduism and Ecology* (Boston, Harvard University Press, 2000), 222–3.

Shiva, Vandana, *Staying Alive: Women, Ecology and Survival in India* (Delhi, Kali for Women, 1988).

Sigdel, Anil, *India in the Era of China's Belt and Road Initiative: How Modi Responds to Xi* ( Lanham, Lexington Books, 2020).

Singer, Milton (ed.), *Krishna: Myths, Rites, and Attitudes* (Honolulu, East-West Centre Press, 1966).

Singh, Daman J., and Aditya Vir, *State of the Environment: Vrindavan* (New Delhi, WWF India, 1994).

Singh, Karan, "Foreword", in Anna Mcdowall and Arvind Sharma (eds), *Vignettes of Vrindavan* (New Delhi, Books and Books, 1987), vii.

Singh, Rana P.B., "Ecological Cosmology in Hindu Tradition for the 21st Century", *Sumangalam: Framing Indian Narrative of Environment*, https://nenp.facebook.com/people/Sumangalam/100084819411949/.

Singh, Rana P.B., *Sumangalam: Framing Indian Narrative of Environment: Ecological Cosmology in Hindu Tradition for the 21st Century* (Varanasi, Sumangalam, 2020).

Singh, Sandeep, "The Electrifying Effect", *Organiser*, 31 July 2016.

Singh, Satyajit, *Taming the Waters: The Political Economy of Large Dams in India* (New Delhi, Oxford University Press, 1997).

Singh, Savita, *Global Concern with Environmental Crisis and Gandhi's Vision* (New Delhi, APH Publishing Corporation, 1999).

Singh, Vijaya Laxmi, *Mathura: The Settlement Pattern and Cultural Profile of an Early Historial City* (New Delhi, Sandeep Prakashan, 2005).

Singh, Yashpal, *Tehri Bandh Pariyojana ki Byatha-Katha* (Rishikesh, 1992).

Singh, Yashpal, *Tehri Bandh Pariyojana: Vivad evam Tathya* (Rishikesh, Tehri Dam Project: Debate and Facts, 1992).

Sinha, Subir, Shubhra Gururani, and Brian Greenberg, "The 'New Traditionalist' Discourse of Indian Enviornmentalism", *The Journal of Peasant Studies*, vol. 24, no. 3 (April 1997), 65–99.

Sirohi, Sanjeev, "Hey Gange", *Organiser*, 30 April 2017.

Sirsikar, V.M., "Political Culture of Maharashtra", in A.R. Kulkarni and N.K. Wagle (eds), *Region, Nationality and Religion* (Mumbai, Popular Prakashan, 1999), 5–17.

Soni, Suresh, *India's Glorious Scientific Tradition* (Delhi, Ocean Books, 2021).

Staples, James, *Sacred Cows and Chicken Manchurian* (Seattle, University of Washington Press, 2020).

Subramaniam, Banu, *Holy Science: The Biopolitics of Hindu Nationalism* (Seattle, University of Washington Press, 2019).

Subramanian, Ajantha, *Shorelines: Space and Rights in South India* (Stanford, Stanford University Press, 2009).

Subramanya, Rupa, "Is India Ready to Be a Solar Power Leader?", *Foreign Policy*, 1 July 2015, https://foreignpolicy.com/2015/07/01/india-modi-bjp-energy-solar-softbank/.

Sud, Nikita, "Constructing and Contesting a Gujarati-Hindu Ethno-Religious Identity through Development Programmes", *Oxford Development Studies* 35, no. 2 (2007).

Sullivan, Bruce M., "Theology and Ecology at the Birthplace of Krsna", in Lauce E. Nelson (ed.), *Purifying the Earthly Body of God: Religion and Ecology in Hindu India* (Albany, State University of New York Press, 1998), 252–3.

Svitil, Kathy A., "The Coming Himalayan Catastrophe", in *Bhagirathi ki Pukar*, vol. 5, no. 8 (October 1995).

Swadeshi Jagaran Manch, *Rebuilding the Nation: A Swadeshi Outline* (Delhi, n.d.).

Swami, Mahanidhi, *Appreciating Sri Vrndavana Dhama* (Vrndavana Iskcon, 1991).

Swarup, Ram, *On Hinduism: Reviews and Reflections* (New Delhi, Voice of India, 2009).

Tanzler, Dennis, and Alexander Carius, "Beyond International Climate Negotiations: Climate Diplomacy from a Foreign Policy Perspective", in Oliver C. Ruppel, *et al.* (eds), *Climate Change: International Law and Global Governance* (Baden-Baden, Nomos, 2013).

Tewari, Indu, *Unity for Identity: Struggle for Uttarakhand State* (New Delhi, K.K. Publishers & Distributors, 2001).

Thengadi, Dattopant B., *Global Economic System: A Hindu View* (Delhi, Swadeshi Jagaran Manch, n.d.).

Thengadi, Dattopant, *Third Way* (Bangalore, Sahitya Sindhu Prakashana, 1991).

Toke, David, *Ecological Modernisation and Renewable Energy* (Hampshire, Palgrave Macmillan, 2011).

Trivedi, V.R., *Autonomy of Uttarakhand* (New Delhi, Mohit Publications, 1995).

Turner, Joe, and Dan Bailey, "Ecobordering": Casting Immigration Control as Environmental Protection", *Environmental Politics,* vol. 31, no. 1 (2022).

U.P. Irrigation Department (UP), *Multipurpose and Hydroelectric Projects in Ganga and Yamuna Valleys* (Lucknow, Irrigation Department, May 1986).

U.P. Vidhan Sabha First Session (Lucknow, Director Printing & Stationary, 1990).

U.P. Voluntary Health Association, *Rehabilitation of Tehri Dam Oustees: Promises and Performance* (Lucknow, 1996).

Upadhyaya, Deendayal, *Political Diary* (Bombay, Jaico Publishing House, 1968).

*Uttarakhand Vikas Vibhag Development 1994–95 and Programme 1995–96* (Lucknow, Uttarakhand Vikas, U.P. Government).

Vaidyaraj, Prashanth, "Decolonising the Village Ecosystem", *Organiser,* 19 August 2018.

van der Veer, Peter, "Hindu Nationalism and the Discourse of Modernity", in Martin Marty and R. Scott Appleby (eds), *Accounting for Fundamentalism: The Dynamic Characteristics of Movements* (Chicago, University of Chicago Press, 1994).

van der Veer, Peter, *Religious Nationalism: Hindus and Muslims in India* (Berkeley, University of California Press, 1994).

Van Dyke, Virginia, "The 1998 General Election: The Janus-faced Policies of the BJP and Religious Mobilization at the District Level in Uttar Pradesh", in R. Roy and P. Wallace, *Indian Politics and the 1998 Elections* (Delhi, Sage, 1999).

Varadarajan, Siddharth (ed.), *Gujarat: The Making of a Tragedy* (Delhi, Penguin, 2003).

Venkatasubramanian, Kalpana, "Examining the Politics of Climate Change: Narratives, Actions and Adaptations in Gujarat, India", Doctor of

Philosophy dissertation submitted to the Graduate School in Geography, The State University of New Jersey, Rutgers (2016).

Vishwa Hindu Parishad, *Braj Rakshak Sena* (Vrindavan, n.d.).

Visvanathan, Shiv, *A Carnival for Science* (Delhi, Oxford University Press, 1996).

*Vrindavan Today* (Vrindavan, Vrindavan Today Foundation, 2022, 2023).

W. Laine, James, "A Question of Maharashtrian Identity: Hindu Self-definition in the Tales of Shivaji", in Meera Kosambi (ed.), *Intersections: Socio-Cultural Trends in Maharashtra* (Delhi, Orient Longman, 2000), 70.

Wagle, N.K. (ed.), *Images of Maharashtra: A Regional Profile of India* (London, Curzon Press, 1980).

White Aryan Resistance, www.resist.com/AryanUpdates.

Wodak, Ruth, *The Politics of Fear: What Right-Wing Populist Discourses Mean* (London, Sage, 2015).

World Wildlife Fund (WWF), *Brij Vrindavan Sanrakshan* (Vrindavan, 1998).

WWF website: www.panda.org.

WWF-India, *Brij Vrindavan Sanrakshan* (Protection of Brij Vrindavan), Background Papers of a Conference (Vrindavan, 8 April 1998).

WWF-India, *Vrindavan Forest Revival Project* (*Brochure 1*) (Delhi, 1993).

WWF-India, *Vrindavan Forest Revival Project* (*Brochure 2*) (Delhi, n.d.).

Yadav, Kushal P.S., "Going Under", *Down to Earth*, 15 January 2002, 21–4.

Yang, Anand, "Sacred Symbol and Sacred Space in Rural India: Community Mobilization in the 'Anti-cow Killing' Riot of 1893", *Comparative Studies in Society and History*, 22 (4), 1980, 576–96.

Zimmerer, K., "Social Erosion and Social (Dis)courses in Cochabamba, Bolivia: Perceiving the Nature of Environmental Degradation", *Economic Geography*, vol. 69 (1993).

# Index